BEHAVE YOURSELF!

BEHAVE YOURSELF!

The Working Guide to Business Etiquette

Elena Jankowic
with Sandra Bernstein

PRENTICE-HALL, Inc., Englewood Cliffs, New Jersey

LIBRARY OF CONGRESS CATALOGING-IN-PUBLICATION DATA

Jankowic, Elena.
  Behave Yourself.

Includes Index.
I. Business Etiquette. I. Bernstein, Sandra.
II. Title.

HF5387.J34 1986 395'.52 86-5033
ISBN 0-13-071721-5

Prentice-Hall International, Inc., London
Prentice-Hall of Australia, Pty. Ltd., Sydney
Prentice-Hall of India, Pvt., Ltd., New Delhi
Prentice-Hall of Japan, Inc., Tokyo
Prentice-Hall of Southeast Asia (Pte.) Ltd., Singapore
Editora Prentice-Hall do Brasil Ltda., Rio de Janeiro
Prentice-Hall Hispanoamericana, S.A., Mexico
Whitehall Books Limited, Wellington, New Zealand

10 9 8 7 6 5

10 9 8 7 6 5 4 3 2 1 (PBK)

ISBN 0-13-071721-5

ISBN 0-13-073925-1 PBK

Design: Janet Eidt
Production: Joanne Matthews
Composition: Attic Typesetting

Contents

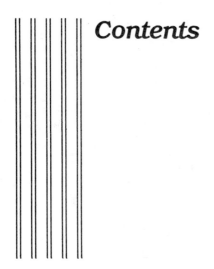

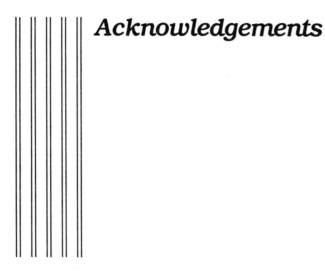

Acknowledgements

I would like to express my gratitude to the wonderful people who brought their talents and support to this book:

Sandra Bernstein, for her superb writing skills and patience, Stephen Lugosi, for his wit, charm and valuable contributions, Gwynne MacHattie, for her support and great coffee, and Iris Skeoch, who was instrumental in initiating this project.

I am eternally grateful to you all.

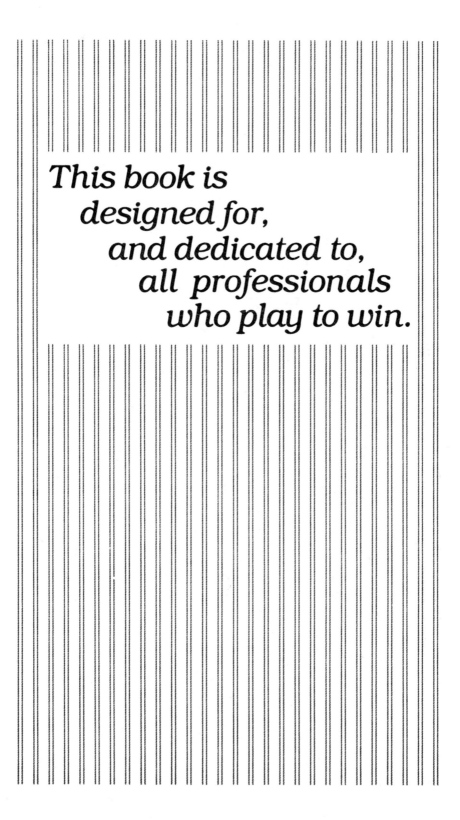

*This book is
designed for,
and dedicated to,
all professionals
who play to win.*

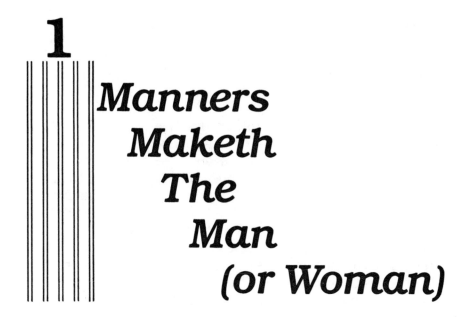

1

Manners Maketh The Man (or Woman)

Whether you're the president of a Fortune 500 company, or a recent graduate starting your first job, every working day offers the opportunity to accumulate one of the most valuable assets a business person can acquire. I'm not talking about money, stocks, or a Savile Row wardrobe, but about goodwill.

Goodwill is not easily defined. You can't touch it with your hand or wear it on your lapel, but its absence is keenly felt and immediately noticed. Without goodwill, a career or business can never grow or flourish. It is an essential ingredient of corporate success.

You earn goodwill whenever you show respect and consideration for others, handle situations with tact and diplomacy, behave like a professional, and give credit where credit is due. In short, when your behavior is such that you inspire confidence, people both admire and trust you.

The executive of today constantly faces situations that were unheard-of twenty years ago. New technologies, the growth of multinational corporations, the changing role of women and diversified management styles have reshaped the

1

corporate environment into a complex arena that demands new standards of behavior, standards that work anywhere from Tokyo to Toronto. As a result, business etiquette has become the new international language. It is one of the easiest languages to learn, and it is an essential attribute of those who want to reach the top.

For example, it is common practice in North America today for employers to invite prospective executives out for dinner. They do not do this because they are hungry. The successful candidate for a key position will represent the prestige and dignity of the firm. Employers want to observe the applicant's social skills, to watch him eating and carrying on an informal conversation. It is understood that good manners and an understanding of business etiquette are not superficial frills. They define business practice, and business practice determines the bottom line. The more prominent the position, the more important it becomes to project a secure, professional image.

Five Popular Misconceptions About Business Etiquette

Most people think they know what etiquette is, but there are a surprising number of popular misconceptions about it. For example:

1. **Social skills are not important in a professional environment.** Wrong. In seminars on professional protocol, hundreds of people have been asked to rate their ease in both a business environment and in a social environment. Without exception, they've rated their professional aplomb higher than their social skills. What they don't realize, however, is that BUSINESS IS THE LARGEST SOCIAL ENVIRONMENT IN THE WORLD TODAY. Remember, a *faux pas* at a business luncheon can cost a young executive more than just the check.

2. **Business etiquette is not important because people will always remember how elegantly you were dressed.** Wrong. Someone might be wearing a $1000.00 suit, but if he has poor table manners, guess what people will remember? It certainly won't be his clothes. For years now, people have been dressing for success, and there's certainly nothing wrong with dressing appropriately and putting your best foot forward. However, to stand out in the crowd, it takes more than costly apparel. It is behavior that makes a person memorable, and inspires confidence.

3. **There isn't the time in most business contacts to make much of an impression either way.** It's true that in business today, most encounters are brief. You might see a client once a month for a half-hour, a vice-president 20 minutes a day, a secretary eight times a day for five minutes at a time, a receptionist when you arrive and leave. But this brevity means that you have to try harder to use your time with people effectively. It makes it more of a challenge to build and nurture relationships, and to leave a favorable impression.

4. **The top brass are the real ambassadors of the company.** Wrong. Every employee is an ambassador of the corporation, no matter what his or her position. Attitudes, the ability to deal with people, and job performance always reflect on the company, whether they belong to a mail clerk or a vice-president. Every move may be observed by someone. It therefore behooves prudent employees to move with the dignity and style that becomes their positions, or the positions they would like to hold.

5. **Good business etiquette will make me a president, and guarantee me a seat on the board of directors.** Wrong. The only thing that makes you a president with a seat on the board of directors (unless you inherited the company) is a combination of skill, achievement, and hard work. But while there is no guarantee that good etiquette training will open

the door to the presidential suite, chances are very good that without it, the door will remain closed. A top executive must be able to move with ease and grace in social and professional environments, and to get along with people.

This fact was brought home to me early in my career, when I worked with a man I'll call Peter.

"Peter" was and is a brilliant marketing executive, with all the right credentials, including an M.B.A. Unfortunately, within three months of being hired, Peter had managed to alienate everyone in his department.

Peter's brilliance worked against him, because it made him intolerant of everyone he considered intellectually inferior. Because he had absolutely no tact or diplomacy, he felt free to criticize others, pointing out their weaknesses in meetings and in front of their fellow-workers. This criticism did not stop at the work at hand, but extended to the individuals personally. Peter appeared increasingly abrasive to senior management. It reached the point at which people were afraid to let him into the board room. Not surprisingly, he was equally unpopular with support staff. The word processing operators who had to put up with his withering abuse never failed to put his work at the bottom of their overloaded in-baskets.

Unfortunately, Peter relied totally on his cleverness as a marketer, and failed to adhere to the established rules. Instead, he foolishly believed that he could write his own. He never recognized that good management requires "people skills," such as effective communication and the ability to motivate others.

Although he had the talent that could have propelled him on a fast track to the top, Peter's behavior held him back. He lasted about a year at the company before he was fired. The last I heard of him, he had gone through at least four more jobs.

Peter has a problem. He can't see himself as others see him.

Like the Wicked Queen in "Snow White," who had to ask her mirror "Who's the fairest of them all?" we can never see our own faces—only reflections in a mirror. The mirror that tells us how well we are behaving, how we truly appear, and how people are perceiving us, is the reaction of others. In business, that reaction determines whether people will like us, whether they will hire and promote us, and whether they will choose to deal with us.

Peter's ignorance of the simplest rules of professional protocol doomed his career almost before it started.

The Corporate Environment

Look at this familiar pyramid diagram, representing a corporate hierarchy:

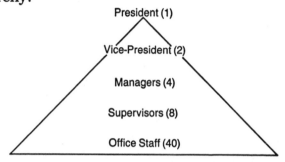

President (1)

Vice-President (2)

Managers (4)

Supervisors (8)

Office Staff (40)

Notice that there is more room at the bottom than at the top. At the bottom it is harder to be noticed, which is fine if you want to take a nap. However, most young people are ambitious, and are not content to stay at the bottom. They want to move up, but find that at each step there are fewer and fewer positions available. As a simple example, in a department of 30 people, there are, not uncommonly, only two managerial positions. The situation is exacerbated by post-war demographics which indicate that a generation unprecedented in number, education and ambition finds itself blocked not only by older managers who have not yet reached retirement age, but by older baby boomers who were the first to reach the upper echelons.

How can you stand out in a crowd, when other people may be better looking, taller, better dressed or have a better education?

The best way is through behavior, which is where business etiquette training comes in. With good etiquette training, you can appear natural and at ease in any situation—able to deal with the expected and the unexpected with equal aplomb. Your behavior tells the world, "I am competent, I am professional, and you can trust me."

Impeccable deportment makes an employee popular with management, peers and subordinates. It helps define your own high standard of performance, and puts you head and shoulders above anyone else. In a heavily competitive environment, those who behave professionally have the edge.

How to Stand Out in a Corporate Crowd

Of course, you could choose other ways to be outstanding in business. As "Peter" dramatically demonstrated, there are numerous practices and characteristics that guarantee senior management becomes aware of your presence. The following tactics require very little effort or awareness.

- Always be late. This is an excellent way to keep your name in front of people. Be late for work, lunches, meetings, even the office party—after all, everyone likes making a dramatic entrance. And it's so gratifying to be missed.
- Keep people waiting at least half an hour when they have an appointment with you. Chances are they will have to leave before you are ready to see them. You can then devote the rest of the day to complaining about the difficulty of getting good service these days. This reinforces your own importance.
- Forget your handkerchief, but don't worry about it. Let management know how resourceful you are by using your serviette or your sleeve.
- Never let your secretary know where you are. This is very effective, because it keeps people guessing about what it is you are actually doing, and about your importance to the company.
- Drop the president's first name every now and then. It can't hurt.
- Forget people's names, and spell them incorrectly on correspondence. It shows how much you care.
- Ignore all letters and memos for at least ten days. People will feel sorry for you when they see the volume of work piling up in your office.
- Enliven your conversation with the odd four-letter word. It tells people how confident you are.

- Scream into the telephone so that not only the other party can hear your conversation, but also the receptionist on the fifth floor and your aged aunt in Des Moines. They'll know you're a force to be reckoned with.
- Have no secrets from your fellow workers. Tell them all how much you pay for car insurance, why your sister needed a hysterectomy, about Junior's dental problems, and how hard it is to get a rotorooter man on short notice. This will keep them from suffering the effects of overwork, and from feeling badly about missing the afternoon soaps.
- Pinch the posterior of the boss's wife at the office Christmas party.
- Chew with your mouth open. This is particularly effective if done in the presence of senior management.

These simple guidelines will ensure that you are noticed in a crowd. In fact, you will be remembered in ALL the places you worked.

Although these may appear humorous in a list, if you look carefully, almost everyone is guilty of at least one such gaffe. When any of them becomes a daily habit, it's no longer a laughing matter.

Of course, there is a better way to be noticed. If you truly wish to improve your chances for success in the corporate world, it takes diligence, sincerity, and an ability to look honestly at yourself. What is the mirror telling you? Are you behaving like a true professional? Are you following the rules? Do you know what they are?

2

Rules of the Game

Whatever the game is—football, chess or stock trading—every professional needs to know the rules. Just as a billiard player is governed by the rules of geometry, so business people everywhere must be governed by the basic rules of professional behavior. These rules determine the actions and attitudes of everyone who wishes to succeed. They apply regardless of any policies and management styles that may exist within any single organization.

The Golden Rule of Business

Everyone is familiar with the Golden Rule: "Do unto others as you would have them do unto you." This rule, which sounds deceptively simple, is extremely important in both the business world and our private lives. Our daily actions invite a response—inevitably, what you give out, you get back. It follows that adherence to the Golden Rule benefits not only those with whom you are dealing, but ultimately benefits you.

Within the corporate environment, we find a variation on this theme, which we call *The Golden Rule of Business.* If you remember only one sentence from this book, make it this one—

```
EVERYBODY IS IMPORTANT
```

Everybody, from the president to the mail clerk, is important and deserves to be treated with the same respect and professional consideration. The smart executive never underestimates the power and importance of this rule. It is the key to building a solid foundation of goodwill, for actions taken today have consequences well into the future.

For example, the receptionist in a client's office may be the purchasing manager next year, and she will remember the one client who called her "Miss Jones" instead of "honey." On the other hand, a person who is snubbed at a cocktail party will return the favor when he is placing his account. A man who insults a junior executive today may be reporting to him tomorrow, or applying to him for a job. The sales representative from a small company whose phone calls you ignore may take on a product that's in short supply, but which is essential to your company's production. The rep will then be in a position to ignore your calls. Remember, what you give out you get back, and it's wise to "be nice to them on the way up, because you might meet them again on the way down."

Five Rules of Professional Behavior

When we talk about professional protocol, many people immediately think of rules dealing with specific "micro" situations, such as choosing a fork at a dinner party or making proper introductions. However, there are "macro" rules which underlie all such guidelines. Understanding these rules enables an executive to behave appropriately in both expected and unexpected situations. The Golden Rule of Business is the primary macro rule. The others are:

1. Be Focused

The focused executive learns to use energy correctly, rather than waste it. You must concentrate on the work at hand, and not squander your attention on irrelevant issues and unproductive activities.

Every organization offers limitless potential for distractions—office politics, gossip and personal animosities. Those who dissipate their energy on these petty matters won't have enough left to do the job effectively.

> Take for example the case of reactive Roger, an assistant sales manager with a large company. Every time someone points out a weakness in his sales reports, or suggests improvements to his management practices, Roger broods on the comments as if they were a personal slight. He soothes his bruised ego by eliciting sympathy and support from his co-workers, through making disparaging remarks about his superiors. He wastes all his energy nursing grudges, instead of correcting the flaws in his work. This leaves him no opportunity to show improvement in his performance, unlike the true professional, who can accept constructive criticism and learn from it.

Focused executives always direct their energy toward their jobs, rather than squandering it on emotional reactions.

Another important aspect of being focused is recognizing that in a professional environment, relationships must remain primarily professional. One of the greatest dangers, however, is that everybody tries to relate to each other on a social level. There's nothing wrong with being warm, friendly and gracious, but the smart executive does not forget that a corporate environment is not a golf course or encounter group.

Allowing the office to take on a social atmosphere may be fun, but it discourages the formality and professional respect necessary to achieve high standards of performance. In such an office, people relate more as friends than as colleagues, which opens the door to serious problems. For example, friends let each other get away with little things. No one wants to upset a friend, let alone fire or demote one. Friends rarely challenge each other, or push each other to higher degrees of excellence. In a corporate milieu, work quality and productivity can slip if employees consider each other as friends first and as colleagues second. The focused executive realizes that this is in no one's best interest, and does not allow it to happen.

2. Be Discreet

Discreet executives keep their business and personal lives separate. They realize that it is both inappropriate and foolish to reveal too many details about one's private life, since these details bear no relevance to one's professional profile. The cost of your mortgage, your mother's retirement plans, and the size of your overdraft, for instance, are not suitable topics for office conversation, and neither enhance your image nor advance your career.

There is also a danger that personal revelations that may not seem important today could come back to hurt you.

> Loudmouth Larry was a loans officer who loved regaling his pals at work with tales of his weekend binges. However, when he was promoted to branch manager, these same pals reported to him, and he found he was unable to command any respect for his authority. They saw him not as management material, but merely as a wild and crazy guy.

Remember, too, that disclosures made to a close colleague may not hurt you directly, but could have damaging repercussions if your friend repeats them to someone who does not have your best interests at heart. For this reason, discreet executives keep criticisms of their superiors or company policy to themselves.

Being discreet also means keeping confidences, both personal and corporate. This ties in with keeping private affairs private; if the boss hears someone discussing the intimate details of last night's date, he may not be inclined to show that person the sales projections for the third quarter. Conversely, if the boss tells an employee in confidence that the president is leaving the company, it is not the employee's place to spread the news.

3. Don't Waste Your Time—or Anyone Else's

In a business environment, time is money. Wise executives realize this and respect not only their own time, but that of others. They learn to budget time effectively, and make the most of their business day. One of the greatest *faux pas,* whether in a social or professional environment, is to be late.

> Take the case of Tardy Ted, an underwriter for an insurance company. Ted is chronically late for everything, from work to lunch. Not only that, but when he does arrive, he continues to waste time. He breaks the flow of meetings by interjecting irrelevant remarks and anecdotes. Ted has what it takes to rise to the top of his profession, but his behavior forces people to regard him as a nuisance. They will never believe that he can accept greater responsibility, as a promotion would merely give him the opportunity to waste time at a higher hourly rate.

People often forget that if everyone in a large corporation wastes only a few minutes a day, the cost is staggering.

4. Be Reliable

One of the marks of a successful executive is the ability to be consistently reliable. This is an extremely important quality, since reliability opens the door to greater opportunity and advancement. Management will never give greater responsibilities to an individual who has not demonstrated an ability to take care of small ones. For this reason, those who wish to rise in the corporation accept full responsibility for their assignments, use initiative to get the job done, don't take the easy way out, and never miss a deadline. If an executive's secretary gets sick and goes home the day a project is due, he finds someone to help him, or types it himself if necessary.

> Professional Paul is the technical support manager for a large computer company. With a major demonstration scheduled for Monday, Paul discovered on Friday afternoon that the system was malfunctioning. He worked straight through the weekend, 12 hours a day, until he found the problem: the microwave oven in the lunchroom was on the same circuit as the demonstration equipment, causing power irregularities. With some fast rewiring, the demonstration went flawlessly, resulting in a substantial order for the company and a promotion for Paul.

5. Be Positive and Acknowledge Others

True professionals—indeed, all healthy people—make an effort to see things in a positive light. They find opportunities in the problems that present themselves, and refuse to dwell on obstacles and minor frustrations. They also encourage others to do the same.

Many employees are too busy complaining about petty grievances to enjoy the challenges, or appreciate the good points, of a company. These negative attitudes not only waste time and deplete energy; they are also highly contagious, and can destroy morale.

> Enthusiastic Ellen was pleased about her new job with an import-export firm, and enjoyed her first few weeks as an administrative assistant. She found her fellow workers to be extremely friendly, and in a very short time was an accepted member of their little group. However, the more relaxed they became in her presence, the freer they felt to reveal their gripes about various company policies. Their complaints ranged from low pay levels to heavy work loads and even the quality of food in the lunchroom. Day after day, their conversation centered on the flaws in the company, leaving Ellen with very few reasons to remain enthusiastic. Within six months, she could no longer remember all the things she had initially liked about her job, and had joined the ranks of the whiners. Had she known the effect her co-workers would have on her morale, Ellen would have turned the conversation toward more positive topics.

Anybody can find problems. It takes initiative and creativity to see beyond them.

3

The Corporate Network

Today's corporate environment is a complex arena. In addition to professional expertise and experience, an executive must be able to function smoothly as part of an organization. One of the most important qualities management seeks when hiring a new employee is the ability to get along with people.

The key to building successful business relationships is understanding what others expect from us. This is largely determined by our role within the company, by our position relative to others, and our own appreciation of others' needs. Department heads have obligations to their own staff that may not apply in their dealings with people in other divisions, or with senior management. Customers have their own expectations of suppliers. And so on.

Outstanding executives do not stop at meeting these expectations, but always seek the "extra step" that puts them ahead of the crowd. This chapter provides an executive blueprint for building a solid network of support. It outlines not only how to fulfil the basic requirements, but how to go beyond them.

Senior Management

Senior management is the core of any corporation. It is usually comprised of the executives who have brought the company to its present degree of success and prestige. Their decisions have shaped the company and set its standards. For this alone, all employees owe them respect and acknowledgement. Show this respect by observing the following behavior.

DO imitate their style. Watch how they dress, how they move, how they conduct meetings. They are the models for the company, and expect those who join their ranks to conform to their style. Although they may be looking for leadership and initiative, chances are they are uncomfortable with anything that is too radical. If you wish to be invited into the boardroom or presidential suite, be prepared to adapt to those surroundings.

> We were recently hired by a financial institution to work with "George," one of their senior executives. Although he was brilliant and quite personable, George had no sense of the correct attire for his position. His clothing was outdated, and his hair was too long. Management did not feel he was representing the firm appropriately, and were uncomfortable when he met with clients and international guests. We visited the company to observe the dress codes in effect there. Then, over a two-day period, we recommended changes to George's wardrobe, hair, and posture. He emerged with a new fashion sense, and management was pleased that he no longer stood out like a sore thumb.

George was fortunate in that his company took the initiative in improving his professional image, and thus his chances for advancement. Not many firms are that considerate.

Remember, a team player can't wear a different uniform. Many qualified people have failed to advance because they did not understand the importance of this unspoken rule.

Similarly, when dealing with senior management of client firms, a guest should try to fit in with their corporate style. An advertising agency may be in the vanguard of fashion, but when visiting a conservative client, its account executive should dress appropriately and wash the green rinse out of his hair. Be sensitive, also, to regional differences: correct business attire in California is often a short-sleeved, open-necked shirt. This manner of dress would not be appropriate in a Boston boardroom.

DO show tact and diplomacy. This is a must. Never insult senior players to their faces or make disparaging remarks about them behind their backs. Don't take it upon yourself to warn other staff members that "the boss is on the warpath this morning." Don't say anything you wouldn't say to your boss directly. And if you think, for instance, that a marketing strategy is outdated, it is unwise to snicker and make unfavorable comparisons with the brilliant case study you did at Harvard last year. MBA should not stand for Most Belligerent Attitude. Ask, instead, what you can learn from senior management. If you do not understand why they are doing something, ask for help instead of reacting with hostility.

DO respect their time. Time is money, and the higher up in the hierarchy, the more it is worth. It is a mistake to try to make a good impression by constantly buttonholing a superior, without having some urgent matter to discuss. For example, you may have a common interest, such as baseball, but that doesn't give you license to discuss it at every opportunity. Nor should you run into your supervisor's office every few minutes to report on the progress of your work. Management is not fooled by someone who is constantly looking for attention and approval. Busy people tend to avoid those who waste their time.

DO keep them informed. This doesn't mean reporting every five minutes, so use discretion. You should let your superior know your progress, what you and your staff are doing, how projects are coming, and any potential problems on the horizon. One effective way to handle this is to leave a memo at the end of each day, briefly summarizing in point form your current status. The supervisor can read this memo the next morning, or at some convenient time. You thus demonstrate your willingness to share information, and your sensitivity to the superior's schedule.

DO respect the hierarchy. The chain of command is there for a reason, and applies to everyone. You may not get along well with your supervisor, who may not be creative or innovative, and may veto every good idea you propose. You'll score no points, however, by taking that brainwave for the spring campaign directly to the vice-president of marketing. If the vice-president mentions it to your supervisor, who knows nothing about it, you're in trouble with both. Remember, it isn't possible to leapfrog in a hierarchy.

DO accept criticism without taking it personally. This goes back to being focused. If management recommends a change in an employee's plans, they must have confidence that the recommendation will be complied with cheerfully. Management has little time or regard for a person who sulks and reacts sourly to constructive criticism. Always seek to demonstrate executive maturity.

DO try to see things from management's perspective. Look beyond your small part of the whole operation, and encourage others to do the same. The mark of a leader is an ability to examine the fuller picture, rather than fixating on one small point.

Although you may not agree with all the rules or policies of the company, it is important to understand that you cannot change them, until you are the responsible member of senior management. *Then* you can make recommendations. Until then, if you can't lick 'em, join 'em. Look for the positive points.

Peers

Peer relationships are not only the most competitive ones in the workplace, but are crucially important to a person's success. They offer a good opportunity to build goodwill, and to establish strong relationships. These relationships can last for years, enriching your experience and strengthening your base of support. On the other hand, underestimating the importance of these relationships can have negative consequences for years to come.

> "Fred" is a young executive in the restaurant industry who has made the fatal mistake of focusing his charm and attention only on those at the top. Among his peers, he is manipulative, and uses people for his own gain. He can be superficially charming, but only to pump others for information about their activities and accounts. His fellow workers grew to realize that any confidential information revealed to him become common knowledge in the executive suite in very short order, usually in twisted form. His main talent is contrasting his own strengths to others' weaknesses. Fred also brags about having contacts with key people in the industry, and often refers to them on a first-name basis, as if to suggest he is their social and professional

equal. Name-dropping is just one of the ways he tries to intimidate others.

Four years after joining the company, Fred is still there, and in the same position. This is because, while management sometimes has uses for snakes like Fred, they certainly don't trust them enough to promote them to their own level. And nobody else in the industry will hire him, simply because many of the colleagues whose positions he undermines have since left to accept responsible positions with competitors. As in so many industries, word spreads quickly among peers. Fred is still digging his own career grave.

In short, it is with their peers that effective executives learn the true meaning of teamwork. They take advantage of their daily encounters to make allies, not enemies, and observe the dos and don'ts of peer relationships.

DO learn from your peers. As you all advance up the ladder, those who climb most rapidly are often those who are able to learn from the mistakes and triumphs of both themselves and others.

DO share and communicate with your colleagues. It is one thing to be discreet, but don't unnecessarily close yourself off, or become extremely secretive. This type of behavior arouses the suspicions of others, leaving you uninformed and unpopular. A confident executive is inclusive, not exclusive, recognizing the importance of sharing pertinent information with those who need to know it. This does not, of course, mean that you should disseminate confidential information among those who are not authorized to receive it.

DO support and assist your peers. Remember that you are building goodwill, and must leave an impression of reliability and integrity with all whom you encounter. However, don't be naive. Support is one thing, but it is not advisable to do someone else's work, cover for an incompetent colleague, or train someone to the extent that your own job becomes redundant.

DON'T take advantage of a colleague's weakness. If a capable fellow-worker is having an off period, talk to him or her about it and try to find out what the problem is, with a view to finding a solution.

DO respect the privacy of fellow-workers. If a person hears that a colleague has been seeking another job or is having marital problems, it is indiscreet to ask direct questions about it or spread the word to others.

Subordinates

As a person advances within a corporation, more and more employees fall under his or her supervision. Effective managers MUST know how to create a satisfying and productive atmosphere among subordinates, while encouraging them to reach their full potential. A good manager works hard to establish a basis of mutual respect and trust.

Although management is the topic of numerous books and degree programs, there are a few basic rules governing behavior to subordinates, that are applicable to all situations.

DO remember the simple courtesies in your dealings with subordinates. The most important words you can use with them are "please" and "thank you." Always say "good morning" and "good night" to them. Smile. When working together from day to day, it is too easy to start taking each other for granted.

DO set the standard. If you value punctuality, be punctual. Employees get the lay of the land by following the example of supervisors. One corporate culture may permit some personal long distance phone calls from the office, personal photocopies, taking home office supplies and so on, while another may not. (Personal long distance calls and photocopies are *not* a good idea, regardless of corporate culture.) The boss's tolerance for cleanliness and neatness becomes that of his or her subordinates. There's no reason why they should exceed your implicit or explicit performance expectations.

DON'T use abusive language or profanity when speaking to staff or in their presence. This is an infectious practice. Others will feel free to follow your example, and before long you'll hear unprofessional discourse when customers and your superiors are present. Remember, abuse is no way to raise morale or productivity, and profanity has no place in any professional environment.

DO keep direct subordinates informed of relevant information. Let them know why things are done in a certain manner, and keep them informed of policies and programs that affect the department's status. You are not obliged to communicate plans with support staff who do not report to you, such as members of a stenographic, data processing or word processing pool. It is courteous, however, to advise supervisors of these departments of any large or rush jobs you will be submitting.

DO acknowledge your subordinates' contribution to the company and to particular projects. If your staff works late to meet a deadline, make sure you acknowledge the contribution not only to them but also to senior management. If your report is praised, mention the people who helped you research, write and type it. An occasional gesture, such as a box of chocolates for the entire group, never goes amiss as a tribute to a job well done.

Never underestimate the power of acknowledgement. Include your staff, and you'll win their support. Pass the glory, not the buck.

DON'T reprimand staff in the presence of others. If you have criticisms, speak only of their work and never criticize them personally. Say "the report was late" rather than "you lazy sod." And remember, the responsibility for any failure is ultimately yours, as supervisor. Don't create an environment in which everyone is afraid to take risks because the penalties for failure are so severe.

DO allow subordinates flexibility in setting their own pace and work habits. It causes a great deal of unnecessary stress if you constantly interrupt with "rush" jobs or ask them to drop whatever they're doing. Similarly, try to think things through so that they don't waste time doing innumerable drafts of every document.

DO delegate as much as possible. Don't keep all the interesting work for yourself or a few favorites. Subordinates should know that good work leads to more interesting and rewarding assignments. Otherwise, they'll feel there's no point in trying. A subordinate who shines reflects well on you. Also, perceptive clients and suppliers will notice if you are not delegating enough, or are constantly taking low-level phone calls while meeting with them. The word will quickly spread, not that you are busy and hard-working, but that you have foolish work habits.

DO look for opportunities to promote from within. You're not likely to be promoted yourself if you haven't groomed a successor. Also, your staff will strive to excel, knowing that their efforts will be rewarded.

DO remember the Golden Rule when supervising. Most people, left to their own initiative, want to do a good job. Constant or electronic surveillance is inappropriate, counterproductive and creates an atmosphere of hostility. Don't initiate a system of supervision under which you yourself would hate to work.

DON'T play favorites. Policies should apply equally to all.

DON'T get unduly personal with subordinates. Maintain a certain distance. Also, you should restrict criticism to matters related to work. We know of one boss who asked a subordinate why she wore a ring showing her Hebrew name carved in silver, since it drew "unnecessary" attention to her Jewish ethnic origin. This is unacceptable behavior.

DO bring in food on your expense account if you ask office staff to work late. Remember, little things mean a lot, and your staff will appreciate the gesture.

DO insist on a degree of formality when visitors are present in your department. Even if your secretary refers to you as JB throughout the course of your working day, she must address you as Ms. Brown in the presence of clients. In most industries, it is not considered professional behavior to be on a first-name basis with your staff.

DO take employees to lunch on their birthdays. Remember the anniversary of their first day of work with your company. (We know of one company that sent a dozen roses to a female executive's home the day she joined the company, to welcome her on board, then another dozen on each anniversary of that date. It may be expensive, but that's a class act.) At the very least, an employee's work anniversary should be acknowledged in a brief and warm letter or card from his/her supervisor.

DON'T ever refer to women as "girls". This shows very little tact. Don't call your secretary "honey," "dear," "my girl" or refer to "a new doll in the office" or "the gals in reception." Don't even THINK things like "are you sure a girl could handle the marketing post?" let alone say them. Aside from being dated, tacky and just plain wrong, this sort of thing can land you in court.

DON'T discriminate against minorities in hiring. Apart from the moral implications, this archaic attitude is illegal in most jurisdictions, and carries severe penalties that may be damaging to you and your company.

Secretaries

Never underestimate your secretary. A good secretary is worth her weight in gold and deserves to be treated with respect and consideration. She can be the greatest ally an executive has.

DO make the job description clear right from the start. Explain your expectations in clear, concise terms, and ask for a response. It is important to establish agreement at the beginning of a working relationship.

The classic example is "making coffee." There are two situations in which this happens. One is for meetings and guests in the office, when the boss is occupied with other people, and the other situation constitutes a personal service when the boss is thirsty. Making or getting coffee in either or both situations may be part of the job description and should be emphasized at the employment interview, in which case the applicants have the choice of accepting or not accepting the work. It should not come as a surprise after the job has been accepted.

DO let your secretary know where you can be reached during working hours, and when you expect to return. Not only is this common courtesy, but you should be able to be reached in case of an emergency. It can be embarrassing and frustrating for her to field questions when she has no idea of your whereabouts. Also, people may start to wonder whether you're renting by the hour at the local motel, or shooting craps at Louie's.

DON'T ask her to cover for you if you are leaving early, taking a long lunch hour, and so on. Take responsibility for your own actions, and don't expect her to lie just because she reports to you.

DO introduce her to guests whenever possible, especially if they will be having future contact with her on the telephone. Use her formal name ("This is my secretary, Mrs. Jones"). Leave it up to her to encourage less formal address.

DO treat her as a professional, not your slave. Don't ask or expect your secretary to do personal errands, such as mend your socks, buy personal presents, and pick up your dry cleaning. Neither should she do errands for your spouse. The company is paying her salary, not you.

DON'T forget that she is an individual, not a word processing unit. Ask her advice and opinion when appropriate.

Let her know you value her contribution. And if she is sporting a new haircut or dress, it is not out of line to pay a (respectful) compliment.

DO maintain your patience if you are a male secretary and all your mail is addressed to "Ms. X." More and more secretarial positions are now being held by men. If you answer the phone and the caller asks for Mr. Z's secretary, don't answer sarcastically. Simply reply, "You're speaking to him."

DO remember Secretaries' Week. Buy your secretary lunch or some flowers. Also, even though there may be an office Christmas party, you should invite your secretary to join you for lunch at some other point during the festive season.

DO read the section in Chapter 4 on "To Screen or not to Screen." Establish a telephone-answering policy that allows both you and your secretary to appear courteous and professional.

Clients

To establish personal credibility with a client or customer, and build a relationship of mutual trust and respect, it is essential to start with an attitude that puts service first. Unless you are selling something unique, clients buy not only a product or service, but their impressions of you. However brief your contacts with customers, your behavior must reinforce their confidence in your trustworthiness and competence.

DO be responsible. Act as your clients' advocate within your company, getting orders filled and making sure their needs are met. If you are planning holidays or a leave of absence, double check that your accounts will be properly serviced while you are gone. Have a personal stake in seeing that they get good treatment.

DO be punctual. Place a value on their time. Don't waste it by being late for appointments or overstaying your welcome.

DO use tact and diplomacy. Deal with irate clients calmly and professionally. Don't be defensive. Remember, without customers, there is no profit. The following example illustrates the benefits of diplomacy.

An industrial coatings manufacturer received a hostile phone call from a customer, claiming that the paint in a recent shipment was peeling off the pieces of heavy machinery to which it had been applied. The supplier, a chemical engineer, knew at once that the problem was with the substrate. However, instead of contradicting the customer or hanging up, the supplier drove five hours to the customer's factory, examined the shipment of steel they had received, and demonstrated that it was covered with an oily film that was preventing the paint from adhering. When the steel was cleaned, the paint no longer peeled. The supplier then offered to provide, at the customer's convenience, a free training session for paint assembly line employees, focusing on quality control and prevention of this type of problem. The customer, instead of being furious at the supplier for causing production problems, was impressed with the service and grateful for the technical advice.

DO keep customers informed. If there are production or shipping delays, raw material shortages, or any other problems that affect the order, let the customer know immediately. Customers should also be kept up-to-date on "specials", promotional tools, cooperative advertising, and the like.

DO respect the rights of customers to run their own business. If you have suggestions to make regarding their business, don't criticize the operation directly. Introduce your ideas as part of a general industry update, as in "I attended an interesting meeting last week about improving line efficiency. The speaker had some intriguing ideas.... What's your opinion?" Small businesses, in particular, appreciate recommendations and information from their suppliers.

DO remember to be friendly without getting too intimate. It's a common and tempting mistake to become too friendly with clients, since this may lead them to develop expectations of special treatment. To be perceived as a real professional, you must maintain a slight formality.

DO keep a card index of customers. It should contain details such as names of children, food preferences, hobbies and so on. Before meeting with them, it is easy to refresh your memory on these points, to personalize your opening remarks.

DO keep abreast of customer accounts. Make sure preliminary accounts receivable letters are courteous and never threatening. Cheques may be lost in the mail or delayed because of an honest mistake. Give customers the benefit of the doubt, at least until they have had a chance to explain and pay up.

DO review your client list from time to time. Are any accounts unprofitable? Has anyone stopped ordering recently? If so, why? Reflect on your dealings with these people to determine whether your attitude or product has caused the problem. Then get in touch with them and try to rectify the situation.

DO remember that ALL clients are important, whether you deal with them once a year or once a month. They all deserve courtesy and attention.

DO encourage feedback from customers about your products and service. It's the only way you can improve and they will appreciate your concern.

DO remember to say "Thank you."

The importance of building customer loyalty cannot be underestimated. Remember, your rolodex is your dowry.

Suppliers

Suppliers are an important part of any corporate network. Many business people do not realize that effective purchasing not only involves monitoring commodity prices, but also maintaining positive relationships with suppliers.

Developing a tie between buyer and seller should not be a one-way street. The following guidelines can help purchasers to do their part to ensure that this relationship is mutually beneficial and productive.

DON'T keep suppliers waiting, and return calls promptly. Their time is just as important as yours.

DON'T treat suppliers as second-class citizens, or as a dumping ground for any disgruntlement you may be feeling at work.

For example, "Harvey" is an ineffectual office manager, working at the headquarters of a large retail chain. He has held this job for fourteen years, and his advancement within the company has ended. In the eyes of his corporate associates, Harvey is a nice guy who is going nowhere. But in the eyes of his suppliers, Harvey is a tyrant who is going nowhere. When suppliers come around to sell coffee, photocopy supplies or stationery, he enjoys power-tripping. He yells at them for petty mistakes, keeps them waiting, takes calls when they are visiting, makes demands instead of asking questions, and always tries to make them feel inferior. He doesn't realize that by being so unpleasant, he puts himself at the bottom of their priority list. They are reluctant to answer his calls, and don't take seriously any complaints he might have. Behind his back, people think of him as the Napoleon of office supplies. His behavior fools no one but himself.

DO inform suppliers immediately of any changes to budgets, orders, promotional plans, and schedules, and so on. Remember, these have a ripple effect among your suppliers, and problems that seem small in your organization may seriously disrupt them.

DO specify your requirements, both verbally and in writing, using as much detail as possible. This protects you both, and it is folly to rely on any person's memory, including your own.

DO see that their bills are paid on time. Approve invoices for payment promptly. Almost every industry is subject to periodic shortages. In such times, it is the reliable customers whose orders are filled. Also, for small businesses in particular, late payments can give rise to rumors that your company is experiencing financial difficulties.

DO express your pleasure at work well done. Make a point of accenting the good as well as the bad. Sending an appreciative letter makes a good impression.

DO be cautious in accepting gifts. Most companies have or should have a policy about gifts from suppliers. Small gifts, such as a Christmas fruitcake and promotional gizmos like bottle openers, calendars and plastic pens, are commonly distributed as a goodwill gesture in the business world. No reasonable person would feel compromised by accepting such a favor. On the other hand, it is unethical to accept valuable gifts or considerations, since the cost of these items is invariably built into an inflated purchase price.

A purchasing agent who accepts gifts like a VCR or a trip to Las Vegas is guilty of serious misconduct which could lead to blackmail or dismissal. If a supplier offers a gift that is out of line with professional standards, you should report it immediately to your superior so that there is no doubt about your integrity.

If a gift arrives with a purchase, it belongs to those who paid for the goods, that is, the owners of the company or the shareholders. The secretary who orders a magazine subscription for the lobby is not entitled to keep the digital travel alarm bonus-with-order that goes with the subscription.

DON'T expect suppliers to take you for lunch all the time.

DON'T be indiscreet about your company's business. The supplier also calls on your competitors.

DON'T put suppliers in an awkward position by asking for specific information about competitors' activities or orders. Nor is it advisable or dignified to knock your competitors in front of suppliers.

DO feel free to ask for advice or general industry news from your suppliers. They often have a broad base of knowledge, through dealing with a wide variety of companies. However, choose a time when the supplier is free to talk with you.

Family

An executive's family can be a great support system. Indeed, the further up the ladder executives progress, the greater part family plays in their professional profile. Senior management feels comfortable with employees who maintain a satisfactory balance between their work and family lives.

DON'T exclude your family from your work. They should feel involved and informed. Let them know periodically what the company is doing, how your day went, and so on. Ask questions about their activities as well. Keep in mind that your work should NOT be your primary focus when you are with your family.

DON'T use your family as a dumping ground for constant complaints about your workplace, or take out employment frustrations on them. Stress positive points about your job, so your family feels proud of you.

DO set aside some inviolable time with your family. There may be occasional genuine emergencies at work, but you should establish a routine that allows you time with your family on a regular basis.

Workaholics give the impression that they lead an unbalanced existence and that they are too inefficient to finish their work in a normal period of time. There is little satisfaction in being able to quote last year's second quarter sales figures, if you can't remember your children's ages.

Family Businesses

Family businesses place special demands on the diplomacy of everyone involved. Not only must family members get along as business partners and employees, playing a double role, but they must work doubly hard to ensure that non-family employees feel part of the enterprise.

DO use businesslike address with family colleagues. It is not appropriate to address the president as "Mummy." Say "Mrs. Jones," when others are present.

DON'T bring in dim-witted family members over the heads of long-term loyal employees.

DON'T side automatically with family members in a dispute. Listen to both points of view and be seen to be fair.

DON'T bring private family problems and grievances into the office. Others are bound to feel acutely uncomfortable in such a situation. Marital discord, for example, is your business, and should not be paraded before employees, customers or suppliers.

DO introduce a profit-sharing or productivity gains sharing scheme, if possible, so that employees don't feel they are slaving to put your kids through medical school.

DO offer qualified offspring of non-family employees summer jobs, when available.

DON'T allow junior family members company privileges that regular employees are not accorded. If punctuality is a company value, cousin Marvin should not stroll in at 11:00. Privileges of senior management should clearly derive from the position in the company, not in the family.

DO take time to communicate, mingle and eat lunch with non-family members. Annual social events such as a Christmas party or summer picnic help build company spirit and goodwill.

DON'T expect non-family members to perform family functions, such as supervising your children during office hours. Professionals are bound to resent being asked to double as domestics, gardeners or delivery services, simply because they work for you in another capacity.

4

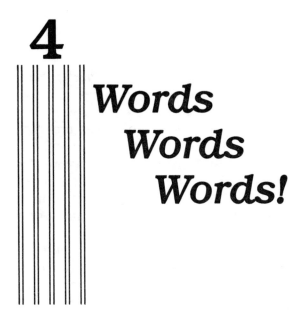

Words
Words
Words!

Effective Communication

Until fairly recently, one of the most important subjects at school was rhetoric. Rhetoric is the art of eloquent persuasion. It involves communicating your point of view, and convincing others to share it. A good speaker uses language to demonstrate knowledge of the subject, and also to establish personal credibility.

It is unfortunate that rhetoric has lapsed in popularity, because the importance of rhetorical skills has in no way diminished. If anything, there is a greater demand today for people who are able to speak effectively, partly because modern communications can reach such a large audience, and partly because the pace and competition of life demands that we choose every word for maximum effect.

Conversation

Conversation is one of the most basic elements of verbal communication and the wise business person recognizes its value. Speaking well is always a great mark of confidence. People with good verbal skills know how to open a conversation, direct its flow, and use it as an important professional tool.

For example, politicians and others who move in the public realm always seem to know just the right thing to say. They develop an ability to put people at ease and to win their support. The person who initiates conversation is immediately perceived as a leader.

However, most people today do not know how to make the most out of their conversations. A good conversationalist always opens the door to a response and invites the other person to participate.

The key to the art of conversation is the ability to listen. One must be able to respond intelligently to the points and objections of others, and adapt one's views when appropriate. Intelligent response is not possible if you have not been paying attention.

Even though we all have two ears, that doesn't mean we're always using them. Instead of listening to our companion's words, we tend to pay attention to a voice that drones on at the back of our head, the voice of our mind. The mind is constantly connecting fragments of conversation with memories, ideas and other associations. It reacts to and comments on an unending flow of perceptions. This is why it takes great discipline to listen to other people and to hear what they are saying.

When someone else is speaking, you should appear interested, open and attentive. Show you are actively involved in the conversation by nodding occasionally, maintaining eye contact, smiling when appropriate, saying "I understand," and so on. It is very disconcerting to speak with someone whose eyes have glazed over and who gives the impression that although the lights may be on, no one is home.

The simplest way to have a conversation is to let the other person do most of the talking. This shows that you respect what you are hearing and find the company interesting. People love to answer questions and give advice. If you learn to ask the right questions, people will tell you anything you want to know.

As sales people can attest, there are two basic kinds of questions: open-ended and closed-ended. Both of these have specific uses. Open-ended questions are used to draw people into the conversation. They leave room for growth and discussion, as in "How did you get into this line of work?" This type of question encourages other people to share information and to articulate their views.

A closed-ended question invites a brief, pithy response that usually ends discussion on the topic. For example, if you stop someone on the street to find out the correct time, you do not wish to initiate a long conversation. Other closed-ended questions include: "How old are you?" or "Where did you buy your shoes?" Such questions leave little room for elaboration or maneuvering. These are particularly effective when talking to a very long-winded person, since they bring a halt to the conversation and allow you to either change the subject or excuse yourself.

When meeting someone for the first time, find some common ground to open the conversation. This could be as simple as the weather, or traffic conditions. It's all right to mention an aspect of the person's outfit, as long as it is not too personal—"I notice you're wearing a Harvard ring. I was in the class of '69. What faculty were you in?"

And remember to use your guest's name in conversation. People like to hear their names mentioned.

The Rain in Spain

Your voice, as well as your words, conveys your message. It should be pleasing to the ear, and well-modulated. Your audience should neither have to strain to hear you nor be obliged to wear earmuffs in your presence.

Listen to your voice, using a tape recorder. Is it nasal? Do you articulate clearly, or do you mumble? Do you speak too quickly? Do you pronounce your consonants? Is your pitch high and squeaky? If you think of your voice as a musical instrument, does it play only one note, or is it playing a melody?

We know one woman who raises the pitch of her voice at the end of every sentence. This makes everything sound like a question? Not only is it maddening to listen to her talk, but nobody takes her seriously, since this affectation makes her sound insecure and immature.

If there are problems with your voice, don't ignore them. They can greatly reduce the impact of your words and presence, whether in a boardroom or on a podium.

Many speech problems can be corrected with practice and simple exercises. Make a conscious effort to improve, and if necessary take elocution lessons.

Language

Keep your conversation clear and simple, to reduce the likelihood of being misunderstood. Long, complex words can be effective seasoning in a conversation, but should not form the basis of it. Use the simplest word that does the job. For example, say "car" instead of "automobile," and "buy" instead of "procure".

Don't use inflated or pompous language to make your point.

Also avoid colloquial expressions that are used exclusively by one generation. Current adolescent slang seldom percolates into the ranks of middle-aged senior management. Conversely, expressions that were popular in the 1950s are meaningless to recent graduates.

Avoid dated slang of any kind. Slang succeeds only in making the speaker look out of touch. Besides, many people are too young to understand. Outdated words and phrases include "rapping", "groovy", "out of sight", "hip", "funky", "sock it to me", "get a handle on this", "soul power", "share these results with you", "airbrush" (a memo or something else that would never be airbrushed), "touch base", "massage the figures", "crunch some numbers", "yuppie", "light my fire", "run this past you", "dynamite!", "all right!", "lay it on me", "let's go for it", and "it's not my bag".

There is no point in speaking if no one can understand you. Remember, it takes two to have a conversation.

Dealing with the Press

The ability to deal with the media in a sophisticated way is a prerequisite to occupancy of today's executive suite. Good press coverage can get your company thousands of dollars worth of free advertising. Bad press coverage can, in extreme cases, put you into receivership.

The first rule, when dealing with the press, is to appear open and courteous at all times. Never be hostile or defensive. Have the facts at hand, or offer to call back promptly with any missing information. Journalists love sensing that a person has something to hide, then finding out what it is. Don't misrepresent the facts, either, although it is natural to wish to present them in the most favorable light. In any case, the reporter will probably call your competition to get the other side of the story.

Courtesy involves showing up for meetings and returning phone calls promptly. Most journalists operate on tight deadlines, particularly newspaper reporters, and if you do not call back, they will try to obtain information from other sources.

Be professional, show style, and nurture your press contacts. Maintain an up-to-date press mailing list. Reporters know who the professionals are, and deal with them again and again. These are the people who get a lot of good press.

When preparing press releases, try to see them from the editor's viewpoint. Look for the "angle" or "hook." What's new here? What's of interest to readers? Why would anyone care about this subject? Have a grabby lead or headline. And make sure press releases are professionally prepared. Grammatical errors and poor writing cause editors to lose interest. Professionally-taken glossy photographs and transparencies, preferably ones that show action, greatly increase a story's chances of making it into the print media.

Give the press as much lead time as possible. Magazines work several months ahead and their feature articles are often decided more than a year in advance (except news magazines, of course).

Don't issue a flood of trivial press releases. When editors get something from a company every week, usually along the lines of "Company X plans extension to parking lot," it isn't long before they start pitching any envelope with your company's logo into the garbage, unopened. Eventually, when you really do have something to say, nobody will read it. As the boy who cried wolf learned, if you haven't got anything to say, don't say it.

If you want a press conference to be covered by television, hold it somewhere that has visual interest. "Good visuals" are the hook that grabs any television story editor. Given the choice between a head shot in a boardroom and a construction site or even an interesting background display, the head shot always loses.

Don't offer a bribe. When launching a new compact disc player, it is not appropriate to tell a reporter from the trade press that you can get her a good price on one.

It is not acceptable to ask to see an article before it goes to print. No reputable publication does this, and the request is considered offensive. The better consumer magazines employ fact-checkers, who call everyone quoted to make sure the words are accurate and to verify statistics.

Watch your language when dealing with the press—don't use profanity, and be careful of grammar and syntax. The print media regularly tighten and edit quotes from casual conversation (without affecting the meaning), so that the subject does not look like a donkey. For example, "ums", "you knows", and "ers" are removed, and grammatical errors corrected. However, if you have made a poor impression on the reporter, he or she may not bother to do this. Sometimes, it's worse to be quoted accurately than to be misquoted. Also, with radio and television, what you say is what you get. The best way to speak well is to try to do so at all times, so that it comes naturally to you in front of a microphone.

Every reporter has a story about an interviewee who went on at great length on some subject, then said, "of course, that's all off the record." Not so. *If you don't specify in advance, it's on the record.* It is always wise to be cautious about issuing off-the-record statements and to bear in mind at all times that you are talking to the press. Remember, too, that a reporter may refuse to interview someone whose entire discourse is off the

record on the reasonable grounds that this is a waste of everyone's time.

In some cases, you may specify in advance that the quote
is "not for attribution," which means that it may be used in the
piece, but the speaker not identified. Journalists may go along
with this if, for instance, they know that identification could
result in the source being fired, and they cannot obtain an
attributable quote from anyone else.

When a reporter is interviewing you, it is not appropriate
to mention that you will sue if you are not quoted accurately.
You must assume that the reporter is well aware of the legal
rights of both sides and it is offensive to imply that he or she is
an unethical journalist.

Corporate representatives should not threaten to pull advertising from a radio or television station or publication if
their company does not receive what they feel is adequate and
favorable coverage. This behavior is waving a red flag in front
of a bull. Most editors will respond by going out of their way to
demonstrate their editorial independence by printing something negative or cancelling a story about your company.

Be well-dressed and well-groomed on television. Look
steadily at the camera or interviewer. Glancing at the off-
screen crew or producer makes you look shifty-eyed. Don't
mop your brow with your handkerchief, even though the
lights may be hot. You will only look nervous. If necessary, take
elocution training to prepare you for radio and television exposure.

Unaccustomed as I am
to Public Speaking...

Sooner or later, every executive is called upon to make a
speech or presentation, whether at an industry conference or
at the company picnic.

Many people become very nervous when they have to
speak to an audience, since they feel uncomfortable being the
center of attention. However, contrary to popular belief, one
does not have to play Hamlet in order to become a successful

public speaker. Keep your speech as simple as possible and present your information clearly, concisely, and with warmth. Use a dash of humor, if appropriate.

Before your speech, practice at home in front of a mirror. When reading a book or newspaper, try reading it out loud so that you get used to projecting vitality into your voice.

Be as prepared as possible. The best speakers do not read verbatim from their notes, but know enough that they can ad lib at appropriate moments. Speaking without notes also frees your eyes from the lectern, so that you can look directly at members of the audience, to command their attention. If possible, eliminate the lectern altogether, since this is a barrier between you and the audience.

If you must use notes, make them small ones that you can hold in the palm of your hand. Large papers tend to make you look unprepared. They also rustle in the microphone, particularly if you are nervous and your hands shake.

Just before you start your presentation, drink a glass of water to relax the throat and stomach and banish those butterflies. (This is why you always see a pitcher of water on the table at panel discussions). Breath deeply and regularly, to help you relax and to slow down the pace of your speech.

Don't be afraid to use your hands when speaking. Hands become focal points, and movements help to create interest and hold attention. Use gestures as you would in normal conversation: for instance, let your hands drive home a point or enumerate a series of items.

Keep your hands out of your pockets and don't fidget. Don't play with your jewellery or your hair. Nervous gestures distract the audience and make them feel uncomfortable.

Listen to your own innate sense of timing, and remain flexible, so that you can adapt your presentation to suit your audience's mood. If you sense they are becoming bored, or you observe people nodding into their dessert, move to another section of your speech that is livelier, or ask the audience questions to revive their attention. Also, if people become restless, if they start coughing a lot and are fidgeting in their chairs, you're losing them. Either change course or draw to a close.

Smile when you speak to your audience, and always thank them for their attention.

Introducing Speakers

When introducing a guest speaker, it is appropriate to give some background about the person's career and qualifications to speak on the particular subject. The speaker or organizers should provide you with a curriculum vitae, in advance, which you should memorize so that your introduction appears warm and spontaneous, rather than forced and awkward. Remember that the mood you set with your introduction is the one the audience will adopt in greeting the speaker. If you sound enthusiastic, they will look forward to the speech.

Pronounce the speaker's names correctly and indicate that you are honored to have been chosen to make the introduction.

Don't go on too long. Four to five minutes is sufficient to warm up the audience and present the background information.

Above all, don't bring yourself into the introduction, except perhaps as the first sentence of an anecdote ("I first met George when we were students together, and since then he has gone on to a brilliant career....") There is no need to outline every moment you spent together since 1960, or to mention that George was best man at your wedding.

When you have finished the introduction, invite the audience to join you in welcoming the speaker and begin applauding as a cue for them to do so as well. When the speaker arrives at the podium, shake his or her hand, smile, and get off the stage.

Professional Correspondence

Correspondence reflects not only the company but the writer. In fact, the written word is one of the most effective tools available to executives, one that offers them an opportunity to demonstrate their superior communication skills and courtesy.

Whether you are writing a letter, a memo or an annual report, use the following guidelines.

- Know what you want to say before you start to write. Drafting an outline of key points and facts helps you organize your thoughts.
- Keep correspondence simple so that your message is clear. If people are not answering your mail, it is probably because they do not understand it. For some reason, people who express themselves very well orally often feel that their prose must be flowery, ornate or excessively technical. Instead, they should use everyday language, avoid jargon and pompous phrases, and say what they want to say as though they were speaking directly to the recipient.
- Avoid inflated expressions such as "with reference to our telephone conversation," unless there is a legal or political reason to include them. Most of these phrases are irrelevant and a waste of time.
- Keep your writing brief. The Procter and Gamble company rule restricting memos to a single page makes a lot of sense. People are likely to read a one-page memo and put all longer ones aside. When writing professional correspondence, always remember that time is money.
- If you are not sure of your facts, DON'T put them in writing. And never write a letter in moments of anger, emotion or passion. If you do, tear it up before mailing. Remember, a letter has a longer life span than your mood. Just ask any lawyer who specializes in litigation.
- Use correct spelling and grammar at all times. It's not easy for many of us; however, most business communication is not complex and anyone who makes a minimal effort should be able to avoid careless mistakes.

No matter what your education, there is no excuse for not caring and not trying. If you are an engineer who can't tell too from two, try composing on a microcomputer and invest in one of the many modestly-priced style and spelling checking programs that have been recently reviewed in computer magazines. Buy and read one of the many books on business communication for background on style, grammar and punctuation. If necessary, sign up for a seminar on the subject. Keep a good dictionary in your office. And until you feel confident, have someone knowledgeable read your mail before it is posted. Otherwise, those who know the rules won't remember the content of your memo, only the fact that you misspelled single-syllable words from a grade three syllabus because you could not be bothered to look them up.

Answer all mail within 48 hours. Make sure you use the addressee's exact name, spelling and title, even if this demands an extra phone call. Add a personal touch, if possible. (See the section on notes.)

Business Letters

A formal business letter sent to someone you have never met starts with one of "Dear Sir," "Dear Madam," "Dear Sir/s and Madam/Mesdames," Or "Dear Sir or Madam" (the last if you do not know who will be reading it.) Unless you are positive the reader is male, NEVER use "Dear Sir/s." These letters should close with "Yours truly," followed by a comma. In the United Kingdom, "Yours faithfully" is more commonly used.

If you are acquainted with the recipient, it is appropriate to address him or her directly by name. Write "Dear Mr. Williams," and close with "Yours sincerely," which is a more familiar usage than "Yours truly." A large number of women prefer the title "Ms.", and their wishes should be respected. Also, if a woman does not specify Miss or Mrs., use Ms.

Letters to friends and acquaintances may begin with "Dear Derek," or "Dear Anne," and close with "Yours," or "Yours ever."

Never draw little pictures or happy faces at the bottom of business correspondence. This is not kindergarten.

A Note on Notes

Most people believe that they don't have time to write anything but memos, reports and other run-of-the-mill business documents.

However, there are three social occasions that demand a written response, in a corporate as well as the private environment. Smart business people don't ignore them. Responding in this manner is an excellent opportunity to demonstrate your professional polish and to appear outstanding.

When we speak of a written response, we don't mean a five-page letter of the kind you might send to your mother in Prince Rupert, or a memo that has been typed by your secretary and photocopied. These situations call for a brief, hand-written note.

When an occasion arises that calls for a note, don't delay. Write it at once and put it in the mail. This takes no more time than a phone call, and the results far exceed the effort required. People may remember the phone call for five minutes, five hours, or five days, but a letter lasts for years—and can last a lifetime.

The first occasion on which you must send one of these notes is upon receiving a gift. You MUST respond with a thank-you note. This applies not only to Christmas gifts from suppliers, but also to internal gifts such as a wedding present from your staff (address the note to the department) or the clock you receive after ten years of service. The latter occasion calls for a note to your supervisor, who made the presentation, and also to the president of the company, thanking him for the gift and for the opportunity to work with the company for ten years. Tell them how much you have enjoyed the experience of working there.

The second occasion that demands a written response is an invitation to lunch or dinner, in a restaurant or somebody's home. Send a thank-you note after the meal, even if it was a business lunch. This doesn't apply to people you see every day or every week, such as the person at the next desk, but you should certainly write a new supplier or a host on an out-of-town business trip. These notes should thank the host, but should not mention business details you overlooked during the meal.

The third compulsory note is the letter of condolence. On hearing of a death, you must write a letter, and it must be hand-written. (Other notes may be typed.) Sending a sympathy card is not appropriate, unless it contains a hand-written message. Approach letters of condolence with sensitivity. Avoid using the words "illness", "death", "tragic loss", and other phrases that reinforce the pain of the event. For example, a vice-president of sales, on hearing that the top salesman at a competing firm was killed in a car crash, may send a letter similar to the one below.

> January 16/1986
>
> Dear Mr. Jones,
>
> On behalf of the XYZ Company, I would like to express our sincere sympathy. Thomas Fisher was respected not only by colleagues at his own company, but by everyone in the industry. His enthusiasm and professionalism were an example to us all. We will miss him.
>
> Yours Truly,
> Doug Campbell,
> Vice-President, Sales.

Note that letters of condolence also demand a hand-written response. They must be mailed within a two week period following the funeral and the writer should simply express his or her thanks for the very kind words and support.

Every executive should invest in a box of good-quality 5" x 7" note paper. The paper may have your name and company name on it, if you wish, but it should not look like official company letterhead paper. It should look like a personal note from you.

The color of this paper is very important. It should be a simple, plain tone, never cute or loud. A bright-red envelope arriving on an executive's desk won't win you any points. A classic taupe with your initials embossed in gold, on the other hand, immediately marks you as a class act. Avoid any color of which you will tire.

Men should never use cream-colored stationery. This is strictly a woman's color. Men can use grey, taupe, blue, green, and even white. Women can use any of these, in addition to cream, pinks, lavenders, yellows, and turquoise.

Writing the compulsory notes is important. However, to take the extra step that makes one truly memorable,

> WRITE A NOTE WHEN YOU DON'T HAVE TO.

Receiving a note out of the blue makes people feel very special. This brings you to their attention and reinforces a favorable impression.

For example, if you invite someone to your home for dinner, social convention dictates that your guest send you a note afterward, thanking you for the evening. This would not be considered exceptional, but would be standard protocol. However, if you were to take the extra step of writing your *guest* a note of thanks for making the evening special, you would be going beyond the norm, and entering the realm of truly extraordinary behavior.

Be alert for occasions on which you may be able to send one of these unexpected notes. For example, it is a good idea to keep your eyes open for magazine or newspaper articles that may be of interest to business acquaintances. Send an article on ballet to a customer whose daughter is studying dance, or an article on the Bahamas to someone who mentioned wanting to go there on holiday. Keep a file of such articles, to send to appropriate people from time to time, with a brief note. They'll feel special and remembered, and will in turn remember you favorably.

Not all situations demand a separate note. It is often possible to add a short hand-written message to the bottom of business letters. One multi-millionaire we know keeps an index file that helps jog his memory for personal details. Every time he meets someone for lunch or dinner or for the first time, he creates a file card immediately on returning to his office. On this card he writes the other person's name, what he or she wore, where they ate, what they ordered, notes on the conversation, and as many other details as he can remember. Before their next contact, although it may be two years hence, he simply pulls the card to refresh his memory. He can then write at the bottom of his letter, "Walked past Fenton's the other day and remembered our delightful lunch there. Looking forward to an update on that totem pole you're carving!" The person feels he must have made quite an impression, even though our hero may not have thought about him since.

```
HUNT, JOAN

Secretary to Vice-President
First date of employment: May 2, 1982
Birthdate: July 11, 1961

Joan is fond of yellow carnations, pizza,
and is very efficient.
```

This method can be equally effective with co-workers. Keep track of the anniversaries of the dates employees joined your staff. Send them a note on each anniversary, congratulating them and thanking them for their hard work. It also builds goodwill if employees receive a birthday card from the president or from their supervisor.

Put Praise in Writing

The motto, "Don't say it, write it," applies particularly to words of praise. If someone works late for you, leave that person a note of thanks—chances are you'll be helped again. If callers mention the efficiency of your new courier, you should mention it—in writing.

A little praise is also effective outside your company. Whether it's your ad agency or a telephone repairman, acknowledge good service in writing. Such actions work to your advantage, in that it almost always ensures that you'll get good service in future.

Remember, to be outstanding, write the note when you don't have to.

Corporate Christmas Cards

Most companies have Christmas cards printed, and distribute them to management for mailing to clients and suppliers. Sign these cards personally before sending them, using your full name.

If your company does not print cards, it is advisable to send some on your own initiative. Choose a design that is simple, tasteful, non-denominational, and represents the image and dignity of your firm. "Season's Greetings" is the most appropriate message. If you choose to purchase cards published by a charity, it should be one that is non-denominational and non-controversial. Sign them with your full name and your company's name.

Send the cards to the recipients' business addresses, unless they are old friends or retired. Always include a brief, hand-written message, such as "all the best for the new year."

Send Christmas cards at the beginning of December, to ensure that they arrive on time. (Check with your local post office for suggested mail deadlines.) Christmas cards that arrive on Valentines Day do *not* bear the message that the sender is on top of things.

Send a personal Christmas card to your boss and his or her family, mailed to their home address. The same applies to any senior management people with whom you have close contact throughout the year, and to any people who report to you.

A boss should never hand out Christmas cards to staff as they are putting on their coats to leave the office on Christmas eve, or at the Christmas party, (unless of course they contain a bonus check). This looks as if he is trying to save on stamps.

It is acceptable for one department of a company to send a card to the employees of another department, thanking them for their cooperation during the year.

A president may send a Christmas card or letter to each department, which they can post for all to read. This should be hand-written and *not* mimeographed, unless the company is the size of ITT.

Hello, Hello,
Is Anybody There:
Telephone Manners

Many business people today do the bulk of their business on the phone. You may deal with important customers and suppliers for a year or more before meeting them in person. The telephone can make your work day much more pleasant and efficient. It can also be a minefield for those who use it discourteously. Observe the following guidelines.

- Answer your own telephone promptly. Letting it ring while you finish a conversation or search through files annoys your fellow-workers and wastes the caller's time. There is also the chance that the caller may hang up.

- Always take a second to set your tone. You should sound both enthusiastic and attentive, whether it is your first or fortieth call of the day.

- Remember, your voice is the key to using the telephone effectively. It creates the image you have in the other party's mind. Your voice reveals both your personality and your attitude toward the caller.

- Always identify yourself when initiating a call. "Hello, this is Mary Black calling. Is Mr. Forsythe available?" Similarly, answer the phone with your full name, unless there is a company policy to the contrary. Naming yourself is a particular courtesy to the caller, especially if your name is difficult to pronounce.

- Be professional, not personal. NEVER address anyone as "honey" or "dear." Also, if you are calling a woman and don't know whether she calls herself Mrs., Miss or Ms., call her company's switchboard and ask. If you can't find out her title before calling her, simply say, "Mary Black, please." It is offensive to call a woman Mrs. simply because you don't know her marital status.

- Unless absolutely necessary, do not put the other party on hold. For waits of more than a minute, it is better to offer to call back. If you must put a call on hold for some reason, make sure it is acceptable. For instance, say "I'm sorry, but the chairman is calling from Budapest, and it takes six hours to book an overseas call there. May I put you on hold, or would you like me to call you back in a few minutes?"

- Resist the impulse to shout or raise your voice, especially on long distance calls. Always speak at your natural volume and pitch, since amplification distorts the voice and shouting distracts your fellow workers.

- In all ordinary circumstances, it is courteous to wait for the caller to say goodbye first. If this is not possible, never sound abrupt, and offer a credible reason for having to hang up. "I'd like to continue this discussion, but I have to take a long-distance call."
- Never slam the receiver, drop it, or knock it against a filing cabinet. Hang up carefully.
- Keep personal calls to a MINIMUM. When you do make personal calls, close the door to your office for privacy and so as not to disturb your co-workers.
- Be courteous to people who have dialed a wrong number, without getting involved in a lengthy conversation. If you have dialed a wrong number, resist the impulse to hang up. Apologize and say goodbye.

To Screen or Not to Screen

Some so-called "time management experts" have wreaked havoc with telephone manners by encouraging executives to screen calls. This arrogant practice may indeed save a few seconds of your time, but it wastes a great deal of the time of both your callers and your secretary. Here is a typical scenario:

Secretary: Mr. Peabody's office.
Caller: Hello, is Mr. Peabody available?
Secretary: Who's calling?
Caller: Fred Wilson.
Secretary: Is there a company name?
Caller: Acme Boomerang.
Secretary: Does he know what you're calling about?
Caller: He should recognize my name.
Secretary: Just a minute please. (long pause) I'm sorry, he's in a meeting. May I take a message?
Caller: No. I'll call back the next time I'm in from New Zealand.

This scenario is by no means unusual. Smart executives never let something like this happen in their offices—let alone encourage it.

For those who persist in playing this questionable game, here are a few thoughts to ponder:

- Nobody enjoys getting the third degree for the dubious privilege of speaking with you. This tactic does not start your conversation off on the right foot.

- Screening calls tells callers not only that you don't care about wasting their time, but you think you are more important than they are—even before you know who they are. Unfortunately for you, they probably disagree. And chances are pretty good that you are NOT that important.
- Either you are in or you are out. Either you are available for calls or you are not. Callers will, understandably, be extremely insulted if they hear that you are out or not available ONLY after the secretary has decided you are not important.
- Perhaps you really prefer to know who is on the other end of the phone, to arrange your thoughts before taking the call. Your secretary may ask "May I tell him who's calling?" AFTER indicating that you are available to take the call. If the party says "no," your secretary should still put the call through, without taking offense.
- In the unlikely event that people call you when they should be calling another party in the company, it takes only a few seconds to transfer the call yourself or to ask your secretary to assist the person in reaching the correct party—after you have courteously given the name of that person.

If you wish to make good use of your time by holding all or almost all calls for certain hours of the day, your secretary must learn how to screen calls courteously. When someone calls and asks whether you are available, she should say, "I'm sorry, Ms. Jenkins is tied up in a meeting," and offer to take a message. If the caller is important, chances are she will recognize the voice, or the name from a list you've given her. She can always see you "just coming out of the meeting," of course.

However, in ordinary circumstances, *answer your own telephone.*

Hello, This is the Recorded Voice of...

During regular business hours, your phone should never go unanswered.

The best message-taking service is a reliable human being. If you can't find such a person (and it's not as easy as it sounds), an answering machine is the next best solution.

The most common mistake people make when using answering machines is buying an announcement tape that is too long. Your message should not exceed 15 seconds, and 10 seconds is preferable. If most of your callers hang up without leaving a message, it may be that your announcement is too long and boring. Although it MAY be cute in a home setting, business callers do not wish to sit through Beethoven's 9th Symphony in order to leave their number on your tape.

Keep your message simple and to the point. For example, "Thank you for calling Sam's Welding Services. Unfortunately, no one is available at the moment to take your call. However, if you leave your name and number at the sound of the tone, your call will be returned as soon as possible."

Also, you should buy a machine that is voice-activated. Callers get rattled and annoyed when they are cut off after 30 seconds and then have to call back and sit through your announcement again.

Electronic Mail: Good Manners in the Computer Age

Electronic mail is a complicated field, as etiquette varies with the various systems and their quirks. There are two main types of systems: those for which someone pays line charges, and internal systems, such as local area networks, on which time is no object.

On local systems, your correspondence may be conversational in tone but not careless. Spelling and grammar should be correct. Avoid tacky shorthand such as "u" in place of "you" and "4" instead of "for."

No matter what the system, capitalize the pronoun I. Remember, you are not e.e. cummings. Besides, sixties-style poetry is strictly passé, and has no place in business communication. If receiving a message costs the recipient money, make your message short and clear. Telegraph-style language is acceptable here. Don't waste words if you can get your message across economically.

Remember, it might be cheaper and as simple to mail someone a report, rather than incur high upload and download costs. Also, long files tie up equipment and phone lines. In a small office, such tie-ups can pose problems. Use electronic mail only when to do so makes sense, for reasons of speed, efficiency or economy.

If the message is very long, make sure the subject field is precise and give the size of the file. These courtesies are important if, as in at least one system, there is a NOPAUSE option for downloading and it can't be aborted once started. It's very frustrating, particularly with 300 baud modems, to start downloading a 30k file, find that it is of no interest, but be unable to stop it without pulling the plug (in which case logout may not function correctly, resulting in extra charges).

Similarly, separate correspondence concerning different subjects into different messages. Separating messages makes each easier to file. Also, if the recipient does not want to read mail on a particular subject, he won't have to download massive files on it to get to another topic.

If the system distinguishes between normal and urgent priority, don't flag frivolous messages as urgent. On some systems, urgent messages pop up on the terminal, replacing the file on which the recipient was working. Don't break someone's concentration to ask about last night's concert.

Use the subject field as effectively as possible. If the destination I.D. is a large organization, use the subject field to identify the specific person.

When possible, create a long message in a file and upload it, rather than write it in real-time while connected to the other party by modem. The exception is when an electronic conversation or collaboration is occuring in terminal mode.

Keep an electronic or hard copy file of important electronic correspondence. A copy allows you to resend if the transmission fails. However, you should regularly purge your files of unimportant correspondence, to save storage space or charges.

Finally, put your electronic mail addresses on your letterhead.

5

What Do I Do Now?

Many people underestimate the importance of the niceties of day-to-day behavior. However, in a competitive environment, these niceties can mean the difference between building successful working relationships and merely being tolerated.

Too often we forget that business is our largest arena for human interaction. When we work with people five days a week, it is easy to take them for granted and forget the common courtesies which should never be forgotten. Effective use of the social amenities in a business environment nurtures mutual respect and appreciation. Small gestures are the bricks that build lasting relationships.

What's Wrong with This Picture?

Gerald is a cost accountant with a sporting goods company. His boss is a woman, and quite often they have lunch together at the local delicatessen, three blocks away. When walking down the street together, Gerald is conscious of his manners, and makes a point of walking on the outside, closer to the curb. Is Gerald right or wrong?

WRONG. The traditional social rule is that a woman should always be placed on the man's right. (At one time, the lady who didn't take this position was considered no lady.) This rule applies in every situation, be it walking down the street, sitting at a dinner table, or standing at a cocktail party. Therefore, Gerald should walk either on the inside or curb side, depending on the direction.

In today's world, however, there are some exceptions to this long-standing rule. For example, in New York and other large cities where crime is a problem, the man walks on the inside, because muggers are more likely to jump from doorways and alleys than from the curb. Another consideration is that a woman may get hit in the head by water dripping from awnings or air conditioners, so it is considered gallant for a man to walk on the inside.

Thirty-five-year-old Anne is a lawyer. When coming out of the subway in the morning, she frequently encounters one of the senior partners from her law firm. Middle-aged and quite formal, he always offers his arm to her when crossing the street. Is he right or wrong?

WRONG. A man does not offer his arm to a woman unless she is an invalid, elderly, pregnant, or if the street is covered with ice or deep snow. (The reason is very practical. If one of you is hit by a car, you don't want to be attached.) Instead, the man should touch the woman lightly on her back or at her elbow for just a moment before they set off across the street together. A man should never grab his companion by the elbow and propel her across the street at a faster pace than she would normally use. This behavior is not courteous.

George and his secretary were riding the elevator to their office on the 25th floor. As usual, it was quite crowded, and when the elevator stopped and the doors opened, George got out first and waited for her to catch up. His secretary was offended and thought that his behavior was rude. Was George right or wrong?

RIGHT. Women don't have to get off first. This wastes everybody's time. When the elevator is crowded, the person who is nearest the door gets off first. However, if the elevator is nearly empty, women should exit first.

Martin was playing host to a visiting female designer from London. They decided to go for lunch, and since the restaurant was on the lower level, he suggested they use the escalator rather than take the stairs. Martin stepped on the escalator first, so she would not have to look up at him while they continued their conversation. He was eager to demonstrate his good manners. Was Martin right or wrong?

WRONG. A woman gets on the escalator first, and a man stands behind her, regardless of whether the escalator is going up or down. Both stand on the right. It is extremely rude for two people to stand together, as the left hand lane must remain clear for people in a rush.

David is a department store clerk who travels to and from work on the subway. Because he gets on near the beginning of the line, he always manages to get a seat during the rush-hour period. Inevitably, the person who stands in front of him is a woman. David pretends not to notice her, since he doesn't want to give up his seat. After all, he has been standing all day and his feet hurt. Is David right or wrong?

RIGHT. Although it is not correct to ignore someone deliberately, David is not obligated to give his seat to a woman unless she is disabled, pregnant, elderly, or carrying a small child or bulky packages. In fact, many women will refuse the offer because they consider it totally unnecessary. (To avoid offending people who do not consider themselves elderly, we suggest glancing at their shoes. Orthopedic oxfords and other sensible shoes are often the mark of a woman who may appreciate a seat.) Women should also give up their seats under similar circumstances.

If David was riding home with a co-worker, and there was just one seat available, it would be polite for David to offer the seat to his companion, male or female.

Lina is a product manager with a small chocolate manufacturer. Last week she was about to present her promotional plans at the monthly meeting when she met Charles, the company president, outside the boardroom door. He stepped aside to let her go in first. She politely said, "after you," out of respect for his position. Was Lina right or wrong?

WRONG. Just because Lina is a product manager doesn't mean she's not a woman. And just because Charles is the president doesn't mean he's not a man. The standard rules of courtesy apply regardless of rank.

Glenn is a new sales rep for a pharmaceutical firm. His first call was to one of the largest hospitals in the city, where he was introduced to a female senior surgeon. Glenn was confused. He didn't know whether to extend his hand in greeting or to wait for her to extend hers. He chose to forego tradition and put forth his hand with a smile. Was Glenn right or wrong?

RIGHT. In business, extending your hand is a professional greeting, and an important sign of trust and respect. It used to be considered a social gaffe for a man to extend his hand to a woman. This is no longer true. The only occasion on which the decision remains the woman's is when the woman is elderly (or the Queen). Otherwise, people should extend hands to each other. This rule includes women, who should extend hands to men and other women.

Barry operates a one-man law office. One day, a woman called asking for consultation on a major lawsuit. Barry agreed to see her at 2:30. When she arrived, he was on the telephone. He didn't get up, but just waved her in and motioned with his finger for her to take a seat. He kept her waiting ten minutes while he finished his call. His client looked offended, but Barry couldn't understand why. Surely, he thought, she did not expect him to stand when he was busy on the telephone. Was Barry right or wrong?

WRONG. Meeting anyone in your office for the first time requires that you stand and offer your guest a seat. This rule applies equally to men and women and should be a very natural, relaxed gesture bearing no resemblance to a jack-in-the-box. Even if Barry were on the telephone, he should have stood when his client entered, smiled and gestured for her to have a seat. He should never have kept her waiting while he finished his call. (In a corporate environment, an employee should stand when the president or visitors enter his office.)

Allan is a plant manager with a soft drink company. One day last week, he returned from lunch to find his secretary crying at her desk. He asked whether anything were wrong. She shook her head and continued crying. Allan was embarrassed, went into his office and closed the door. Was Allan right or wrong?

WRONG. Don't ask whether something is wrong when it is obviously the case. Allan should have called her into his office and asked whether there were anything he could do. He then could have given her a few minutes alone in his office, to catch her breath and pull herself together. If there were a serious problem, he should have given her time away from her desk or offered to let her have the afternoon off.

Margaret is the supervisor of a typing pool. She recently discovered that one of her staff was pilfering stationery supplies. Margaret was furious. She called the woman into her office and threatened her with dismissal. Was Margaret right or wrong?

WRONG. Emotional scenes and threats have no place in a professional environment, and problems of this nature must be handled carefully. Margaret should have called a general staff meeting, discussed the problem without mentioning names, and asked for cooperation. This approach lets the person know the shrinkage has been noted and should put an end to it. If the problem persists, Margaret would have to follow her company's personnel policy for such cases.

Nancy is a sales representative with a commercial sign company. Although her boss is a nice enough guy in other respects, he is always making sexist remarks about women in business. He talks about the "little girl" on the switchboard, and constantly reminds his secretary, in front of the rest of the staff, that he hired her because she has "good legs". The last time Nancy landed a large order, he joked about her "methods of persuasion" with her male clients. Nancy is offended by these comments, and wants to set him straight once and for all. Is Nancy right or wrong?

RIGHT. Just because she reports to him, she doesn't have to put up with offensive personal remarks. However, she should speak to him privately, in his office. She should address her criticisms to the remarks, not to her boss as a person. She should make it clear that she finds his comments offensive and embarrassing, and that as one professional to another, she is asking him to stop.

Janet is a dietician at a local high school. Quite often, she encounters male teachers and support staff on her way to the cafeteria. They make a point of holding the door open for her, which she feels is quite unnecessary since she is perfectly capable of doing this for herself. Last week, one gentleman held the door open and then turned and said, "you're welcome," after she had walked through. Janet could not believe that he expected her to thank him for this unsolicited gesture. Is Janet right or wrong?

WRONG. Courtesy from anyone should always be acknowledged with a polite "thank you." Also, it is still appropriate for a man to open the door for a woman, and women should not take offense at this gesture.

Making Introductions

Making gracious introductions used to be considered the mark of a cultured individual. Unfortunately, today one is lucky to be introduced at all, because the art of introductions has been almost entirely lost. We often end up introducing ourselves because nobody else has bothered.

The most important part of making introductions is showing consideration for and interest in the people being introduced, and maintaining a courteous tone. For bonus points, you may do it correctly, by remembering two simple rules:

1. A man is always introduced to a woman. Say the woman's name first, as in, "Miss Rogers, may I present Fred Astaire." This rule applies regardless of rank. For example, when introducing your mother to your company president (male), her gender takes precedence over his corporate status: "Mother, may I introduce John Smith, our company president. John/Mr. Smith, this is my mother, Mrs. Green."

2. When introducing two people of the same sex, present the younger to the older. Say the older person's name first, as in "Dr. Brown, have you met my fiance, James Ott?"

Always add a little information to go with the name (if possible), so that the people have a springboard for conversation. For example, "John has just returned from a month in Greece," or "Ellen is our new in-house counsel."

If an occasion arises in which you must introduce your companion to someone whose name you have forgotten, say simply "Have you met my associate, Jane Fredericks?" This is a cue for the third party to introduce himself to Jane. If not, Jane may ask, "and your name is...?" A similar technique is useful when you suspect that your companion or spouse has forgotten the name of an acquaintance. "Of course, dear, you remember my assistant, Arthur Williams."

If someone has forgotten to introduce you, take the initiative to introduce yourself. Smile, extend your hand, and say "My name is... I don't believe we've met."

Visitors to Your Office

When a visitor comes to your office, you should extend the same care and consideration you would show toward a guest in your home. There are many practical ways to express this consideration.

Make sure you have adequate seating, and that chairs are not piled high with file folders and sales brochures. It is not professional to have to run and grab your secretary's chair while your guests stand and wait. This wastes everybody's time, leaves the impression that you lack foresight and suggests that you can't count very well.

Never keep a visitor waiting. If you know you will be detained, call in advance and request a change in the appointment time. If you are delayed and the guest has already arrived, send your secretary to make your apologies and to offer a magazine or a cup of coffee or tea.

Try to greet all visitors in person, and escort them from the reception area to your office. If this is not possible, send your secretary. Greet them with a smile and a firm handshake. (Men must wear their suit jackets.)

Remember to take your visitor's coat and HANG IT UP. Never sling it over the back of a chair.

Have ashtrays available in case your visitor is a smoker. If smoking is not allowed on the premises, or if you have a medical problem, make sure that "No Smoking" is clearly posted, to avoid embarrassing your guests. If, however, your guest is a heavy smoker, you don't mind smoke, and your office is in a non-smoking area, you may suggest moving the meeting to a smoking area such as the cafeteria.

Don't smoke without first asking your guest's permission. Needless to say, if the visitor indicates, however mildly, that he or she finds smoke objectionable, refrain from smoking. Many non-smokers hesitate to force the issue on someone else's territory but appreciate your consideration.

Offer your visitor a cup of coffee or tea. Use a china mug and real (not artificial) cream, if possible. Paper or styrofoam cups, as well as chipped or less than perfectly clean mugs, should never be used. (One successful entrepreneur has an executive secretary who notes on an address file the way all visitors to the office take their coffee. After the first visit, she can offer coffee to the visitor's taste.)

Give your visitor your undivided attention. Don't accept telephone calls or interruptions unless absolutely necessary.

Don't waste time. Stick to business, after the usual introductory amenities, and encourage your guest to do the same.

Don't be afraid to end the meeting if the visitor has stayed too long. Do so tactfully but firmly.

Don't expect your visitors to wander through the halls. Either show them out yourself, or ask your secretary to accompany them to the reception area. Rise to say goodbye, and offer a warm, firm handshake.

Hosting
Out-of-Town Guests

Out-of-town guests require special courtesy and consideration, since they are unfamiliar with your city and may not know many people there. Your duty is to make them feel welcome.

Arrange for out-of-town guests to be met at the airport, unless they will be renting a car. Such arrangements are appreciated by overseas visitors and people for whom English is a second language. If your guest is renting a car, be sure to provide good directions for getting to your office.

Send a fruit basket or a note of welcome to the guest's hotel room, to be waiting on arrival. Include numbers at which you can be reached both at home and during the day, if you feel this is appropriate. If you haven't heard from the person after a reasonable length of time, call to make sure the accommodations are satisfactory and to ask whether there is anything you can do.

While visiting your offices, it is courteous to offer the guest the use of a desk and telephone.

The considerate host also asks guests how they are enjoying the city, and what activities they have arranged for the evenings. Be prepared to offer suggestions of plays, night clubs, restaurants, theatre, and so on, as the disoriented visitor is often at a loss. Do take the guest to lunch. Don't feel, however, that you have to take the guest sightseeing during the day.

On the day of departure, if the guest is in your office, offer to call the airline to check the departure time, and arrange transportation to the airport.

We Have to Stop Meeting Like This

Meetings are a way of life in the corporate environment. Once you have decided that a meeting is necessary, the key to making it a success is planning.

1. Prepare an agenda and circulate it well in advance, ideally two weeks ahead of the meeting. The agenda should include the purpose of the meeting, a list of participants, the date and location, and start and end times. Also include a list of topics, and the length of time dedicated to each topic. Agenda items should be listed and discussed in order of importance, so that key issues are handled while people's attention is fresh.

2. Start and finish meetings punctually, unless some-thing extraordinary is happening. If you discipline the discussion you will earn the appreciation of all present.

3. Don't invite people who are unlikely to make impor-tant contributions to the discussion and will only waste everyone's time. If people need to be informed, make sure they receive copies of the minutes.

4. Minutes should summarize decisions and specify any action to be taken, the individual responsible for it, and the agreed deadline. Minutes should be dis-tributed within 48 hours of the meeting.

5. Don't hold meetings at all if the possible benefits don't merit the cost of the participants' time. Con-sider the alternatives of a conference call, informal discussion or electronic mail.

Marks of the Meeting Misfit

The Meeting Misfit is often cleverly disguised as a working executive. But you can spot one by looking for the following characteristics.

- arriving ten minutes later than everyone else;
- bringing a pad of paper to the meeting and then doo-dling all over it;
- not paying attention;
- cleaning their nails with a match;
- bringing their lunch in a brown paper bag or Snoopy lunch box, and asking whether anyone minds if they go ahead;
- staring out the window while colleagues are making their presentations;
- frequently interrupting with irrelevant comments and anecdotes;
- asking people to repeat statements that have just been clearly and concisely presented;
- constantly dropping their pencils on the floor;

- going to the washroom more than three times;
- asking whether anyone has an extra cigarette while the guest speaker pauses for breath;
- falling asleep during the slide presentation;
- breaking their styrofoam coffee cups into little pieces and flicking them into the ashtray (usually missing it);
- taking out the morning newspaper to while away the time.

Power Seating

Just as some people wear certain colors to be noticed, it is wise to choose your location in a meeting room with care, since some seats command more attention than others.

The seats on either side of the chairperson are reserved for senior management. It is not considered proper behavior for lower-ranking individuals to sit in them. The next most desirable seats are the ones next to these. The least desirable are those toward the foot of the table, which are far from the action, and those which have their backs to the door.

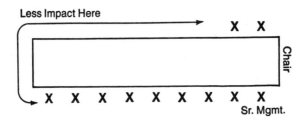

Don't sit right at the foot of the table, unless you are prepared to be extremely attentive, meet the chair's eye, and nod from time to time. In this position, you are right in the chair's line of vision, and your every move will be observed.

One common mistake women make in the board room is to sit beside another woman, as if forming a ladies' auxiliary. Particularly if there are only two women present, they should sit on opposite sides and opposite ends of the table. This increases their impact.

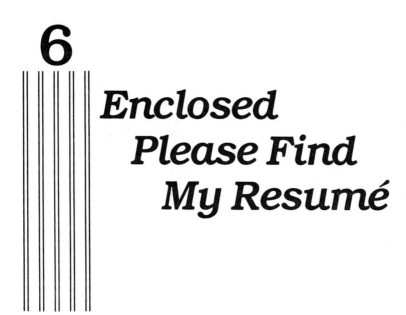

6

Enclosed Please Find My Resumé

When we consider how much time we spend on the job, it's amazing to think that most people choose careers and jobs almost by chance. People tend to take advantage of the first opportunity that arises without considering either where the job leads or whether it is suited to their abilities and ambitions. Too many people go after a job instead of going after the right job.

The first and most important step in any job search should be choosing a direction. Focus on what you want to be, where you want to be and how you want to get there. Don't limit your imagination. Take an honest look at your employment history. Have your jobs been satisfying, or have you harbored other ambitions? Are you excited about your work or just marking time?

What Do You Want?

As a first step in determining a career direction, write down everything you want from a job. What's important to you? What is fulfilling for you? What motivates you? Do you need an exceptional benefit package or high remuneration? Do you want a salaried position or the challenge of bonuses and commissions based on performance? Is prestige important to you? Job security? Upward mobility? Are you prepared to move up a hierarchy or do you want to be your own boss? Don't listen to what anyone else tells you—these are important decisions, so be honest with yourself.

Now take responsibility for your own career. Determine what steps are necessary to achieve your goals. Do your goals require that you take intermediate steps or acquire further education? Are you prepared, financially, emotionally and professionally, to pursue whatever course is required?

Be realistic. There's no point dreaming about being a lion tamer if you're 45, your background is in accounting, you have three small children, and your wife does not work outside the home. Consider all the factors carefully, and discuss them with your spouse. Choose your career as carefully as you would any major purchase, since this is the largest investment you will make in your life. People who have successful careers seldom achieve them by chance. Thought, care and planning mark every move they make. Be prepared to devote a great deal of time and energy to a job search. This move will affect your entire career, so don't be lazy about it. An hour here and there isn't enough. Treat your search as an important job in itself, one that must be approached with enthusiasm and dedication.

Once you have determined what you want out of a career, consider where appropriate job opportunities exist. What kind of companies offer them? How can you take advantage of them?

The first thing most people do when considering changing jobs is open the newspaper. Unfortunately, the possibility of finding a good job in this way is extremely remote. It's a place to start, but no more. Nevertheless, a careful reading of these advertisements can work to your advantage. They tell you who is hiring, what qualifications employers are seeking, how many and what types of openings exist in your industry, what the salary levels are, and so on. Keep a file of interesting job ads, even if you don't apply for them. This helps you keep abreast of employment trends.

Sending unsolicited resumés is another overused tactic, one with a rather poor success rate. Corporations may receive in excess of 100 resumés per week, most of which end up in the circular file. This approach should never comprise the main thrust of your job search. If you wish to give it a try, remember that sending unsolicited resumés requires careful and thorough planning. First, make a list of all the companies for which you would like to work and spend some time on the phone finding out the correct names and titles of the people responsible for hiring at your level. They aren't necessarily the personnel officers. Then send each of those people a copy of your resumé with an appropriate covering letter. Now cross your fingers—but don't hold your breath—and wait.

It's far more effective to get acquainted with potential employers in such a way that you are not perceived as a supplicant. For example, an excellent way to build your network and make yourself known is to become active in an industry organization. Try to hold office, so that your name appears on newsletters and the like. Offer to sit on committees populated by influential executives from other companies. Try to be named a speaker at conventions, meetings, and panel discussions. (Needless to say, this strategy demands that once you are in the limelight, you present a competent, self-assured image.)

Another technique is to call an executive you admire and respect, and ask whether he or she can spare a few minutes for coffee or a drink. Always offer to make the appointment at a time and location convenient to the other person.

Indicate when you call that you understand the person is an innovator in the industry and that you would very much appreciate his or her advice. Tell the person that you have been thinking about increasing your involvement in that particular field and would like to get some background on the latest trends. When you get together, ask the person such questions as how he or she got started, where the industry is going, which companies are expanding or hiring at the moment, which employers encourage growth and challenge for their executives, and so on. Don't take up too much of the person's time. When the discussion is over, thank the person for his or her time. The following day, send a note of thanks. In this way, you not only acquaint yourself with some movers and shakers and with the industry, but also build a network that will tip you off to job openings. If you do get a job, inform the people who have been helping you and keep in touch with them. Return the favor when you can.

Another alternative is placing your own classified ad in the "employment wanted" column. Many small business people skim these ads looking for qualified individuals. Keep your ad small, concise and dignified. Resist the impulse to be cute or dramatic.

Don't expect your campaign to pay off immediately. It may take two years and hundreds of contacts before you get the job you want. Don't rush to take the first offer, if there's a little voice inside you telling you something's wrong. That little voice seldom makes mistakes. The world is full of people who are unhappy and unfulfilled because they are in the wrong jobs.

Finally, don't give up!

The Resumé

A good resumé probably won't get you a job, but a bad resumé will almost certainly knock you out of the running for any job for which you apply.

Remember, a resumé is not an autobiography or an encyclopedia of your experiences. It is a piece of marketing communication and should be crafted as carefully as any direct mail campaign. The purpose of the resumé is *to get you an interview*, not to provoke a job offer. It should pique the reader's interest. Most people need more than one resumé, tailored to various types of companies or highlighting particular skills.

A resumé should be on heavy, good quality, 8½ x 11″ paper that photocopies well. It should not be on colored paper and should not contain your photograph unless you are applying for a job as a model. If it has been photocopied, make sure it was done on a good-quality machine. It is less than impressive to receive a resumé that looks as if it was from a print run of a thousand, or was run off for a dime at Woolworth's.

The typing, spelling and layout must be impeccable. It should attract the eye and the main points should be clear. People reading resumés usually read a large number at one sitting and get impatient quickly. Don't waste their time and don't do anything to irritate them, such as submit a resumé in longhand.

The resumé should be *concise* and highlight your accomplishments. It should not exceed one and a half pages in length, and if possible should be one page long. A short paragraph is not enough and suggests a life devoid of activity.

Keep the tone businesslike and positive. Two-thirds of the resumé should concern itself with relevant work experience and achievements. Educational history is secondary although important and should include only post-secondary information. Personal data should be kept to the minimum—nothing irrelevant. Your name, address, phone number and date of birth should be at the top of the resumé. If possible, list historical data chronologically, starting with your most recent position. Function-oriented resumés, which group accomplishments together regardless of chronology or company, are very confusing, difficult to skim, and suggest that the applicant has something to hide, such as long periods of unemployment.

Do not indicate the salary you earn or desire or list references on a resumé. These things are more appropriately discussed in the final stages of negotiation, after the company has decided to make you an offer.

Do not describe yourself in the third person, which suggests a mental disorder ("He held three positions in XYZ company..."). On the other hand, don't use the pronoun "I" to excess, as you are obviously the subject of the resumé, and so there is no need to labor the point.

The Covering Letter

When applying for a job, a covering letter should accompany your resumé. It should be short (no more than one page long), simple and to the point.

The letter should be impeccably typed, using a carbon ribbon. It should be on good-quality paper—never perforated computer paper—and in an equally good envelope. If the stationery is your letterhead, it must be businesslike.

Keep the tone professional, never familiar, chatty or cute. Avoid phrases like "Dear Sir, This is your lucky day!" or "I am the actuary of your dreams!" Be assertive. Don't use sentences like, "Although I am not really qualified, I would be interested in discussing the position."

If the letter responds to a blind box, or if you were unable to find out the name of the person who will receive it, address the letter "Dear Sir or Madam," never "Dear Sir/s".

Refer to the job advertisement, if there was one, and note any aspects of your experience that make you particularly desirable to the company in question. Respond to any points in the advertisement that are not covered in your resume. For instance, if experience with particular equipment is required for the job, mention that you have it. Don't outline your salary expectations on a resumé, even if asked. High or low salary expectations may cause your resume to be discarded before you have a chance to speak with a prospective employer. However, if you obtain an interview, you will then have the opportunity to make them want you on your terms—at which time you'll be happy to discuss salary expectations.

Next Please!

The job interview is crucial to a job hunt. Never refuse to go to an interview, even if you're not interested in the job. You may get interested once you begin to discuss the position. Consider it at the very least as an opportunity to practice your interviewing skills. You'll get familiar with different interviewers' styles and with handling difficult questions. Remember, actors audition for as many roles as possible because gaining skill at auditioning is as important as being able to act in a real production.

We recently spoke with a woman who was sent to Vancouver to open a western sales office for her company. She interviewed more than 300 applicants for the 22 positions available and told us she was appalled by their lack of personal presentation skills. Even top executives had trouble participating effectively in the interviews. Here are some of the most common problems she encountered.

1. **Lack of focus.** People did not answer questions directly or satisfactorily. They wandered off on tangents and tried to divert her attention to other areas of their resumes.

2. **Lack of confidence.** This created an overall impression of insecurity. People were hesitant to talk about their abilities or goals.

3. **Poor dress.** The interviewer was amazed at how many people were dressed inappropriately, or had not taken the time to pay attention to the details of their appearance that could give them the edge over a field of equally-qualified candidates. One woman even came in with bags full of shopping, explaining that she had stopped for groceries on her way to the interview. Poor posture and nervous demeanor were rampant.

4. **No one asked for the job.** An interview is like a sales presentation. Always ask for the sale, by indicating you are definitely interested in the job.

Before going to an interview, do your homework. Find out as much as you can about the corporation—its financial history, officers and corporate culture. Being knowledgeable allows you to feel confident and to ask questions that are informed and pertinent.

Dress neatly and conservatively. Choose your clothes carefully, since this is your only opportunity to make a favorable impression. Your grooming must be immaculate. Accessories must be tasteful. Jewellery should be kept to a minimum. Men should wear dark blue or grey two-piece suits and white shirts with an appropriate tie that is not flamboyant in color or pattern. Women should not wear shoes that are too high and should choose a good-quality, tasteful outfit. A silk dress with a jacket or blazer is always appropriate, as is a well-cut, dark, two-piece suit with a good blouse (never a sweater).

Make sure you have a good pen on hand. You may have to fill out forms and it leaves a poor impression if you have to ask the interviewer or a secretary to lend you a pen.

Be prompt and find out ahead of time how to pronounce the interviewers' names. When you arrive, remember that you are being observed at all times. We know of one personnel manager who keeps his office door open so he can observe applicants as they arrive in the reception area. He isn't interested only in their best behavior, but also in their "normal behavior." What is their posture? Do they fidget or look bored or nervous? How would they respond if asked to wait a few extra minutes? Do they smile at the receptionist, or try to pump her for information? How do they treat the other applicants? The interview, in effect, begins outside the door, not in the interviewer's office.

When greeting the interviewer, smile and shake hands. Don't take a seat until invited to do so. One sales manager deliberately piles the only other chair in his office with samples and sales material when interviewing a prospective sales representative. He watches to see how the person reacts when told to sit down. If the candidate looks helpless, he or she has had it. This manager is looking for someone who is willing to take control by saying, "Would you mind if I moved these to your credenza?" and moving the material.

Unless everyone else is smoking and you have been invited to do the same, it is not advisable to smoke during a job interview.

Be prepared for the questions you may be asked about your work history. For each of your past jobs, make a mental note of four things you accomplished and ask yourself "Why did I leave? What did I learn? How did I grow?"

The interviewers will ask questions not only about your employment background, but also questions designed to reveal the type of person you are. They want to know whether you are well-adjusted and a team player. How ambitious are you? Will your family obligations interfere with your career? How well do you get along with your fellow-workers? Be prepared to answer some of these standard interview questions.

1.   "What do you look for in a job?" Employers prefer someone who seeks challenge and responsibility rather than benefits and a good retirement plan.

2.   "What are your strengths and your weaknesses?" On the positive side, employers are looking for good organizational and people skills, initiative, responsibility and stability. They also anticipate that an ef-

fective employee be mature enough to recognize his or her own weaknesses. However, we don't recommend that you mention serious faults at this time, such as mental instability or an adverse reaction to authority.

3.   "Where would you like to be in a year, five years, and ten years?" Interviewers are looking here for a combination of financial and career goals. "In ten years I expect to be earning $100,000 and to be a top-performing salesman." Don't mention that you want to be president of the company or start a competitive business.

4.   "Why do you think you are the best person for this job?" This question gives you an opportunity to reiterate, clearly and concisely, your accomplishments to date and to underline the fact that you are eager to accept the responsibility and challenge of the position.

5.   "What are your interests and hobbies?" Management wants to make sure that your interest in macrame won't dominate every waking hour. On the other hand, it is good to mention active interests that demonstrate leadership qualities, such as participation in a charity or service club, community or sports activities.

6.   "Why did you leave your last job?/Why are you seeking a new job?" Never be negative. Highlight the positive things you've learned, but indicate that you are seeking new challenges and new opportunities for growth. Do not mention that your boss was a monster or the company was run by incompetents. If you were fired, be honest and mature. Discuss the circumstances openly and without rancor.

Never attempt to invoke the pity of the interviewer. Show, instead, what you can offer the company.

Remember, your objective during the interview is to appear articulate, self-assured and positive. Be aware of your posture and your body language and don't fidget. Everything you say must be considered and must serve to promote your interests, while showing a clear understanding of the company's needs.

After the Interview

After a job interview, be sure to write a note expressing your interest in the company and the position and thanking the interviewer for his time. This approach means you will be remembered even if you were number three of 15 applicants and would normally have been forgotten by the end of the day. Remember you are writing a thank-you note. Don't use it as an opportunity to clarify something you said in the interview, or to bring up a point you'd forgotten. It should be typed.

Here is an example:

Dear Mr. White,

Thank you for taking the time to meet with me yesterday. I found our discussion both stimulating and informative, and would like to take this opportunity again to express my interest in the position of Controller.

I look forward to future discussions. If you have any further questions, please do not hesitate to contact me at 555-1234.

Yours truly,

Jane Olynyk

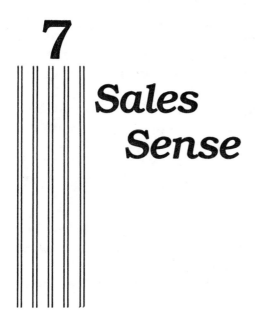

7

Sales Sense

Richard Lowe wakes up at 7 o'clock every weekday morning. He showers and puts on a crisp white shirt with elegant cufflinks, a clean silk tie and an impeccably-tailored wool suit. He checks to make sure his shoes are shined and in good repair. He has breakfast with his wife in the kitchen of his luxury condominium and quickly reads the Wall St. Journal. He then picks up his leather attache case and drives his late-model, mid-sized car to the office, arriving at 8:30. Richard is well-liked and respected by his co-workers. He gets a warm welcome from the receptionist, stops to pick up a cup of coffee and proceeds to his office where he spends twenty minutes organizing his day.

Is Richard a lawyer? The president of a company? A stockbroker? No. He's a top-performing sales representative and everything about his appearance and demeanor attests to his professional success.

Gone are the days of the stereotypical pushy salesman with the loud, tasteless clothes and manners which consisted of slapping backs, telling off-color jokes and speaking too loudly. Today's sales person is more likely to be eloquent, educated, well-dressed and polished, with outstanding people and communications skills and considerable technical expertise.

The sales field has opened up to include women as well. Many women have found commissioned sales to be their ticket to high incomes and career satisfaction since sales ability is easily quantifiable, achievement is immediately rewarded and the challenge is unlimited.

Whether male or female, professional sales people hold one of the most important positions in any company. They are also among its highest earners, since they generate revenue for the company and maintain the company's relationship with customers. A good sales and marketing record is often a prerequisite to entering the executive suite. Sales is also one position that will never be replaced by a microchip, as a good sales representative is more than an order-taker. The true key to success in sales is the ability to deal with customers, listen to their needs and help them solve problems.

However, there is no foolproof formula for successful salesmanship. Nor is there any one way to build goodwill. Rather, goodwill derives from a large number of small gestures. Take that extra step. Remember, all the sales techniques in the world will never take the place of a salesperson's sensitivity and innate sense of timing.

That First Impression

Impressions are a chief stock in trade of sales people who, after all, represent the company in the marketplace. Not only must their dress be impeccable at all times; the manners and professional behavior of salespeople constitute equally essential components of their image. First impressions, in particular, are critical. You must look like a winner.

Dress, as they say, for success. It is essential that all your accoutrements be of top quality. Similarly, your car should be quite new, clean and rust-free. It should be larger than a subcompact and conservative in color. People want to deal with a person who looks successful and established, not somebody who is new on the job or must make a sale, any sale, to pay his rent. A successful image tells people that you are good at your job, give good service and represent a good product.

The Rule of Twelve

As almost every sales textbook mentions, you can control that critical first impression by observing the following guidelines based on the "Rule of Twelve," which suggest that we first notice and remember three things about people we meet.

- the first twelve inches from shoulders up.
- the first twelve steps a person takes.
- the first twelve words a person speaks.

The first rule of twelve tells you that people notice everything above the shoulders of your jacket—your tie, tie knot, how well-pressed or creased your collar is, the length and neatness of your hair, your complexion, your eyes and your smile. Men should pay particular attention to ensuring their shoulders do not display dandruff—people will remember you for it. For women, the advice is similar. Their hair should be neat, their earrings not distracting or dangling and they should wear something brightly colored at the neck, such as a silk scarf or bow. This attracts the customer's eye to the face. Women should never have a pen or eyeglasses dangling from a string or chain around the neck. Nor should salespeople wear sunglasses—on their faces or on the top of their heads— when meeting with a client. Remember to smile, as this is a key factor in creating that critical first impression.

The second rule of twelve tells you to enter a room with confidence, and to look as if you both have a reason to be there and are happy to be there. Smile and extend your hand. Keep your shoulders back and stand up straight. Carry your attache case and samples in your left hand so that the right hand is ready to shake the prospect's hand. Remember to remove your gloves before shaking hands. Never enter an office holding out your business card. After you have taken a seat, take out your card and put it on the desk.

The third rule suggests that your first twelve words should always include a "thank you" of some kind. For instance, you could thank the customer for taking the time to see you, indicate that you're glad you could finally get together, or mention that you've been looking forward to meeting the person for a long time. Your words should invite the customer to respond in kind, for instance by saying "you're welcome," or thanking you for dropping by. This approach puts everyone at ease and opens the appointment on a friendly footing. Remember, first impressions are lasting, so give those first twelve inches, twelve steps and twelve words everything you've got.

Meeting with Customers

Once you've made your first impression, every subsequent visit and action should serve to reinforce your professional image. Every gesture builds both your reputation and your business relationship.

- Be on time. If you can't make an appointment, call in advance to reschedule it, not after it was supposed to start.
- Always look well-groomed for a meeting with a client. If necessary, take a moment to freshen up in a hallway or coffee shop washroom, before going into the waiting room.
- Remember that good manners begin in the reception area. Be courteous to the receptionist. Don't fling your coat and attache case over other chairs, tie up the visitors' phone or hog all the magazines in your lap. When you are through with a magazine, put it back in the pile, rather than leaving it on your chair.
- Be organized. Don't waste the customer's time. If you're dealing with a new prospect, have all the required background information prepared, as well as a list of questions you want to ask. If it's a long-standing customer, have the company's ordering history at your fingertips and have in mind any recommendations you wish to make during the call.
- Your air should be professional and unapologetic. A sales person should never appear embarrassed to be selling or act as if he or she is infringing on the prospect's time. Move with confidence, speak with authority

and let your words and gestures indicate that you have an important reason to be there.

- Show that you are keeping the customer's interests at heart. Don't appear to be pushing products that aren't suitable. Take the time to show the customer how the product can benefit his or her operation and outline its advantages over competitive products. Be patient and speak slowly, clearly and concisely. Remember, your customer is not as familiar with your products as you are, nor has he heard your pitch as many times as you have.

- Be polite. Never forget to say please and thank you. Don't assume you can address the customer on a first-name basis before you have been invited to do so. Also, don't take a seat in the client's office until you are offered one.

- Respect your customer's privacy. Don't make comments if you happen to overhear the end of a conversation. We know of a young salesman who lost an account because he read a memo (upside down) on the customer's desk and proceeded to comment on it.

- Stick to business. Make your pitch, ask for the sale, deal with objections, close the deal and get out. Too many sales representatives overstay their welcome with busy customers. Take the time, however, to end all conversations (in person or on the phone) on a friendly and more personal note. "Have a good weekend," "Enjoy your vacation," or "Congratulations again on your promotion," are a few examples. *Never* say "Have a nice day." This is overused, overrated, and sounds insincere.

Back at the Ranch

When you get back to the office after meeting a customer for the first time, send a note thanking him or her for spending time with you. Indicate how much you enjoyed the meeting and that you look forward to working together in the future.

Enclose any information you promised, such as brochures or price lists. Send the note even if you didn't get an order—this time.

Update your records. Keep a file card on your clients, including such information as the names of key people in the organization (your contact and his secretary, the plant manager, etc.) This information will help you make a favorable impression on your next call.

Take responsibility for servicing your accounts. Make a point of checking that the order is filled promptly and correctly, particularly when dealing with new customers.

Always analyze your day's work. Look for your strong points and weaknesses. Is your performance in line with your goals and forecasts? What can you do to make tomorrow a better and more profitable day?

Cold Calling

Cold calling, whether by phone or in person, is the hardest part of any sales person's job, and its greatest challenge. If you can face nine rejections and still make that tenth call that could result in a sale, you have the determination that marks you for success.

When speaking on the phone, remember that your voice creates an impression. It should always sound fresh and enthusiastic. Give the person you are speaking to a reason to see you, such as offering to improve efficiency or lower costs.

When calling in person make an appointment first, when possible. Busy executives consider it the height of rudeness if a salesman bursts in on their schedule and expects them to drop everything to hear about the latest in photocopiers or postage meters.

Always thank the prospect for the time you have been given. Apologize if you have unintentionally interrupted something and ask whether you may call back in the future.

And learn to deal with rejection gracefully. It's part of the job. Remember that people aren't rejecting you personally, but the idea of seeing a sales representative at that moment.

Telemarketing

Telemarketing can be an effective marketing tool—otherwise it wouldn't be so popular. Unfortunately, telemarketers have a very poor reputation, largely because some of them behave insensitively and a minority are fly-by-night operators working out of phone booths. It's not an easy profession, but those who succeed at it do so by showing such courtesy that they avert negative reactions.

Tone of voice is crucial. The caller must sound professional and be able to read the script convincingly and authoritatively. He or she should sound proud of the product, not embarrassed about the job. Hire callers who speak distinctly and train them to understand the product. Don't hire people who lack the intelligence to improvise if the other party deviates in some way from the script. Train callers to handle various objections and to wing it if necessary.

Callers should show courtesy and consideration to secretaries and receptionists. Don't treat them as if they were unimportant. Nor should you be hesitant in offering information, such as your name and that of your company. You may arouse their suspicions and prompt them to screen your call.

Telemarketers should not use underhanded methods to get through to an individual in a particular company. For example, don't call during the lunch hour to find out the name of the purchasing manager, then call back after lunch and ask for the person by his or her first name, implying that you know the person. If the party you are trying to reach is too busy to talk, apologize for disturbing him or her and ask for a convenient time to call back. Then get off the phone. Don't refuse to leave your name and number, unless doing so is against company policy.

Telemarketers who engage in direct sales to consumers must remember that they are intruding on people's scarce leisure time, so they must behave at all times with sensitivity and discretion. Otherwise, they will create massive ill-will. Always identify your company before proceeding to your sales pitch. If a woman answers the phone, and the call list specifies only an initial, don't say "Mrs." And don't start by asking whether she is the lady of the house, particularly before identifying your name and company.

Don't ask, "Am I calling at a bad time?"; the answer will invariably be "yes." Instead ask, "Am I calling at a good time?" Extend this courtesy, rather than launching insensitively into a pitch.

Computerized telemarketing, which uses machines instead of people, is generally annoying. Even if they are not yet illegal in your jurisdiction, never use the kind of equipment that ties up the line until the end of the pitch, even if the other party has hung up. This is not only ill-mannered, but can also be dangerous in case of an emergency.

8

Fish Forks and Canapés: Table Manners

Sharing food is one of the most deeply-rooted rituals in any society. For this reason, it is important that we learn how to conduct ourselves properly at the table, and acquire the skills that elevate our behavior from mere eating to fine dining. The thousand or so meals we eat in a year should each be regarded as an opportunity to polish our dining expertise, and to leave a positive impression with our fellow diners.

Good table manners are always a sign of breeding and education. Manners reveal a great deal about our backgrounds. If a person is disorganized, greedy, insensitive, scattered, ill at ease, or insecure, these qualities will always be evident in his behavior at table. We have all had the experience of eating with someone whose table manners were poor, and can attest to the fact that not only was this offensive and embarrassing, but it is a difficult memory to erase.

Fortunately, the rules of dining etiquette are straightforward and easy to master. It's rather like learning how to drive a car. Until you know what you are doing, it's very distracting to keep it all straight. You feel as if you can't operate the car and watch the traffic at the same time. With a little practice, however, the moves become mechanical actions, and you are free to concentrate on the road. Similarly, once you learn how to behave at the table, your manners become as automatic as shifting gears on a car. From that point, you no longer need to think about them, and you are free to enjoy your meal.

For example, a junior executive, who recently attended one of our dining seminars, told us that before enrolling in the course he had been extremely ill at ease when dining with clients or senior management of his company. Instead of being able to concentrate on the conversation, his attention was constantly distracted by such questions as which fork to use, how to cope with a crusty roll, and when to take the napkin from the table. At the back of his mind he was always worried that people were watching him, and that his manners might be making a poor impression. He felt that his awkward behavior was affecting his credibility as a professional. However, once he had learned the skills of correct dining, he felt much more confident and his mind was free to focus on business. His overall demeanor became much more polished.

This chapter outlines the major rules of correct dining etiquette.

The Napkin

A napkin is not a blanket, a face cloth, or a bib. Many people, men in particular, fail to appreciate this. You should not attach it to your clothing with a tie clip, or loop it through your belt buckle to make sure it doesn't fall off your lap. Neither should you tuck it into your collar. (Exception would be made in the case of messy sea foods, like crab or lobster. Many restaurants will provide customers with bibs to eat these dishes).

The correct way to handle the napkin is to take it from the table, and using both hands, give it a slight shake under the table and lay it across your lap. The napkin should be half open, with the fold toward you. Resist the impulse to open it fully and never wave it in the faces of your dining companions. They will not award you a boy scout badge for semaphor if you make this mistake.

An exception to the above occurs when the napkin has been folded accordion-style in your wine glass, which signifies that it is the waiter's responsibility to remove it from the glass and place it on your lap. If you are seated so that the waiter won't be able to reach you, wait until he has placed the napkin for someone else at the table before removing your own. Otherwise, people may follow your lead.

If you are called away from the table during the meal, place the napkin on the left side of your plate, in loose folds, or on your chair. It is not correct to take it with you to the telephone or washroom.

The purpose of the napkin is to remove any particles of food that may have attached themselves to your face in the course of the meal. Do this by dabbing at your mouth with a very delicate action that should in no way resemble polishing a car.

It is considered déclassé to dip the napkin in your water glass to clean the silverware or your fingers. Similarly, never use your napkin to blow your nose or clean your ear. Neither should it be a receptacle for inedible objects such as olive pits or chicken bones.

When finished, place the napkin to the left of the place setting in loose folds. NEVER crumple up a napkin (paper or cloth) and put it in a heap on top of your plate.

The hostess or host takes the napkin from the table first. This is a signal to the others at the table to do the same.

Cutlery

Most people know how to set a table and in which order to use cutlery. Forks are laid to the left of the plate, tines up. (The exception to this is the small fish fork, which is always set to the right of the place setting.) Knives are at the right of the plate, blades turned towards it. To the right of the knives are the spoons, bowls facing up.

When using cutlery, the rule is to work from the outside in. Choose the fork on the extreme left, and the spoon or knife on the extreme right. Cutlery will have been set so that if this rule is followed, diners will have the correct utensils for each course.

A very common mistake that people make is holding cutlery incorrectly. The essence of good table manners is to be

as unobtrusive as possible, and holding cutlery in an unnatural position appears awkward and draws attention to your hands.

For example, many people tend to make a fist around the handle of the utensil, (particularly the soup spoon), which is the gesture of a toddler. Another error is holding the cutlery near the base, like a pencil or pen, sometimes with the index finger near the prongs of the fork. Others cut their food incorrectly by holding the fork and knife perpendicular to each other, stabbing with the fork and sawing with the knife, as if playing the cello.

The correct way to hold cutlery is at a slight angle. It is positioned between your thumb, first and second finger, with the end of the handle resting lightly on your palm, near the base of your fingers. However, when raising a soup spoon to the mouth, the same three fingers hold the handle, but the end rests on the forefinger to keep the spoon level.

There are two acceptable ways to use the knife and fork: continental fashion, which is more prevalent in Europe, and American standard. Choose the style to which you are accustomed, and which will draw the lesser amount of attention to you at table. Don't awkwardly try to follow continental style in Europe, if you're not comfortable with it. If your own etiquette is consistent and correct, you can't go wrong.

In continental fashion, the diner holds the utensils at all times. The diner cuts the food, usually one bite at a time, and uses the fork in the left hand, tines pointing down, to spear the food and bring it to the mouth.

The American standard style calls for cutting a few mouthfuls of food, then laying the knife across the top of the plate, with the serrated edge pointing toward the center. The fork is then switched to the right hand, tines pointing up, and used to bring the food to the mouth. The left hands rests on the lap while the fork is used. The diner switches cutlery from hand to hand in this way throughout the meal.

Remember never to cut more than three bites at one time. It is not considered good etiquette to cut all your food up into itty bitty pieces at the start of the meal.

If there are any utensils at the top of the place setting, these are not salad forks or coffee spoons that have gone astray. They are to be used for dessert, and may comprise a spoon, a fork, or both, depending on the type of desserts served. (Your coffee spoon is either at the right of your plate or will be brought with the coffee.)

In North America it is becoming increasingly popular to eat dessert with a spoon *and* fork. They are being used to eat anything from pie with ice cream to lemon mousse or walnut torte. When it is time to use the utensils, they should not be lifted off the table. One handle faces each hand, and the correct method is to take hold of these handles and slide each down so that the fork is to the left and the spoon to the right of the plate. The spoon is used to break the food (one bite at at time), and the fork acts as a pusher by pivoting rhythmically from the wrist. The diner then uses the spoon in the right hand to lift the food to the mouth.

The correct way to indicate that you have finished eating a course is to place your cutlery on your plate, in a clock position of approximately ten to four, with the handles in the four

position. The knife goes down first, with the sharp edge toward you. The fork then goes beside it, closer to you. This is a signal that you have finished eating and that the waiter may remove your plate.

Left-Handed Diners

Left-handed diners should use continental style, to reduce the number of movements necessary. If possible, they should choose a corner seat with the left side open, so that their arm movements won't disrupt the adjacent person. A left-handed person should not rearrange his place setting or reach for his beverage with his left hand.

Chopsticks

Every cosmopolitan person knows how to dine with chopsticks. Using them is really quite simple once you get the knack. If you aren't familiar with their use, we suggest you buy a pair for your home and eat only with chopsticks for a single weekend. This should perfect your technique.

The method for eating with chopsticks is as follows: hold them slightly below the midpoint, one on top of the other, with the pointed ends toward your plate. The bottom chopstick never moves, relative to the other chopstick. It is held tightly between the middle finger and the thumb joint, and rests on the fourth (ring) finger. The top chopstick pivots up and down, so that its point moves toward and away from the bottom chopstick to grasp the food. Hold the top chopstick between the inside end of the thumb and the side of the index finger, and wiggle the index finger to effect the pivoting motion.

When using chopsticks to eat rice from a bowl, it is customary to lift the bowl from the table and bring it closer to your mouth.

Passing Fancies

When first passing main dishes, bread baskets or salt and pepper shakers at the table, always pass to the right. (This rule applies equally to left-handed people.)

Salt and Pepper

The correct way to pass salt and pepper is together. It is easier to keep track of their location on the table this way. Your fingers or hands should not touch the top of the dispenser; hold them at the bottom.

If the table is set using salt cellars, you may use the tip of your knife to serve yourself if a tiny spoon is not provided. If the salt cellar is for your individual use, you may also use the tips of your fingers.

A note for salt addicts: Some people feel their food must be coated with a fine layer of white before they are able to eat it. It is particularly risky to smother your food with salt when lunching with your life insurance agent, who may become alarmed and raise your premiums. It is also considered a social lapse to salt your food before you have tasted it. In restaurants and particularly in someone's home, where the chef has gone to a great deal of trouble to season the food correctly, such behavior is insulting and further suggests that you have no appreciation of good food.

Little Pitchers

When passing a dish such as a creamer, syrup pitcher, or gravy boat, pass it with the handle pointing toward the recipient. Needless to say, fingers should not touch the spout. If the pitcher has a liner (small plate), pass it on the liner, handle toward the recipient. The liner is there to prevent spills onto the tablecloth.

When pouring, lift the liner and dish together, holding the liner under it as you pour. Then pass both to your right, as you received them, without putting them down first.

Your Bread and Butter

As everyone knows, most dining establishments supply a basket of bread and butter as a light snack while the meal is being prepared. If the basket is placed in front of you, it is courteous to open the napkin that covers the bread, and pass the basket to the person on your right. If there are two of you, offer it to the other person before helping yourself.

The correct way to eat bread is to place a piece on your bread plate. Take butter, if desired, and place it on your bread plate as well. (Use the butter knife if there is one. If not, use your dinner knife, never your fork.) Break the roll in your hands, unless it is so hard that a knife or chisel is required. Tear off a small piece of bread, not more than one or two bites in size. Butter this piece, and eat it. Food you pick up for any reason (except to break it) should not be returned to the plate. Nor is it correct to pick up an entire piece of bread and butter it flat in your hand, in mid-air, or over the dinner plate. The same rules apply when eating a bread stick. Remember not to wave it like a baton as you are speaking, or to let it make a nose dive for the butter.

Toast and garlic bread, however, may be eaten in larger pieces. Since these are served already buttered, it would be messy to break them frequently in your hands.

It shows a lack of finesse to stuff oneself with bread and then ask the waiter to bring more. Restrict yourself to one piece, until the meal is served.

In the Soup

The correct way to eat soup is always to spoon it away from you. Lean forward slightly with your back straight, and bring the soup up to your mouth. Avoid hunching over the bowl. The bowl of the spoon should be held so as to allow you to sip from the side of the spoon rather than the tip. However, if the soup contains large pieces of meat, fish, or vegetables, you may have to adjust the angle of the spoon. Don't slurp.

If there is a little soup left in the bottom of the bowl and you want to finish it, tip the bowl away from you. But don't scrape cutlery against the side of the bowl.

If the bowl has handles, use your spoon to take two or three mouthfuls. It is then acceptable to lay your spoon on the liner, use the handles to raise the bowl to your mouth to drink the soup. Use this method for THIN clear soups only. Always eat a thick soup with the spoon, even if it is served in a cup or bowl with handles. (Also, if you are eating in a Japanese restaurant, use chopsticks to eat solids in the soup, such as noodles. Then drink directly from the bowl. It is not appropriate to ask for a spoon.)

Often, people order French onion soup or cream of asparagus soup *au gratin*, i.e. with broiled cheese on the top. Anyone who has ever eaten them knows that they present problems for even the most elegant diner. The cheese is either infinitely expandable when it melts, or congeals to a rubbery consistency that is impossible to cut. The best way to eat soup au gratin is in private. We do not advise that you order it in a public place unless you are confident that you can handle it with aplomb. If an au gratin soup is served at a banquet, try using the edge of your spoon to break the cheese. Resist the temptation to whip out your Swiss army knife.

When you have finished eating your soup, place the spoon on the right side of the liner. If there is no liner, place the spoon in the empty bowl.

Salad

Salads are served before the main course, with the main course, or after the main course, and should be eaten with a salad fork or a dinner fork.

Most of us have been in the situation of ordering a green salad and receiving half a head of lettuce, or vegetables served in enormous pieces.

In the distant past, it was considered a *faux pas* to cut salad at the table, more out of courtesy for the hostess than because it was a boorish table manner. This taboo developed because the acid from vegetables and dressing could discolor silver. Since the advent of stainless steel, silver is no longer commonly used, and seldom by people who would dump half a tomato in a salad bowl. Therefore, there is no longer any reason not to cut that lettuce or tomato. It's far better to do that than to try to stuff it in your mouth, or to spear it on your fork, suspend it in the air, and proceed to nibble away at it until it is a manageable size. (However, you should not cut your entire salad into small pieces at the beginning of the meal.) Also, twirling a piece of lettuce as if it were spaghetti is unnecessarily theatrical.

Drinking Wine

Many people are not aware that red and white wine should not be served in the same type of glass.

A red wine glass has a very round bowl and a fairly short stem. The correct way to hold it is delicately with your fingers at the base of the bowl, since red wine is served at room temperature and the heat from your fingers will not adversely affect the flavor of the wine. It is not appropriate to grasp the glass with your entire hand, nor should you use two hands to lift the glass to your mouth.

White wine is served in a glass that is larger and longer-stemmed than a red wine glass. The correct way to hold it is with your thumb and first two fingers, at the base of the stem. Your fingers should never touch the bowl, as heat from the body may affect the flavor of slightly chilled wines. The same rule applies to champagne, rosé, and other wines served below room temperature.

Coffee
and Tea

It is not appropriate to blow on a hot beverage to cool it, or to sip it from a spoon.

When served a cup or pot of tea containing a tea bag, wait until the tea is strong enough, then lift the tea bag and gently squeeze it against the side of the cup with your spoon, to remove excess liquid. Then lay the tea bag on the side of your saucer. If the tea was served in a mug, place the tea bag on the side of your bread and butter plate.

If you are served coffee in a mug, and you use a spoon to stir it, it is permissible to wipe the spoon clean between your lips and lay it down on the table. If a table cloth is used, however, lay the spoon face down on your plate.

Should you spill coffee or tea into your saucer, you may use a dry paper napkin to blot the excess. If paper napkins are not available, it is acceptable to pour the liquid from the saucer back into your cup. Never use a linen napkin or a corner of the tablecloth to soak up the extra liquid. And never drink from the saucer.

When individual portions of sugar are provided, wrapped in paper, either fold the paper and leave it under your dinner plate, or place it on the table, to the upper right of your place setting. Don't put it in the ash tray, where it could pose a fire hazard, or leave it folded on your saucer. Resist the impulse to play with it.

Food
Glorious Food

In the course of our seminars, we are often asked the correct way to eat certain foods. Here is a list of some of these.

Apples and Pears   These are usually served at the end of the meal, and should be quartered, cored, and then peeled (peeling optional). The quarters may be eaten with fingers, or cut into small pieces with a knife and eaten with a fork.

Artichokes   Whole artichokes are a finger food. Pull off one leaf at a time, and dip it in the sauce provided. Pull the leaf between your teeth to remove the fleshy edible part. When you reach the centre of the artichoke, scrape away the rough part with a knife, and eat the heart with a fork and knife.

Asparagus   Asparagus can be a finger food, although many people prefer to use a knife and fork. Start at the top, and if it starts to get stringy, stop. Normally, asparagus toughens about ¾ of the way down, depending on the manner of preparation; good chefs remove the tough ends before serving.

Bacon   Bacon should be eaten with a knife and fork. However, if it is very crisp and could disintegrate at the touch of a knife, it should be treated as a finger food.

Bottled Drinks and Cartoned Beverages The correct way to drink these is in a glass. If one is not available, the least offensive alternative is to use a straw. Never drink directly from the container or bottle, particularly at the table.

Cake Cake is usually eaten with a fork. However, if it is very solid, like Christmas fruit cake, it may be picked up with the fingers.

Chicken, Fried or Barbequed Unless served in a basket or at a barbeque, chicken, like spare ribs, is not a finger food. It is not considered good manners to pick food up in your hands from your plate. Eat as much as you can with your cutlery. Then wait until someone else at the table picks his up, or ask permission of your hostess to do so— "This chicken is so delicious. Would you mind if I used my fingers to finish it?"

Corn on the Cob Corn on the cob is a very difficult food to eat, which is why it is never served at a formal dinner. The trick is not to run it through butter or lather butter on the entire cob, which would almost certainly end up smeared all over one's hands, face, and cuffs. Salt and butter a small section at any one time, not more than you could eat in two or three bites. Then whether you choose to eat from left to right like a typewriter carriage, or in a circular fashion as if peeling an apple, is entirely up to you. It is not appropriate to cut kernels from an ear of corn at the table.

Eggs A hard-boiled egg in the shell may be eaten with the fingers. Tap it gently with your knife, to break the shell, and peel it. Place the shell on your bread plate or at the edge of your dinner plate. Soft-boiled eggs are usually served in an egg cup. Cut the tip off, using your knife, and use a teaspoon to mix the white and the yolk. Add salt and pepper, if desired, and eat it from the shell, using your teaspoon. Eggs cooked in all other ways are eaten with a fork.

Escargots Escargots, when served in the shell, come with special tongs. Grip the shell in the tongs, which are held in the left hand if the diner is right-handed. Then use the small fork provided to remove the snail from the shell and eat it.

Fish—Whole When a fish is served whole, it should be cut lengthwise along the upper edge, and the top fillet of meat lifted off. You then remove the entire skeleton and place it aside. The fish may then be eaten with a knife and fork. It is acceptable to ask a waiter to fillet the fish for you.

Garnishes Carrots are considered finger food. So are cherry tomatoes, which you should pop in your mouth whole. Parsley or watercress may be picked up with the fingers and eaten, if desired. (If you have eaten garlic, parsley cuts the aroma on your breath.) Radishes, pickles and olives may also be eaten with the fingers.

Grapes The correct way to eat grapes is to tear a small twig off the bunch. Never pick them off one at a time and put them in your mouth. When eating grapes with seeds, drop the seeds back into your hand, then discreetly onto your plate. Don't spit or swallow them.

Gravy Gravy should be poured directly onto the meat, not on top of potatoes, rice or noodles. It is considered déclassé to pour gravy (or ketchup) over your entire dish. You must also avoid "mopping" up the gravy with a piece of bread held in your hand. The correct way to do this is to place a small piece of bread in the gravy, and eat it with your knife and fork.

Ice Cream Some people make this mistake when eating ice cream—they move a large spoonful of it in and out of their mouths, taking a bit each time. (Food that goes into your mouth should never come out again, unless it's inedible, such as a fish bone or olive pit.) Instead, take smaller spoonfuls so that you can eat each in one bite.

Lemon If you are served a segment of lemon with a fish dish, hold it in your left hand and use your fork to pierce the membrane. Then cup your hand over the segment as you squeeze it, so that it doesn't squirt anyone in the eye. Place the segment on your bread and butter plate when you are finished with it.

Lobster Better restaurants serve these already cracked, for the convenience of the customer. Use the lobster cracker to make any other breaks required, and the oyster fork to pry the meat from the shell. Place empty pieces of shell on the plate provided for that purpose. When you have removed a large piece from a claw, or the meat from the body of the lobster, put it on your plate and use your knife and fork to eat it. Never spear a piece of food and allow it to hover in the air while you nibble at it.

Mussels You may use a fork to remove mussels from the shell. Then they should be eaten in one bite. Also, you may suck the mussel off the shell, as long as you can do it without making noise or spilling ANY juice or sauce on your face.

Oranges   Oranges should be peeled with a knife, then pulled into segments and eaten with the fingers. Alternatively, they may be peeled, cut in half horizontally, and eaten with a knife and fork.

Oysters   Hold the shell with the left hand, and using the oyster fork, lift the oyster whole from the shell. Dip it in the sauce provided, and swallow it whole. The above also applies to clams on the half shell.

Pie   Pie is usually eaten with a fork, unless it is served a la mode, in which case a spoon should also be used. Start with the point, and work toward the crust.

Pizza   Pizza is a finger food. If served in a restaurant, use a knife and fork for the first few bites, then pick it up with your hands.

Sandwiches   Sandwiches, of course, are eaten with the hands. If, however, the sandwich or hamburger is extremely messy, it is safer to use a knife and fork. Very thick sandwiches may be cut into halves or quarters for easier handling, and held in both hands.

Shrimp   If possible, shrimp should be speared with the fork, dipped in the cocktail sauce, and then eaten in one bite. A knife and fork may be used if the shrimp is served on a plate, and not in a cup. If the shrimp is not shelled, remove the shell with your hands by splitting it open as daintily as possible. Place the shell on your bread and butter plate.

Spaghetti   The correct way to eat spaghetti is with a fork only (never a fork and spoon). This is easily accomplished if you hold your fork at an angle at the side of the plate, and turn it. When you have enough on your fork, you can easily cut it against the edge of the plate and put it in your mouth. This allows you to control the amount of spaghetti on your fork.

Spare Ribs   See chicken, above.

Stewed Fruits   Stewed fruits may be eaten with a spoon, or a spoon and a fork. Pits are daintily dropped back into the spoon and deposited at the side of the plate or liner.

Sushi Sushi and sashimi are normally eaten in two mouthfuls, using chopsticks. If you can't use chopsticks, it is preferable to use your fingers than a knife and fork. Splash a little soy sauce on your plate, if desired, and dip the sushi in it.

Toothpicks

Never use toothpicks at the table. If there is a piece of food caught between your teeth, excuse yourself and remove it in the washroom. There is nothing more offensive than watching someone clean their teeth at the table. Also, never make it obvious if you have to wiggle your tongue in an effort to pry food loose.

Smoking at the Table

Smoke, if you must, at the end of the meal, and only with the permission of your host or companion, after everyone has finished eating. Do not light up between courses, or leave a cigarette burning while you are eating.

Spills at the Table

If you spill food on your tie, use a clean piece of cutlery to scrape it off. Alternatively, you may dip a small corner of your napkin into your water glass, and use it to sponge the food off. Never moisten the napkin in your mouth. When the spill is severe, it is better to excuse yourself and go to the washroom. The table is a poor place to do your laundry.

Should you spill a beverage on the tablecloth, use your napkin to blot it, and bring it to the waiter's attention. If the spill occurs in a private home, clean it up immediately and offer to cover any laundry or replacement costs.

Fifteen Definite No-Nos

1. Don't put liquid of any kind in your mouth while there is still food in it. Swallow first. The only exception is if hot food is scalding your mouth and a cold drink is applied as first aid.

2. Don't spit inedible objects into your palm and put them back on your plate. Use an inconspicuous motion to remove the fish bone or whatever with your thumb and forefinger. Then place it on your bread and butter plate.

3. Don't chew with your mouth open.

4. Don't replenish the supply of food in your mouth before you have swallowed the previous mouthful. You are not a coal furnace.

5. Don't try to talk with food in your mouth.

6. Don't use your napkin, handkerchief, the tablecloth or anything else to clean your cutlery. If it isn't clean, ask the waiter discreetly for another piece.

7. Don't fiddle with your cutlery. You will look nervous and make others edgy.

8. Don't leave the coffee spoon in your cup while drinking from it. Similarly, don't treat the spoon and cup as a musical instrument, making clinking noises as you stir.

9. Don't try the "boarding house reach." Ask someone to pass you whatever it is you want.

10. Don't smack your lips and heave a sigh of satisfaction after swallowing.

11. Don't share someone's food by spearing it with your fork and guiding it across the table like a toy airplane. The correct way is to pass the person your bread plate or main plate, and request that a little of the food be put on it.

12. Don't mash all your food together in the center of your plate.

13. Don't dunk!

14. Don't apply cosmetics at the table—not even lipstick.

15. Don't lean back on the rear legs of your chair. You could break the chair or your neck.

9

Restaurant Savoir-faire

Eating out is rapidly becoming the number one form of entertainment for many people throughout the world. Apart from their social and culinary attributes, however, restaurants are also becoming favored venues for conducting business. For this reason, restaurant savoir-faire has become a highly prized commodity for today's executives.

Just as dining etiquette is important at the table, a thorough knowledge of restaurant etiquette is required of both hosts and guests. This savoir-faire helps ensure that the business meal runs smoothly and that the outcome is a desirable one.

Are You Ready to Order, Sir?

Though placing an order in a restaurant often seems confusing, there are simple guidelines you should follow. Knowledge of these rules demonstrates courtesy and respect both for your fellow diners and for the waiter who is serving your table.

1. When a man and woman are dining together, the man always orders on behalf of the woman. He does *not* choose her food, but simply places her order with the waiter. There is a practical reason behind this. Good staff in restaurants are trained to deal with one person at the table, and like it or not that person is still the man. The correct way for a gentleman to handle it is to ask the woman what she would like to have. When the waiter asks, "Are you ready to order now, sir," the man replies, "Yes, the lady will have tomato soup and the roast turkey sandwich, and I will have the steak and kidney pie." However, when further choices are required, such as salad dressings, type of bread or potato, the woman responds directly to the waiter. It is not appropriate to go into a comedy routine in which the man echoes each of her choices to the waiter as if she required an interpreter. (These traditions may appear unnecessary to some women, but protesting or making a scene won't put a guest at ease or help you attain your objectives for the meal.)

2. If two men or two women are dining, the guest places his or her order first. If there is no guest, the older person orders first, and the one who is paying for the meal says "one bill please." The waiter then knows that it is to go to him or her.

3. If one man and two or more women are dining together, the women place their orders first on an individual basis.

4. When groups of men or women are eating together, each orders for himself or herself.

5. If a party occupies a large table, everyone at the table orders individually, in order of their seating. It is too much to expect a poor waiter to run to all the women first then run back to the men. Also, when dining in a group, let the waiter know before you order whether you desire separate cheques.

If there is to be one bill with people paying their own shares, each person should make a mental note of approximately how much his order costs, before the menus are removed. It is not considered good etiquette to whip out a calculator or lap computer at the end of the meal. If everyone in the group has eaten a similarly-priced meal and run a similar bar tab, it is appropriate to suggest splitting the bill evenly.

Choosing
a Wine

It is always a sign of savoir-faire to be able to choose an appropriate beverage for a meal.

At a very good restaurant, it is considered gauche to drink hard liquor before dinner, as this numbs the taste buds for the feast to follow. Similarly, sweet wine before a meal diminishes the appetite. It is more appropriate to order a dry aperitif such as vermouth, campari or dry sherry.

The wine should be selected after the meal has been chosen. It is always polite for the host to ask for the guest's preference, before making a selection.

If you are not familiar with the wine list, ask the wine steward to recommend a red or white wine as you peruse the list. Point to a label with the approximate price you wish to spend, to let the steward know subtly that you are willing to pay up to, say $30, but need his advice. Indicate whether you would like domestic or imported wine.

The traditional rule is that white wine is served with white meat, and red wine with red meat. White meats include chicken, fish, veal in cream sauce, fish paté, and shellfish. Red meats include beef, pork, game, duck, and meat patés. If both red and white meats are served, still rosé is a good middle-of-the-road choice. Sake is an appropriate drink with Japanese food, and beer with curry.

Champagne is appropriate with all foods and throughout the meal. The only caveat is that it should not be ordered when to do so seems ostentatious or too personal. Junior executives may seem to be abusing their expense accounts if they order champagne, unless some special occasion is being celebrated, such as closing a huge deal. When dining formally, however, it is not unusual to have champagne served with each course or with dessert.

When the wine is rare and expensive, the wine steward will bring you the cork. You are supposed to sniff this under (but not touching) the nose, to make sure the wine has not spoiled. The color and texture will also indicate whether the wine has been stored correctly. However, unless you are a connoisseur, you should avoid making comments such as, "Yes, it smells like a very good year," or "Good, I like a damp cork." This makes you look like a bozo instead of a beaujolais expert.

Pardon My Confusion: Menu Terms

There are two basic types of menus. One is a la carte, which means that you select items from a list of dishes, and pay the price listed beside each individual dish. When ordering a la carte, you must pay separately for each vegetable, for instance.

The second type is table d'hôte, or prix fixe, which means that there is one set price for the entire meal, regardless of how many of the courses you choose to eat. Usually, the single price is indicated at the top of the menu, or beside each of the choices of main courses. There is no price listed beside the choices of appetizers, soups, vegetables and desserts, since they are included with the meal.

A hybrid menu has individually priced appetizers and desserts, but coffee or tea may be included, and vegetables and potatoes served as a garnish with the main course.

Garçon!

Never snap your fingers, clap your hands, hit your glass with your knife, or wave your napkin, to get a waiter's attention.

The correct way to signal a waiter is to catch his eye and nod your head, or to say pleasantly, "Excuse me," or "Waiter—" if he is within hearing. It is not appropriate to bellow across the restaurant. If he catches your eye across the room, you may raise your index finger.

If your waiter has disappeared into the kitchen, it is acceptable to ask another member of the staff to request that he or she come to your table.

There's a Fly in My Soup

A customer is not obliged to accept food if it has been prepared incorrectly, seems spoiled or unclean, contains a foreign object, or is not as described on the menu. If you ordered your steak rare and it arrives well-done, send it back. If your meat cannot be cut with any normal utensil, send it back. If you ordered something with wild mushroom sauce and the wild mushrooms seem to have escaped, send it back. However, send it back as soon as it is placed in front of you, or after one or two bites. People who eat three quarters of a meal before complaining about it appear ridiculous. Be polite as you draw the problem to the attention of the waiter, and don't make a scene or indignantly raise your voice. If you point out the problem, most waiters will be apologetic, and immediately replace your order. In the case of wildlife or short hairs, try not to put your fellow diners off their food. Don't shriek or faint. Ask the waiter to remove the plate and bring a new one.

Some situations may be unpleasant but tolerable. If a piece of leaf lettuce contains sand, you may choose to set it aside rather than disrupt the meal by sending back the dish. On the other hand, if you find china or glass in your food, tell the kitchen as soon as possible; it is probably in other diners' food as well, and could cause an accident.

If the food is clean and acceptably prepared, but you don't care for it, tough luck. You are not entitled to send it back.

Tipping

Tipping is literally putting your money where your mouth is, and an acknowledgement for work well done.

If the service and food were good, tip 15 percent. Good service should be encouraged, and is in the interest of all concerned. If the food and service were excellent, a tip of 20 percent is not inappropriate. Tipping exorbitant amounts such as 40–50 percent has a Klondike air, and while the waiter may appreciate it, your companions will consider this to be flaunting your wealth.

If you receive loose change from your bill, don't leave it as a tip. Remove the change from the table, then leave money from your wallet as a tip. Small change, particularly pennies, constitutes a slightly insulting tip.

Don't scrimp on the tip. Ten percent is too low for acceptable service. It suggests that either the service was somewhere between good and unacceptable, or that you are cheap. If you can't afford to tip the correct amount, eat at a less expensive restaurant. Only the ill-mannered accept good quality and service, then leave a miserly tip for a hard-working waiter who probably earns a minimum-wage base salary.

Don't feel, however, that you must always tip. If the waiter was surly, you waited two hours for your menu, the food was thrown in front of you, or you stared at your used plates for an hour, leaving a tip merely suggests that you find this treatment acceptable. Make your point by leaving no tip, but don't leave 25 cents, which simply adds insult to injury. Do not hesitate to mention to the manager or maitre d' that you left no tip because the service was offensive. It is not your responsibility, though, to point out the waiter's shortcomings to his or her face.

When sales tax applies to restaurant meals, tip on the amount of the order, not on the amount with tax. Many restaurants present a credit card invoice with the tax space empty, and the total amount with tax as the food total, to encourage you to tip more. Be aware and be careful!

A helpful wine steward should receive 15 percent of the wine bill as a tip, at the end of the meal. In the unlikely event that the steward is unavailable when you end the meal, leave the tip with the maitre d'.

It May Look Like Lunch, But It's Still Business

The important thing to remember about business lunches is that they are still meetings, ones that require even more planning than a meeting in the office.

By taking care of details ahead of time, an executive can ensure that nothing will interrupt the lunch, or distract the diners from the objective of the exercise, which is business.

Preliminaries

When extending an invitation for a business lunch, always inquire whether your guest has a preference for any particular restaurant or type of food. He may be a vegetarian or keep kosher, and your consideration sets off the relationship on the right foot. If your guest has no preference, be prepared with the names of a few good, conveniently-located restaurants. Ideally, these should be establishments you have visited, and in whose food and service you have confidence. Your choice should reflect your good taste. We know of one businessman who lost an account because he took the customer to lunch in a strip joint.

Always make reservations, in your name. It is annoying to arrive at a restaurant and have to wait twenty minutes for a table—a situation which can be avoided with a simple phone call. If you know the restaurant, it helps to request a particular location. If you don't, let the reservations person know that it is a business lunch, and you would like a quiet table. Planning ahead helps eliminate the possibility of being placed in a high-traffic area, such as by the kitchen door, washroom, or cash register.

Be on time, and greet the client in the foyer, never seated at a table or in the bar. The only exception is when your guest is late, and you are in danger of losing the table.

If you are both going to be late, always call the restaurant as a simple courtesy. Your consideration will be appreciated by the maitre d'. You can't expect restaurants to hold a table indefinitely for an apparent no-show. If you are unavoidably detained, call the restaurant, and ask that your guests be seated, told of your delay, and offered drinks.

Every table in a restaurant has a power seat. The power seat faces the "audience," so that its occupant can see everything that is going on in the restaurant. This seat is the favored seat at any table. (This is based on military lore, in which a wise general would never sit with his back to the door or to the main body of a room.) Always give this seat to your client and take the inferior seat yourself. Women in business, however, may take this seat, which is traditionally offered by men to women.

It is inadvisable to take a client to an extremely expensive restaurant. First, unless your dining etiquette is flawless, you will not feel comfortable in this setting. Waiters and guests will sense that your behavior is awkward. You will *not* score points. Take clients to a good, moderately-priced restaurant where the food is of good quality and service is reliable. Ideally, you should be able to make useful recommendations from the menu ("The antipasto here is terrific"), so that the client feels you are at ease in this setting. Attention to detail also helps you maintain control over the meeting.

Ordering

Although it is a business meal, the rules of gracious dining still apply, which means that regardless of who is picking up the cheque, the man should place the order on behalf of the woman.

Don't order anything that is heavily laced with onions or garlic. Although garlic bread and caesar salad are popular items, they are not suitable for a business lunch. It is very difficult to convince someone who is close to fainting to place a $100,000 order with you. Also, the aroma carries over into your afternoon meetings. It's better to indulge in these flavors at home or on weekends.

Neither should you order anything too exotic. If you are trying a restaurant for the first time, order menu items with which you are familiar. This is not the day to try the duck feet at your favorite dim sum palace. Even if you like them, your companions may be so mesmerized by what's on your plate they won't listen to what's on your mind. Food at a business lunch should never be distracting.

Avoid food that is very messy, like ribs, spaghetti, French onion soup, or crab in the shell. The corporate law of gravity states that the more important the guest, the more food your tie will attract. It is almost impossible to maintain your dignity with sauce all over your hands or your lap.

Watch the booze. The days of the liquid lunch are gone, and three martinis are no longer considered the hallmark of professional behavior. Your guest may think you're great socially, but who wants to place an account in the hands of a drunk? If you must order a drink, make it just that—*a* drink.

We are often asked, "If a woman has invited a man for a business lunch or dinner, who orders the wine?" First of all, a bottle of wine is too much for a business meal for two people. A small carafe or single glasses are much more appropriate. However, any ordering should be done by the man.

During The Meal

Pleasantries are fine as openers, but the primary focus of conversation at a business lunch should be business. Don't make the mistake of having a drink and moving into a relaxed atmosphere. It is very easy to lose control of a situation by spending too much time talking about baseball, your children, or your vacation plans. Remember, your companion is a business associate, not a social acquaintance, and the rules of professional behavior apply as much in a restaurant as in a board room. It is a mistake, for instance, to start talking about any frustrations you might have at work. Similarly, be cautious that you don't reveal too much about your personal life.

Watch the time. No one will be impressed if you linger over lunch for three hours. Executives believe a competent person is a busy person. At a business lunch, respect your own time as well as that of your guest. Every meeting has its peak point, which your own inner sense of timing should identify. If the meal is over and the conversation is starting to drift into other areas, it is time to pay the bill and subtly end the lunch. If your guest shows no sign of wanting to leave, say, for example, "Bill, I wish I had more time to spend with you. Unfortunately, I must excuse myself to attend a meeting at 2:00. It's been great seeing you. Where are you parked?"

The Bill

One of the most important details of a business lunch is paying the bill. A mark of the polished host is to ensure that the bill never comes to the table. If you frequent a particular restaurant, inquire about establishing an account there. Otherwise, we recommend that you arrive a few minutes ahead of your guest, give your credit card to the maitre d' for imprint, and excuse yourself briefly at some point after the meal to sign the invoice. If, as you leave, your guest expresses concern that nobody has paid for the meal, you can say simply that "it's been taken care of."

Many women create a serious *faux pas* when it comes time to pick up the bill, (assuming that this has not been arranged before hand, as described above.)

> "Sally Jones" invites her major supplier, "Fred Brown," for lunch at an elegant restaurant. The meal goes well, but when the bill comes, Sally is enjoying herself so much that she ignores it, letting it sit in the middle of the table. There is plenty of time, she figures, to pick it up, and when the waiter comes over she asks for more coffee instead of laying her credit card over the bill. She continues in full rhetorical flourish, while Fred gets more and more distracted. His attention fades, as he becomes wrapped up in moral dilemmas about the bill. As a gentleman, he feels it would be an appropriate gesture to offer to pay. On the other hand, he recalls that she had invited HIM for lunch.

Sally handled the situation poorly. When the bill arrived, she should have placed her hand on it, pulled it to her side of the table, smiled, and said, "My company would like to

buy you lunch." This would have removed any personal connotations from the matter, and alleviated any embarrassment
Fred might have been feeling. The point is that *either* sex
should pick the bill up quickly. This is appropriate. Fred
might be as ill-at-ease if a man left it, but most men know not
to.

Fred could have given her a hint by simply saying, "It's
been so long since anyone treated me to lunch. I've thoroughly
enjoyed it." This would have been her cue to look after the bill.

After the Lunch

Remember to send your guest or host a personal note after the
lunch, thanking him for his time and pleasant company.

A Checklist For Business Lunches

- Make reservations.
- Be prompt.
- Order familiar, easy-to-eat foods.
- Watch the booze.
- Keep the conversation to business, after opening
  pleasantries. Don't get too personal.
- Don't loiter after the meal.
- Use savoir-faire in paying the bill.
- Tip adequately.
- Send a thank-you note.

Cafeteria Conduct

Many companies that in the past may have opted for executive
dining rooms, are now encouraging all employees to eat in one
company cafeteria.

Just as there are rules for behaving in other parts of an
office building, there are guidelines for appropriate behavior in
a company cafeteria. These are:

- **DON'T hold up the line.** Read the list of specials before you get in line, if possible. It is not considerate to take ten minutes to decide on a sandwich filling while others are waiting.
- **DO treat cafeteria employees as human beings,** not slaves. Don't expect them to run over with the ketchup just because you forgot to ask for it earlier. Also, however tempting it may be, refrain from making jokes in their hearing about the quality of the food.
- **DON'T force yourself on senior management.** They will signal you if they wish you to join them. Also, it is not appropriate to mention the revised media budget as you waft by carrying your macaroni and cheese.
- **DON'T make your lunch group look like a secret powwow.** Cliques make people feel excluded, uncomfortable and nervous.
- **DON'T flirt.** This is still a professional environment, not a bar.
- **DON'T make derogatory remarks** about other people's food, whether it be quantity, quality or type. For example, if the company's overweight mail clerk wants to eat chocolate cake for dessert, it is his business. It is not appropriate to comment, especially in front of others.
- **DON'T sit alone, reading a book.** Use the lunch period to get to know employees from other departments as well as your own.
- **DON'T make a mess with your food.** Clean your place when you are finished, and remove your tray.

10

The Pleasure of Your Company

Cocktail Parties

The cocktail party is an effective way to bring groups of people together in a relaxed atmosphere, for a limited period of time. As such, it is a popular form of business entertaining, particularly at conventions and other large meetings.

The purpose of attending a cocktail party is to mingle. Guests must make an effort to talk with as many people as possible. The person who sticks with his or her spouse or a few favorite cronies all evening misses the point.

Similarly, food or drink should not be considered the main event at a cocktail party. Limit yourself to two or three drinks, and don't expect the food to substitute for dinner. It is hard to imagine anything less gracious than a person devouring all the hors d'oeuvres.

Cocktail food is always finger food, and a paper napkin is usually provided. The napkin serves as a plate, so be careful when you are maneuvering through a crowd with it. Also, cocktail food is deliberately heavy in oil, to slow down the absorption of alcoholic beverages. It is, as a result, rather messy to eat, so mind your face and hands.

If you must smoke, pick up an ashtray for your use as you wander the room. Don't drop ashes in plants or on the floor, and be aware of the direction your smoke is drifting.

Don't overstay your welcome. Usually, a time span is specified on the invitation, and should not be exceeded even if you would like another drink or are having a good time.

Office Parties: Dos and Don'ts

Office parties serve a valuable function in a company. They improve morale and build goodwill, promoting a feeling of esprit de corps. They are also a good opportunity for employees from different parts of the company to mingle.

Here are some dos and don'ts for correct behavior at these functions:

- **DON'T** let planning an office party come ahead of high-priority work, such as serving customers.

- **DO** attend—it is not optional. It is the duty of employees at all levels to attend company functions cheerfully.

- **DO** look as if you are enjoying yourselves (this goes for you and your companion/spouse.) Even if square dancing is not your idea of a good time, you must participate with a smile.

- **DO** be on your best behavior. You are being watched, and don't want to be remembered as the one with the lampshade on your head.

- **DO** watch the drinking—yours and your companion/spouse's. People never forget a lapse in this area.

- **DON'T** discuss business. It is a social occasion, and an important opportunity to get to know some of your fellow employees. Try to circulate among individuals from a variety of departments, rather than sticking with your day-to-day colleagues.

- **DON'T** make a pass at one or more of your fellow workers. For some strange reason, co-workers look infinitely more attractive at company parties than they do at the photocopy machine. Suggestive remarks and fondling are as out of place at the office party as they are in the office.

- **DON'T** tell off-color or ethnic jokes or stories. These jokes may offend others.

- **DON'T** make derogatory comments, jokes or slurs against the company. You will be insulting your host, and these jests will not be forgotten in the morning.

- **DON'T** air grievances against the company. Keep the atmosphere light and festive, and save your complaints for your annual review.

- **DO** respect the hierarchy. Don't call company presidents by their first name or refer to the vice-president of finance as "pal."

- **DO** speak to children ahead of time, if they have been invited. Stress the importance of "please" and "thank you." (If children are too young to be discreet, this is the time you may start to regret gossiping about fellow-workers in front of them. If a toddler says to your boss "Are you the one who yells all the time?" you have only yourself to blame.) Make sure children are well-behaved and, if necessary, discreetly disciplined, at the party.

- **DO** make a short speech, if you are the president of the company. The speech should thank the members of the organizing committee for their efforts, thank everyone for coming, and express the hope that everyone has a good time.

- **DO** send a thank-you note to the organizing committee, AFTER the party, if you were not a committee member.

Dinner at the Boss's House

The important thing to remember about having dinner with the boss is that BOTH YOU AND YOUR SPOUSE/COMPANION ARE BEING OBSERVED. Such dinners are occasions for playing the role of the perfect guest. When small courtesies are required, such as helping people with coats, lighting cigarettes, and pulling out chairs, snap to it.

You are usually invited with your spouse, and unless absolutely unavoidable, both of you must attend. Remember, you have not been invited but *instructed* to appear.

Have your car washed before the dinner.

Men should wear a good dark suit, unless of course the dinner is black tie. Women must dress tastefully. This is not the place to wear your backless, frontless chiffon number, or your new leather pants and rhinestone belts.

Arrive promptly (never more than ten minutes late) and bring a gift. Flowers or top-quality chocolates are good choices. Never bring dessert or wine, since your host/hostess may feel obliged to serve them, and they may not complement the menu. A bottle of good liqueur is acceptable, but hard liquor is not.

Compliment the host/hostess at least once on the dinner and their home, but don't overdo it so that you appear sycophantic.

A dinner invitation does not mean that you are necessarily on a first-name basis with your boss. Similarly, if your boss is a man, address his wife formally, not by her first name (even if you call him Frank at the office), unless invited to do otherwise.

Don't bring up business unless the boss does. Don't use this opportunity to air grievances or gossip about other employees. Neither should you make jokes or comparisons between your salary level, home or lifestyle and your boss's. Stick to social conversation. Make an effort to speak with everyone, not just the boss or your companion. Men, in particular, should remember to include women in the conversation.

When speaking with your spouse, there should be no personal slights, bickering, contradiction, or demonstrations of boredom.

Watch your dining etiquette. Don't ask for seconds unless offered. Eat the food you are given, unless you have a life-threatening allergy. Neither you nor your spouse/companion should be dieting during this particular meal. Don't drink too much, and don't smoke unless others do.

Don't ask to watch television, even if there is a big playoff game on that night.

Don't overstay your welcome, and don't be the last to leave.

After the meal, the woman of the couple should send a thank-you note to the hostess. It is improper to mention or brag about your invitation to dinner back at the office.

Spouse Activities at Conventions

It is common for executives to attend conventions, annual meetings and trade shows with their spouses. Appropriate behavior and dress is required from both, at all times, during the event.

The first thing to remember is that you are both on duty, and you are both being watched. A husband or wife should complement the spouse, not detract from his/her reputation. Management loves to see a happy couple. Whatever your differences, present a supportive, united front. Never bicker in front of others.

Neither should you put on a honeymoon act. Sexual innuendos, particularly when leaving a party to go to bed, are not appropriate.

It is a mistake to be exclusive. Both spouses should make an effort to speak to everyone at least once, not just old friends or people they consider "important." The wife of one successful businessman we know describes what she calls the "working wives," women who try to curry favor with her in order to advance their husband's position. Be gracious, but not grasping. People are bound to see through it and react with distaste.

Employees shouldn't stick with each other, and spouses with each other, with ne're the twain meeting. Avoid these groupings by including spouses in the general conversation. Too often they are ignored—and function more like props than people.

Try to remember the names and faces of associates' spouses. When in doubt, play it safe. Don't say, "Dora, you look marvelous!" or "Donald, you've lost weight" until you're sure Dora or Donald hasn't been traded in for a newer model. Meeting planners should provide a list of attendees, with the full names of spouses, in the registration kit to help jog people's memories.

Often, members of a trade organization meet annually over a course of decades. When a middle-aged colleague arrives with a new companion it is no one's place to gossip or to snub the newcomer—that person should be made welcome. References to the previous person should be taboo.

Participate actively in all activities, looking attentive and interested whether they interest you or not. If people are dancing, dance. If it seems that spouses of all the other people at your companion's level are participating in some way, such as organizing or chairing spousal sessions, make sure you do the same.

It often happens, although thankfully less than it used to, that "spouse activities" are designed for an outmoded "dim-witted housewife" stereotype. Consequently, they bore and insult the vibrant women who are forced to attend them. Women who find it excruciating to sit through a three-hour session on "ring around the collar" should try not to gripe during the event. The organizer may be sitting in the seat ahead, and she may be the president's wife. It is better to offer to sit on the steering committee, and organize more interesting and appropriate sessions for next year.

Avoid excessive use of alcohol at all times, as this can lead to indiscretions and coarse language. As they used to say during wartime, loose lips sink ships.

A spouse should not take the opportunity to air grievances with senior management, particularly after a few martinis. One wife of a company president told us that she is frequently buttonholed by wives complaining that their husbands have to work late too often. She never knows what to say to them, particularly as many of these husbands are NOT working late. Similarly, it is completely inappropriate for spouses to lobby for higher salaries or more rapid advancement.

A spouse should not slip into a coffee party mentality. This is not the place to provide other wives with details of gynacological or fertility problems. If other people start doing it, don't feel you have to join in. Change the subject. It is no one's business but your own.

When single business people, or people whose spouses are not free to travel, are asked to attend couple-oriented functions, they are due the same respect and consideration as if they were in a couple. They should never be made to feel excluded.

11

*What's a Nice Girl Like You Doing in a Place Like This?**

The twentieth century has brought tremendous changes for western women—changes that encompass the spirit of Rosie the Rivetter, the intellect of Margaret Mead and the dynamism of Tina Turner. Seventy years ago, women did not have the vote, but today Margaret Thatcher is prime minister of Britain and it is her husband Denis who attends the spousal functions at Commonwealth conferences.

The liberating movements of the last two decades have given women choices they did not previously have. Today, there are plenty of very intelligent, ambitious and assertive women armed with MBAs, legal and medical degrees whose careers are advancing very rapidly. They know where they want to go and they're determined to get there.

For many, this includes a decision not to marry or bear children, but to concentrate solely on their careers. Even those women who choose to combine family and a career now realize that working is not a temporary situation, but something that is likely to continue throughout their lives. All working women must learn to regard a career as a kind of marriage—one that also involves a lifelong commitment.

*I own it.

Although women have always worked, whether in the home, as domestic servants, teachers, governesses, nurses or farm workers, it is only in this century that they have come to play an important role in business. Nevertheless, women still face many obstacles in rising above the lower levels and even those in professions find it hard to establish lasting credibility among men. One reason for this is that men's perceptions and attitudes have not kept pace with women's achievements and qualifications.

For example, very few women in corporations are groomed for advancement as men are. They traditionally start in lower positions and remain at lower salaries. The work they do is often undervalued or overlooked. And many double standards persist. For instance, when looking for a job, a male executive can cite his wife and children as evidence of his reliability, maturity, and willingness to accept responsibility. However, a woman with a family is not considered serious about her career.

Socially, relationships between the sexes have become very muddled. Men don't know how to deal with modern women, privately or in business. They project their insecurities, inadequacies and fears onto their female colleagues, and call it "the problem of women in business". And like any powerful group, they are unwilling to share that power.

These obstacles should not discourage motivated women from reaching for their goals. Working women today must realize that they are in a transition period. The problems they face in business will not be faced by women twenty years from now. Change takes place slowly, but it is happening. Women today are creating new role models that are helping to make these changes possible. That is why it is important that women demolish archaic stereotypes by demonstrating impeccable professional behavior.

The Fiction

In North America today, approximately 50 percent of women work outside the home. While there are still some men who feel women belong in the kitchen, it is more common for businesswomen to encounter archaic attitudes and false preconceptions about their role in the business environment.

In years of experience consulting to industry, we have heard the same complaints over and over:

"Women are too emotional on the job." Any sign of anger or frustration in a woman points to her "emotional nature". When her work is criticized, it is expected that she will burst into tears or have a temper tantrum, and may refer to "that time of month". Of course, when a male executive shows anger, it has none of these connotations. A woman must combat this attitude by keeping outbursts private and her temper under control. She does not have the luxury of blowing up in the office environment. It is preferable to leave the room rather than express feelings which will not find a sympathetic audience. We know of one female executive with a major corporation who keeps two tennis balls in her desk drawer. When things bother her, she closes her office door, takes out the balls and squeezes them hard in her hands, to vent her frustration. (We leave her thoughts to your imagination, but the point is that she indulges in them privately.)

"Women cannot take pressure as well as men." This prejudice no doubt arises because men tend to view women as the weaker sex, and expect that stamina in the workplace is somehow related to stamina on the football field. (For a real lesson in stamina, men should try spending a day with three pre-schoolers!) Whatever its origin, because of this perception women have to take that extra step to stay cool when the pressure is on in the office. If an important meeting is 10 minutes away, the figures for the meeting have just been changed, and the photocopy machine is broken, a woman can't allow the situation to disrupt her composure. She must remain calm, even though her male counterparts may be tearing their hair. She should also make a point of never raising her voice unnecessarily, unless she wishes to be called "hysterical".

"Women bring personal and family problems into the workplace." Many men believe that a woman's private and professional worlds occupy her thoughts concurrently, and that her status as a professional will always take second place to her role as a mother. They anticipate that if a child gets a nosebleed at school, a mother may have to leave suddenly to pick him up. If she has a fight with her husband or junior has the mumps, they fear that she won't be able to concentrate on her work. Of course, many men are able to separate their work and home lives only because they have the luxury of a wife looking after the home front. Also, working couples often decide to let the woman take time off to deal with domestic crises because she earns less: a vicious circle. The correct way for women to deal with this perception is to make a point of keeping their business and private lives separate. Women shouldn't offer a running commentary on their family's development nor expose family problems at work. An employer should be told in advance, when possible, of any absence, and time missed should always be made up. Stealing time for personal or family business is the same as stealing money.

"Women are more likely to watch the clock." A male executive may work till 6:00 or 6:30, while some women find it necessary to leave at 5:00 to begin their "double day" of doing household chores. If this is the case, the woman should leave promptly, without justifying it with excuses such as "Sally has the mumps". However, women who wish to advance in a corporation must demonstrate their willingness and freedom to work late if required. This may necessitate hiring outside help to deal with domestic demands.

"A women accepts and makes far more personal phone calls than a man." It may be that management notices more when women do it or that more men have private offices. In any case, personal phone calls should not be made on company time. Restrict them to your lunch hour and keep them brief. If the call is of a private nature, close your office door.

"Introducing women into a male office or boardroom may create sexual distraction." Oddly, few men have ever suggested solving this problem by having an all-female board! While they cannot take responsibility for the thoughts in men's minds, women should be particularly careful that their dress or demeanor does not invite suggestive comments.

Double Crossed by the Double Standard

When travelling through Saskatchewan a few years ago, we picked up a flyer published by the Women's Division of the Saskatchewan Department of Labour which quotes "Anonymous" as writing:

A businessman is aggressive; a businesswoman is pushy.
He's good on details; she's picky.
He loses his temper because he's so involved with his job;
she's bitchy.
He gets depressed from work pressures;
she has menstrual tension.
He's a man of the world; she's been around.
He's confident; she's conceited.
He drinks because of excessive work pressure; she's a lush.
He isn't afraid to say what he thinks; she's mouthy.
He's enthusiastic; she's emotional.
He exercises authority diligently; she's power mad.
He's a stern taskmaster; she's impossible to work for.

Offensive and ill-conceived as these perceptions seem, the bottom line is that they persist and are likely to do so for a number of years. Many men believe the fiction and are ready to place this interpretation on the behavior of the women with whom they work. They bemoan the fact that a woman "can't be more like a man", yet when she comes close, they panic. Women should not be intimidated by this type of thinking. If one of the above labels is applied to you, examine your behavior honestly to determine whether there is any truth in it. If not, peel the label off and throw it away.

The Fact

The fact is that women in business are here to stay and they're on their way up. Companies that fail to recognize this are depriving themselves of the greatest natural resource on the market.

More and more women are getting impatient with the restrictions that all too often characterize the corporate environment and are starting their own businesses—often in competition with their former employers. Women are taking the opportunity to use their talents to the fullest capacity and to develop their abilities as responsible professionals. Statistically, the small business success rate is much higher when the owners are women than men.

Women are the new players in a different game and they're writing the rules by which we will all play in the future.

The Advice

The Competition

Women have never been encouraged to be competitive. Women's education has encouraged them to nurture others, not to vanquish them—particularly if they're male. It was once considered in poor taste for a woman to beat a man at any game. "Smart" girls hid their intelligence and creativity so as not to threaten males. Needless to say, these attitudes are no longer appropriate, professionally or personally. Women must realize that the corporate environment is fundamentally competitive. If a company is uncompetitive, it generally goes out of business and its employees become unemployed. The same thing can happen to a career.

As they climb the corporate ladder, women find themselves in competition with fellow workers for a reduced number of higher-level jobs. Those who leave their careers to chance lag behind. Therefore, it is crucial that women in business take responsibility for their own careers. Set your goals, and go after them. Nobody will hand success to you on a platter.

Advancing in a corporation takes strategy. You have to plan your moves astutely and take advantage of opportunities. Start by asking yourself, when faced with a choice, "How will this help me?" For example, we recently spoke to a commissioned sales representative who had been offered an assistant sales manager position at a fixed salary. After carefully reviewing both the offer and her own goals, she realized that the security of an inside job could never compensate for the lost income potential and would restrict her contacts in the industry. She turned down the job and it was awarded to a male sales representative. Two years later, her income had tripled and the man had not progressed.

Women are well-advised to sharpen their competitive instincts by participating in sports or other games of strategy. Chess and bridge are good mental training for thinking two or three steps ahead—another area in which women's education is often deficient. In business, it is necessary to learn to anticipate the moves of others and to test our mental agility by responding to these.

Another aspect of competition is competing with yourself. The focused businesswoman sets her own goals, quotas and standards and then competes with them. She's not afraid to push herself, to do more than the minimum required. She's not interested in competing with someone else's mediocre achievements. She sets her own standard of excellence and strives to meet it.

For example, one of the areas in which women have excelled is multi-level marketing—companies like Avon and Mary Kay. These companies combine supportive sales teams with a drive for individual performance. The force that motivates the women in these businesses is money and the companies that have appreciated and harnessed that force usually find their balance sheets to be very healthy indeed. Just as we admire men who desire financial success, so there is nothing wrong with a woman who wants financial independence—and a woman should never feel ashamed of, or shrink from, ambition and success. Successful life insurance salespeople may talk about helping their customers gain peace of mind, but if salespeople weren't interested in the money they can earn in the process they'd join the Peace Corps or become missionaries. Women must learn to be honest about their desires. If money is a motivating factor, admit it and set your goals accordingly.

On Aggression

Traditionally, aggression has been associated with macho, masculine behavior. Unfortunately, there are a few women who feel that to succeed in business, they must imitate this quality and present a warrior-like image. But women always appear undignified when they imitate men, whether it be by swearing, drinking to excess, speaking too loudly, or dressing in drag. Aggression is no more appropriate in a women than in a man. Assertiveness, however, is desirable for both. Women should never hesitate to assert themselves in the business world. If you are being assertive and men complain that you are being aggressive, they are simply trying to manipulate you into backing down. Don't fall for it.

Ask What Your Company Can Do for You

Many women fail to realize that it is not only acceptable but desirable to take advantage of all the learning opportunities a company offers. Don't think just about today, but look down the road and acquire the skills you will need to qualify you for future positions. Keep asking yourself, "How will this help me—today and tomorrow?" Here are some steps you can follow that may pay future dividends.

- Observe your boss and other senior officers. Learn as much as you can about the way they handle various situations. Mold yourself on their behavior—people promote in their own image.

- Attend as many seminars as possible. Even if some aren't directly related to your present job, outline for your boss the ways in which your attendance will benefit your department in the long run.

- Order as many useful trade publications as your company considers worth buying—and read them. Keep current. If necessary, consider doing it at your own expense as an investment in your career.

- Make sure you are on the circulation list of relevant business and professional periodicals. When you see something of interest, mark it in the margin with your initials and a note ("Note: new product on p. 8—J.B.")—people may notice that you are keeping abreast. Keep photocopies of useful articles for your personal files.

- Take advantage of any company subsidies for extension courses at local educational institutions.

- Join professional organizations and attend the meetings and seminars they offer. This offers you a profile in the industry and allows you to build contacts.

Use these opportunities to become more valuable to the company. You'll show management that you have both initiative and the ability to learn and you'll make yourself eligible for promotion.

Business is Business

Remember, business is not a cocktail party or coffee klatch. You are not there to mingle. Nor should women play the role of wife and mother. Socially and educationally, women are raised to feel comfortable in these roles, but in a corporate environment you must resist them. Men will try to slot women into these roles but if you play along, you'll be trapped. Women are not there to listen to people's problems and console them, to supply muffins, or to sew buttons on coats. If you have extra energy, use it in professional ways within the organization—to your own advantage and to gain visibility.

Similarly, if asked to do a traditionally female task, such as advise on a color scheme for the office or plan a reception, consult with male colleagues. Do not act as if you are genetically predisposed for these tasks.

The Garbo Syndrome

Greta Garbo's famous line, "I want to be left alone," sometimes seems to be the theme song of many businesswomen. Women often operate in isolation because they are reluctant to delegate hard-won authority and feel personally responsible for all the work.

Unfortunately, there are several flaws in this attitude. The first is that management values team players, not individual stars (which is one of the reasons business people tend to conform to dress codes rather than flaunt personal style). Women should learn to get along with others and to collaborate with colleagues. At higher levels of management, it is essential to be able to interact effectively with people. In addition, the higher you climb, the less it will be possible for you to do everything yourself. Managers must learn to delegate, and to motivate others to do work at an acceptable standard.

If someone dumps a lot of work on you at the end of a day, don't be the one to work till late at night to finish it. Ask others to help you. Show you are willing to work longer hours, but don't be a martyr or take on work that should be delegated to others. Remember, too, that if you wish to be promoted, you must groom a successor. Those who report to you should be trained to perform some of your duties—not just the unpleasant ones, but also those that will develop their skills and allow you to delegate effectively.

There is another aspect to avoiding the Garbo syndrome. Women should cultivate professional contacts within their company and industry. In this way they will be able to keep abreast of new developments, and to hear about opportunities. Build up your profile with senior management whenever possible. Get involved in committees and task forces that will allow you access to senior executives. Remember, nobody will promote you if you're invisible.

Don't make the mistake of regarding your boss as the most important person in the company. We recently spoke with a young woman who worked hard at cultivating a good relationship with her boss. He was so pleased with her work and her abilities that he regarded her as indispensible to his department. When opportunities for promotion arose, he never considered recommending her. She made the mistake of making sure that he alone knew about her abilities—no one else did.

The bottom line is that women have a choice. They can work alone, taking personal responsibility for everything and living with the illusion that they are in complete control. Alternatively, they can learn to delegate and become a team player. In this way, they truly are in control, because they are free to dedicate the time and energy they save to developing their own careers, becoming more visible while learning new skills.

Protect Your Interests

It's often up to you to negotiate and renegotiate your salary and benefits packages. Always choose a good moment to ask for a raise. For example, broach the topic when you have successfully taken on extra responsibilities or have saved the company a lot of money by making shrewd suggestions—don't ask immediately after returning from vacation or if you have recently made some bad decisions that have reflected poorly on your monthly report.

Married or not, working or not, statistics indicate that most women end up alone and that old women tend to live at or below the poverty line. Protect yourself. Take advantage of company pension plans if the employer makes contributions or if the rate of return is good. Contribute to your own tax-sheltered retirement fund. Don't put your entire paycheck in your joint account or spend everything on the children—invest some money in your own future. You aren't being selfish if you do, just being smart.

Calling Foul

When women encounter unfair behavior that offends their principles as women, they should deal with the situation maturely and never resort to slogans or name-calling ("You male chauvinist pig!"). Some discriminatory situations are illegal, or contrary to contracts or collective agreements and there are dignified, effective and legitimate ways to deal with these.

A Summary

- Be a team player.
- Learn to delegate.
- Take advantage of all opportunities for professional development.
- Stay calm in the face of crisis.
- Keep your personal life out of the office.
- Be willing to work late when necessary.
- Keep personal phone calls brief.
- Don't imitate male behavior, particularly in its more lamentable aspects.
- Hone your competitive skills.
- Avoid stereotypical roles.
- Take responsibility for your own career.

12

Close Encounters

In the 1960s, there was a very popular song called "Where the Boys Are" and where the "boys" are today is in corporations. The "girls" are there too. Throw in a few desks side by side, add a dash of working late, a pinch of travelling out of town and voila! the office affair is born.

The best advice we have for anyone contemplating this concoction is "DON'T GET INVOLVED."

These three words describe an ideal situation and the basis for truly professional behavior. Unfortunately, although the phrase is short and the words are simple, many people have trouble understanding the message. In the exciting real world of business, office affairs do happen. It is natural that people who work together from day to day sharing ideas, triumphs and disappointments, develop a professional intimacy. In such an atmosphere, a spark of attraction can easily ignite an affair.

Office affairs tend to be short and sweet. While the sweetness lasts, it's hard to foresee the nasty repercussions that generally follow. Few participants live happily ever after. If people realized the consequences of their actions, they would nip passion in the bud and sublimate their libidinal energies.

Unfortunately, being human, some are bound to ignore the traditional wisdom. They think they are the elect who can handle it.

If you feel you must act on impulse, make sure you think it out very carefully and understand the ramifications an office affair will have. And, if you break the first rule, which is not to do it in the first place, follow these guidelines.

1. **Be Discreet.** Resist the impulse to discuss the affair with friends or co-workers. It is your business. Even so, people are bound to suspect that there is something in the air. Lovers have a certain energy—they want to spend extra time with one another, to have one too many lunches together, to pass in corridors, hang around the other's desk, and rub elbows in elevators. They call each other over trivial matters. All of the above are inadvisable. Men should be aware that female co-workers are likely to pick up non-verbal signals and see telltale signs of an affair in the slightest, most innocuous actions. Don't meet at restaurants or bars frequented by fellow workers. And don't take your vacations at the same time.

2. **Don't Let Your Affair Affect Your Work.** One problem with affairs is that they inevitably affect one's performance in the workplace. The proximity of a lover is bound to distract a person. After all, it's much more exciting to daydream about romance than do a bank reconciliation. The point is that you're being paid to do the reconciliation.

3. **Don't Lose Your Objectivity.** Lovers must make a supreme effort to respond to each other in a business context. They must be objective, which is often very difficult, since attraction heightens response and predisposes you to favor the loved one. It is important, however, not to show partiality toward the lover's work or ideas or withhold constructive criticisms because you don't want to hurt his or her feelings. When your lover faces criticism from co-workers, you should not be the one to spring indignantly to the defense. For example, Karen was having an affair with a man in her department. One day her boss criticized her lover's quarterly report.

Instead of responding objectively, Karen replied that "Jack" was a sensitive, considerate and loving person and did not deserve to be ridiculed behind his back. Apart from making it obvious that she was involved with Jack, Karen's unprofessional behavior cost her her boss's esteem.

4. **Conduct Your Affair Away From The Office.** Affairs should never take place on company time or company premises. Don't risk tarnishing your professional image by indulging in hanky panky in the office supply storeroom. The corporate law of attraction states that the moment chosen for a quick feel by the coffee machine is the very moment the boss chooses to get two black and one double cream. Besides, it is always a good test of affection to see whether you can stand each other in a different environment. At the office, you are two co-workers sharing an exciting secret. In public, you are two adults having to behave in a mature fashion and woo each other without the benefit of subterfuge. A man who seems charming at the office may behave like a boor at a concert and a woman who is enticing at a desk may be a bore on a long weekend.

5. **Don't Reveal Confidential Information.** If you must bare your secrets to a lover, make sure they are your own, not your employer's. Otherwise, at best, your loved one will learn that you are not trustworthy. At worst, the confidential information, or merely the fact that you disclosed it, leaves you open to trouble if the affair turns sour. There is always the danger that your lover, male or female, is using you to get to the top. Also, an innocent little aside may come back to haunt you. For example, Jim works in the personnel department and was involved with one of his firm's project managers. He casually told her that one of her co-workers was going to be fired because of a drinking problem. His lover felt obligated to warn her colleague, out of sympathy for his situation. The next day, the man in question stormed into Jim's office and demanded an explanation. Jim was left in a very awkward position. The

moral of all this is that, just as your affair should not take place at the company, the company should not have a place in your affair.

6. **Don't Confuse Your Motivation.** We are often attracted to people at work whom we wouldn't even notice anywhere else. Be careful, though; familiarity breeds attempt. Attractions in the office are often based on feelings that have little to do with love and a lot to do with comfort, which is why it is advisable to have a normal social life outside working hours.

7. **Hands Off Your Boss and Senior Management.** Managers and senior executives are the power players in a company. They are in a position to hurt you and damage your reputation if an affair doesn't work out. Even if it does work, they rarely use their position to help you. Also, these people are often married, and their families are an important part of their corporate profiles. If anyone finds out, not only will you look as if you are sleeping your way to the top, but you will also look like a homewrecker. It is better to worship from afar than stare unemployment in the face.

8. **Discuss the End in the Beginning.** Don't be naive. All office affairs have a shelf life. While it's still "Best Before", approach your lover as one adult to another, and agree upon your treatment of each other should the affair end. When it's over, it's over. Both parties should agree to remain friends and not mention it to others or to each other. If it turns out that one of you gets involved with someone else at the office, the other should not display jealousy or make catty remarks. If you find this discussion distasteful, consider the true story of "Sylvia", a market researcher who had an affair with her boss. It lasted about four months, before he broke it off. Soon after, he was taking "long lunches" with his new administrative assistant. Sylvia felt it was only fair to write an anonymous letter to his wife, asking whether she knew her husband was having an affair.

The fact is, business and pleasure don't mix, and combining the two often makes a Molotov cocktail. If you must proceed, be warned that an office affair will almost certainly damage your reputation and jeopardize your chances for advancement.

A Note to Women

Women who are considering an office romance should be particularly careful. Sex in the office is, for females, almost always career suicide. When the affair ends, the junior person generally has to go and business being the chauvinistic environment it is, that person is usually female. If the man is the woman's boss, he may start criticizing her work and finding fault. There are a thousand ways he can make her work life unpleasant. Or he can fire her outright, if he thinks he can get away with it. Either way, she winds up with no job and no reference.

Remember, major appliances last much longer than the average office affair. Always ask yourself: Is this guy really worth risking having my furniture repossessed?

Unwanted Advances

Most light, flirtatious behavior in an office is harmless and not serious. It is a mistake to overreact to a co-worker's flirtatious style, since, in most cases, what you hear is not what you get. However, when faced with persistent and aggressive unwanted advances, the best initial tactic for a person of either sex is to ignore them as long as possible. No response is the best response and should be sufficient to cool someone's jets.

If not, speak to Casanova privately (not too privately!), and make it clear, with all the politeness you can muster, that you are not interested and that you do not appreciate the extra attention. Don't list personal criticisms or the particular reasons you find him or her unattractive. In extreme cases, it may help to invent an existing relationship, to ease the situation. In all cases, be careful that your demeanor and body language do nothing to encourage these flirtations. Remember that the slightest suggestive gesture says "come hither" to a conceited office Romeo or Juliet.

A particularly difficult situation arises when the unwanted advance comes from the boss's spouse, perhaps at a company party or picnic. This person is in a position to put a detour sign on your career path, so slow down and approach with extreme caution.

If it's a single pass, ignore it. Don't panic, and above all, don't fall for it! Simply excuse yourself as graciously as possible, and walk away. (Everyone should be allowed one indiscretion, especially after he or she has been drinking.) The next time you see the person, you should be as professional and as cordial as possible, and your demeanor should never suggest that you remember the incident. Sly winks and nudges are a big mistake.

If these advances persist, and you find yourself pursued, for instance, with telephone calls and letters, you have no choice but to deal with the situation. Tell the person that you are very flattered by these attentions, but you have too much respect for the person and his or her spouse to allow this to continue. Don't say "I'm happily married", and don't embarrass the person. Deal with the situation calmly and sensitively, so that both parties may maintain their dignity. Then make no mention of the episode—ever. Never give anyone occasion to be vindictive.

13

On the Road Again: Corporate Travel

It is no longer possible or necessary for most people to restrict their business activities to their home towns. Our global marketplace dictates that we travel, and travel places new demands on today's executives. It also allows them to take advantage of opportunities that lie beyond our own borders.

Planning a Trip

Careful planning is the key to successful business travel. It allows you to make the most of your time and energy, and affords you peace of mind.

Plan your itinerary, obtaining reservations for hotel, car, and so on as far in advance as possible. (Remember that in Europe, it is also necessary to reserve a seat on most trains.) You should have a written copy of this itinerary, complete with phone numbers, as should your secretary and your family. Make sure at the time of reservations that the hotel accepts the credit card with which you plan to pay your bill. Also, if you plan to arrive after 6:00 p.m., your reservation should specify "guaranteed" as otherwise the hotel may not hold your room.

For overseas trips, check with the embassy, consulate or tourist office of the country concerned to make sure you have not planned your trip during a religious or civic holiday, or other inappropriate time. Also, find out from them what weather you can expect at that time of the year.

Should you require special food or medical facilities on a flight, specify these when you make your reservation. Then, 48–72 hours ahead of departure, re-confirm with the airline, NOT your travel agent, whose computer may not be able to record such requests.

Before leaving, obtain sufficient travellers' checks for your trip, and a day or two's supply of cash in the currency of the destination country. Don't rely on using the change facility in the destination airport: your plane may be delayed and although many change facilities are open 24 hours, the one you need may be closed. It is hard to conduct business when you don't have enough cash to get downtown.

Luggage

Your luggage should be lightweight and in good repair. It should not be so tattered that a luggage strap holds it together, making you look like a refugee. On the other hand, it is foolish to use very expensive-looking luggage such as leather, particularly when travelling by airplane. Baggage handlers are too rough. Also, your luggage or its contents are more likely to be stolen if they attract attention.

Rugged garment bags with side pockets are a practical alternative to checked baggage, for short trips. They can be carried onto many aircraft and hung in cabin closets. However, some airlines have recently cracked down on this, after business people started hauling 40-lb garment bags on board. If you have packed valuables in a carry-on case of this kind, make sure before you leave that carrying it is permitted, to avoid hasty re-packing while standing in the check-in line.

Smart Packing

Pack lightly—no steamer trunks.

Plan the activities in which you will engage during the trip, then bring clothes suitable for each occasion, whether it be squash, a business meeting, or an elegant dinner. Men should bring a versatile dark suit that would be as appropriate in an office during the day as in an elegant restaurant at night. A woman can bring a good-quality silk shirtwaist dress and blazer, which can function as a suit during the day and, minus the jacket, as a suitable dress for evening.

Take comfortable shoes and clothing, since you can't go home to change. Don't risk bringing clothing that is impractical just because it looks great. Also, choose clothes that do not show dirt, since you may not be able to get them cleaned at your convenience. Leave that white suit at home.

It's hard to avoid creasing clothes in a suitcase. Well-chosen fabrics can help: wool doesn't usually crease, for example. Pack things that might crease folded over tissue paper, or roll them around a paper towel tube. Stuff underwear and socks in your shoes, to help them keep their shape. Pack shirts folded from the laundry service. Don't overstuff your suitcase. It is better to take two smaller cases than one large one that cannot be closed without jumping on it.

If your clothes arrive creased, and there is no valet service in the hotel, ask whether housekeeping can lend you an iron and ironing board. We also recommend that you invest in a lightweight, inexpensive travel steamer, which removes creases from clothes—preferably one that doesn't require salt or distilled water. You should also be able to rinse some items in your hotel room if necessary, as not all hotels offer convenient laundry services. For this reason, we recommend that you travel with a small packet of washing detergent, in a plastic bag. Most business trips are too hectic for a side trip to the supermarket.

Pack your money, important personal or business documents, travellers' checks, medication, essential toiletries such as your toothbrush, or valuables such as jewellery in a carry-on bag, your pockets, or an attache case, as appropriate. Never put these things into checked baggage. Also carry with you the names, addresses, and telephone numbers of the people with whom you are to meet. And don't carry excessive amounts of cash.

A lap-computer with built-in modem and dual voltage is a very desirable tool for the frequent business traveller. If you have an electronic mailbox in which you can dump notes for future retrieval, so much the better. (Many airports now have electronic mail terminals for sending and receiving messages.) Before using electronic devices in the air, however, check with a flight attendant to make sure it will not interfere with the plane's communication systems.

Always travel with a compact alarm clock. Many pocket calculators have this feature. It is unwise to rely solely on hotel wake-up services.

Remember that all travel appliances should have dual voltage or an adapter, unless all your travelling is in North America.

At The Airport

Always dress well en route. You never know whom you'll meet on the plane or at the airport.

Modern security measures and stopovers between flights mean that travellers now spend a lot more time in airports. Because of this, airlines are starting to accommodate business passengers by providing special facilities. Some airlines allow you to book executive suites or conference rooms, and even provide telephones and secretarial services. Such facilities are usually available only to first-class passengers, but check with your carrier. You no longer need to fritter away your time in the bar or in the duty-free shop.

Many executives like to play an infantile game. They try to see how close to departure time they can arrive without missing the flight. Such behavior is inconsiderate to staff and fellow-passengers, and many airlines are getting very tough about locking the doors five minutes before departure. Consider that at 7:00 a.m. in a busy airport, two dozen jets may be departing. The first one onto the runway saves thousands of dollars in jet fuel, and is most likely to arrive on time. The late-arriving passenger, on the other hand, may be voted least likely to arrive on time.

When arriving at an airport, read the signs. If you are flying business class, don't get in the first-class lineup. Everyone is in a hurry at airports, so don't waste your time or that of others.

Airline employees can always identify a successful executive by his or her behavior. These are people who never miss their hellos, thank yous and you're welcomes. They are kind to everybody they encounter among airline staff. Also, they never underestimate the power of airline personnel to assist them. In case of overbooking, upgrading, rerouting, and meeting connections, staff can move mountains for anybody who treats them with common decency.

Airline personnel are only human. Computers are programmed to provide the best available seating, but people who behave rudely at the check-in counter may find themselves with the worst seats on the plane. Such people are far more likely to be bumped off an overbooked flight than to be enjoying caviar in the first class cabin.

If your departure is delayed by poor weather, you are not entitled to compensation. However, if you are bumped because the flight was overbooked, or delayed by mechanical problems, you will probably receive accommodation, meal vouchers, credit and/or cash compensation (cash within the U.S. only). It does no harm to ask (politely) for these.

In the Air

Your behavior in the air is as important as your behavior on the ground. Just because you may be among strangers is no excuse to behave poorly.

Only boors smoke in non-smoking sections. Don't light up while the no-smoking sign is on, and butt out graciously when requested to do by a flight attendant.

Try to avoid eating too much, as internal organs expand when you are in flight, and you can become uncomfortable.

Also, avoid drinking more than one alcoholic beverage. Most people don't realize that alcohol has four times the impact on your system in the air as on the ground, and exacerbates jet lag. It is better to drink soda water, as flying is very dehydrating. And remember, if you must drink alcohol, that certain flight restrictions do apply.

For instance, we once saw a couple of airline travellers practically assault a flight attendant for refusing to serve them a drink while the plane was experiencing some turbulence. These passengers insisted that the attendant disobey both her supervisor and the law, possibly risking her own safety and the safety of all passengers, merely because they wanted a drink. They were so abusive that the steward finally had to threaten to call the police at the destination airport. Such behavior can only be described as inexcusable.

Arriving

You should never arrive looking as if you have slept in your clothes. If you have no checked baggage, about a half-hour before arrival (before the seat belt sign is turned on), go to the washroom and freshen up—women should check their makeup, men should shave if it's been a long flight. Also, comb your hair and brush your teeth.

If you have checked baggage, wait to do these things until you have landed (unless someone is meeting you right at the gate as is permitted in a few airports). Your baggage won't appear for at least 10-20 minutes, so use the time to visit the airport washroom where you can clean up in more space and comfort than an airplane washroom allows. You can then stroll down, refreshed, to collect your luggage.

If your luggage is lost, remember that getting angry won't make it appear. Nor is the lost luggage clerk personally responsible. If you're reasonable, the clerk is likely to do everything possible to assist you. If you're abusive, your claim will likely go to the bottom of the pile.

Most major European airports (Zurich, London Gatwick, London Heathrow, Frankfurt, Brussels) are connected to the city center by frequent train or subway service, so it is a waste of time and money to take a taxi. There is always the chance that the cab driver will use a rather roundabout route. It is much better to take the train to the city center, and a cab from there, if nobody is meeting your plane. It is wise to have the approximate locations of your hotel and of your meetings handy, so that you can find your way there.

Hotel Savvy

If you travel to a city frequently, and you are fortunate enough to find a hotel that suits you, stay there on every visit. This way the staff gets to know you and if there is a concierge service it will keep track of your preferences (foam pillows rather than feather pillows, and so on).

If you are visiting a particular company, choose a hotel that is conveniently near that company. If necessary, ask your contact there to recommend one. Choose a centrally-located hotel if you have business with a number of companies. Don't stay near the airport or in the suburbs just because it is less expensive; it will only mean wasting a lot of time and energy driving on unfamiliar roads.

Obtain telex confirmations of your hotel reservations and carry them with you.

All other things being equal, your travel agent may be able to recommend a hotel with non-smoking floors, or health-club facilities, if these amenities are important to you.

Never stay in a hotel with an unreliable message service when travelling on business, no matter how good all the other services and furnishings are.

When you check in, confirm that you can put room, restaurant and bar service on your account, based on your signature. Many people don't realize that this method of payment is not universally applicable.

Take advantage of any services the hotel offers, such as clothes cleaning, pressing, and shoe polishing. The cost is usually fairly reasonable, and failing to do so is a false economy. It is extremely important to maintain a well-groomed appearance when representing your company.

Don't leave valuables in your hotel room while you are out. Put important personal and business documents, visas, passports, jewellery, cameras, traveller's checks and cash in the hotel safe. Indeed, valuables may be left there while you are in the room, if you fear burglary.

Tipping

Tipping in hotels, as in restaurants, shows appreciation and ensures good service in future. Tip the bellboy $1 per bag, or equivalent. Tip the chambermaid $1-2 per day, depending on the length of your stay and whether you have left the room particularly messy. If you have used any hotel services, such as shoe shining, tip in advance. Put your shoes outside the door of your room at night, with a tip inside them in a small envelope.

Room service of any kind requires a tip. The amount depends on the nature of the order and the standard of the hotel. A veal sandwich in a motel may demand $1, while an elegant meal at a first-class hotel calls for a lot more. If the meal is served by a waiter from the restaurant who has had to leave his station to make up and deliver the trolley, 15 percent is not inappropriate, particularly if you stay at the hotel regularly.

If you frequently stay in a hotel that is small enough for the staff to remember you, it is worth tipping generously. Generosity is one way to ensure that you are always welcome.

It is a good idea to carry a number of small envelopes when travelling to Europe or the Orient. These are used in hotels, when tipping for housekeeping and related services. Also, if you use taxis, tip between 10 and 15 percent of the fare.

Foreign Travel

When travelling abroad it goes without saying that your passport, visa, immunization and documentation should be in order well ahead of your trip. Also, make sure you have health insurance that covers any medical expenses while travelling. Your company should pay for this insurance, as you are travelling on its behalf, but if they don't, buy it yourself.

Find out from the appropriate government body about any health hazards particular to the country you are visiting

(If necessary, be prepared to drink bottled water, avoid salads, and shake out your shoes before putting them on.) Carry antacid tablets and a good supply of any other medication you require, along with your eyeglass or contact lens prescription.

It is particularly important, when travelling in a foreign country, to ensure that all your reservations have been confirmed in writing, and that you have these documents with you.

Plan to arrive a day ahead of an important overseas meeting, so that you are rested and not drowsy and jet-lagged.

Many businessmen underestimate the effect of jet lag and fatigue on business trips. They wait until they come home to make notes on events, and find they can't remember important facts. It's advisable, instead, to write as many notes as possible at the end of each day you are away, for review and assessment. Also, make a note of details such as the names of acquaintances' spouses and children, which can help you make a favorable impression on your next visit.

Don't Forget

Business entertaining is an important aspect of most trips. Whether one person is host and the other guest, or one person selling and the other buying, the point to remember is that one party should not do all the giving and the other all the taking. The guest should take the host party to lunch or dinner at least once during the visit, in a style that matches the hospitality extended. (If no hospitality has been extended, the guest should still make a point of taking the host out).

Always maintain formality and show respect when dealing with staff at your host's company. Never call them by their first names until invited to do so. Even if your host calls his secretary "Toots", you should call her Mrs. Schmidt until she suggests otherwise.

Don't expect your host's secretary to do personal errands for you, such as change money or make appointments, even if you don't speak the local language well.

If you have been using the offices of a business contact during a stay of several days or more, or if your contact's staff has extended special courtesies to you (supplying morning coffee, photocopying documents) be sure to bring a suitable gift for the department on the day of your departure. A large box of chocolates or sweet biscuits is appropriate.

After Hours

Business travellers are ambassadors of their company and their country, and as such should use discretion in after-hours activities. Your evening plans should leave you fresh and alert for the next morning. Besides, a traveller should not put his local contact in the position of having to bail him out (legally or otherwise).

People should not reveal too much about their business activities during evening socializing. The cute stranger in a bar may work for a competitor, and in the morning his boss will know not only that you do a mean rhumba, but all about the products you plan to launch. If a stranger starts asking you specific questions or directing the conversation to business, watch out. (Conversely, when talking with business associates, it is not appropriate to reveal too much about one's personal life.)

Women

It is now common for women to be sent along on business trips. Indeed, some hotels have all-women floors and other services catering to this growing sector.

Whenever possible, women should arrange to do business on the customer's premises. Female commercial travellers who must conduct business in a hotel room should rent a suite and keep the bedroom door closed, so that they never appear to be entertaining in a boudoir. Even if the meeting occurs after hours, they should maintain an atmosphere that is totally professional. If the customer requests a drink, it is preferable to suggest going down to the bar after the business has been completed, than to order a bottle of scotch from room service.

At conventions or other large meetings, a woman should never make her room the site of impromptu parties. She should let somebody else play host, in their own room, so that she is free to leave if the evening gets out of hand or drags on all night.

As a woman alone, it is appropriate and acceptable to have dinner in a restaurant if you feel comfortable doing so. If not, order room service. Your evenings are your own, but remember not to do things that might have embarrassing or dangerous repercussions. In dangerous cities, take cabs at night, and wear shoes in which you can run.

Two's Company

When more than one person from a company is sent on a corporate business trip, there are certain guidelines that should not be neglected.

Junior executives accompanying senior executives on a business trip should always be on their best behavior. They should not keep their companions waiting, should not get too personal and should remain focused on the purpose of the trip. For example, when attending a conference in New York, it is inappropriate to show more enthusiasm for your Broadway tickets than for the panel discussions.

It often happens that a man and a woman working for the same company must travel together on business. In such cases, it is better to err on the side of propriety than to overlook potential sources of embarrassment. For example, reservations should be made primarily in the names of the individuals, not of the company, to avoid confusion when checking in. Another advantage of this system is that their company can easily reach either party through the switchboard.

It is not appropriate for these parties to share a room or a suite. Even if a suite is required for hospitality at a convention, economy does not demand that both sleep in one two-bedroom suite. Instead, the senior employee should occupy a one-bedroom suite, and the junior employee take a single room. Some companies insist that they be on separate floors, and this is not a bad idea.

There is nothing wrong with having a drink or dinner together in the evening, as long as both parties remember that the purpose of the trip is business. All socializing should occur in public places, never in a hotel room. Also, even if the other person is your only acquaintance in the city, it is not appropriate to spend every waking moment together unless business demands it.

On returning to the office, neither party should make public reference to the swell evening they spent together at the theatre or Sardi's. However innocent it may have been, this is no one's business but your own, and is bound to be misinterpreted by co-workers.

Should other staff snicker or tease a female employee, implying that some hanky-panky has occurred, it is important that she ignore this and not fall for the bait. Professional demeanor and references to a heavy workload during the trip should reduce the incidence of wisecracks.

Conventions

In the last two decades, conventions and trade shows have become extremely popular because they are an efficient way to meet a large number of suppliers and prospects in a concentrated period of time.

The person who cuts loose at conventions has become a stock comic character in the theater of business. Nobody should aspire to be remembered as the convention clown. Like other aspects of business travel, trade shows call for professional demeanor at all times. Nothing can ruin a reputation more quickly than making a fool of yourself at an industry party.

Planners for a large convention should distribute a list of registrants, with their corporate affiliation, spouse's name if present, and the name of their hotel. This helps everyone save time and facilitates making business contacts.

Convention hospitality suites are established so the host can get to know you, not just to provide an open bar. Don't abuse them. Also, if you are stomping among many such suites during the day, stick to mineral water so you can stick to business.

Finally, one sure way for a business person to look ridiculous is to continue wearing a convention identity badge after leaving the convention centre. This is particularly inappropriate when going on to an elegant dinner, the airport, or a shopping plaza.

14

International Protocol

If you do a lot of international travel, it is worth investing in one of the books that specialize in the topic so you can periodically update your knowledge. However, this chapter offers a brief introduction which should help the occasional business traveller.

General Advice

In most countries, business relations are approached with a high degree of formality. The common courtesies become extremely important, and a business person's knowledge of protocol, or lack thereof, can seriously affect business dealings abroad. For example, in Europe and Latin America, all dealings with women must show respect. The director of a large company may consider it a personal insult if a visitor doesn't seat his wife at table, if she is placed to his right.

Remember you are a guest in the other country. Be sensitive not only to business protocol, but also to cultural differences. Try to accommodate yourself to local customs—"when in Rome", as the saying goes. For instance, many countries close to the equator have a siesta after lunch and begin work early in the morning while it is still cool. The gracious visitor follows this schedule.

Show appreciation for the host country's customs and heritage. Make a point of trying local foods, rather than eating steak and potatoes or hamburgers everywhere you go. Also, respect the religious traditions, dietary customs and holidays of the country you are visiting. When in doubt, follow the lead of your host.

Try not to show offense at something foreign or something you don't understand. Seeing sacred cows wandering among the hungry may offend westerners, but it makes plenty of sense to those who understand the importance of the cow's milk and dung (as fuel and fertilizer) to the survival of many communities. Don't criticize the host culture or make unfavorable comparisons with your own. Above all, never insult the government of any country.

In many places (Arab nations, Turkey, the USSR, Greece, much of Europe, Saudi Arabia), business does not begin until food or drink is offered to the guest. Never refuse this offer of hospitality, as this could be interpreted as a slap in the face or unwillingness to do business. If you don't like the food, eat as much as you can.

In most countries, with the exception of Portugal, the bulk of the adult population smokes, and the concept of non-smokers' rights simply doesn't exist. Whereas people in North America don't hesitate to tell friends or strangers to put out a cigarette, such behavior is largely unknown in other lands. Try to stay calm and situate yourself upwind if smoke bothers you. If you have a serious respiratory ailment, you might try explaining your situation politely. Reasonable people usually defer to such a request. On the other hand, if you are a smoker, being in the majority does not eliminate the necessity for YOU to ask permission before lighting up.

It is unfair to expect North American standards in parts of the world that do not have our degree of educational funding or technological development. Also, cultures vary in the importance they accord to business. Business is everything in Hong Kong, while other nations try to balance the arts of living and commerce.

You should also have realistic expectations about communication links with other countries. Allow plenty of time for mail to arrive. Cables may not be delivered overnight, and take as long as three days in many places. Use telex or electronic mail whenever possible, if speed is required.

Try not to stick out like a sore thumb. Slinging a camera over your shoulder makes you look like a tourist, not a business traveller. Also, find some simple formula for currency conversion. You will not only save time but appear to be on top of things. Don't flaunt large amounts of cash or jewellery, particularly in poor countries. This sort of behavior is not only ostentatious, but dangerous—life is cheap in many parts of the world. And last but by no means least, don't deal on the black market. You may wind up as a commodity.

Be Formal

The use of correct titles is very important in many cultures, particularly in Europe. In France or Italy, for instance, one does not address business acquaintances by their first names. Although familiar forms of language may be more common in social life, it is better to wait to be invited to use the familiar form of address (such as "tu" in French). The English, too, prefer "Mr and "Mrs" to first names, until better acquainted. Also, in England and many European countries the president of a company is called the "managing director" while the position of "president" is a sinecure. American company presidents travelling in these countries should refer to themselves as Managing Director (MD). In Germany, executives are often addressed by their position, such as Herr Engineer. English-speaking North Americans frequently underestimate the extent to which incorrect or disrespectful titles can constitute a *faux pas*, even an insult. When in doubt, err on the side of formality.

Correspondence in other countries must also be approached with great formality and conventional language. Phrases such as "my most esteemed sir" and "your humble servant" are common and appropriate in many cultures.

Be Considerate

North Americans tend to waste energy, because it is plentiful and relatively cheap. However, it is bad manners to waste energy in other countries—particularly when your host is paying. Turn off lights and heaters when you leave a room. Don't ask a host to turn up the heat. If you're cold, put on a sweater. Other nations are accustomed to cooler indoor temperatures, and your host would be uncomfortable in a warmer room. Similarly, in many places phones are metered, and you should not spend long periods on the phone at a colleague's office without offering to pay.

Be punctual at all times and in all places. Allow extra time for traffic; in most major foreign cities, traffic is always congested.

Tipping

Tip as you would at home, rather than basing tips on your estimate of gross per capita income in the host country. The hospitality industry is sufficiently cosmopolitan that people are likely to recognize and take offense at a low tip. Ask yourself what, in the other person's situation, you would consider a fair amount.

It is not necessary to tip when a service charge has been added to the bill. However, it is advisable to leave a small (not minuscule) amount to show your appreciation for good service.

Also, it is thoughtful to leave a cash tip in foreign countries when paying a restaurant bill by bank credit card, even if doing so means tipping from your own pocket. The waiter is then assured of receiving the full amount immediately.

When visiting less developed nations, it is a good idea to bring a number of gifts that are inexpensive without being insulting. An example is a metal ball point pen with digital time display, which is a popular small present for people you may encounter on your travels. Such a gift will be appreciated by the hotel receptionist, who may be inspired to give you a superior room, or a chambermaid who has given excellent service.

Language

Don't assume that everyone you meet speaks English, even though English has become the universal business language.

When approaching foreigners ask, preferably in the local language, whether they speak English. Be humble—they are doing you a favor by communicating in your language.

When speaking to people whose English is poor, always speak slowly and distinctly. We know of a cable television executive from New York who was invited to speak at a conference in Switzerland because he was the only one the organizers met who bothered to slow his speech out of respect for his listeners. It does not help to shout. On the contrary, North Americans abroad should use modulated tones. A voice speaking another language stands out in a crowded room as it is. Don't draw undue attention to yourself.

If you do a lot of business in a particular linguistic region, your business card should be printed on the reverse in the second language, particularly if it uses a different alphabet. The Japanese, for instance, notice and appreciate this courtesy.

Last but not least, smile, say please, and say thank you.

Europe

Throughout Europe, handshakes are frequent and important. However, the old conventions for handshakes between men and women apply there. Men should not extend their hands in greeting until women do so first. Also, in Mediterranean countries, it is not unusual for men to greet each other with a kiss on both cheeks. Never look offended if this happens to you.

Europeans, like people of most cultures, respect the elderly. They express this by waiting for them to extend the hand in greeting, standing when an elderly person enters the room, allowing the older person to initiate the conversation, and using formal address. Visitors should follow these guidelines as well.

Dress

Throughout Europe, business people place great value on being well-dressed. They expect visitors to have well-polished shoes, white shirts (on men) and a good haircut. Women should not wear slacks or sleeveless dresses as street wear, or at the office. A skirt, blouse and jacket is usually appropriate.

Most Europeans of all social classes are interested in the arts, and are likely to invite visitors to attend a cultural event. The most elegant of these is the symphony concert. Dress for this is quite formal. If you don't have a tuxedo, you should definitely wear a dark suit. The safest bet for women is a black cocktail dress. Theater attire varies, as in North America, but when attending a world-renowned theater, such as the Comedie Française, casual clothing is not appropriate.

Dining

In Europe, the evening meal is an event, and dinners can last two to four hours. When invited to a private home for dinner, it is always a gracious gesture to send cut flowers to the hostess before you arrive or to bring them with you. The only other acceptable gift is chocolates. Never bring wine, liquor or cookies.

Once there, it is gracious to compliment your host's home. Do not expect to be shown more than the living room and dining room, and in summer perhaps the garden. It is rude to ask to see more. Europeans would be dumbfounded by the American custom of giving a grand tour of the house.

On the continent, aperitifs, not hard liquor or cocktails, are drunk before supper. These include Campari, Dubonnet, and Ouzo. If in doubt, ask your host to recommend a local specialty.

You should not start eating until everyone else has been served, even though the hostess may invite you to do so. Starting a meal before everyone else labels one a boor.

In many European countries and in Israel, the woman of the house serves the meal even if someone else prepared it. If you wish second helpings, ask her for more, after she has finished eating. It is not acceptable to help yourself. Always compliment the food, and eat a reasonable amount, even if you don't like it.

In many lands, including Greece and Cyprus, coffee means the small cups of sweet, black, murky brew we generally call "Turkish coffee". Needless to say, you should not ask for cream or milk. Drink it until you get to the grounds near the bottom of the cup. In other parts of the world, including Europe, if you want the pale, weak coffee most North Americans prefer to continental roasts, ask for American coffee/café americain, or Nescafé, which will be understood generically.

The meal is over when the man of the house breaks the table. If you have to leave before that, ask permission.

Finally, do not overstay your welcome. The meal is the main event, and you should not linger in someone's home.

United Kingdom

The British tend to be more formal and reserved than North Americans,and these attitudes permeate every aspect of their business dealings. It is important to respect British regard for protocol, and a visitor should never make the mistake of crossing over into familiar behavior unless invited to do so. Slaps on the back, arms around the shoulder and two-handed handshakes are inappropriate. Physical contact is best kept to a minimum.

Privacy is valued in Britain and discretion is expected. Don't ask personal questions or volunteer personal information, since this may make others uncomfortable. Well-bred English people become acutely uncomfortable when Americans turn the conversation to personal intimacies. Don't make the fatal mistake of glancing at mail or memos in an office or asking questions about areas of the business that do not concern you.

Punctuality is very important and should be the rule. If you have some distance to travel to a meeting, leave extra time to accommodate the always-heavy traffic. "Sorry, but I was stuck behind a bus..." is a poor excuse when offered to someone who deals with heavy traffic every day. Also, remember that cars are driven on the *left* side of the road.

Phones are metered in the U.K. and the rates vary according to the time of day. Mornings are most expensive, afternoons cheaper, and evenings and weekends cheapest. If using someone's phone, bear the cost in mind.

Dress is quite conservative. The three-piece pinstripe suit is the norm in the City (financial district of London) and good tailoring is noticed and expected. A dark suit is always more appropriate than lighter colors. Men should leave their bracelets and diamond rings at home; a man who wears excessive jewellery is not trusted. When outdoors, it is advisable to carry a good quality (conservative) umbrella at all times, since British weather is unpredictable.

The English like to work a regular working day, which starts and ends slightly later than the North American 9-5 routine. In keeping with their respect for privacy, it is unlikely that British executives will invite overseas guests to their homes for dinner, but rather leave them to their own devices. Business entertaining generally occurs at lunch, and it is not uncommon to be invited to the neighborhood pub where lunch is eaten standing up. If you are invited for a pub lunch, know the terms. Beer is served in pints or half pints ("halfs"). It is served at nearly room temperature and it is gauche to complain that it isn't cold. You'll score points and enjoy a treat by asking for any "real ale" on tap. Typical pub grub includes the "ploughman's lunch" (bread and cheese with mustard or chutney), "scotch eggs" (hard-boiled egg covered with sausage meat, breaded, deep fried and served cold), and cornish pasties (a meat turnover). Pub lunches are quite inexpensive, but you will find that there is little between the very cheap restaurants and the very expensive ones. Brace yourself for occasional whopping bills.

A few notes on tea: In Britain, tea is always served very strong and with milk. "High Tea" refers to a rather formal light meal of sandwiches and perhaps fruit cake (known sportingly as British Rail cake) served in the late afternoon. High Tea is still served at the upper levels of some corporations. "Cream Tea" is served at the same time, usually in exclusive restaurants and hotels and consists of tea with cream cakes (pastry with whipped cream) or scones (tea biscuits) with whipped double-milk fat cream and preserves. When a worker says it's time for tea, he means a hot supper, not cucumber sandwiches or a tea break. It is considered gauche to drink tea after late afternoon, and restaurants may refuse to serve it after supper. Coffee is the appropriate beverage for this time of day. Coffee with milk or cream is "white".

It is normal for executives to take the tube (subway) or a British Rail train to work in the City, unless they have a car and a driver or have arranged parking. When walking in London, which is a great pleasure, always carry a good map: the *London A-Z* is the choice of residents and comes in a complete or central London version. The streets change names every few blocks and can be confusing for all but taxi drivers. In London, the city shuts down with the underground, so it isn't the 24-hour city New York is.

The English spoken in England is not North American and words don't always mean the same thing. "Pants" are underpants, not trousers, which has caused many a foreigner embarrassment. "Knock me up" means "knock on my door to wake me up". "Suspenders" mean garters, which hold up socks (which the British call stockings), not the elastic that holds up American trousers (which Brits call braces). A suspender belt is a garter belt. A vest means an undershirt, not the part of a 3-piece suit that would be called a waistcoat in England. Pudding can mean any kind of dessert other than cake, which is often called "gateau." In London, rather than say you were "going downtown", you would say "to the City" (financial district) or "to the West End". Here are some other examples of different usage.

English	American
subway	pedestrian underpass
tube, underground	subway
traffic circus	traffic roundabout
bonnet	hood of a car
dynamo	generator
boot	trunk (car)
lorry	truck
boiler	furnace
valve	tube
mains, point/power point	electrical outlet, hydro
the bill	the check (restaurant)
guard	railway conductor
unit trust	mutual fund
chemist's shop	drug store
personal call	person to person
chairman (business)	president
football	soccer
fortnight	two weeks

Many London bookstores carry pocket-size English-American dictionaries which are quite helpful. A traveller should become familiar with common expressions so as not to commit any embarrassing blunder or take undue offense of a host's usage. One final note: Absolutely *NO* jokes about the Queen.

France

A business trip to Paris is everyone's dream come true. However, to keep it from becoming a nightmare, it is important to be on your best behavior, since many French people are quick to take offense at the lapses of foreigners.

The French are very serious about their work. The business day starts at 8:30 with a break for lunch at 12:30 and then resumes at 3:00 or 3:30 and runs until 6:00 or 6:30. The polite business visitor must be prepared to entertain himself during the lunch break since many people use this time to go home for a meal and a short rest.

The French are very cautious about dealing with strangers who walk in off the street and offer to do business with them. They have a great respect for the old-world convention that demands that companies, as well as individuals, be properly introduced. Therefore, it is important that you be referred to new business contacts by people they know and respect. For this reason, prior appointments are a must and should be confirmed in writing if possible. Remember that formality is the rule. Never use first names unless invited to do so and always address your associate's staff as Monsieur and Madam rather than Jean and Marie. And you *must* shake hands when meeting and also when leaving—to forget to do so is extremely insulting.

Subtleties play an important part in your business dealings. Be especially aware of your body language and facial expressions. The French are famous for their cautious approach and their careful examination of every fact and figure. Be prepared to discuss even the smallest point at great length and have your information up to date and close at hand. At no time should you show impatience or irritation. Such behavior is considered out of line in a professional environment; the French do not like to feel rushed and do not respond to high pressure tactics

Correspondence is valued, and the French like to confirm details in writing. Write in correct French, if possible, using the appropriate and ornate conventions of formal business letters.

Business attire in France is always formal and conservative: dark suit, white shirt and tie are a must for men; women should always be well dressed. It is not proper to arrive for a business meeting wearing a leisure suit and turtleneck sweater. Women should never wear slacks.

It is rare that the French invite business guests to their homes. (If this does happen, don't forget to bring flowers or chocolates for the hostess.) They prefer to entertain in restaurants and are flattered if visitors request that they choose food on their behalf. Dinner promises to be a leisurely meal and the guest must show appreciation for the food. Note that in France salad is served *after* the main course. Remember too that any wine you drink must be sipped appreciatively and never gulped. The French are very proud of their wines.

Also, if you extend a dinner invitation to your business associates, be prepared to go to an *expensive* restaurant. This is an important part of protocol. An inexpensive establishment shows a lack of respect so be careful in selecting an appropriate restaurant and don't gulp when you get the bill.

Italy

The business traveller in Italy is sure to receive a warm reception. Italians are famous for their generous hospitality and will go to great lengths to make a visitor feel welcome, which ought to inspire a desire to reciprocate with gracious behavior.

Business attire is conservative and elegant. Suits, ties and white shirts are the rule for men and women are advised to dress smartly. We recommend wearing a dress and blazer or stylish skirt and blouse rather than a business suit, unless the suit is very chic.

Italians have an extended work day which runs from 9:00 a.m. to 8:00 p.m. and is broken by a lunch break of 3 hours between 1:00 and 4:00 in the afternoon. This break is not normally used for business discussions and the travellers will be left to their own devices during this time.

In Italy, many professions carry particular titles that are recognized as a sign of professional respect. For example, doctors or engineers should always be introduced and addressed as *Dottore* or *Ingegnere*, rather than Signor, and many businessmen qualify to be called *Commandatore*, a title given by the government in recognition of their achievements. These titles are important and failure to use them constitutes an insult or lapse. Also, when meeting or greeting anyone, a handshake should be automatic. This is an important gesture of trust and Italians are suspicious of anyone who does not offer to shake hands.

Because their mail service tends to be unreliable, Italians do not set great store on correspondence and conduct much of their business by telephone. To use a pay phone in Italy, you must purchase tokens in advance. These are available at post offices and tobacconists, and are called *gettoni.*

Italians, like the French, do not generally entertain business acquaintances at home until the relationship becomes one of personal friendship. If you are invited to an Italian's home, *you must* accept the invitation since it is insulting to decline. Be sure to bring a gift for the hostess and make a point of complimenting the house, the children and the decor. Your hosts may feel they have offended you if you are not forthcoming with this praise. And always compliment the food and eat what you are given. It is considered an insult to refuse food.

When dining out, take note that it is gauche to order both soup and pasta in Italy. Pasta is an appetizer. After the pasta, the meat is served by itself. If you wish something to accompany the meat, you must order it separately. As in France, salads are served after the meat course.

Italians consider it in poor taste to drink milky coffees such as capuccino or caffèlatte after 10:00 a.m. After this hour, coffee is always served black.

Heavy tipping (20 percent) is appropriate in this country, where waiters are highly trained and service is invariably impeccable.

West Germany

Formality and protocol reign in West Germany. The business traveller should never make the mistake of becoming familiar or casual with his German hosts or moving to a first name basis without invitation Such behavior is regarded as unprofessional and can seriously undermine a business relationship. Germans are very cautious in all their business dealings and trust and confidence must be nurtured with great care.

All appointments should be made well in advance. Germans hate surprises and prefer to conduct business with someone who has been introduced by a recognized colleague. References and goodwill are very important here.

Work habits are very efficient so don't waste time and please be punctual. Arriving late for an appointment is a serious error; the Germans are more likely to consider it a lack of respect than a reflection of your sleeping habits.

German business attire is extremely conservative—dark suits, ties and white shirts for men and tasteful, almost subdued, clothing for women. (A business trip will often include an invitation to the symphony or opera so men should pack an extra suit and women should be prepared with a long dress or skirt.)

On the rare occasion that you are invited to an associate's home, you should bring a gift for the hostess, such as cut flowers. Take care to compliment the house and the food. This is not the time to discuss business. Dinner tends to be a very social affair and the conversation is bound to include a discussion of cultural events, so be prepared. Afterwards, send a thank-you note.

Greece

Businessmen in Greece are very formal, while businesswomen are extremely rare. However, observance of protocol toward women is both noticed and valued.

In Greece, it is considered a mistake to discuss business over lunch. Greeks believe that lunch is for enjoyment, and for getting to know one another better. Don't try to negotiate or close a deal over your moussaka. Business should be conducted in the office.

If a Greek man plays with worry beads while he talks with you, it is not a sign of boredom, but a customary way of reducing stress. Don't let it distract you.

As in Italy, certain cafes are reserved strictly for men, and women will get a very cool reception if they enter.

Most Greek food is served lukewarm, and it is not appropriate to send it back to the kitchen. If you crave hot food, order fish or omelettes, which are cooked to order. In some "bouzouki bars" in Greece, it is traditional for diners to smash plates and glasses against the wall. Before you get carried away, find out how much will be added to your bill for each one you break. If we're talking about Royal Doulton, you could be in for a nasty shock.

If there is a busboy, his tip is left on the table, whereas the waiter's tip goes on the tray on which the bill arrives.

The U.S.S.R.

When planning a business trip to the Soviet Union, you must start making arrangements weeks in advance, since all visa applications and travel plans must be approved by Soviet officials. Arrangements should be made through a travel agent that deals with *Intourist,* the state travel agency, and the business traveller must be prepared to pay for hotel and car in advance. (As a matter of fact, officials will not issue visas until hotel reservations have been confirmed and paid for.) The visitor must realize that all the details of his trip will be planned and approved and he is expected to stick to his outlined schedule—even dinner invitations to business associates must have prior state clearance. The Soviet Union and spontaneity are not words that go hand in hand!

It is extremely important to respect the political system of the U.S.S.R. It is in bad taste and very dangerous to make unfavorable comparisons between the East and the West and you should not say anything in private that you would not say in public. And don't compromise people you meet by eliciting or making comments that may land them in hot water with the authorities. Bear in mind that no matter what business brings you there, the U.S.S.R.'s unique position in the world today casts political overtones on all our relationships with them. Visitors should never forget to act as ambassadors of both their company and their country.

The Soviet people on the whole are very sincere and warm. Their work day usually begins at 9:00 a.m. and goes to noon; an hour is taken for lunch and then business resumes until 6:00 p.m.

Business attire is conservative to the point of dullness and the visitor should wear a dark suit, white shirt and tie and sensible shoes.

All business appointments should be made well in advance (and approved by officials) and confirmed in writing. Make an effort to be on time since punctuality is highly regarded.

Remember to refer to The Soviet Union—never Russia. And don't make jokes or call your associate "comrade" since this word is used only by members of the communist party.

When dining out, it is recommended that you bring cash since many restaurants do not accept credit cards. Usually all charges will be included in your bill since tipping is generally discouraged, but it never hurts to leave a small amount of money on the table.

Israel

"Shalom" is the universal greeting in Israel. It means peace, hello, and goodbye and is appropriate in both professional and social situations.

The Israeli work week observes the sabbath, which officially is from Friday sunset to Saturday sunset. Unofficially it runs from Friday noon to Sunday morning. Israelis tend to be very impatient, so don't waste time. The work week begins on Sunday. Business hours vary but there is a lunch break of two to three hours during which many Israelis go home.

Israel has no dress code. It is probably the least formal country in the world for the business person. Short-sleeved shirts, shorts, no jacket and no tie are common among members of the Knesset (parliament). A tie provokes stares, and formal dress stops traffic.

Most Israeli restaurants are kosher, that is, they follow the dietary laws of Judaism. Pork is not served in Israel. Under kosher rules, dairy and meat are not mixed. If you have eaten a meat meal, you should not ask for cream or milk for your coffee, or butter for your bread/sandwich. Remember that shellfish is not kosher. Israelis used to find tipping objectionable, but this is no longer the case in the service and hospitality industries.

Israelis commonly entertain in their homes. If you are invited to someone's home to greet the sabbath (Shabbat) on Friday night, be sure to bring flowers and something for the children. Chocolate or candies are appropriate. Israel is a very child-oriented society and parents would rather see their children pleased than receive a gift themselves.

When leaving Israel, arrive at the airport two hours early *without fail*, for security clearance. However, if you are flying El Al, Israel's national airline, you may check your baggage through the night before at their downtown terminals, which will reduce your check-in time to one hour.

The Orient

In most oriental countries, the corporate hierarchy is extremely well-respected. The further up the ladder, the more formal the demeanor required. Thus, visitors should be polite to all, but abide by the professional caste system of the host. For instance, in Japan it is not appropriate to chat with a business contact's receptionist, as one might do in North America. It is more appropriate to sit and wait quietly in the reception area.

Japan

Business never stops in Japan. And it is not unusual, when conducting business in Japan, to open the day with a tea ceremony. Westerners fortunate enough to be present for a tea ceremony should follow the lead of their host and participate. When this is over, business begins in earnest.

Manners are very important to the Japanese. Bowing is not as prevalent a custom as it used to be, but when a person bows to you, you should return the bow immediately. Bow from the waist, while lowering the head approximately one foot, and place your hands together. Also, remember that while North Americans tend to measure honesty and square dealing by direct eye contact, the Japanese consider too much eye contact offensive. It is considered a sign of humility to cast the eyes down occasionally.

It is still traditional to remove your shoes in homes and some restaurants, although this is no longer the case in a business environment. Make sure your socks are presentable in case you find yourself at a threshold where shoes must be removed.

Correspondence is much valued in Japan. Be sure all business dealings are confirmed in writing. Also, before your trip, send a schedule of the points you hope to cover, and ask whether these are acceptable to your host. Above all, be on time—the Japanese are fanatics for punctuality.

It is very unlikely that a business guest will be invited to a Japanese home. Restaurants are the scene of business entertaining. Always call ahead for reservations in Japan. Many of the expensive restaurants there are like private clubs, and it is hard to get a reservation for a first-time customer who isn't known.

At the best Japanese restaurants, no money changes hands between Japanese. The customers have accounts, and a representative arrives in person at the end of the month to settle the account. Bills are not sent by mail. A visitor with a reservation should pay cash. In matters where extreme protocol is required, we suggest that a visitor carry new currency that is sequentially numbered. When the bill arrives at the end of the evening, it comes in an envelope. The money is placed in this envelope. The Japanese do not like to see cash on the table when they are dining. Your change, also in new bills, will be returned in an envelope. Only when you have become known to an upscale establishment may you use a credit card. (In major American hotels in Japan, credit cards are more readily accepted.)

Japanese stationery stores sell special small envelopes, usually brightly-colored or flowered, which are used for tips. Leave the tip on the table in this envelope. You are expected to bring your own envelope. Some restaurants also like you to bring your own toothpick and napkin, so it is advisable to carry a large linen handkerchief, just in case.

It is a mistake to ask to bring your wife to a business dinner. Women are still not welcome at these traditionally male events. Professional hostesses, known as Geishas, still serve at a number of restaurants. It is incorrect to assume that they are anything more than hostesses. Heavy drinking is also customary at Japanese business dinners.

If your Japanese associate wishes to pick up the tab, don't fight over it, but remember to reciprocate during your visit and when your guest comes to your country.

Japanese culture sets a high store on gifts. If you are visiting a company for the first time you should bring a tasteful gift, perhaps something representative of your country or culture. A coffee table picture book or characteristic figurine is appropriate. Scotch whiskey is an excellent present, as it is very expensive in Japan. On leaving, it is courteous to send a gift, such as candy, to the office staff.

The Japanese business uniform consists of classic, understated dark blue or grey suits with white shirts—nothing flamboyant or double-breasted. Make sure your grooming and personal cleanliness are impeccable.

Japan is very densely populated, so it is wise to prepare yourself for the crowds, particularly in Tokyo. If you have to take public transit, be aware that there are people whose job it is to push people into the Tokyo subway. Tokyo is also very polluted. Bring along extra clothes, or be prepared to have them laundered more often, because of the dirt in the air. And don't be unduly alarmed by masked figures on the street. The Japanese wear surgical-type masks when they have an infectious disease, such as a cold or the flu. These masks are worn as a courtesy to others.

Hong Kong

Business in Hong Kong is a 24-hour-a-day, 365-day-a-year activity. Don't assume your Saturdays and Sundays will be free for shopping. If you want time off, book yourself in for a few extra days.

Women are accepted on an equal basis in the Hong Kong business world and most business people there speak English. Remember, though, that when doing business with Europeans in Hong Kong, European protocol applies.

Be prepared for the traffic congestion in Hong Kong, and the different standards of hygiene and table manners that exist there. The Chinese don't consider it rude to slurp soup or noodles and they do eat with their hands.

Although the climate is tropical and the humidity usually around 97 percent, white suits and dresses are not appropriate, as white is the color of mourning. White shirts, however, are fine.

Australia

Australian business is male-dominated. However, attitudes toward women and minorities notwithstanding, Australia prides itself on being democratic. You will find this a very friendly and open place to do business.

Dress is very casual: shorts, no jacket, no tie. But at the upper echelons of international business, greater formality persists.

Australian English is substantially different from that spoken anywhere else. Australian-English phrasebooks are available in some places, and they make fascinating reading.

Islamic Countries

The following rules apply throughout the Persian Gulf, with the exception of Bahrain, where general international rules apply.

Blasphemy is not tolerated in Muslim countries. Neither is alcohol, which should not be consumed or carried into these countries. Muslims do not eat pork. Tipping is frowned upon, although many hospitality and service industry workers in the Gulf come from lands which accept it. Smoking, too, is unacceptable.

Women are not included in business in the Persian Gulf—indeed in many places women aren't allowed to walk about on the street.

Business is not conducted between Thursday night and Friday night in Islamic countries. Make sure you do not try to do business during other holy times, such as Ramadan, the 30-day fast that occurs during the ninth month of the Islamic year. Remember that the Islamic calendar is different from the western calendar, so the business traveller should double check dates in advance.

The large international hotels are the base for most business activities in these countries. You seldom need to leave this part of the city. All kinds of foods, not just local specialties, are available in these hotels. When being entertained by a business contact from an Arabian country you should never refuse any food or drink that is offered to you. A refusal would be interpreted as an insult.

Dress is formal and modest. Shorts and short sleeves are generally not permitted.

Latin America

In Latin countries, correct protocol toward women is important. Walking with the woman on the wrong side of you can hamper a business deal. Remember, though, that women are respected as escorts, not as business people.

Dress is very formal in this region: you should always wear a white shirt with a dark suit.

Latin Americans are very hospitable, and are likely to open their homes to guests. When visiting a home in any Latin country, compliment something about the home. You should also bring a gift.

Don't smoke at the table in Mexico, South America or any Latin country. Another thing to be careful about is looking at your watch while in company. It is offensive to Latin Americans.

Tipping is very heavy throughout central and south America.

Handshakes are a very important sign of male camaraderie. Men shake hands several times a day.

15

Professional Style

It is your appearance that creates that all-important first impression, so it is crucial that you think about the message you wish your clothing to convey. Start by taking a look in the mirror. Do you look like everyone else, or is your appearance outstanding? Do your clothes and grooming express your own high standards? Do you look like a successful, competent executive?

Just as you would give plenty of consideration to the packaging of a new product, so you should package yourself to achieve your own goals. Clothing should work in your favor, enhancing your image rather than detracting from it in any way. When you are talking with people, they should never be distracted by something inappropriate in your appearance.

You should dress for the position you would like to occupy, not your current position. A person is unlikely to be promoted to a position if he doesn't look the part.

One of the most important aspects of business dress is consistency. Always dress as if you were representing the company to customers, shareholders, or on a business trip. Otherwise, no one will have the confidence to send you on such a mission. If you arrive at work wearing jeans one day, that is the way people will remember you.

Your
Business Wardrobe

In planning a business wardrobe, it is advisable to choose one basic color and work around it. You will then be able to mix and match effectively without having to invest in an extensive wardrobe. Make sure the color you choose is flattering.

Always buy quality; consider your clothes an investment in your career. Better-quality clothing saves money in the long run because it lasts longer, is usually based on classic designs and doesn't go out of fashion and holds its shape. Good clothes also fit better.

Wearing expensive clothing, however, is not the same thing as being well-dressed. Your wardrobe has to suit you. Dressing appropriately and with flair is an acquired skill. If you have trouble in this regard, purchase a book that covers the subject in depth or seek the advice of a reputable tailor.

Male Office Attire

The recent interest in dressing for success indicates that more and more men are becoming aware of the importance of being "well suited" for the job.

Men's business suits should be conservative in style, pattern and color. Pure wool is the most appropriate fabric.

Business shirts should generally be white. Unless the wearer has an acute fashion sense or is acting on the advice of his tailor, it is safer to leave colored shirts for leisure wear. Short-sleeved shirts are acceptable attire in the summer months only. Shirt collars should never be too tight. It is not becoming to look as if you are being strangled. Turtleneck sweaters, while comfortable, do not present a professional image for work. An exception may be certain "creative" fields, such as advertising. Take your cue from top management.

Even if you have only two good suits, don't scrimp when you buy your ties. Men's suit styles don't change much over time, so impact is often created by the tie. A poorly-knotted tie makes a lasting impression, but it may not be the impression you wanted to make. Since ties are so noticeable, make sure they are clean. Don't wear your tie once too often without dry cleaning it

Women find it very sexy to see an attractive man with his tie loosened and the top shirt button undone. You may have success with this at a bar, but nevertheless it is not appropriate for a corporate environment—it suggests casualness and laziness. Your tie should remain neatly knotted unless you have stayed late to work and there are few people around. The old saying still applies: If the man is not comfortable in his tie, he is not comfortable in his executive role.

The old college tie and the conservative stripe are always appropriate, but don't be afraid to get more creative. Working with your tailor, choose colors you've perhaps never worn before, that will help you stand out in an acceptable way.

Don't wear a tie made by your children in batik class, to the office. Also avoid tasteless ties and tie-tacks, such as those featuring nude women, horses, or slogans such as "I visited Disney World."

Coordinate your shoes to your wardrobe. A navy blue suit and brown loafers do not belong together. Black shoes are appropriate with a navy, grey or black suit. Shoes should always be clean and well-polished.

Wear black socks with a black suit, dark navy or black socks with a navy suit. Do not wear dark brown, white, red or argyle socks with any of the above. Socks should be of one solid color. Leave patterned hose for wearing in your leisure time. Remember to keep an eye on the condition of your hosiery. Nothing is more eye-catching than an otherwise well-dressed executive with a worn-out sock heel. And don't wear short socks; it is very distracting when an executive crosses his legs to expose a few inches of pale skin at the ankle.

Ten Inappropriate Items For Men's Office Wear

Safari Suits
Polyester Leisure Suits
Nehru Jackets
Medallions/Chains
Short-Sleeved Jacket with Long-Sleeved Shirt
Ill-Fitting Toupees
Undershirts with Sleeves
Jogging Suits/T-Shirts
Sweatbands
Corduroy

Hats The streets of New York, London and Paris are full of men wearing hats to the office, theater, dinner and other occasions. These hats are decorative, as opposed to a toque worn to keep the head warm. As part of an outfit, hats can be very chic, as long as you remember the etiquette associated with them.

A man should never wear his hat into a church, office building, institution, upscale restaurant or private residence. Remove it as soon as you step inside the door. Removing one's hat remains a gesture of respect even though men may no longer tip their hats to ladies. Hats should never be worn in a concert hall or theater where they may obstruct the view of other patrons. Baseball and cowboy hats may be worn in fast food restaurants, suburban shopping malls, the oil patch, and bars catering to exotic clientele. A Stetson looks ridiculous on a man who has obviously never been nearer to a steer than eating a steak. And remember, men wear hats tilting down to the left of the face.

Other Accessories To paraphrase the old saying about chains, an outfit is only as strong as its weakest link. People notice the small details—particularly if they are jarring. Once you have invested hundreds of dollars in the basics of a good business wardrobe, don't destroy the effect by choosing inappropriate accessories.

The handkerchief for the breast pocket should be either white or a color that harmonizes with the tie. It is worn only for appearance, and is never used to blow your nose. Men should invest in three or four good-quality white linen handkerchiefs. These are always kept out of sight in your pants pocket when not in use, never tucked in your sleeve or your inside jacket pocket. If you don't like using handkerchiefs, use man-sized disposable tissues. A male executive should never use little colored tissues to blow his nose.

Do not wear a digital watch with a built-in calculator, computer, modem, transistor radio or television set. Only divers need watches that glow in the dark. Instead, choose an analog watch in good taste. And invest in a good-quality pen. It is not impressive to negotiate a large deal with another executive, then hand him a 39-cent plastic medium-point pen to sign the deal.

Belt buckles should be understated and of classic design. They should not be in the shape of cowboy hats or sailing ships.

Jewellery should be simple and elegant. Many people find an excess of jewellery on men to be in very poor taste and even a simple gold bracelet can be distracting in a corporate setting. Heavy chains and numerous rings or earrings are not appropriate office wear.

A beaten-up attache case detracts from a business person's overall presentation. Leather products should be of good quality and well-maintained.

Female Office Attire

Few sights are more impressive than a well-dressed, well-shod woman moving with an air of confidence. The smart female executive uses her clothes to project a secure, professional image.

Appropriate fabrics for office wear include pure wool, fine cotton, silk, and cashmere. Suits should be avoided unless they are of top quality, excellent cut, and perfect fit. Poorly-fitting, inexpensive suits look dowdy and detract from one's image. Women should never wear three-piece or corduroy suits.

To have impact in a corporate situation, it is preferable to wear a well-cut dress in a good fabric, worn with a blazer, or well-fitting classic coordinates. This distinguishes you from the rest of the suited female crowd.

Well-tailored lined wool trousers can look terrific on a tall, svelte woman who is wearing appropriate shoes, but very few women wear trousers well. At the executive level, they are appropriate only in artsy industries such as film and advertising and then only on thin women. Anyone over a size 8 should opt for skirts.

You may prefer to spend your leisure time in jeans and football sweaters or gold lame pajamas, but classic conservatism is the rule when dressing for work. High fashion suggests flightiness, and a woman will never be taken seriously if she shows up each week sporting a different fad.

Be discriminating when choosing summer fashions. The office is no place for a bare back, a halter dress with a plunging

V neck, and so on. Remember, only mailmen wear shorts to the office. You don't, however, have to wear a wool suit in hot weather. A smart cotton dress with a matching jacket is fine.

The point is that female executives must dress with a sense of decorum. Save slit skirts, flowers in the hair, plunging necklines, and see-through blouses for the disco. If you have a bra, wear it; if not, buy one.

We're not suggesting that dowdy, severe or straight-laced clothes are required in a professional environment. Today's fashions allow women great flexibility and expression in choosing clothes. A woman should dress with a sense of style, always asking herself: "Does this make me look like the professional I am?"

Some Inappropriate Items for Women's Office Wear

Lamé
Chiffon
Taffeta
Double knits
Bulky Fisherman Knit Sweaters
Sweaters, except under skirted suits (shouldn't be too tight)
Extremely high-heeled shoes
Thongs
Ballet Slippers
Running Shoes
Mules
Exercise Sandals
Plastic shoes of any kind
Toreador Pants
Harem Pants
Shawls
Garish floral prints or patterns
Flowers in hair
"Little-Girl" Styles
T-Shirts
Jeans
Cords
Buttons bearing slogans, such as "Rock and Roll Lives"
Hippie Attire

Hats Hats have returned to women's fashion after an absence of some 20 years, following the influence of Princess

Diana. Hats should be considered an accessory to an outfit, like jewellery. If you have never worn a hat, it is wise to invest in a smartly-styled model and learn to wear it with panache. A hat draws attention to a woman, and makes her more conscious of her demeanor.

Unless a woman is wearing a balaklava, she does not have to remove a hat while dining in a restaurant. She may wear her hat to the office, but never at her desk. When calling on a client, a hat should be removed in the reception area.

Some men are intimidated by women in hats. Avoid large-brimmed hats which obstruct eye contact. Never wear a large-brimmed hat for a business meeting. You are not attending a garden party. A small hat fitting snugly to the head may be left on as long as it is not distracting to you or the other people.

The old rules about hats still apply. Don't wear a large, broad-brimmed hat after 6:00 p.m. These are considered day-time attire. The exception is functional hats worn in cold weather, such as fur hats, but these should be removed at the door. Otherwise, after six, small cocktail hats are appropriate and look very chic for a night on the town. Women's hats are always worn tipping down to the right of the face.

Other Accessories Accessories should be understated and classic in design. They should not draw undue attention, and should enhance the wardrobe rather than overpower it.

Tasteful silk scarves are appropriate for the office and can add color to an outfit. Men's ties are not appropriate, however fashionable the tie may become.

Plastic drop earrings and numerous bangle or charm bracelets are not appropriate boardroom attire. Stay away from junk jewellery. It has a dime-store look. Jewellery should be simple and elegant. If you wish to add impact, a brightly-colored bag and shoes work much better than large, garish jewellery. Don't wear more than one earring per ear. Pearls are a suitable gem for office wear but whisper chains and hair-thin rings are not appropriate. Avoid wearing jewellery shaped like hearts or the signs of the zodiac.

The advice to men on leather accessories and pens applies equally to women. Don't wear shoulder bags made of cloth, denim and raw leather. A large jelly-plastic basket is *not* a purse—handbags should be small, plain and neat, demonstrating that the owner is organized. We recommend a smart shoulder bag or a small clutch that fits in your attache case.

Stockings are always a point of issue for some reason. There should be no issue. Working women should always wear stockings in summer. You never see men wearing sandals with a three-piece suit because shoes and socks make them too hot. Bare legs, no matter how tanned and well-groomed, belong at home and at the beach. Sockettes are not appropriate either.

Winter boots, unless decorative and part of the outfit, don't belong in the office. Keep a pair of pumps (the most suitable office shoe) in your desk drawer, and remove your boots when you arrive.

Puttin' on the Ritz

If a man is invited to an evening function, he should wear a good quality dark suit with a white shirt, a dark tie, dark socks and black shoes. This will usually prove appropriate, unless black tie or "formal attire" have been specified on the invitation. However, executives must be prepared to attend formal dinners and receptions.

A "Black Tie" invitation means a tuxedo (dinner jacket) is required. Traditionally, these are black and black remains the most suitable color. A tuxedo has a single or double breasted jacket worn with cuffless pants that have a stripe of satin down the side. Tuxedos are worn with a white dress shirt with studs and cuff links, black silk socks, and black patent leather shoes. With a single breasted jacket, there is no belt, but a "cummerbund" which matches the bow tie. Traditionally, cummerbunds are black, but in recent years red and deep maroon cummerbunds have become very popular. Some European designers have created cummerbunds in bright turquoise, emerald green and even lurex. These flamboyant designs may be stylish, but they are probably not appropriate for your boss's country club.

"White Tie" means a white bow tie and tails instead of a dinner jacket. The shirt, pants, socks and shoes are the same as worn for "black tie". Either a white vest or a cummerbund completes the outfit.

If the invitation says "formal" but does not specify black or white tie, wear a tuxedo. You can't go wrong this way. On the other hand, if you are the only one who shows up in tails, you may appear pompous and overdressed—or you might be mistaken for the cocktail pianist.

For a formal evening function which is described as such on the invitation, a woman should wear a long dress. However, when attending a cocktail party, mid-afternoon event or the theater with a man who is wearing a tuxedo, a formal ballet-length (above the ankle) or cocktail-length (below the knee) is acceptable.

Women should dress with a sense of decorum, particularly for functions connected with business. Avoid very low cut, slinky gowns and very high cut, slinky skirts. Evening pants are not suitable for company functions. With formal wear, women should consider having peau-de-soie shoes dyed to match their dress. Leather pumps and silver or gold slippers are usually not appropriate. You may wear evening sandals with sheer evening hose.

Grooming

You cannot afford to ignore the fundamentals of good grooming. Your clothes may not be expensive, but they must be neat, clean, crisp and fresh. Deodorant is a must. Deodorant stains and ring-around-the-collar are no-nos.

Use a lint brush to remove dust and hair from your clothes, particularly if you are wearing dark colors. Make sure your hands and nails are clean. Do *not* bite your fingernails. Both men and women should have a monthly manicure.

Your shoes should always be clean and well-polished. Heels should not be allowed to wear out. Have them replaced once wear becomes visible; remember the expression "down at the heels"? Shoes should never have split seams or holes in the soles.

Keep hats cleaned and brushed. If they lose their shape, they can be blocked and steamed by a hatter. Some tailors offer this service as well. You can do a quick home treatment by holding the hat over a steaming kettle.

If you wear glasses, keep them clean and well-tightened.

Perfume

Perfume, cologne, and men's aftershave, if worn, must be of good quality and remain extremely subtle. A person should notice it only as a pleasant surprise when he or she hugs you.

The person next to you at the office should not be able to smell your cologne. Your fragrance should not precede you into a room or linger there after your departure. It detracts from your image. Remember, too, that if you customarily wear a fragrance, you won't notice it after a while. Ask someone you know to tell you if it is overpowering. Bear in mind that many people are allergic to perfumes, which are normally suspended in a highly-allergenic substance. If people start sneezing the minute you enter the board room, the message is obvious.

For Men

Make sure your suit is pressed. Wearing it that extra week is a big mistake. Shirts should be pressed, crisp and bright. Ties, as we've noted, should be clean.

Conservative haircuts are the norm in almost all offices. If you have a moustache, beard and/or sideburns, keep them neat and trimmed. Be aware of facial hair when eating food. It is very distracting to talk business with someone whose beard looks like a pizza. Muttonchop sideburns or sideburns that attach to a moustache look affected on most men. Generally speaking, it is better to be clean-shaven unless you have a weak chin.

For Women

Keep your hair neat and trimmed. Avoid punk or frizzy hairstyles, ponytails, childish bangs and little girl hair decorations such as ribbons, velvet bows and plastic barrettes. Hair should be shoulder-length or shorter, but not cropped close to the head.

Four-inch nails look as if you never worked a day in your life. Also, chipped nail polish must be repaired immediately.

Check the heels and soles of your shoes every morning before you leave for work. Make sure your slip and bra straps aren't showing. Repair hems—and we don't mean with cellotape or safety pins. If a button is loose, sew it on.

If your blouse pulls apart at the bust, choose another, move the buttons, or wear a vest if the problem is chronic.

Wear seamless bras and briefs, not bikinis, under knits.

Makeup

A moderate amount of makeup is appropriate office wear. Keep in mind, however, that work is not a hallowe'en party. You should not wear too much makeup, makeup that draws attention to itself, or makeup that is years out of date. For example, heavy eyeliner was stylish in the sixties, but it is no longer fashionable. Makeup should be refreshed several times a day to avoid streaks or cracks.

Office Emergency Kit

Keep a few cosmetic items in a drawer of your office for emergencies. Your kit should include a toothbrush and toothpaste, a comb, a pocket mirror, a lint brush, a moist towelette, and one of those little sewing kits they give out in hotel rooms. Men should have a fresh shirt or two (wrapped from the laundry) and women a new pair of neutral pantihose, nail polish in the shade usually worn, an emery board, lipstick and blusher. If women keep hand cream in this kit, it should be unscented so as not to make the office seem like a powder room.

Colors

People seldom take full advantage of the benefits offered by color. Colors should flatter your hair and skin tone and should be appropriate to the occasion.

Color is the first thing the eye sees and should never be overpowering. In any outfit, one color should dominate the eye and all other colors should merely accent the principal one. Also, remember that the colors you choose affect people in certain ways, both optically and by association.

Red Red is a very physical color, symbolizing vitality. However, be careful how you use it. Red has no soothing qualities; too much of it can be intimidating. If a person is having a bad day or has a headache, being with a person wearing a lot of red can be subconsciously irritating.

Red is the best color to wear if you want to stand out in a crowd. If a man wants to be noticed at an important board meeting, he should wear a white shirt and a red tie (provided of course that it goes with his suit). Women can achieve the same effect by wearing a red blouse, blazer or scarf.

Orange Certain shades of orange are very popular, particularly for decoration in waiting rooms and other high-traffic areas. However, orange is a very difficult color to wear. It can be very stimulating, but in an office environment one must avoid looking like a pumpkin. Most oranges quickly prove tiresome to the eyes.

Flecks of orange in a tie pattern can be interesting, but unless your taste is flawless and you are acting on advice from a good tailor, stay away from it altogether. Similarly, suits should not have any orange overtones, unless worked very subtly into a tweed fabric. Burnt orange shirts have no place in the office.

Yellow Yellow is a very crisp color. A bright lemon-yellow tie against a white shirt makes a man look alert and immaculately-groomed.

Women should be careful about wearing too much yellow, as it makes many complexions look sallow. If in doubt, stick to yellow accessories such as belts and brooches.

Green Green is not considered an appropriate color for a man's business suit, although green-toned tweed jackets may be acceptable leisure wear.

Green is a very difficult color to wear because it is hard to match shades of green. Almost every woman has a green handbag in her closet that clashes with every green item she has bought since. If you choose to wear green, be very careful when selecting a tone. Some shades of green are associated with service industries because many hotels, hospitals and cleaning services outfit their staff in green uniforms. The ambitious executive should note these associations and choose colors carefully.

Blue Blue is the most popular, easy-to-wear color in the world. It is non-threatening. A person entering a room full of strangers often gravitates subconsciously toward a person dressed in blue. Wearing a blue (not navy) suit or blouse is advisable if you are dealing with a sensitive situation, such as reprimanding an employee.

However, be careful with blue if you want to make an impact. You might blend in *too* well, to the point of becoming invisible.

Brown   At one time brown was a very popular color. However, this is no longer the case. For some reason, many inexpensive, synthetic suits are brown. With a few exceptions, brown now suggests that the wearer is a plodding individual who is not conscious of his dress, perhaps someone who went to sleep ten years ago and has not observed that styles have changed. A brown suit is not effective unless it is of high-quality fabric and an excellent, up-to-date cut. Some light brown tones, such as beiges and taupes, are classic year-round colors. Brown shirts, however, have no place in the office.

White   White can be dazzling and is extremely effective as a background color. It is the most appropriate color for men's business shirts. However, white suits, shoes and ties do not belong in a corporate environment.

White comes in numerous tones, and it is worth taking the time to discover which shades suit the individual best.

Beware: If you are wearing white, make sure it *is* white, not grey. If your shirts are 100 percent cotton, they should be professionally laundered. Dry cleaning turns white cottons grey. Similarly, home washing machines often leave a soap residue on whites that gives them a tinge.

Grey   Grey is still a very popular color, one that signifies success. It expresses solidity, trustworthiness and a methodical nature. If you are wearing a grey suit, choose a bright color for your tie or accessories to liven your image.

Black   Black is the new power color, the color for leaders. Many businessmen, particularly in Europe, are making quite an impression by wearing black suits, softened by a carefully-chosen tie in, say, rose, pale yellow or soft turquoise.

The color black can be put to good advantage and help you look secure and confident. But be careful—black, perhaps more than any other color, demands a strong fashion sense. Don't wear black unless you are a very dynamic person who feels comfortable as the center of attention. Otherwise, you may be mistaken for an undertaker or a maitre d'. Large men must be careful in their use of black, as it can make them appear so intimidating that people will find it difficult to approach them.

Some people appear washed out in black, because of their coloring. Nevertheless, most of us can include some black in our wardrobes. For example, an executive can wear a black blazer and grey slacks, or black slacks and a grey-black tweed or houndstooth jacket.

Any black item of clothing should be of high quality, of well-chosen fabric. Cheap black suits or blouses look terrible. Black should have a very crisp, coordinated look. Ask your tailor for advice.

Body Language

Have you ever been in the situation of meeting people for the first time, and feeling ill at ease before they even open their mouths? Or have you ever made a polished sales presentation throughout which you were certain the customer wouldn't buy, even though he or she agreed with everything you said?

Feelings like these are generally a reaction to non-verbal signals. Whether speaking, listening, walking, eating, or partying, our body gestures carry a message that can speak louder than words. These gestures can make others feel comfortable and included or uneasy and rejected. It's important, therefore, to be conscious of both our own signals, and those of the people around us.

Posture

Many people are not aware of the impact of their physical presence and how to utilize that impact effectively. Your posture reveals your mood and your level of confidence.

When sitting, keep your back straight, and don't slouch. Slouching suggests casualness and laziness. At a meeting, sit resting your forearms on the table, hands folded lightly in each other or with the tips of the fingers touching pyramid-style. This allows you to lean forward slightly, and presents a picture of attentiveness, interest and consideration.

Never stand with one hand on your hip. This reminds most people of mother's posture when you got into the cookie jar at age six. For this reason, it is a particularly inadvisable stance for women. It immediately puts people on the defensive and invites a negative reaction.

Don't slouch in someone's doorway. You will give the impression that you have nothing to do and are wasting time. If you have something to say, enter the office with confidence and deliver your message directly to the person. Blocking an open doorway can make people uneasy and distracted, as they may be aware of events beyond the door but are no longer able to see them at a glance.

When walking up stairs, keep the back straight. Don't lean forward or pull yourself up by the bannister, unless your legs have some disability that demands this method. When you walk, do so with purpose and intent. You should always appear to have a destination in mind. Always enter a room unhesitatingly, as if you have a reason to be there.

If you must bend to pick something up, bend your knees. It is undignified to stick your rear end up in the air, or to go down on your knees.

Learn to read the signals in others' posture. If you are speaking to someone who unconsciously leans forward, resting his forearms on the desk or boardroom table, he is probably interested in what you have to say. You have captured his attention, and he is eager to hear more. If on the other hand the person leans back pensively in his chair, he is probably not impressed with your remarks, and is spending more energy thinking about his rebuttal than listening to you.

Similarly, a person who rapidly taps his foot or flexes his ankle while you are speaking is reacting negatively, and you are in trouble. Stress positive points until you see signs that he is relaxing.

Gestures

Be aware of your facial and hand gestures. Hands are strong symbols of power and of your personality, which is one of the reasons we recommended manicures in the "Grooming" section above. Use your hands wisely for expression, to involve your audience and make points. However, keep hands away from your face and hair. Women, in particular, sometimes have a bad habit of putting hair in their mouths. Also, if you find yourself pushing up your glasses, have them tightened so that they don't slip down.

You shouldn't fidget with your nails, straighten paper clips or tap the table with your pen. All these gestures indicate nervousness, boredom and/or hostility.

If a person rubs the side of his nose, it generally means that you can keep talking till the cows come home, but he won't change his mind. Folded arms also suggest a closed mind. If a person scratches his head, it means either that his head is itchy or he doesn't understand. To be safe, find a way to re-emphasize your points.

Power Stance

It used to be considered powerful for an individual who was making a presentation to stand hands on his hips, feet a foot-and-a-half apart. People thought this warrior-like posture conveyed an impression of strength and reliability. Unfortunately, this is not the case. It merely suggests the inflexibility of an impenetrable stone wall, and intimidates people.

The new power stance still keeps the feet approximately a foot-and-a-half apart. However, the right foot is now placed slightly forward of the left foot. This posture allows the flexibility of slight movement by shifting weight. You can move forward to stress a point, or rest comfortably with your full weight on your left foot. Hands are held at your sides, not at your hips, unless required to illustrate your speech. This posture says "I'm flexible, I'm open to hearing your contributions, I'm confident and I'm approachable."

Shaking Hands

As everyone knows, handshakes are much more than an expression of polite greeting. Handshakes are your first way of connecting with a person. Touch creates bonds, and should open communication. However, a poor, limp, moist handshake can close the door to an enthusiastic response. When you shake hands, people make an immediate judgement about your character and level of confidence. It is a mistake to shake hands from a limp wrist. Shake with the full arm, keeping the wrist and elbow firm. Your arm should not resemble a flapping chicken wing.

Another error is extending the hand with the fingers curled, so that the only way a person can grasp the hand is by linking fingers, as in some childish secret society. The hand should be in a straight line, extended very slightly in on an angle. The angle is particularly important when men are shaking women's hands, as many men don't know their own strength. A hand extended straight out can break bones or crush her rings into her fingers. The slight angle allows a firm grip without damage. The grip should not last an undue period.

Two-handed handshakes, in which the left hand covers the back of the other party's right hand, are becoming increasingly popular. This gesture is too intimate for a man to employ when meeting a woman. Those not running for public office should use such a handshake with extreme caution, as it can appear insincere.

Handshakes used to be a sign of camaraderie chiefly among men, but women today should get used to extending their hand to both men and other women. Many women, however, are notorious for poor handshakes. Some even extend the hand straight, parallel to the floor, as if expecting to be kissed. Women in a corporate environment should know the proper, professional way to shake hands.

Men should never wear gloves when shaking hands. The only woman allowed to do so is the Queen.

Kissing on the face when meeting may be correct protocol in some countries and in the entertainment industry, but it is not otherwise common in North American business. Save it for your spouse.

Your Home
Away From Home

An office should enhance the image of an executive. Treat your office as an important aspect of your corporate profile and dress it as carefully as you dress yourself. Every item in your office should be tasteful, simple, and well-placed. Each should convey the message: "I have high standards and I choose to surround myself with objects of excellence." Plants, for example, should be either healthy or discarded in favor of dried or silk flower arrangements. A dead rubber tree suggests to visitors that you allow responsibilities to wither on the vine.

An office should appear neat and clean. It should not be piled with magazines, file folders and other papers. If these accumulate, hide them in a hanging file cabinet or credenza. Keep ash trays clean and remove used coffee cups promptly.

Hand lotion, lucky charms, half-eaten boxes of cookies and the like should be kept out of sight. Executive toys, however engaging, suggest you regard your office as your personal sandbox.

Limit family pictures to one or two, always in classy frames. Keep family snaps on the credenza, not your desk, where they appear to distract you from your work. No pictures of pets, please.

Decorate your walls with attractive photographs—no velvet paintings, or drawings of cutesy little girls in huge bonnets. Art should be tasteful, non-threatening and uncontroversial. We once met a man who worked for a major newspaper, and whose office was decorated with a photo of two nude women embracing. Erotic art, pinups and centrefolds, male or female, have no place in a professional environment and may offend others.

Have at least two guest chairs, if possible. This allows you either to seat two guests, or to create an informal atmosphere by joining a single guest on the other side of your desk. Do not buy cute little cushions to put on these chairs.

Finally, always have enough hangers. Even if you use a coat rack, coats and jackets should be hung on hangers, not over hooks.

Home, James

Company cars are now a fairly standard executive perquisite. If you are fortunate enough to have been given the use of a car, there are certain points to bear in mind. First of all, the *company* owns the car. It has merely been lent to you. Treat it as you would treat any borrowed item. Keep it washed and the interior clean and tidy. Any maintenance or repairs that are your responsibility should be dealt with promptly. Keep the insurance premiums up to date unless the company pays them. And since the company has gone to so much expense to get you to work, don't be late.

Your 16-year-old-son should not be allowed to drive a company car, particularly if he is not covered by the insurance. Nor should any driver drink and drive. And while we are not naive enough to suggest that people never use company cars for personal business, you should not use it to drive 3000 miles for your Florida vacation.

The car should reflect the company's image. Refrain from decorating it with fuzzy dice or doggies with nodding heads.

Be prepared to lend a company car to a co-worker during the day, if it is needed for business and your insurance covers it. Keep the trunk and interior free of personal debris.

16

The Mailbox

Dear Miss J,

Our company has a strict "no smoking" policy. In fact, that's one of the reasons I decided to work there, as I have asthma. The trouble is that one of the senior vice-presidents constantly smokes cigars. He also believes in management by walking around, so his habit bothers a lot of people. These cigars smell foul and I'm unable to concentrate on my work because the smoke makes me so uncomfortable. I'm just a word processing operator and I don't feel free to complain about this. What should I do?—Wheezing in Washington

Dear Wheezing,

If being near him bothers you, go to the washroom or remove yourself from the room as unobtrusively as possible. Let your supervisor know this is why you leave when he comes in. Unfortunately, you are not in a position to lay down the law.

Dear Miss J,

I'm a senior lawyer in a large firm. My secretary is having an affair with a married junior partner. I'm concerned that they are both making a mistake. How do I handle this?—Q.C., Montreal

Dear Q.C.,

You don't. The affair is their personal business unless it is interfering with their work. If it is, speak to the junior partner and point out that it has spilled over the borders of discretion and is affecting billings. Otherwise, mind your own business unless either one asks for your advice.

Dear Miss J,

I was recently promoted. A secretary came with the job. (She worked for my predecessor.) The problem is I can't stand her. She makes an incredible number of mistakes, can't spell, and has the I.Q. of a rutabaga. I'm wasting far too much time supervising and correcting her work, at the expense of my own. Is there anything I can do about this?—Fuming in Fort Frances

Dear Fuming,

You could get in touch with personnel, say you would like to restructure your department and recommend that she be transferred to another division. She has no doubt sensed your displeasure anyway and would appreciate a move. If this is not possible, bring her into your office and explain as graciously as possible that your management style is different from your predecessor's. Explain your expectations clearly and ask for her response. Focus your remarks on the work at hand, not your personal feelings towards her.

Dear Miss J,

In my industry, heavy drinking is common during business entertaining. I'm not a heavy drinker, and anyway I'm supposed to watch my weight. Is there a tactful way I can get out of this without seeming like misfit?—A.A., Dallas

Dear A.A.,

Yes. Keep a glass in your hand, filled with mineral water, soda or juice. When pressed, the most diplomatic way to get out of ordering alcohol is to smile and say, "No thank you, I'm watching my weight" (unless you're paper thin or the other person is obese), "No thank you, I'm driving", (if it's true) or "No thank you, I'm on medication and it's not compatible with alcohol". Sometimes a little white lie eases a situation. Never say "No thank you, I don't drink". This sets up a social barrier which says "I don't and you do (you lush)". Better to say "No thank you, but go ahead".

Dear Miss J,

What is the correct way to interrupt a meeting? I'm a secretary/receptionist, and my boss is often in meetings when things come up that require his immediate attention.—Charlene G., L.A.

Dear Charlene,

First, make sure the event is important enough to warrant interrupting the meeting. If so, the way to interrupt a meeting is to knock on the door. If someone is speaking, apologize to the speaker. Otherwise, apologize to the room. "I'm sorry to interrupt. However, I have an urgent message for Mr. Jones". Place the message beside him on a piece of paper, face down. Don't announce the message to the entire room. Leave the room with a "thank you".

Dear Miss J,

What is the best way to ask for a raise?—M.G., New York

Dear M.G.,

The best way to get a raise is to apply for a promotion within the company. A promotion not only offers more money, but offers more interesting work, makes you more visible and demonstrates your satisfactory performance.

Otherwise, proceed carefully. Never ask for a raise without giving the matter great consideration, planning and preparation. You must be able to justify an increase with valid reasons other than the length of time you've been there, your need/desire for more money or comparisons with other workers.

The best time to ask for a raise is when you've just had a great idea, made a big sale or otherwise distinguished yourself, or when you've been asked to take on new responsibilities and proved you can do them satisfactorily. You should be getting along well with your boss and working in an atmosphere of mutual trust and respect. Don't ask for a raise when your work has recently been criticized.

When you're ready to ask for a raise, first document your current salary level, the work you do over and above your present job description, any additional responsibilities you are prepared to handle and your recent contributions to the company. Then request a meeting with your boss to discuss your job, your contribution and your goals. Indicate the amount of raise you consider fair.

If you receive an attractive outside offer, you can explain the situation to your boss and ask frankly what your possibilities are in your present position. Never threaten to leave if you don't get a raise. It's better to look around discreetly while still employed. Often, young people can increase their salaries more by changing jobs than by staying with one company.

Dear Miss J,

My boss is great but his wife is a real witch. She treats me like dirt and sometimes I wonder whether she suspects me of having an affair with him (not true). When she comes into the office, she commandeers my phone so I can't do my work or take his calls. Is there anything I can do about this?—L.F., Denver

Dear L.F.,

Stop reacting. Do your work and be as gracious as possible. It is not your place to confront her or to complain to your boss. Two wrongs don't make a right, so there is no excuse for rude behavior on your part. Be as polite and good-natured as possible—and cheer up, you're not the one who has to live with her.

Dear Miss J,

Our receptionist is a nice enough person but she chews gum when she answers the phone. I don't like to get personal, but I'd like her to stop. What should I say?—Disgusted in Detroit

Dear Disgusted,

Unfortunately, in a situation like this someone has to get personal. Use tact and diplomacy. Tell her that a number of callers have told you that they've noticed she's chewing gum, and you think she's far too intelligent and/or elegant to be remembered for something like that. Besides the fact that it's not a good image for the company, it's not a good image for her.

Dear Miss J,

I work with a guy who is all right, except he's a garbage mouth. The language that comes out of him is unbelievable. Also, I'm offended by blasphemy. How can I get him to stop without becoming the object of ridicule?—Born Again, Calgary

Dear Born Again,

This is an area that requires great tact. Most people are not aware of their language, because it is habitual. To confront them directly can embarrass and antagonize them. The best way to handle it is to put the focus on yourself. Say something like, "My wife mentioned to me the other day that I'm swearing too much around my daughter. I'm trying to break the habit. If you ever notice me doing it, promise me you'll point it out". This may make him aware of his own vocabulary. At some later point, you could suggest that his swearing is making you pick it up and ask for his cooperation in reducing it.

Dear Miss J,

I work in the shipping department with a guy who hums to himself all the time. It drives me nuts. How can I get him to stop?—F.M., London

Dear F.M.,

You could turn a radio up and try to drown him out. Otherwise, you're stuck with telling him directly, but as tactfully as possible, that his humming is distracting you from your work. Remember, there's no law against humming. If he insists on humming, it's his choice. However, if he's aware of your feelings, he may choose to consider them.

Dear Miss J,

I'm a salesman. Customers are always dumping on me for things beyond my control, such as screwups in shipping and on the order desk. I understand their frustration, but I don't feel I should have to take the brunt of other people's goofs. Would it be ok to refer them to the people who made the mistakes?—W.L., Chicago

Dear W.L.,

No. As a salesman, you are liaison officer between the company and the customer. It is your job to handle problems and complaints tactfully, and to do your best to allay the customers' concerns. Screwups in shipping and the order desk are internal problems that should be solved by you or the management of your company. They should not become the customer's problem.

Dear Miss J,

What do you say when you see a man walk into the boardroom with his zipper open?—Distracted, Halifax

Dear Distracted,

"Feel a draft?"

Dear Miss J,

I've been a mail clerk here for six months now (my first job), and my salary is rock bottom. It seems like every couple of days somebody here hits me for a few bucks for an office present, such as a wedding, baby shower, retirement, etc. I haven't even met some of the recipients, and those I have met usually are earning three times my salary. Also I'm a confirmed bachelor and don't expect to retire for forty years, so it's unlikely I'll be on the receiving end of any of this in the foreseeable future. Would it be ok for me to refuse to give to some of these collections?—Broke in Boston

Dear Broke,

Yes. If you feel you need to explain, just say "I'm sorry, I'm not able to contribute at this time." No other explanations are necessary.

Dear Miss J,

At our firm, executives are encouraged to play in a company golf league. As it happens, I am a very good golfer. However, I'm not the president—I'm a division manager. Should I just do my best, which usually means beating the pants off my boss and other big cheeses, or should I fake it sometimes and let them win?—Par 3, Westchester

Dear Par 3,

Although it's a golf game, it's still business. Use it as a platform for tact and diplomacy, not a showplace for your golfing expertise. Use your discretion. Remember, it's preferable to beat them by a point than by a humiliating margin. If you're that good a shot, you should at least be able to arrange this.

Dear Miss J,

Our office Christmas party is coming up soon. Spouses are traditionally invited. I recently hired a young cost accountant. Although he is discreet about his private life, I have heard on the grapevine that he lives with his gay lover. Should I invite his "spousal equivalent?"—Liberal in Seattle

Dear Liberal,

Yes. Extend the invitation for him to bring a "date". It is therefore up to him whether he chooses to come solo or bring a friend.

Dear Miss J,

Several times a year, our company has a big bash for the employees. For example, there is a field day with a dinner and dance at a country club.

The problem is that although most of the people here are married, I'm single and not seeing anyone regularly. Even if I were, I'm not sure I'd want to inflict a company do on a date or a friend, since people often talk shop and it can get quite boring. Also, I don't want to become the subject of gossip.

Should I go along, facing the embarrassment of buying half a couple's ticket? Or should I skip it? Please advise.—Hers and Hers, Toronto

Dear H&H,

Most company celebrations are of great interest to company people. If you do not want to "inflict" this event on a friend or a date, it is better to buy a single ticket and make an appearance. Stay an hour or two, then leave, claiming another function.

Dear Miss J,

I recently hired a bright young man who has some good ideas. However, he has a habit that annoys me. He often sits with his feet on his desk and as his office has a large glass window, everyone can see this. I've no evidence that this posture is having a poor effect on his work, but to me it looks unbusinesslike. Would I be out of line to ask him to stop?—Out of Joint in Pittsburgh

Dear Out of Joint,

Is this against company policy? If not, it should be. It's very difficult to respect a professional if you're forced to look at his feet to see his face. By all means ask him to stop this practice, without treating it like a capital offense.

Dear Miss J,

I'm a male secretary. Sometimes my boss suggests we go for lunch together. We go to places that are more expensive than I would normally choose, given that I don't earn much. Should I offer to pick up the tab sometimes? Or to go Dutch?—M.M., Fargo

Dear M.M.,

Better yet, ask for separate checks.

Dear Miss J,

My boss is ok, but he's a slob. He wears terrible clothes, his shoes are always scuffed, he has food on his tie and grease in his hair. I doubt he takes a shower more than once a week. How can I get the message across without getting fired?—Fumigating in Toledo

Dear Fumigating,

You can't. Obviously, his style is acceptable to management. It is not your place to point out his flaws and poor grooming habits.

Dear Miss J,

What are the rules regarding funerals? If an employee dies, how do you decide whether to close the office for the funeral or allow time during the day for employees to attend? What if a spouse, child or parent of an employee dies? Should friends from the office be given time off to go? What if it's a company's busy season and the owner doesn't feel everybody should leave?—Personnel Manager, Deep River

Dear Manager,

There's no set answer for this. It is up to the discretion of management. There should be a company policy to deal with these situations. Usually, if the president dies, the company closes for the day of the funeral. If the owner dies, it may be closed longer than a day. If the deceased is a recent and junior employee, a company representative who knew him, such as his supervisor, should attend the funeral. If the employee dies on the premises or in particularly tragic circumstances, the company may use its discretion to vary the rules. We know of one major entertainment corporation in New York which held a special memorial service for a manager who was murdered on the street.

Dear Miss J,

I'm getting married in a few months. We're having a small, family wedding. If I invite a few of my co-workers to the reception, do I have to invite all? What if they want to come to the ceremony? Usually, they collect for a present or give a shower when people get married here.—Blushing Bride, Portland

Dear B.B.,

It's up to you to decide whom you want to invite to your wedding. Don't feel you have to invite the entire company. If a few workers are particularly close friends, everyone will understand if you invite only those few. Acknowledge all gifts with a prompt thank-you note.

Dear Miss J,

My boss runs a small photography business on the side. This has nothing to do with the business of our company. He gets a lot of personal business calls during the day, which I'm supposed to handle and he gives me typing to do for this business. I'm busy enough with my own job and resent this imposition. Is there anything I can do?—Ticked off, Oklahoma City

Dear T.O.,

Yes. Simply let your boss know, as tactfully as possible, that you do not appreciate the extra work, but more importantly, that you cannot get involved with any other business. The sooner you do this, the better. Postponing this discussion does no one any favors.

Dear Miss J,

One of my co-workers has a big mouth. He not only spreads gossip about people in the company, but talks about company business in public places such as lunch counters. Is there a tactful way to discourage this?—D.B., L.A.

Dear D.B.,

Yes. Don't listen if he's spreading gossip and change the subject if he raises proprietary information in a public place. He'll get the message.

Dear Miss J,

My boss and I have a friendly relationship. However, this seems to encourage him to ask a lot of personal questions. He wants to know about my love life, investments, how much I got when I sold my house, and so on. Can I discourage this without spoiling the atmosphere at work?—T.T., Vancouver

Dear T.T.,

Answer as vaguely as possible ("I did ok on the sale.") Remember, you are never forced to reveal the answer to personal questions, even if he is your boss. If he persists, simply say, as politely as possible, "Fred, you know I never talk about my personal life".

Dear Miss J.,

I'm a purchasing manager with a staff of four. Last Christmas, a large basket of gourmet foods arrived as a Christmas present from a major supplier. I took it home and my family enjoyed serving the goodies during the festive season. However, I got some dirty looks from my staff when this happened. Should I have distributed them? The package was addressed to me.—J.S., New York

Dear J.S.,

Sorry, but you should have shared with your staff. The gift was corporate, not personal. Also, your thank-you not should have mentioned that both you and your staff enjoyed the present greatly. A copy of this note should have been placed on file.

Dear Miss J,

My secretary is intelligent and capable but she is always late. It annoys me to have the phone unattended, and work undone. Should I force this issue?—Frazzled, Miami

Dear Frazzled,

Yes. Remember to mention, as you lay down the law, how pleased you are with the work she does when she's there.

Index

198

The Art of Naming

The Art of Naming

Michael Ohl
translated by Elisabeth Lauffer

The MIT Press
Cambridge, Massachusetts
London, England

This book was set in ITC Stone by Toppan Best-set Premedia Limited. Printed and bound in the United States of America.

Library of Congress Cataloging-in-Publication Data

Names: Ohl, Michael, author.
Title: The art of naming / Michael Ohl ; translated by Elisabeth Lauffer.
Other titles: Kunst der Benennung. English
Description: Cambridge, MA : The MIT Press, [2018] | Originally published as
   Die Kunst der Benennung. 1. Aufl. Berlin : Matthes et Seitz, 2015. | Includes
   bibliographical references and index.
Identifiers: LCCN 2017036352 | ISBN 9780262037761 (hardcover : alk. paper)
Subjects: LCSH: Biology--Nomenclature. | Biology--Classification.
Classification: LCC QH83 .O3513 2018 | DDC 578.01/2--dc23 LC record available
   at https://lccn.loc.gov/2017036352

10 9 8 7 6 5 4 3 2 1

Contents

Prologue: The Beauty of Names

Nature is complicated. All of our efforts to experience and understand its elements and phenomena are channeled through words, whether spoken or written. In no instance is this more evident than in natural history collections. Drawers upon drawers, cabinets upon cabinets of butterflies, insects, fish, and worms—large and small, colorful and plain, unremarkable and exotic—fill the great halls. Natural history museums, each a microcosm of the world, house millions of creatures, but none of the individuals stands for itself alone. Each one has a name, which is usually provided in the form of a label. It is through its name that the individual is bestowed with meaning, and it is through its naming that it becomes part of our perception of nature. Names perform the function of verbal tags that can apply to any imaginable biological entity. Species, which serve as the most important unit of generalization in the natural sciences, thus command the most space in this regard. The standardized and distinct linguistic designation of species follows right on the heels of scientific discovery: one can only name what has been discovered and recognized.

But beyond the sciences, we also name the diversity of organisms in our world, in order to speak about them. Many common names, or even components of names, originate in the distant past of our language, and we must rely on historical linguistics to reconstruct their meaning. Given their largely organic emergence and usage, along with a continuous dynamic of change, vernacular names—compared with scientific labels—are not a suitable standard for the uniform naming of biological species.

Why not? Because there are so many of them. Too many to surrender to the whims of everyday speech. Approximately 1.5 million species have been identified, cataloged, and named, but an additional three, five, ten, or even 100 million are still waiting to be found. And named.

For this reason, organisms are given scientific names that can be used around the world. Scientific names can seem foreign within everyday speech because they're typically formed with classical linguistic elements following classical linguistic rules. Scientific naming seems to exist at a distance from the public sphere, perhaps even constituting its own hermetic world of specialists. Yet species names are everywhere. They're on the endangered species list. They're displayed on potted plant markers in every garden shop, like *Petunia*, *Iris*, and *Chrysanthemum*. They can even be found in children's books, because what dinosaur-obsessed kid doesn't know about *Tyrannosaurus rex*, *Triceratops*, or *Velociraptor*?

Indeed, this is where most people will first experience the delight of scientific names. As though they were secret incantations, these names grant access to the world of those extinct behemoths. Mental images of prehistoric landscapes take shape at the sound of their names, and we feel we are among the initiated, the entrusted, the knowing. For those who know its name, it becomes possible to experience and possess *Spinosaurus*, that fearsome predator of the Cretaceous Period. It is here that insiders break from the wannabes, those in the know from the amateurs. Thus, the formal name not only reveals the scene of an organism living in its own world, it ushers us into the world of science. A species name conveys authority and knowledge, structuring the living world according to science. A scientific name is, therefore, the culminating point of a range of impressions and connotations, knowledge and interpretations.

Yet scientific names are even more than that. For all their alienness, they are linguistic beauties. Once one has learned to recognize and formulate their component parts, there is no end to the kaleidoscope of words and delightful puzzles they present. Working with names, one enters a complex area of systematic biology and linguistics. The imaginative invention of scientific names for newly discovered species is an especially joyful ritual. The intrinsic satisfaction in naming arises not least from the fact that a name is for eternity—or at least for as long as humans continue speaking about nature.

Thus, the ideas presented in this book are outlined. Scientific naming is relevant and important, it's ubiquitous, it's easier to understand and use than one may think, and it's fun. Because subjective and emotional stakes invariably play a part in naming, the art of naming should be told through the example of the artists—that is to say, the taxonomists for whom the perpetuation of the "catalog of life" quite often constitutes the center of their own. These people change and enrich our understanding of nature through their discovery and naming of such creatures as the giant panda, the *Triceratops*, and the pygmy hippopotamus (not to mention the great many insects, slime molds, and flatworms that don't exactly win points for charisma).

Even my perspective is subjective, emotional, and not always unintentionally informed by my zoological and entomological interests, which are largely defined by "winged things that sting"—that is, wasps, bees, and ants. Wasps are where I make all my discoveries, however, because they are my primary focus as a scientist. I regularly discover new species, and some have even attracted attention outside the scientific sphere, like *Megalara garuda*, known as the "warrior wasp" or "king of the wasps" because of its impressive size, or *Ampulex dementor*, which was named after the dementors of *Harry Potter* notoriety. But my personal proclivities represent only one of the reasons for the animal and insect-heaviness of this text. There is no other organism group as species-rich as insects, and the need for names is accordingly high—as it always has been.

Many people think that the age of discovery and naming of species has passed. On the contrary, we are right in the middle of it. Every year more new species are discovered and cataloged than ever before, and the key to this ever-growing diversity is scientific names. This book tells their story.

Acknowledgments

Although I wrote the majority of this book at home, overlooking the out-skirts of Berlin with my library at my back, it's the nature of a project like this that many people contributed to its completion and success. I hope to name all of those people here, and please pardon any unintentional omissions.

Elisabeth Lauffer undertook the sometimes challenging translation of this text-heavy book, with its many German examples and expressions, with care and sensitivity. Beth Clevenger and Anthony Zannino from the MIT Press oversaw the project, helping polish the language and content of the English version, including providing additional images. Thanks to Liz, Beth, and Anthony, this book has become more than a mere translation.

I wish to thank Hanns Zischler for our many inspiring conversations and his unique perspective on natural history. He directed me to Rebekka Göpfert at Agentur Göpfert literary agency, to whom I am indebted for her generous support, interest, and—last but not least—facilitating my connec-tion with publishing house Matthes & Seitz Berlin. Many thanks to Andreas Rötzer and his publishing team for their friendly, positive support, and in particular to editor Tilman Vogt, who handled the manuscript with impres-sive care, patience, and sensitivity.

Thanks to Professor Damaris Nübling at the University of Marburg, who is a true authority on the study of names and who patiently answered my probing questions—which must have seemed naïve from the perspective of a linguistic pro—and who probably remained convinced that biological species "are no more special than a batch of freshly baked rolls."

Special thanks to biologist and historian Carsten Eckert, who was always willing to share his impressive knowledge of the history of biology, and especially the history of the Berlin Museum für Naturkunde.

Doug Yanega (Riverside, CA) and Neal Evenhuis (Honolulu, HI) carefully corrected the English translation of chapter 1. Janet Monge (Philadelphia, PA) provided background information on Edward Drinker Cope's skull in the University of Pennsylvania Museum of Archaeology and Anthropology.

Many friends and colleagues shared published and unpublished anecdotes and wonderful name constructions with me, generously passing along their own knowledge of names and naming and providing me with relevant literature. Thanks to Ulrike and Horst Aspöck (Vienna, Austria), Sören Flachowsky (Berlin, Germany), Claus Bätke and Jörn Köhler (BIOPAT, Germany), George Beccaloni (London, UK), Wolfgang Böhme and André Koch (Bonn, Germany), Neal Evenhuis (Honolulu, HI), Anke te Heesen (Berlin, Germany), Rainer Hutterer (Bonn, Germany), Michael A. Ivie (Bozeman, MT), Volker Lohrmann (Bremen, Germany), Wojciech J. Pulawski (San Francisco, CA), "Theo" Michael Schmitt (Greifswald, Germany), Frank Steinheimer (Halle, Germany), and Holger Stöcker (Berlin, Germany).

I sincerely thank all colleagues who provided me with images and reproduction permissions, particularly Sabine Hackethal (Museum für Naturkunde, Berlin, Germany) and Editha Schubert (Senckenberg Deutsches Entomologisches Institut, Müncheberg, Germany).

I am especially grateful to my colleagues at the Museum für Naturkunde in Berlin, who happily shared the most wonderful stories about the collections and objects in their expert care. There's no better workplace to study the diversity of nature, accompanied by *Archaeopteryx* and *Brachiosaurus*. The museum wouldn't be the place it is without the following individuals: Renate Angermann, Peter Bartsch, Oliver Coleman, Jason Dunlop, Carsten Eckert, Sylke Frahnert, Johannes Frisch, Christiane Funk, Matthias Glaubrecht, Ursula Göllner, Peter Giere, Rainer Günther, Sabine Hackethal, Anke Hoffmann, Frieder Mayer, Wolfram Mey, Birger Neuhaus, Christiane Quaisser, Carola Radke, Mark-Oliver Rödel, Frank Tillack, and Johannes Vogel. I also thank the team in the museum library, who helped me tremendously with the literature: Martina Rißberger, Hans-Ulrich Raake, and Annegret Henkel. In the final months of writing, Caroline Ring helped with research, bringing her own brand of energy and enthusiasm to the project, as well as an eye for good stories.

I had intended for a number of friends and colleagues to serve as sympathetic but noncontradictory listeners, as I outlined my conviction that names are important and provide the key to taxonomy. Few performed their task to my satisfaction, but those who did helped me refine my own view of things—for the better, I hope—with their critical discussion points and questions. Many thanks to Matthias Glaubrecht, Anita Hermannstädter, Ina Heumann, Annette Kaufhold, Volker Lohrmann, Carsten Lüter, Katinka Pantz, Gerhard Scholtz, Georg Töpfer, and Hanns Zischler.

Thanks to Carsten Eckert, Matthias Glaubrecht, Rebekka Göpfert, and Caroline Ring, who read the manuscript with critical and expert eyes, pointing out all manner of discrepancies and inconsistencies. Katinka Pantz— observant, curious, ingenious—created a piece of art with her revisions.

My wife Daniela was my most untiring and critical reader, mercilessly combing every version of the manuscript for rambling or redundancies, ultimately wresting a slimmer, unquestionably better version from me.

Finally, my gratitude goes again to Daniela and my children Yannika, Mattes, Merle, and Mina, who uncomplainingly spent their days not only with me, but with Alexandre Girault, Francis Walker, and other eccentrics. At this point, my kids can't understand how a person could possibly be bored by etymology.

Note on the Images

The collections housed in natural history museums aren't just collections of objects. They are also collections of names that take the form of labels and inscriptions attached to every object, every drawer, and every case, extending beyond to rooms, halls, and even whole wings. The physical and typographical appearance of the names' material textualization can be as varied as the names themselves, and often with its own particular beauty.

Among the images in this book are those of objects housed in the collections and exhibits of the Museum für Naturkunde in Berlin, where I photographed them (figures 1.1, 1.5, 1.6, 1.8, 2.6, 2.7, 3.1, 3.3, 3.5, 3.6, 4.7, 4.9, 5.1, 5.4, 6.1, 6.7, 7.2, 7.3, 8.1, 8.3, 8.4, 9.2, and 9.6). The goal was to present this textualization of scientific names (in a place of such taxonomic influence) in all its diversity and beauty. The collection pieces were not arranged, cleaned, or otherwise moved into frame. Instead, they were selected on the spot and photographed with a smartphone (Samsung Galaxy S4). There was one exception: the alcohol-filled storage jars pictured had to be moved from their home in the east wing of the museum and arranged elsewhere because fire code prohibits photography in that area.

To this English edition of the book have been joined additional images, from far beyond the walls of the museum in Berlin—photographs from archival collections, figures from published species descriptions, artistic renderings of key species, portraits of the scientists under discussion on these pages—at passages where the textual description was suited to augmentation by visual reference.

1 Hitler and the *Fledermaus*

On March 3, 1942, a brief item with a rather peculiar headline appeared tucked away in the *Berliner Morgenpost* newspaper. "*Fledermaus* No Longer!" the bold letters proclaimed. The following short text was printed underneath:

At its 15th General Assembly, the German Society for Mammalogy passed a resolution to change the zoologically misleading names "*Spitzmaus*" [shrew] and "*Fledermaus*" [bat] to "*Spitzer*" and "*Fleder*." *Fleder* is an old form for *Flatterer* [one that flutters]. The *Spitzmaus*, as it happens, has borne a variety of names: *Spitzer* [one that is pointed], *Spitzlein*, *Spitzwicht*, *Spitzling*. Over the course of the conference, several important lectures were held in the auditorium of the Zoologisches Museum [...].

To this day, despite the problems announced by Germany's leading specialists on mammals on the pages of one of the capital's daily papers, *Fledermaus* and *Spitzmaus* remain the common German names for bats and shrews. Neither dictionaries nor specialized nature guides contain entries for *Fleder* or *Spitzer* (provided one disregards the primary definition of *Spitzer*, which is a "small implement used for the sharpening of pencils").

Indeed, a swift response to the item in question arrived from an unexpected source. Martin Bormann, Adolf Hitler's private secretary, sent a message on March 4, 1942, to Hans Heinrich Lammers, head of the Reich Chancellery. The missive contained remarkably unambiguous instructions from Hitler:

In yesterday's newspapers, the Führer read an item regarding the changes of name ratified by the German Society for Mammalogy on the occasion of its 15th General Assembly. The Führer subsequently instructed me to communicate to the responsible parties, in no uncertain terms, that these changes of name are to be reversed immediately. Should members of the Society for Mammalogy have nothing more essential to the war effort or smarter to do, perhaps an extended stint in the construction battalion on the Russian front could be arranged. Should such asinine renam-

Figure 1.1
One of several types of specimens of the Usambara three-horned chameleon (*Chamaeleon deremensis*, today part of the genus *Trioceros*), described in 1896 by Georg Friedrich Paul Matschie, then curator of the mammal collection. Museum für Naturkunde Berlin, M. Ohl photo.

ings occur once more, the Führer will unquestionably take appropriate measures; under no circumstance should terms that have become established over the course of many years be altered in this fashion.

There's no question that the "responsible parties" understood and responded to the injunction, which could hardly have been misinterpreted. On July 1, 1942, at least, a notice was printed in the *Zoologischer Anzeiger*— at that time, the "organ of the German Zoological Society"—that comprised a scant five lines. The notice has no byline and can most likely be attributed to the journal's publishers:

Regarding the discussion [in earlier issues of the *Zoologischer Anzeiger*] about potential changes to the names *"Fledermaus"* and *"Spitzmaus,"* the Editors wish to make public that terms that have become established over the course of many years are not to be altered, following an announcement by the Reich Minister of Science, Education, and National Culture, as per the Führer's directive.

It's conceivable that Lammers forwarded Hitler's instructions (which had reached him by way of Bormann) to Bernhard Rust, the Reich Minister of Science, Education, and National Culture. Rust will then likely have ordered one of the "parties responsible" for the unpopular initiative to publish the retraction in the appropriate platform. The *Zoologischer Anzeiger* fit the bill, considering the fact that by 1941 it had already featured two articles debating whether the name *Spitzmaus* should be changed.

What *is* the problem, though, that veteran scientists have with *Spitzmaus* and *Fledermaus*, those innocuous terms for the shrew and the bat? And how could it come to pass that Adolf Hitler—preoccupied as he was in 1942— should personally join in the campaign for the correct classification of these small mammals?

Bones of Contention

The common thread in these two unremarkable and familiar terms is of course the second word component, *Maus*, or "mouse." This part of a compound word—or a word formed by joining substantives—is known in German grammar as the base or determinatum. The base, which is always located at the end of the word, determines both the denotation and grammatical gender of the compound. The word to the left of the base, the determinative or determinant (which can also be multiple words), defines the base more precisely. Thus, an armchair is first and foremost a chair

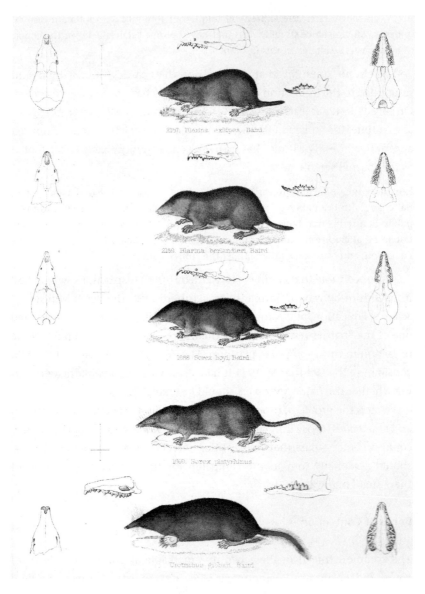

Figure 1.2
North American Insectivora. Four shrew species and the shrew mole (bottom) in an engraving from 1859. Baird, S. F., Mammals of North America, Plate XXVIII (Philadelphia: J. B. Lippincott, 1859). Library of the Museum für Naturkunde Berlin.

with the more specific attribute of possessing arms. As far as our mice are concerned, the *Gelbhalsmaus* (yellow-necked mouse) is first and foremost a mouse. Many species of mice exist, therefore the name specific to each requires an element that limits or modifies the base. Because this species has yellowish neck coloring, the general term "mouse" is narrowed by means of the preceding word element, thus generating a clear term—the yellow-necked mouse—for a specific species of rodent.

The process is much the same for the *Fledermaus* and *Spitzmaus*, which are (linguistically) first and foremost mice. By referencing certain characteristics in these compound words (*Fleder* comes from *flattern*, "to flap"; *Spitz*, or "point," refers to the shrew's pointy nose or rather head shape), it becomes possible to provide a clear name—or almost clear, at least, because there are many bat and shrew species, but more on that later. Both names, of course, imply affiliation with mice, and that's the sticking point. In zoological terms, mice are a group of rodents known at the higher level of classification as Muroidea, "muroids" or the "mouse-like." The group includes quite the mix of animal groups, with occasionally curious names like zokor, blind mole-rat, spiny tree mouse, and Chinese pygmy dormouse, not to mention our pet hamsters and those domestic but unwelcome mice and rats. Common to all muroids are sundry and complex structural features in the skull, coupled of course with the oversized, continually growing incisors typical of rodents. Beyond that, although endless evolutionary gimmickry can revolve around this mouse theme (long or short legs, different fur colors and tail lengths, and much more), and even without biological expertise, most muroids tend to be identifiable as mice, if only vaguely.

Zoologically speaking, a mere mouse-like appearance is insufficient to denote a muroid. Instead, the specific anatomical features of the skull must be in evidence. The underlying idea of systematic biology is fairly simple and obvious. Over the course of evolution, plants and animals have developed new characteristics and passed them on to their descendants. Thus, parallels between species living today might indicate ties back to a common ancestor, from which each adopted these traits. The similarity between such species is therefore the result of an evolutionary event that occurred so far in the past that it remains accessible only by means of scientific hypothesis. Groups of species are described as "natural" when evidence exists of an ancestor common only to them; systems of organisms comprised solely of such groups are designated in the same way. These stand in contrast to artificial groups and artificial systems, in which the species' linkage is based on congruities that can be shown not to have emerged from a unique evolutionary change in the most recent common ancestor. A natural system of organisms thus represents the most plausible course of evolution, whereas an artificial classification illustrates humans' arbitrary notions of what makes sense in grouping. Systematic biology today tends to prefer the reconstruction of natural systems of organisms.

Reconstructing these systems is complicated by the fact that not infrequently evolution will unexpectedly quit the beaten path. There have been instances in which a trait gained by one species will disappear in later species or reappear in new form. This means that the identifying characteristics of a species today will not necessarily be there tomorrow. The high art of systematic biology consists of using all of these traits to formulate well-founded hypotheses of lineage and bring clarity to the "tree of life."

But back to mice and the specific anatomical features of their skulls. Because these characteristics are present in nearly all muroids but absent in their relatives, phylogenetic researchers have concluded that they have originated as an evolutionary trait in the common ancestor of the muroids, the "ur-mouse." Therefore, these features of the skull allow systematic biologists to identify a natural grouping among the muroids. The ancestor of all muroids that inherited these features represents the starting point, the root of the mouse's rather complicated phylogenetic tree, which ultimately encompasses about 1,500 species—which happens to be a quarter of all mammals on earth. To say that a certain rodent belongs to this group amounts to little more than saying it is one of the many descendants of the last common ancestor of the whole mouse superfamily. Field, house, and deer mice are familiar to many North Americans, although they typically live hidden away, and we don't often encounter them. These animals with the "mouse" base in their name are truly mice in the zoological sense.

The same cannot exactly be said for the bat and shrew—the *Fledermaus* and *Spitzmaus*—despite their names. Neither of them is even a rodent or, consequently, a muroid. Then what are they? In the classification of mammals, a whole series of groupings is traditionally distinguished, usually assigned the rank of order within the class of mammals. Depending on scientific opinion, there are twenty-five to thirty of these orders of mammals. Rodents comprise one of these orders, to which muroids and several other groups of mammals belong. Bats, meanwhile, are typical representatives of the order of flying mammals. Their scientific name is Chiroptera, from the Greek words *chiros* (hand) and *pteros* (wings). Chiroptera, then, means "hand-flier," which is a fitting name for bats and their closest relatives, flying foxes. Both have wings formed by the typical membrane spanned between elongated digits. They are the only mammals to have developed the faculty for active flight. Other mammals that seem capable of flight, such as flying squirrels, are passive gliders. With more than 1,000 species known to date, Chiroptera is the second largest group of mammals after rodents. However, bats are missing the features particular to muroid skulls, and they also possess the traits unique to Chiroptera, such as the "hand wings." Bats undoubtedly belong to Chiroptera.

The systematic placement of the shrew, or *Spitzmaus*, is determined in much the same way. They, too, fail to possess the mouse characteristics in question, although they do share traits with moles and hedgehogs, as well as with the solenodon (meaning "slotted tooth"), which is a venomous critter native exclusively to the Caribbean islands. They are now situated under the wondrous designation Eulipotyphla, but only since 1999. How they are related—along with ties to an array of other mammal families, such as tenrecs, desmans, and golden moles—has not been conclusively explained, however, and an overwhelming glut of designations is assigned to various combinations of these animal groups. Dating back to Carl Linnaeus's 1758 coinage, the most widely used term for shrews, hedgehogs, moles, and all manner of more or less exotic animals is Insectivora, or insect eater. The idea that they can be traced to a common ancestor—that is to say, the idea that Insectivora comprises a natural, evolutionarily justifiable unit—is viewed today as improbable. Unquestionably, however (and this is what's of greatest interest to us here), shrews are not connected to either rodents (even muroids) or bats.

Eu Talkin' to Me?

And now, a short excursion following the tracks of Eulipotyphla. The prefix eu- is used frequently in scientific names, and the meaning in Greek is "normal or typical," as opposed to sickly or deviant. Eu- is usually prepended to a name to express that a group has united the actual or real (in this instance) Lipotyphla. Lipo- does not derive from *lipos*, meaning fat or oil, but from the verb *leipo*, which means "to be missing or abandoned."

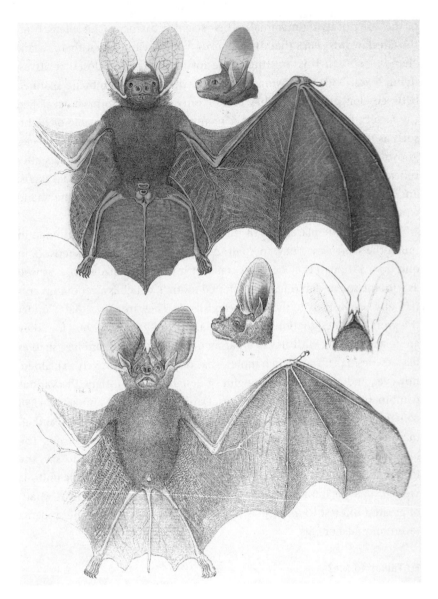

Figure 1.3
The pallid bat (*Antrozous pallidus*, LeConte, 1856) and the California leaf-nosed bat (*Macrotus californicus*, Baird, 1858) in an engraving from 1859. Baird, S. F., Mammals of North America, Plate LXI. (Philadelphia: J. B. Lippincott, 1859). Library of the Museum für Naturkunde Berlin.

Finally, the Greek term *typhlos* means blind or dark, represented in medi-cine by the term "typhlon," for appendix or "blind gut." Lipotyphla are thus distinguished by the absence of the appendix, and it follows that the Eulipotyphla are those "truly without appendix." Unsurprisingly, perhaps, they have close relatives called Menotyphla (from *meno*, meaning to stay or abide), which have an appendix, whereas the division of insectivores into those with and without the appendix dates back to Ernst Haeckel in 1866.

Within the context of phylogenetic research today, the prefix eu- plays a big role in the creation of new names because many systematic biolo-gists have a tendency to name all—or at least many—of the numerous interlacing branches of complex phylogenetic trees. Spiders, insects, crabs, and their kin are customarily designated as Arthropoda—jointed animals or, literally, jointed feet. The arthropods, with their rigid exoskeleton and eponymous multijointed appendages, are closely related to velvet worms (Onychophora, or "claw bearer") and water bears (Tardigrada, or "slow step-per"), two groups of soft-skinned organisms with simple, inarticulate legs that don't seem arthropodic in nature. Most systematic biologists would argue that in the animal system, this central relationship between velvet worms and water bears, on the one hand, and articulated arthropods, on the other hand, should also be reflected in appropriate names. There are two ways in which this can be accomplished. Solution 1: Velvet worms and water bears are thrown in with the arthropods, thus expanding the seman-tic field of Arthropoda. The price paid: the erstwhile arthropods—that is to say, those with "real" jointed appendages—will require a different, new name. Solution 2: The old arthropods stay arthropods but acquire a new superordinate name, along with the velvet worms and water bears.

In the systematic biology community, the majority opted for Solu-tion 1. Arthropoda will henceforth include velvet worms and water bears, those soft-skinned relations. The true jointed animals, once known as arthropods, will get a new name formed by placing eu- in front of the old Arthropoda: Euarthropoda. As stated earlier, the eu- means normal and typical (with the connotation of good and beautiful), suggesting that, as a newly named subgroup of Arthropoda, Euarthropoda could be viewed as the "good" arthropods—that is, those that distinguish themselves through their possession of the "proper" characteristics of articulate animals. The Greek language actually requires that the prefix eu- be pronounced as ev- when preceding a vowel, meaning that when speaking about the subgroup out loud, the name should sound like Ev-arthropoda, instead of You-arthropoda—a rule only followed by a small handful of linguistic purists. In the meantime, the you-arthropods scuttle blithely around talks and lectures with or without the nod of Attic approval.

Experts have known for a long time—since Linnaeus's *Systema Naturae* at the latest—that neither bats nor shrews are related to mice, to which common parlance pays no heed. The *Fledermaus* and *Spitzmaus* comfortably maintain their spots in the lexicon. The superficial similarities in appearance are astonishing, however unspecific, which happens to apply to other animals that also have the word "mouse" in their name but aren't mice. The sea mouse, an unusual marine bristleworm the size of a mouse, with a shimmering mantle of bristles, just barely resembles a mouse and doesn't have a tail. The titmouse, a small woodland bird whose name can be traced back to the Middle English "mose," cognates with the German *Meise*.[1] Although the original etymology of "mose" is unclear, the bird's small size and quick, mouse-like movements either gave rise to the word or aided in its corruption. The tendency to call something a mouse can thus be triggered by rough structural likenesses or linguistic derivations, whereas the reasons behind the *Fledermaus* and *Spitzmaus* are perfectly obvious.

Scientists are assuredly willing to acknowledge that shrews resemble mice superficially, but their life's work as systematic biologists is aimed at being scientifically exact and unequivocal. Not only in their scientific work—that goes without saying—but especially in the scientific designations they employ for organisms. Comprehensive guidelines such as the International Code of Zoological Nomenclature, often known simply as "the Code"—a complex system of conventions that the zoological community has agreed on—serve the single purpose of determining clear names that everyone can understand.[2] The rules are edited by the International Commission on Zoological Nomenclature, a board of about thirty members from different countries who represent a range of disciplines within zoological taxonomy. The Code is about as riveting to read as a piece of legislation, but for zoologists it serves as the framework within which all of zoological taxonomy is housed. Keeping this background in mind, it's understandable that some systematic biologists would like to broaden the reach of these strict standards to apply to nonscientific, common names. This certainly plays a special role with regard to well-known animal groups, such as Central European mammals and birds, which all have German names.

Figure 1.4
Hermann Pohle with his assistant Inge Pasemann in front of a cabinet with genet skulls in 1939. Museum für Naturkunde Berlin, Historische Bild- u. Schriftgutsammlungen (MfN, HBSB), Bestand: Zool. Mus., Signatur: B III/1260.

One of the first mammal biologists to campaign for the standardization of German mammal names was Hermann Pohle. Born in Berlin in 1892, Pohle remained faithful to the city until his death and spent a large part of his life working at the natural history museum there. His career as a mammal biologist started early, when as a university student he worked as an unpaid hireling in the museum's famed mammal collection. Through diligence, endurance, and scientific acumen, he worked his way up to head curator of mammals. He thus held one of the most influential positions, of both national and international significance, in the field of systematic mammal research. In 1926, Pohle—along with Ludwig Heck, the former director of the Berlin Zoo, and a number of other colleagues—founded the German Society for Mammalogy, of which he was the first head. Pohle thus had his finger on the pulse of mammal research, as it were, and he followed the history of the society over the next five decades "with keen interest," as one biographer noted.

In addition to his work as a researcher and curator of the mammal collection at Berlin's Museum für Naturkunde (Museum of Natural History), Pohle's interests also lay with German mammal names. Not only did he push for standardization of names, Pohle also campaigned to have existing names assessed for scientific plausibility and changed, should they not pass (his) zoological muster.

In 1942, Pohle published a summary article addressing the question, "How many species of mammals live in Germany?" He appended a comprehensive list of all German mammals, each with its correct "technical name," as Pohle called it, as well as its corresponding German name. When it came to the various species of *Spitzmaus* (of which the Germans have eight, incidentally, despite the long-standing impression that there is "the" one and only shrew) and the sixteen species of bats that have the base word "*Fledermaus*" in their name, Pohle consistently uses alternative terms. The eight shrew species thus became *Waldspitzer, Zwergspitzer, Alpenspitzer, Wasserspitzer, Mittelspitzer, Feldspitzer, Gartenspitzer,* and *Hausspitzer*.[3] For the bats, the base of their compound name was changed to *Fleder: Teichfleder, Langfußfleder, Wasserfleder,* and so on, all the way to a term of particular elegance, *Wimperfleder*.[4]

Pohle's article, which predates the society's 15th General Assembly and Hitler's emotional veto by more than a year, is a particularly interesting source because he also shares his actual motivations for the suggested changes. His emphatic objective is to see "the term '*Maus*' disappear, responsible as it is for laypersons' wont to lump the animals together with actual mice." In the estimation of these laypersons, mice are something "ugly and destructive that must be fought, or ideally exterminated." Shrews and bats, harmless as they are to humans, are thus subject to the same brutal fate. Pohle hopes for a "shift in perspective" to occur, once the endangered animals are no longer referred to as mice. What to do, then? Pohle would prefer the term *Spitz* for *Spitzmaus*, but it's already been assigned to a dog breed. *Rüssler* could also work, only it already applies to some other insectivore. That leaves *Spitzer*, a name that emphasizes the pointy head as a distinguishing characteristic and is still available. Pohle wants a name for bats without "*Maus*" but happily with a nod to the animals' flying ability. Most names of this kind are already employed for birds, and "*Flatterer*" or "flutterer" could only logically be used for a certain population of bats, namely, those bad at flying. "*Flieger*" or "flyer," another hot candidate, is also in use by various other animal groups. But why, Pohle asks the reader, would one even need to say "*Fleder*maus," when "*Fleder*" actually makes perfect sense? Pohle mentions that the original meaning of "*Fleder*" was different, but few people were aware of this fact anymore. On the off chance that he was correct in this assessment, let it be noted that *Fledermaus* can be traced back to the tenth century, to the Old High German "*vledern*" or "*flattern*" (the infinitive form of "*Flatterer*"). The image of the bat as a "fluttering mouse" has existed since this time in many languages, including "flittermouse" in English. A number of other German terms exist for bats. In some regions of Germany, such as Rhineland-Palatinate and Southern Hesse, the Old High German "*fledarmus*" is said to have been used to describe nocturnal creatures, such as moths. There, bats were apparently called "*Speckmaus*," instead of *Fledermaus*, because while hibernating, they could be seen hanging like pieces of bacon (*Speck*) in the smoke.

Pohle's dedication to promoting the protection of bats and shrews through a bold name change reached its temporary culmination a year later, when—at the 15th General Assembly of the German Society for Mammalogy in Berlin—a resolution was passed on a universal and binding adoption of the *Spitzer*- and *Fleder*-based names Pohle had suggested. The results are known: *Hitler was not amused.*

At this juncture, it should not go unmentioned that a few years after the described events, in 1956, Pohle—together with a number of notable

German mammal researchers—published a fundamental and summary proposal for "The German Names of Mammals." Any talk of "*Spitzer*" or "*Fleder*" had long since vanished. As from time immemorial, all shrew species were named *Spitzmaus*, all bat species, *Fledermaus*.

Domestication of Names

It is unlikely that Hitler's furious intervention in favor of the *Spitzmaus* and *Fledermaus* had wide-reaching impact on the names' actual usage. The scientists responsible can't have spent much time deliberating between abandoning *Spitzer* and *Fleder* and being elsewhere "employed." At the same time, it cannot be assumed that a notice in the *Zoologischer Anzeiger*—or similar appeals in other outlets or on the occasion of later conferences on mammal biology—would have any far-reaching influence on the usage of common names.

In contrast to the names in all the following chapters, in which scientific nomenclature is explored, *Spitzmaus* and *Fledermaus* are elements of German vernacular or everyday language. The formal nomenclature of scientific names was instituted at a distinct point in time—in the case of animal names, almost exactly 250 years ago. Nomenclature rules can change, and in fact they do, in a strictly formalized process of reformulating (or formulating anew) various components of the guidelines, comprehensible only to those who find it interesting. In many cases, this involves adapting or amending legal texts. Moreover, a feature of scientific names is the fact that their individual moment of emergence can be ascertained precisely. They only begin to exist once they've been published.

Everyday speech and its linguistic elements are subject to thoroughly different influences and have their own history of emergence, which by its nature is not formalized. The origins of the German spoken today—which is known in linguistic terms as New High German—can be traced back to 1600, but the customs and words used now have changed drastically since then. The same applies to Modern English, which developed from Early Modern English in the seventeenth century. Changes to words, formation of words, loss of words, and the adoption of words from other languages (loanwords) have occurred throughout history, although today's fast, worldwide communication channels have seen new words seep into

German, English, and other languages faster than ever before. Thus, compared with scientific nomenclature, colloquial terms are not borne of a dateable act of linguistic creation. Rather, over the course of time, they've been influenced on many sides as they pass through a complex linguistic process to arrive at their current form.

For the most part, animal names used in everyday speech aren't simple words—or simplicia, as linguists say—but rather combinations of multiple expressive elements. These compounds can either be "closed," in which the component parts are combined without spaces or hyphenation, or "open," in which the parts are written as separate but associated words. Upon dismantling compound words into their component parts, one can often see their linguistic origins immediately, as well as their meaning. In a typical example, a specific word element will be appended to a general, simple base word such as mouse, duck, or clam, which allows for necessary precision in the labeling of a given animal: house mouse, ring-necked duck, razor clam. Through the addition of further word elements or even adjectives, otherwise similar species can be linguistically distinguished: red-bellied woodpecker, great blue skimmer, golden silk orb-weaver. If one wonders why the *Feldhase* (brown hare or "field hare") is called by that name, the answer seems fairly intuitive. It's a hare—zoologically speaking, too, as it happens—that, as a denizen of open spaces, prefers spending its time in agricultural areas, surviving off the crops planted there.

Considerably more challenging, however, is the linguistic derivation of the individual elements that comprise such compound animal names. The derivation of a term such as *Feldhase* is as intuitive as the words *Feld* or *Hase* are opaque. Admittedly, these questions aren't easy, and even with the tools of a biologist with a penchant for languages, they're impossible to answer. The problem at hand is a change in the meaning or usage of a word that occurred a long time ago, a change that is inaccessible before the backdrop of our current vocabulary—at least without some extra effort. *Hase*, or hare, serves now as little more than the label for a certain type of mammal characterized by long ears, big eyes, and powerful hind legs. One must always assume that in its original usage, a word such as *Hase* may have had a different meaning or been carried over from a different language or context and applied to these creatures. New creations of words— that is, the total invention of a new sound sequence—do occur, but they are extremely rare. The reconstruction of words' complex provenance and historical development constitutes the research domain of etymology, the oldest of linguistic disciplines.

The *Feld* in *Feldhase* is drawn from a different context than zoology and serves here as a special designation for a particular hare. This information is nowhere near adequate, even for amateur linguists, and we therefore turn to the *Etymological Lexicon of the German Language* by Friedrich Kluge (respectfully and endearingly also known as *"der Kluge,"* or "the brainiac") to learn that *Feld* originally meant "of an outspread quality, or plain," and was already in use in the Old High German of the eighth century. Evidence of the word *Hase* also exists in eighth-century Old High German, and its original meaning was "the gray one."

The meaning of the animal name *Maus*, however, isn't as easy to trace. In the form of *"mus"* or similar, the mouse appears to be evident in all Indo-Germanic languages. It also reaches at least as far back as the Old High German of the eighth century. Of further interest is the fact that in Latin, mouse is also *mus*, which can still be seen today in scientific names such as *Mus musculus*. Therefore, the possibility cannot be ruled out that the Indo-Germanic *mus* originated as a loanword from Latin. Thus, the linguistic derivation. What, then, is the original meaning of *mus*?

Kluge, ever true to his name, tells us that while the details of the meaning and origin of *mus* are contested, an "appealing" explanation must exist. To that end, he writes that *mus* must be traceable to the Old Indo-Germanic *mŭs*, which means "to steal," and could refer to mice's pesky habit of helping themselves to our food. However, a connection to the Old High German *chreo-mosido*, which signifies the "robbing of a corpse," cannot be ruled out.[5] As if this explanation were not "appealing" enough already, the story grows more complicated. According to Kluge, one must not ignore the fact that the other past connotation for the word "muscle" points to a different context altogether. Many Indo-Germanic languages feature words derived from *mus* that refer to muscles, whether in general or specific terms. Therefore, it is conceivable that the animal name can be traced back to the according definition of "that which moves." In this scenario, the Latin verb *movere* (known to us today in the English terms "to move" and "movement") is also related to *mus*. Kluge concludes that a decision as to whether the content of "mouse" is derived from "to steal" or "to move" cannot be made. At least it shows us—through the example of "mouse," a simple word learned so quickly in early childhood—just how complicated etymological derivations can be.

Despite the many general etymological dictionaries that exist, no summary scientific study of the origins of German animal names exists. Helmut Carl's *German Plant and Animal Names: Explanation and Linguistic Order*, which is considered a rather popular work and has appeared in multiple editions since 1957, presents a wonderful overview of the diversity of names for organisms in German. Carl groups the names primarily by word content, that is, by the meaning derived from the component words in compound names. As a result, the chapters bear names such as "Nature Spirits, Innocuous and Noxious," "Holidays of the Year," and "Dying and Death." An enormous collection of names, their derivation and meaning.

The etymological reconstruction of the German bird and mammal names, at least, can be traced back—in both Carl and Kluge, as well as in other etymological dictionaries—to two interesting books. In 1899, the Finnish philologist Hugo Palander released part of his dissertation with a Darmstadt-based publishing house. The work is titled *Old High German Animal Names, Volume I: The Names of Mammals* and was supported—if not formally supervised—by Friedrich Kluge. Palander was born in 1874 in the southern Finnish city of Hämeenlinna, which happens to be the birthplace of probably the most famous Finnish composer, Jean Sibelius, who saw the light of day just five years before Palander. Little is known about Palander. Upon completing his undergraduate and master's studies in 1896 at the University of Helsinki, he obtained his doctorate from the same institution in 1901. The topic of his dissertation was the etymology of German animal names, and his occupation with German philology led first to a stint as docent and later to full professorship at the University of Helsinki. He held that position until three years before his death in 1944. As a seeker of buried knowledge, he could not even be stopped by his own surname, which had been Latinized in the seventeenth century. From 1906 onward, he published under the surname Suolahti, his family's original Finnish name.

For this reason, the books of greatest interest to our topic were published under two different names. Especially Palander's book from 1899, which was slated as Volume I of what would have been at least a two-part series, has not been reprinted since and has largely faded into obscurity. This fact is regrettable because the work provides an engaging and informative foundation for discovering the origins of old German names for mammals. A nice example, which Palander expands on, is the word *Pferd*, or horse. The word is said to derive from the Late Old High German *pfarifit*, which corresponds to the Middle High German *pferfrit*, *phärit*, and *pfert*. In this historical usage, it actually means a "courier's horse" specifically, and it wasn't used in general terms until later. It is highly likely, however, that these German names were plucked from Medieval Latin at a much earlier point in time and can probably be traced back to *paraveredus*. The word for mail pony in Latin, however, is *veredus*, and a *paraveredus*, with the prefix para- (meaning "beside"), is a reserve horse kept beside the actual courier's horse during mail delivery. *Paraveredus* ultimately gained acceptance and morphed into *Pferd* in early German, most likely because it was a simple dialectal shortening of the word. However, the path into the history of *Pferd* continues: the Latin term *veredus* can be traced back to an older Celtic word. The Welsh word for horse is *gorwydd*, which is evidently a combination of the sounds *wo* or *we* (meaning "under" or "by") and the Celtic word *reda* ("chariot"), which has an Old High German equivalent in *rida*, meaning "to ride, drive, or move." In addition to *pfari-frit*, *paraveredus*, *veredus*, and *gorwydd*, the word *Pferd* is thus also related to *reda* and *rida*.

Palander's second book, *German Bird Names: A Linguistic Study*, appeared in 1909 under his Finnish name Suolahti but also in German. The book—which relies on historical sources to trace the usage of all bird names and their changes over the course of time back to the Middle Ages—is much more extensive, which comes as no surprise because there are far more species of birds than mammals in the German-speaking realm (and world-wide). As such, it is no less delightful to read.

As fascinating as the etymology of Old High German animal names is, the *Pferd* example makes one thing clear: even for those who have a good command of Latin and Greek vocabulary, the art of name derivation remains largely inaccessible. This pertains in particular to animal names that are no more than German base terms, themselves old, not compounds, and whose original meaning cannot easily be derived from our current understanding of language. Many examples are available: *Aal, Adler, Ameise, Egel, Forelle, Geier, Hamster, Kröte, Schnecke, Storch, Unke*, and *Wespe*,[6] to name just a few of these "simplicia." Interestingly, although many of the English counter-parts of these words are of Old English origin, they ultimately derive from Old High German, such as eel, ant, hamster, snail, stork, and wasp.

What's more, these simple, noncompound words all entered our language at different times. The prevailing practice in historical linguistics is to search for old written sources in which a certain term appeared for the first time. Scientific works about the historical origins of words, like Hugo Suolahti's study of German bird names, often consist largely of references to historical literature and the names found there. One of the oldest and most important sources regarding the origins of bird names are the *Leviticus Apostils*, which probably date from the eighth century. In linguistic history, an apostil is an annotation or explanation of a word or difficult section of text. The *Leviticus Apostils* elucidate the translated words included in an appendix to chapter 11 of the Old Testament Book of Leviticus, as the Third Book of Moses is also known. This book addresses ritual purity requirements, in particular rules regarding the consumption of permitted animals and avoidance of those prohibited. The author of the apostils is Theodore of Canterbury—also known as Theodore of Tarsus, named after his place of birth in what is now Turkey—who was Archbishop of Canterbury in the latter half of the seventh century and is recognized as one of the founding fathers of the Church of England. Theodor was called to Canterbury, accompanied by Hadrian, a native of North Africa and abbot of a monastery near Naples. The *Leviticus Apostils*, which present a compilation of Latin and Old English bird names, were most likely penned by the pair. The reason behind the collection was a practical one: Christians voyaging to Palestine, who were unfamiliar with the local cuisine, needed to know which birds they could eat with confidence and which were to be declined. Given their North African-Byzantine origins, Theodore and his trusted associate Hadrian were believed to be familiar with the biblical animal world of Asia Minor. Thanks to this culinary dictionary, we thus have access to one of the earliest enumerations of a great many bird names.

The sources that linguistic historians use extend back to the eighth century, their numbers increasing from older to more recent eras. The invention of the printing press in the mid-fifteenth century revolutionized the production of books from the ground up, and with the increasing number of publications appearing in subsequent centuries, researching animal names has also become much easier over time. Finally, the Internet provides access to digitized printed works through its global network, as well as lists of names, catalogs, and directories, making even recent changes in word usage easy to research.

In this way, it becomes possible to establish a chronology mapping the latest possible points at which certain animal names could have appeared in the German language. For instance, it's known that the name *Kabeljau* ("cod") was already in use in the twelfth century, whereas *Delphin* and *Antilope* aren't traceable until the nineteenth century. Similarly, the literature will sometimes reveal the circumstances under which a name found its way into our vocabulary. Numerous significant events in the history of our cultural realm have led to the immense enrichment of our store of biological names, simply as previously unknown biodiversity gradually became accessible. From the Migration Period to the deepest Middle Ages, traders and travelers transported medicinal plants and spices from southern Europe to Germany. The Crusades and knighthood opened the plant and animal worlds of the Orient to exploration and exploitation, and many animal names, such as *Giraffe*, *Papagei* (parrot), and *Dromedar*, originated during this time. In the Age of Discovery, starting around the sixteenth century, exotic animals and plants finally made their way to Europe, quickly gaining entry into occidental cuisine. The explorers brought back many new names used by the indigenous peoples in the areas in which the animals were found. Other names, meanwhile, were new creations.

Linguistic Evolution

We can see, then, that over a period of more than a thousand years, animal names from countless sources have entered the German language and undergone their own changes. The question remains, however, as to how the linguistic creations were reached for the animal names in use today. In this regard, linguists outline a series of possibilities. The creation of a truly new name—that is, an entirely new invention of a certain sound sequence, without building on existing words—is rare. The only animal names that have good reason to be considered real new creations are imitative or, in linguistic parlance, onomatopoeic words. The mimicry of sounds plays the biggest role in the animal names that have arisen this way. The cuckoo is doubtless the best-known example, but several others exist: chickadee, towhee, bobwhite, bobolink, whip-poor-will, and the Chuck-will's-widow. Interestingly, *Möwe* (seagull) is believed to derive from the Middle High German verb *mawen* and the Modern Dutch *mauwen*, both of which signify the meowing of a cat, meaning that an onomatopoeic term has been

Figure 1.5
Eggs of the brown-hooded gull (*Larus maculipennis*, Lichtenstein, 1823, today in the genus *Chroicocephalus*) and other gull species. Museum für Naturkunde Berlin, M. Ohl photo.

transferred from one animal to another. There do not seem to be any onomatopoeic mammal names, and even for birds, there are few further examples than those listed here.

Birdsong and birdcalls, in particular, are so characteristic that beyond the real onomatopoeic words, names exist that may not mimic the birdcall but describe it. Examples include the warbler, as well as the mourning dove, mockingbird, and song sparrow, which are easy to understand when broken into their word components.

More common are the loanwords and foreign terms that have usually been brought from the animal's place of origin and introduced to the English language. The axolotl (also known by this name in Mexico), jaguar (from the South American indigenous Tupí-Guaraní language family), jackal (Indian), impala (Zulu), iguana (Arawak), and salamander (Persian) are some of the many animal names that originate from other languages. Some have entered English unaltered and are therefore considered foreign words, whereas many others have been adapted in various ways to conform to English sound conventions (e.g., the cassowary, a large, flightless bird from the Malay name *kasuari*).

The simplest and most common way to arrive at new words, however, consists of combining old—that is, already existing—words to create new ones. While English names include barn owl, moon jelly, water spider, mountain quail, or digger wasp, in German—a language known for its plasticity in compound word formation—there must be several thousand compound names, such as *Rotkehlchen*, *Trompetentierchen*, *Kompassqualle*, *Wasserspitzmaus*, *Flohkrebs*, *Azurjungfer*, and *Grabwespe*.[7] The list could continue almost infinitely because the general linguistic rule regarding word formation also applies to animal names, and their appeal lies in the way we are able to understand both their literal sense and definition through defining their word components—the base word and determinative.

In creating new terms, the possibilities for combinations are nearly boundless because the word components may originate from any number of sources. Given the erratic history of the German language, the components that comprise compound words can change to become so unrecognizable over time that they are nearly impossible to comprehend within the context of today's vocabulary. When new German names are created these days, they are almost always compound words, in which the base word is qualified through the inclusion of certain features, such as geographical origin or special physical traits. Only a few years ago, two new dolphin species were discovered off the coast of Australia, and in both cases the authors of the species descriptions immediately suggested common names (in English, to start) in addition to the scientific names. *Orcaella heinsohni*, described in 2005, is called the Australian snubfin dolphin, while *Tursiops australis*, described in 2011, is known as the Burrunan dolphin. The first name includes a nod to both its geographic origin and small dorsal fin, while the Burrunan dolphin was named after a local Aboriginal term for dolphin. Most animal names today are created in this or a similar fashion. Further examples anon.

It is interesting to consider animal names that have changed so significantly over the course of their history that our *Sprachgefühl* suggests a meaning that has nothing to do with the original. This is because foreign or unfamiliar words are sometimes treated along the lines of known, similar words to make them more understandable in a way. This form of "clarification" will not infrequently yield semantic reversals and new word formations. The linguistic term for this is folk etymology or reanalysis. A good example of a folk etymological change in meaning is the crawfish.[8]

Old English first borrowed the Old French term *crevise* (or *écrevisse* in Modern French) for these freshwater crustaceans, mispronouncing it "cray-VIS." Before long, the bastardized *crevise* morphed into "crayfish." In Louisiana, where both crayfish and French are found in abundance, folks couldn't help but notice that these "fish" don't swim but crawl. Thus, the craw(l)-fish was born.

Vernacular names are used especially for the representation of animals in popular science, which finds its widest reach in the form of field guides and animal encyclopedias. The *National Audubon Society Field Guides*—which cover far more than birds, documenting all manner of animal groups as well as trees, fossils, mushrooms, and the night sky—are hugely popular among amateurs and pros alike. In reference to vertebrates, or at least to mammals, it is best practice to provide a common name for every species. A wide range of Internet-based articles on animal species exists these days, the best known including the individual entries on Wikipedia or Wikispecies, which is currently under construction. The range of Wikipedia pages on animal species is growing constantly, and theoretically, at least, Wikispecies would like to provide a page per species in the distant future.

One of the most important and comprehensive animal encyclopedias ever published is *Grzimek's Animal Life Encyclopedia*, which appeared in thirteen volumes between 1967 and 1972 and has been translated into many languages, including English. (The updated and expanded second edition, which encompasses seventeen volumes and more than 9,000 pages, is now available online by subscription.) With its descriptions of more than 8,000 animal species, *Animal Life* still represents an impressive work of collaboration among numerous specialists from around the world. The encyclopedia was conceived by Bernhard Grzimek. As zoo director, documentary filmmaker, and television host, "Animal Uncle" Bernhard was one of Germany's best-known animal rights advocates for years. *Ein Platz für Tiere* (*A Place for Animals*), the documentary series he hosted on public television from 1956 onward—producing 175 episodes over thirty years—reached millions of viewers in Germany and made Grzimek a TV star. His trademark was putting live animals such as monkeys and cheetahs on camera, providing viewers with firsthand exposure. His old-fashioned, stiff grandfatherly charm, nasally voice, and standard greeting, "Good evening, dear friends," were unmistakable. Grzimek was particularly fond of the African megafauna, and he advocated intensely for preserving Serengeti National Park. His biggest

Figure 1.6
Bernhard Grzimek with a living cheetah during the German television show "Ein Platz für Tiere" in 1977. Courtesy of Hessischer Rundfunk/Pressestelle/Kurt Bethke.

documentary films, *Bambuti* (also known as *No Place for Wild Animals*, 1956) and *Serengeti Shall Not Die* (1959), were filmed in Africa and present a moving image of both the beauty and endangerment of the big animals of the Serengeti. After he surprisingly won the Oscar for *Serengeti Shall Not Die*, Grzimek became internationally recognized and deftly used his popularity for countless conservation initiatives. As director of the Frankfurt Zoo from 1945 to 1974, he contributed significantly to implementing modern, species-appropriate living conditions for animals in captivity.

Grzimek knew how to use television—still a new, unexplored medium in the 1950s and 1960s—to his advantage, but he also wrote a series of popular books. To this day, *Animal Life* has seen the most sustained success of all Grzimek's book publications. It also became well known because of its style, which is both scientifically correct and rendered as popular science. In doing so, Grzimek wanted to distinguish himself—respectfully but decisively—from *Brehm's Animal Life*, in which descriptions that now seem naïve, judgmental, and not seldom vilifying were standard issue.

Grzimek's modern work would be as unlikely to describe the "unspeakably dumb-looking head atop the ostrich's long neck" as it would be to portray creatures as dull, stupid, smart, tender, or chivalrous. These descriptions were judgmental from the human perspective, which did not align with Grzimek's efforts to establish a new objectivity.

As it was, the popular presentation of scientific content stood at the fore-front of Grzimek's characteristic style: scientifically precise and up to date but also easily understood by the nonscientifically trained reader. For this reason, Grzimek issued three important linguistic directives. First, all foreign or technical expressions were to be avoided or, if there were absolutely no other way, reworded using more familiar terms. Second, words that Grzimek felt carried a negative or pejorative connotation, such as *"Maul,"* *"saufen," "fressen,"* and *"verenden,"* were to be replaced by the corresponding terms used for humans: *"Mund," "trinken," "essen,"* and *"sterben."*[9] Finally, of the many animals included in *Animal Life*, all the vertebrates, at least, were to have a vernacular name. He was such a thorough "animal uncle" that at the end of each volume, he included an "animal dictionary," where in addition to the German he recorded the English, French, and Russian animal names. This move put pressure on the authors, who were responsible for the individual chapters on assigned animal groups. Not only did they now have to research the everyday names for their species in four languages, they were often confronted with the problem that no common names were to be found in the existing literature—or at least not in every language. In these instances, they were obligated to invent fitting names.

The "animal dictionaries" attached to every volume thus became a wonderful catalog of intricate compound animal names, composed of elements describing traits, origins, and other features. The large-toothed bandicoot, curl-crested manucode, little five-toed jerboa, and chestnut-bellied sandgrouse[10] are just a few of the gems in *Grzimek's Animal Life*.

A number of years ago, the authors of the monumental monograph *Mammals of Africa* faced a similar problem. In six volumes and more than 3,500 pages, *Mammals of Africa* was intended to collect everything known up to 2012 about the 1,160 species of African mammals. From the species name to drawings of the skull, from distribution to behavior patterns, *Mammals of Africa* is an impressive example of an encyclopedia for every single mammal group, with an emphasis on detail if not completeness. Because mammals are so popular, common names for many species already exist in many languages, and a number of them were supposed to be used in the six-volume opus, at least in species lists. The chapter authors' task consisted, in part, of compiling the English, French, and German collo-quial names for all African mammals. A group of specialists took care of the shrews alone, among them Rainer Hutterer from Germany, who also researched and published the first study on Hitler's intervention regarding the common German names for shrews and bats. The result of their work was sobering: 150 shrew species live in Africa, which is enormous, compared with the 15 European species, and they all deserved a unique English name. Some shrews had long-established names, whereas others had no vernacular name at all. In these cases, Hutterer and his team usually translated the scientific name. If the same name had already been used for another species, then they invented a new one. The shrew specialists resolutely saw the project to completion, and thanks to them, through a combination of English and Latin translations and adjustments made to homonyms, we now have the first complete and—what's more—beautiful list of English names for African shrews. Their list is a joy to read, and for that reason it should be honored in full here:

Aberdare Mole Shrew

African Black Shrew

African Dusky Shrew

African Giant Shrew

Ansell's Shrew

Armoured Shrew

Asian House Shrew

Babault's Mouse Shrew

Bailey's Shrew

Bale Shrew

Bates's Shrew

Bicolored Shrew

Blackish Shrew

Bottego's Shrew

Buettikofer's Shrew

Cameroon Shrew

Cameroonian Forest Shrew

Cinderella Shrew

Climbing Dwarf Shrew

Congo Shrew

Crosse's Shrew

Cyreniaca Shrew

Dark-footed Mouse Shrew

Dent's Shrew

Desert Shrew

Desperate Shrew

Doucet's Shrew

East African Highland Shrew

Egyptian Pygmy Shrew

Eisentraut's Mouse Shrew

Eisentraut's Shrew

Elgon Shrew

Etruscan Dwarf Shrew

Fischer's Shrew

Flat-headed Shrew

Flower's Shrew

Fox's Shrew

Fraser's Shrew

Geata Mouse Shrew

Glass's Shrew

Goliath Shrew

Gracile Naked-tailed Shrew

Grant's Forest Shrew

Grasse's Shrew

Grauer's Large-headed Shrew

Greenwood's Shrew

Greater Congo Shrew

Greater Dwarf Shrew

Greater Forest Shrew

Greater Large-headed Shrew

Greater Red Shrew

Greater Shrew

Greenwood's Shrew

Guramba Shrew

Harenna Shrew

Heather Shrew

Hildegarde's Shrew

Howell's Forest Shrew

Hun Shrew

Hutu-Tutsi Dwarf Shrew

Isabella Forest Shrew

Jackson's Shrew

Johnston's Forest Shrew

Jouvenet's Shrew

Jumping Shrew

Kahuzi Swamp Shrew

Kihaule's Mouse Shrew

Kilimanjaro Shrew

Kilimanjaro Mouse Shrew

Kivu Long-haired Shrew

Kivu Shrew

Kongana Forest Shrew

Lamotte's Shrew

Large-headed Shrew

Latona's Shrew

Least Dwarf Shrew

Lesser Congo Shrew

Lesser Dwarf Shrew

Lesser Forest Shrew

Lesser Grey-brown Shrew

Lesser Red Shrew

Long-footed Shrew

Long-tailed Mouse Shrew

Long-tailed Shrew

Lucina's Shrew

Ludia's Shrew

MacArthur's Shrew

Macmillan's Shrew

Makwassie Shrew

Mamfe Shrew

Manenguba Shrew

Mauritanian Shrew

Montane Shrew

Moon Forest Shrew

Moonshine Shrew

Mount Cameroon Forest Shrew

Mount Kenya Mole-shrew

Naked-tailed Shrew

Nigerian Shrew

Nimba Shrew

Niobe's Shrew

Nyiro Shrew

Oku Mouse Shrew

Phillip's Congo Shrew

Pitman's Shrew

Polia's Shrew

Rainey's Shrew

Rainforest Shrew

Reddish-gray Shrew

Remy's Dwarf Shrew

Roosevelt's Shrew

Rumpi Mouse Shrew

Rwenzori Mouse Shrew   Telford's Shrew
Rwenzori Shrew   Thalia's Shrew
Saharan Shrew   Thérèse's Shrew
Sahelian Tiny Shrew   Thin Mouse Shrew
Savanna Dwarf Shrew   Turbo Shrew
Savanna Path Shrew   Ugandan Lowland Shrew
Savanna Shrew   Ugandan Shrew
Schaller's Mouse Shrew   Ultimate Shrew
Schouteden's Large-headed Shrew   Upemba Shrew
Sclater's Mouse Shrew   Usambara Shrew
Short-footed Shrew   Voi Shrew
Small-footed Shrew   Volcano Forest Shrew
Smoky Mountain Shrew   West African Pygmy Shrew
Somali Dwarf Shrew   West African Long-tailed Shrew
Somali Shrew   Whitaker's Shrew
South African Mouse Shrew   Wimmer's Shrew
Swamp Shrew   Xanthippe's Shrew
Taita Dwarf Shrew   Yankari Shrew
Tanzanian Shrew   Zaphir's Shrew
Tarella Shrew

And those are just the shrews. Compound names such as these exist for each of the 1,160 known animal species in Africa, as outlined in *Mammals of Africa*. Popular African megafauna, such as the giraffe and its many subspecies (including the reticulated giraffe and the Nubian giraffe), have long had widely established vernacular names. The many smaller, lesser known mammals, however, were long neglected and had to make do without proper names.

But what is a "proper" common name anyway? The authors of *Mammals of Africa* doubtless wanted to ensure that at the very least, the base word of the compound name would indicate the zoologically correct animal group. The person using the name should be able to rely on the fact that a Climbing Forest Musk Shrew is truly a shrew. The rest is at the discretion of the respective specialists, who—beyond borrowing from existing scientific and English names—will often be swayed by their own gut feeling. For example, about fifteen species within the mouse genus *Praomys* are known as "soft-furred mice" in English. The name "woodrat" is also used for several species within this genus, which some specialists consider more fitting. The control committee that ultimately decides what is a good and fitting name—and what isn't—is the editorial team of *Mammals*. Beyond that, no truly binding rules exist, and the authors enjoy almost unlimited freedom.

It is interesting, too, to question the purpose of creating standard colloquial names for African mammals. Who even uses them? It's worth distinguishing whether the names have already become an established part of the vernacular. English-speaking researchers, zoogoers, and tourists in Africa will surely refer to *Panthera leo* as "lion." The same applies to any number of the well-known and popular large mammals of Africa. It can be helpful to review a list of these common English names in *Mammals* to confirm certain names in moments of doubt. But what about the overwhelming number of African small mammals known and recognized by specialists alone? Furthermore, it's doubtful that such word monstrosities as "Geoffroy's Trident Leaf-nosed Bat" and "Hayman's Lesser Epauletted Fruit Bat" play an important role in African research projects. Scientists will instead refer to *Asellia tridens* and *Micropteropus intermedius*. Who knows, perhaps the rapidly growing and universally used online encyclopedias such as Wikipedia, Wikispecies, and the *Encyclopedia of Life*—which draw on the knowledge of competent sources—will ensure that in the future the Hayman's Lesser Epauletted Fruit Bat finds its way onto a tablet or smartphone, finally crossing the lips of many a nature-loving tourist in Africa.

The creation of common names for African mammals is thus not governed by any central rulebook. Instead, scientists may carry it out according to their own whim. Whether a name gains acceptance or is ousted by another option is determined by the authors or editors of standard works, along with the wider "scientific community"—the network of scientists interested in African mammals—who will ultimately use (or not use) the name. Naturally, this applies to African mammals as well as animals worldwide.

Birds, however, are the exception, having long enjoyed popular standing with scientists and amateurs alike. With more than 10,000 worldwide and more than 900 in North America, the number of known species is relatively manageable, at least compared with the global figure of more than one million known animal species. It's safe to assume that these numbers come close to the true count of existing bird species. The study of birds has a long history in our culture, and humans have always paid special attention to them, whether as a source of food, a feature for aesthetic improvement in the home, or a research topic. Birds are closely followed by amateur ornithologists worldwide, and for many European bird species, distribution reports exist that often date back to antiquity or at least the Middle Ages. Scarcely any other animal group has been so widely represented, whether in colorful monographs or long species lists that exist for nearly every region on earth, and the number of books published on birds—let alone scientific articles—is utterly unfathomable. Furthermore, the ornithologists of the world are impressively well organized in global and regional societies that vigilantly track developments in their areas.

It therefore comes as no surprise that bird taxonomy is considered well established and encompasses a long tradition of widely used common names. The linguistic origins and development of bird names are also well known in many languages. The world's ornithologists have established various independent commissions on colloquial bird names. Since 1990, the Standing Committee on English Names has been working on an official list of the world's English bird names. This complex and time-consuming project resulted in the 2006 volume *Birds of the World: Recommended English Names*, published by ornithologists Frank Gill and Minturn Wright for the International Ornithological Congress (IOC). Given the many future changes that can still be expected, the online IOC World Bird List provides a regularly updated catalog of standard English names (www.worldbirdnames.org). In both printed and digital editions, the list is prefaced by the various rules the authors followed. The IOC appears prudent in its deliberation here, and it also considers wider usage because it will accept well-established—albeit zoologically unfitting—names. For example, common names such as warbler, which is occasionally applied to species in totally unrelated bird families, such as the Parulidae (New World Warblers), Sylviidae (Old World Warblers), Phylloscopidae (another branch of the Old World Warblers), and others, are accepted for the list when their long-time usage can be established, even though they're zoologically inaccurate.

These examples demonstrate that the emergence and development over time of English animal names can be researched and often reconstructed retrospectively, but that the actual creation of names—the actual act of naming—is not governed by any objective set of rules. This arbitrariness, particularly with regard to common names, doesn't present any issues in everyday life and is strengthened by a further phenomenon. At the heart of the argument is the way that animal names in modern English are used, particularly in written English. Across the English-speaking world, many

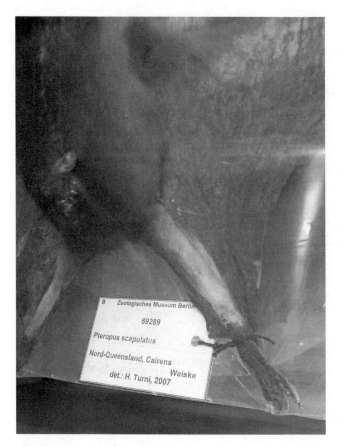

Figure 1.7
A little red flying fox (*Pteropus scapulatus*, Peters, 1862) in a plastic bag in the mammal collection. Museum für Naturkunde Berlin, M. Ohl photo.

common and well-known animal species have different names in the regional dialect. Yet again, even when it comes to regional names, ornithologists are pioneers in comprehensive cataloging. In an unbelievable feat of diligence, the Swiss ornithologist Michel Desfayes gathered the common names of European bird species in the European languages and dialects available to him. The result was a two-volume work, each about 1,200 pages long, titled *A Thesaurus of Bird Names: Etymology of European Lexis Through Paradigms*, published in 1998. The first volume addresses the bird names. For each species, under its scientific name, the common names are given in a variety of languages. Within languages, Defayes lists regional

names and usages, indicating the respective region. An example would be
the Great Titmouse, known by its scientific name as *Parus major*. The Great
Titmouse is common in Europe and has been known to humans since time
immemorial because the birds are common garden visitors. Therefore, it
comes as no surprise that the Great Titmouse has many unique regional
names. Desfayes starts by listing names in forty-one different languages,
from English, German, and Spanish to Kurdish and Georgian. Many languages include a wide range of regional names, and in the English-speaking
world alone, Desfayes tallies sixty names that are at least partly deducible
from one another. Regional names are followed by a note on the area or
city to which the name can be traced. This list of English names for the
Great Titmouse, in alphabetical order and without reference to geographical origins, follows:

bee-bird	*kue-te-kue*
bee-biter	*oaxee*
bee-catcher	*oxeye-tit*
bell-bird	*oxey-eye*
big bluebonnet	*sawfich*
big tit	*sawfiler*
blackcap	*sawfinch*
black-capped billy	*saw-sharpener*
black-capped lolly	*saw-whet*
black-capped tit	*saw-whetter*
blackhead	*sharpie*
black-headed bob	*sharpsaw*
black-headed bodkin	*sit-ye-down*
black-headed tomtit	*tam-tiddymouse*
blackskull	*tet*
blackytop	*thomas tit*
charbonniere	*tide*
great tit	*tinker*
great titmouse	*tinker-tinker*
greater blackcap	*tinner*
jacksaw	*tit*
jorincke	*tita*
jorinker	*tite*
king charles	*titmouse*

titnaup	*tommy-titmouse*
titteribum	*tom-noup*
tittymaw	*tomtit*
tittymouse	*tom-tub*
toddiel	*tydie*
tommy-tit	*tydife*

If a linguistically minded ornithologist wants to know the Basque name for the Great Titmouse before going on vacation, he or she need look no further than Desfayes: the standard Basque term is *Kaskabeltz auni*, although more than fifty other regional names exist within the language.

The second volume of the *Thesaurus of Bird Names* is possibly more unusual. In this section, Desfayes analyzes the structure, origins, and meaning of names and name elements according to a range of criteria. There are long lists of historical bird names in Sumerian, Persian, Greek, and other classical languages, and the list of Sanskrit names alone comes in at around 1,100 entries; a Spanish-French lexicon of falconry terminology is included, along with an extensive catalog of French and Spanish names of non-European origin. The *Thesaurus* is a wonderful book, provided one has a penchant (if not an outright obsession) for encyclopedic lists and catalogs. Beyond that, however, it's unclear who the readers of this monumental opus might be. That doesn't matter because Desfayes makes at least one point abundantly clear: standard animal names in everyday English represent a single facet of common names. These names are typically tied to a great many regional names; in many cases, there are few who know these names anymore, if they haven't already disappeared from the active lexicon.

Let's come back just one more time to the *Fledermaus-Spitzmaus* dispute between Hermann Pohle and Adolf Hitler. We can only guess at what Hitler's actual motive was in issuing such drastic threats to prevent the name alterations proposed by the German Society for Mammalogy. It could have been his outrage that in 1942—hard times because of the war—leading German intellectuals were concerned with something so unimportant and banal as the appropriateness of animal names. Perhaps this anecdote is just a further example of Hitler's hostility toward intellectuals. It is ultimately unclear, even, to what extent Hitler was the driving force behind this directive or whether this is a case of subordinates "working towards the Führer," as historian Ian Kershaw describes it. Conceivably, after reading the *Berliner*

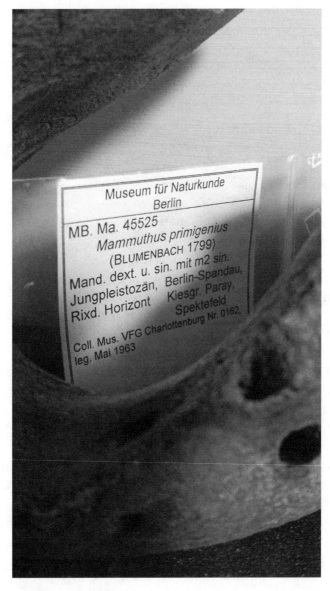

Figure 1.8
Mandible fragment of a fossil woolly mammoth. Museum für Naturkunde Berlin, M.
Ohl photo.

Morgenpost, Hitler may have remarked negatively regarding the zoologists' plans. His circle—in this case, Bormann—may have immediately interpreted this as "the Führer's will" and sprung to action accordingly. As for Pohle and his colleagues, it can't have mattered much whether the "invitation" to the Eastern Front came directly from Hitler or was communicated in an act of premature obedience.

Whatever the case may be, Pohle's suggested name changes did not fail because of Hitler's intervention, which presumably resonated as little with the German-speaking public as the original notice. Pohle failed because he wanted to take the basic idea of a standardized naming system out of the scientific context and transfer it into the realm of vernacular. Everyday German is not formally and officially regulated, and like every other vernacular, it follows different rules than scientific speech. It is shaped by a multitude of factors and influences that have their own unpredictable dynamic, which leads to some word usages changing while others stabilize. In kindergarten, we learn that small, furry four-legged animals with a tail are "mice." This act of naming fulfills the exact function expected of it. It "tags" specific linguistic content—a meaning—that is generally understood. The difference between muroids and insectivores, which is important to zoologists, has no application in everyday confrontations with "mouse-like" animals and makes no difference to most people. A mouse is a mouse, whether a striped field mouse or a shrew.

Perhaps Pohle was well aware of the problem with everyday speech and anticipated the creeping process of scientific language bleeding slowly into the vernacular. Had this been the case, Pohle could have ventured a first step toward standardization among his science colleagues, allowing *Spitzer* and *Fleder* to find application in scientific works—maybe sparingly at the outset but with growing frequency. Had these names first made their way into science, it's entirely possible that they would soon be found in popular publications such as field guides or other animal books. Had they secured their place in a new edition of *Grzimek*, who knows, maybe there would be talk today of *Spitzer* and *Fleder*. The fact that this will never move beyond speculation, and that changes of this sort cannot be planned or predicted, is an essential trait of vernacular. And for this reason, everyday speech is ruled out as a source for the definitive and universal naming of animal and plant species.

2 How Species Get Their Names

He was promised "tea and refreshments." But on March 11, 1869, Father Armand David could scarcely believe what he got instead. He had actually set out to gather plants that day, but the animal world had recently begun to interest him as well. David was on his second trip—or let's just call it an expedition—to China's unexplored wilderness. Born in the French Pyrenees in 1826, David developed a passion for natural history from childhood onward, which was supported by his father, who was studied in both science and medicine. He studied philosophy in Bayonne, not far from his hometown of Espelette. In 1848, he joined the seminary of the Order of Saint Vincent de Paul—the Lazarists for short—and was ordained three years later.

David spent the next three years working as a natural history teacher in a Lazarist secondary school in the northern Italian city of Savona. In 1860, when the Lazarist Order—with support of the French government—extended its reach to China, David volunteered to travel to Peking, as Beijing was known to Europeans at the time. The Lazarists had founded a school there, and David was enlisted to teach, gather plants and animals, and establish a natural history museum. At that time, the Chinese empire had been accessible to Europeans for a scant two decades, and large areas remained scientifically uncharted. As such, David was thrilled at the chance to visit one of the scientifically most significant frontiers on earth. In preparation for his journey, the order dispatched him to Paris, where he met with scientists at the French Academy of Sciences and the Muséum National d'Histoire Naturelle, France's national museum of natural history. From Sinologists to natural historians, all were impressed by the young priest's charisma and persuasiveness. He was thus sent on his way with the French scientists' best wishes and the express expectation that he

Figure 2.1
Armand David in Mandarin dress. Courtesy of St. Vincent DePaul Image Archive,
reproduced by John Rybold.

contribute significantly to the exploration of China through his gathering operations.

Upon arrival, David began to study the surroundings of Peking. In some cases, he would travel for weeks on these gathering missions, provided his teaching schedule allowed for it. He sent the compiled plant and animal specimens to the museum in Paris. Paris was impressed, and Henri Milne Edwards, the director of the museum, sensed that he had sent the right man to the right place. Not only was the material flawlessly preserved and suited for scientific study, but the sheer abundance of new forms was breathtaking. By way of the French government, Milne Edwards urged the Superior General of the Lazarists to release David from his teaching duties and instead send him on an official, government-funded *mission scientifique* to Inner Mongolia. The trip was to begin in February 1866 and last several months before returning to Peking.

David's second journey into the interior of China, from 1868 to 1870, took him to Mupin—known today as Baoxing—in Sichuan. The trip took such a toll on his health that, for the next two years, he stayed in France to recover. From 1872 to 1874, he took his third and final expedition to China. After that point, his health would allow for no further journeys. David remained active in his studies until his death in 1900, undertaking a number of smaller excursions to Tunisia and Turkey.

His second voyage was unquestionably the most important with regard to natural history. Not only did he gather materials in superabundance, it was during this expedition that he made his most important discoveries. On the aforementioned March 11, 1869, he first laid eyes on the most extraordinary animal he had ever seen, a creature utterly unknown to the Western world at the time. He had installed himself at the Catholic mission connected to Dengchigou Valley Cathedral, an impressive wooden structure that is now a cultural monument in Sichuan province. With this as his home base, David studied the area and gathered thousands of plants and animals. A local landowner named Li had invited him over for tea, and at his house, David spotted a bearskin, the likes of which he had never seen. Most of the body was white, similar to that of a polar bear, but all four extremities were black, as were a wide band over the shoulders, the area around the eyes, and the ears. A large, black-and-white bear. David, who possessed a profound overview of Chinese mammalian life, knew that there were no black-and-white bears in China. Or had thought he knew, because the counterevidence lay before him. He sensed and maybe already knew that he was on the tracks of a zoological sensation. What he couldn't have sensed, however, was that more than a hundred years later, this animal would become an object of obsession around the globe. It would become a political issue, a symbol of habitat destruction and species conservation, and a teddy bear, jovial and laid back. Over "tea and refreshments" in Mr. Li's tea parlor, David had discovered the giant panda.

Now, David hadn't truly discovered pandas because the local population already knew of them. He soon discovered that virtually everybody in Sichuan was familiar with them, although the seemingly easy-going bamboo munchers did their best to avoid humans, who rarely glimpsed them. Following tea with Li, David used the time until dinner to summon his hired hunters—Christian hunters, as he repeatedly emphasizes in his journal. They accepted their assignment calmly. David later wrote in his journal that he had been relieved by his hunters' assurance that they could quickly procure one of these animals. By tomorrow even, easy. A few days later, the proud hunting party returned with a large animal they had suspended between bamboo poles. Unfortunately, it turned out to be an immense black wild boar. David was disappointed and, together with his servant, set out for the high icy peaks of Sichuan himself. A hellish climb that nearly cost them their lives, and all in vain because not a single panda was found. Exhausted and disheartened, they returned to the mission, where David's hunters were waiting for them with the near-frozen body of a young panda they had just caught. Because transporting even a young panda requires considerable effort when it's still alive, they had simply killed it. Father David was nonetheless delighted, and the hunters were able to sell the panda at a "very dear" rate, as David later reported. Over the next two weeks, the hunters caught two more pandas, both females, which they brought living to David. On April 7, 1869, he recorded in his journal: "This animal is not fierce in appearance and behaves as a young bear. Its paws and head exactly resemble those of a polar bear. Its stomach is full of leaves." Given that David was able to report on the contents of its stomach, the captured panda didn't remain a living panda for long. David dissected the pandas on a table in the mission, preserving the valuable skins according to the standard methods he had used so often. He rolled up the panda skins, packed them in a box with the skeletons and skulls—so important for taxonomy—and sent everything, along with an accompanying letter, to Alphonse Milne-Edwards in Paris.

Alphonse was the son of Henri Milne Edwards, the museum director and head of the division for birds and mammals. Father and son both worked as renowned zoologists, curators, and professors at the museum in Paris, and each presided over the institution at different times. Alphonse was the first to introduce the hyphen to the family name, however, and provided proper spelling is used, the two can thus be distinguished from one another. This isn't always easy in the literature because both men worked with Father David's findings from the Chinese highlands. Henri, the father, was thus responsible for describing the famous Père David's deer or milu, which he named *Elaphurus davidianus*, in honor of Armand David. A remarkable story lies behind the discovery of Père David's deer, but more on that later. Son Alphonse described and named the golden snub-nosed monkey (*Rhinopithecus roxellana*), a slim monkey species with golden yellow fur and light blue face that is known for its extraordinary tolerance to the cold temperatures of China's high mountain ranges. Alphonse described dozens of other new mammals that David sent him from China.

There was one species that the busy priest sent him, however, that he could not describe. David was well aware of the significance of his discovery of the giant panda. The Western world had never seen such a bear, and as its discoverer, David claimed the naming rights for himself. In 1869, he published the third part of a report on his Chinese expeditions in one of the scientific magazines printed by the Muséum National d'Histoire Naturelle in Paris. In his travel report, he included excerpts of two letters he had sent Alphonse Milne-Edwards. In the first letter, David described his discovery of an unusual goat relative, which he described in just fifteen lines following the excerpt. He named it *Capricornis milneedwardsii*, after Alphonse. It is known today as the mainland serow.

In his second letter, David reported on further finds and closed with the remark that considerable time would pass before his collections reached Paris, and he requested that the description of a bear be published that was new to contemporary science. Based on a number of footnotes inserted by Milne-Edwards, it appears he had taken on the publication for the priest, who was still in China. Thoroughly common practice. Milne-Edwards thus compiled David's travel report, excerpts from the two letters to himself, and several of his own footnotes, along with the two species descriptions and published the text in David's name.

David, convinced he had a true bear on his hands, named it *Ursus melanoleucus*, which translates literally to "black-and-white bear." His description, which comprises a mere sixteen lines, contains little useful information beyond an explanation of the unique color pattern and his suspicion that this was a new species. The animal was said to be "very large," with "short ears and very short tail." The black-and-white pattern appeared to be consistent, he wrote, because both available specimens—the juvenile animal and the female—were essentially identical, save the slight yellowing of the older animal's white fur.

Despite his being an experienced and avid natural historian who knew his Chinese mammals and could be certain the giant panda had not yet been described, David was a far cry from a scientifically trained mammal specialist. He could not perform the actual scientific interpretation of the findings, thus enter Alphonse Milne-Edwards. Once the skeletons and skins finally reached Paris, it quickly became clear to him that this was not a true bear species, as David had believed. Another bear-like mammal had been described by Frédéric Cuvier in 1825. Cuvier had placed the lesser or red panda in its own genus and named it *Ailurus fulgens*. The specimen—that is, the documentary evidence—for the species description can still be found in the Paris museum. After comparing the skulls of both species, Milne-Edwards concluded that a close relationship between the giant and lesser pandas was likely. Not close enough for a shared genus, however. In 1870, without much detail, he thus moved to describe the genus *Ailuropoda*, borrowing linguistically from *Ailurus*. To this day, the giant panda is named *Ailuropoda melanoleuca*, in which the original *melanoleucus* changes to the feminine form *melanoleuca* to match the grammatically feminine genus *Ailuropoda*.

True or False: A Panda Is a Bear

A word regarding the panda's phylogenetic relations, a question that long went unanswered and was the object of much controversy. For some time, the giant and red pandas were actually considered close kin and were the sole members of the Ailuridae family of predators. The predominant similarity between the two species is a second "thumb" on the front paws that, despite its thumb-like qualities, is not a real sixth digit. Instead, it's a finger-like extension of the so-called sesamoid bone, an otherwise unobtrusive small carpal bone. This "pseudo thumb" is used to grasp plants while eating. According to modern scientific findings based largely on DNA analyses,

Figure 2.2
The first natural image of a giant panda based on the furs, skulls, and skeletons sent by David to Paris. Milne Edwards, H., Recherches pour servir à l'histoire naturelle des mammifères (Paris: G. Masson, 1868–1874). Library of the Museum für Naturkunde Berlin.

however, the giant panda is better grouped with the polar bear, brown bear, two black bear species, sun bear, sloth bear, and spectacled bear in the Ursidae family, the true bears. The red panda, meanwhile, would be a closer match with the procyonides—which include raccoons, martens, skunks, and even seals—than with the true bears. Yet its position in the phylogenetic tree of predators is by no means secured. However isolated the giant panda's position may be within the Ursidae family, David was not so amiss in his classification of the panda as a bear.

Over the course of the 150 years that have passed since David's description, *Ailuropoda melanoleuca* has been more intensively and carefully studied than most other predators. It's hard to believe, but zoologically speaking, this portly, easy-going vegetarian is actually a predator. Among its relatives in the predator family, the panda is a distinctive species, given countless physical peculiarities, along with unique behaviors, physiology, and especially food preferences. David's original description makes no

mention of these. It's just a black-and-white bear with characteristic pat-
terning. The most beautiful of all bears, his panda, David wrote. Thus, the
description was emblazoned with the new scientific name as its headline:
Ursus melanoleucus.

Although the brief description contains little more detailed information,
it's more than enough to secure David's naming right, which forever makes
him the original author of the giant panda. Whatever should happen to
the panda taxonomically in the future, there's no getting past David. For
this reason, and to secure the unambiguousness of the species name—that
is, *melanoleucus*, which can readily be used for other animals—the extended
version of scientific names includes the author and publication year. *Ursus
melanoleucus* David, 1869. This is the panda's long-form name, and if specialists like Milne-Edwards had it right and the animal belongs not to the
bear genus *Ursus* but instead to *Ailuropoda*, the brand-new panda-specific
genus, then both the species name and the author are drawn along with it.
Ailuropoda melanoleuca (David, 1869) is its name today, the parenthetical
David indicating the changed genus affiliation.

A quick side note here. As the observant reader will have noted, the
term "species name" can be used in two ways. This is common in biology, albeit undesirable, because its imprecision represents a potential source
of misunderstanding. On the one hand, the species name is the two-part
name, such as *Ailuropoda melanoleuca* in this instance. The first of these
two parts is the genus or "generic" name, which is always at the front and
capitalized. This is followed by the "specific name," which is always lowercase, and it's here that the double meaning of species name is buried.
In one instance, it's the whole binomial; in the other, it's just the latter
part. In the zoological field, it was once suggested that the name components be called the first and second names, which never gained traction.
In botanical nomenclature rules, the problem was solved by referring to
the specific name instead as the "specific epithet." An epithet is generally a linguistic attribute that qualifies another word or sentence, which
is actually the function of a specific epithet as it reflects back onto the
generic name. There are many bears in the genus *Ursus*, and the specific
epithet tells us exactly which bear is meant. The term "epithet" is much
less common in zoology and does not appear in the nomenclature rules.
In general texts on zoological naming, however, it is used fairly often for
linguistic precision. I will also use it here, whenever it comes down to the

difference between the species name as the binomial and the species name as the epithet.

The Devil in the Details

David's description of the giant panda shows us that under certain circumstances, the valid naming of a new species is not that complicated a process. This was the case in the nineteenth century, and it's no different in the twenty-first. The foundations of biological nomenclature are fundamentally simple, however more complex and detailed the standardized rules have become in many areas over the course of their 250-year history. The standardized binomial nomenclature—that is, the principle of naming species with a two-part name comprised of the generic name and specific name—can be traced back to Carl Linnaeus. Latin was the international language of European scientists in the Middle Ages, and well into the eighteenth century, the majority of scientific texts were written in Latin. This was also the case for books on herbs and other registers of flora and fauna, which started appearing in greater numbers following the invention of the printing press in the fifteenth century. Following contemporary linguistic convention, natural historians before Linnaeus used Latin names for plants and animals, many of which had been used by the Greek and Roman academics of antiquity. For example, *Crex*, the generic name of the corncrake, can be found in Aristotle's *Historia animalium*, but it wasn't formalized as a genus name until 1803 by ornithologist Johannes Matthäus Bechstein. *Crex* also happens to be a so-called onomatopoeic name, that is, one that aims to mimic the birdcall linguistically. These names will come up again later.

Into the early eighteenth century, as with *Crex*, many organisms were given uninominal names, which could be extended with an adjectival specific name as needed. In his 1555 bird book *Avium natura*, nature researcher Conrad Gessner named the coal tit *Parus ater* to distinguish it from other titmice, such as the Great Titmouse, *Parus major*, which we encountered in chapter 1. Both names, along with many other animal names that Gessner coined, remained in use into the eighteenth century, at which point Linnaeus and other nature researchers adopted them in their works, thereby validating the terms in the nomenclature. Gessner, however, also used three- and four-part names. For instance, he named the mallard *Anas fera torquata minor*, which amounts to "lesser wild duck with necklace." The

Figure 2.3
Carl Linnaeus in an oil painting by Alexander Roslin, 1775. National Museum of
Fine Arts, Stockholm, Sweden. Accession number NMGrh 1053. Transferred from
Gripsholm Castle, 1866. Nationalmuseum press photo.

reason behind such names was not just to assign a proper name as an unambiguous linguistic marker; it also had a diagnostic function. Polynomial names of this sort contained relevant, recognizable traits and thus served as quick descriptions of the respective species. With the further discovery of new species, the diagnoses became more elaborate, the names longer. Names could become polynomial to the point of no return, rendering them virtually unusable. The honeybee, for example, was known to some authors into the seventeenth century as *Apis pubescens, thorace subgriseo, abdomine fusco, pedibus posticis glabris utrinque margine ciliatis*. Literally, the "furry bee, grayish thorax, brownish abdomen, back legs smooth with hair on both sides," which isn't a bad quick description. Linnaeus truncated this diagnostic name to one as short as it is elegant, *Apis mellifera*, the "honey-bearing bee."

Just as a side note, these names have been extensively discussed. Linnaeus must have sensed that the meaning of the name *Apis mellifera* did not truly convey what defines a honeybee. Bees do not bear honey; rather, they carry the pollen and nectar they've gathered from the blossoms of plants. Honey is produced when the bees mingle this nectar with juices naturally produced in their bodies, then allowing the mixture to ripen in the honeycomb of the beehive. Thus, honeybees don't bear honey—they make it. For this reason, presumably, in his 1761 *Fauna Svecica*, a full catalog of the Swedish animal world, Linnaeus changed the honeybee name he had first published to *Apis mellifica*, the "honey-making bee." In terms of the name's meaning, this alteration was justifiable. However, it is important to emphasize that while the meaning of scientific names can be traced back linguistically, they are not necessarily tethered to their actual definition, which logically refers to a characteristic of the thing named. It certainly can be the case, and taxonomists will usually try to say something about the species they're naming in the names they assign. Should this attempt go sideways, the name will still fulfill its use as a linguistic reference to a species, as was the case with Linnaeus's honeybee. However incorrect the meaning of *Apus mellifera* may be, it is and always will be the first and thus oldest name ever given to our famous honeybee, meaning it will always remain the valid name. Unfortunately, a great many authors of the eighteenth and nineteenth centuries actually used *Apis mellifica*, whether because they didn't want to cast doubt on Linnaeus's authority and correction of his own "mistake" or found the name more fitting. To this day, the *mellifera-mellifica* conflict continues to haunt the bee world, despite priority long having been assigned the Linnaean *mellifera*.

Linnaeus was thus firmly rooted in the tradition of Latin scientific language. One of the key innovations of the Linnaean system—that which formed the foundation of its success—was its simplicity. Following a few basic principles, just about anyone could give an organism a Latin name and count on its permanence. Linnaeus's greatest service was therefore establishing the cogent standard used throughout most of his own works. Linnaeus first used this system for animals consistently in the tenth edition of *Systema Naturae* in 1758, and the publication of this work is thus considered the inception of today's nomenclature rules. To settle the matter clearly and conclusively, the understanding is that *Systema Naturae* was published on January 1, 1758. In accordance with the nomenclature rules, and with but a few exceptions, the names and authors published before 1758 are thus considered invalid, whereas all post-1758 count.

To this day, the simple principle of binomial species naming forms the backbone of the scientific naming process. Even before the backdrop of today's highly formalized and detailed rules, only a few elements are required for a name formulated according to these guidelines to become a valid scientific name—a description of the new species, to which no conditions regarding the extent or accuracy of details apply. The geographic origins are unarguably important and usually included in the species' description—and maybe additional information, such as lifestyle or the potential for confusion with other species, provided this information is available and desired. Get the lot printed and published, and before you know it, the name is in use, and you're the author. Eternity included.

The devil is, as always, in the details. Taxonomy, the science of species naming, isn't always so simple, after all, because any number of hindrances can get in the taxonomist's way. In the vast majority of cases, two particular problems must be eliminated before a new species can be described with a clear conscience. For one, there's the question as to whether it's actually an undescribed species. David had no doubts in this regard—with good reason. Thanks to their size and conspicuousness, large mammals are the object of a long-standing tradition of research and have, in many cases, already been discovered and reasonably well studied. This was already the case by the mid-nineteenth century. Although new mammal species will occasionally

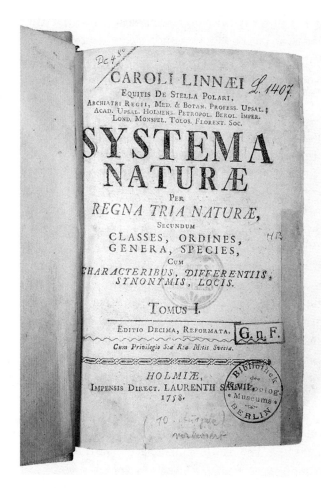

Figure 2.4

The title page of the tenth edition of Linnaeus' *Systema Naturae* from 1758. Library of the Museum für Naturkunde Berlin.

be described today, these are special and rare discoveries that often amount to zoological sensations. One example is the Vietnamese spindlehorn or saola, which was named *Pseudoryx nghetinhensis* after its characteristic horns were discovered in 1993 by the team of authors around Vu Van Dung.

The other hurdle that significantly complicates and slows the taxonomic exploration of the Earth's diverse organisms is the scientific names and descriptions that have already been published. Since 1758, new species have continuously been described, and, especially in older literature, these descriptions are often less detailed and well hidden. Thus, one must first track down every last name published in the literature since 1758 and then use the description to try to understand whether the newly found species might not have been discovered, described, and named in the past. This would be a problem because in cases of double namings—which the experts do their utmost to avoid, if chiefly for scientific reasons—it's the first name that counts. Fall into this trap, and bid eternal fame adieu. There was little to worry David in this regard, either. He knew the scope of the bear diversity in the region, and in his estimation, there was no chance of confusion with one of the other species, so he didn't have to pore endlessly over the literature, comparing his bear to the others. David was thus spared the bother of the two problems central to discovering and describing the planet's biodiversity. He could solve them without hesitation.

The majority of new zoological discoveries, however, are found in animal groups that aren't as well researched as mammals. Maintaining an overview and finding out which species names from the given animal group have already been published is anything but easy. A complete record of every species name ever published in the given animal group is an important foundation for the naming as well as the basis for approaching the ultimate goal of taxonomic work, namely, creating a complete picture of the group's actual diversity.

To achieve this complete taxonomic record, taxonomists and the other experts who describe, discover, and *know* the species will work hard, intensively, and often their whole life on a certain animal group. This intensive work with a narrow segment of the natural world makes taxonomists real authorities in their area, often even "world authorities." This amounts to saying that these people know more about their animal group than anyone else. If people want to know something about the taxonomy of a certain animal, it's only a matter of time before they arrive at such an authority. "World authority on booklice" isn't a conferred title or a job description. "Allow me to introduce myself: Dr. Miller, world authority on booklice" is nigh unthinkable. One achieves this status through endlessly inspecting the world of booklice, which includes reviewing all publications since 1758, visiting all the great booklice collections in the world, and constantly publishing on booklice. As Richard Fortey of the Natural History Museum in London has observed, world authority is "one of those titles that cannot be bought, nor traded, nor given away; it just arrives, like grey hair."

These specialists will often wear their unique competencies as a sort of honorary badge. The German woodlouse expert Christian Schmidt was introduced as the "Pope of Woodlice" in a daily newspaper. In large taxonomic research institutions such as the Berlin Museum für Naturkunde, as in other museums, there's the "bug guy" and the "fish guy." Some scenes are more specialized, so there might even be the "Carabidae guy," a specialist in ground beetles.

The Routes of Nomenclature

The typical process of scientific work in preparing a species description and naming is essentially as follows: gather all names for presumed close relatives of animal in question; reconstruct what our ancestors may have meant by these names; and, finally, compare own animal with the old original descriptions and, where possible, original specimen. It should then become clear whether one is looking at a new species and, if not, then which of the old names applies.

The first step unavoidably leads to the library—or let's say to the various places that store all the publications that have ever dealt with the animal group. This is not necessarily a library in the traditional sense. A significant amount of both historic and current taxonomic literature has been digitized in recent years and is available on the Internet. One of the best sources of historic literature on biodiversity is the Internet portal Biodiversity Heritage Library (BHL). A lot of zoological and botanical taxonomy literature can be found there in various digital formats, provided no rights held by publishers or authors restrict free online use. BHL has revolutionized access to old literature, allowing research and reading to occur beyond the library. But to save on time and effort, many taxonomists will still curate their own specialist libraries, in which they collect the untold masses of scientific articles on their subject—as hard to research as they are to find.

The goal of researching the literature is to achieve a total overview of the species that have already been described in the target group. Once they've all been gathered, or close, the comparison begins. One's own animals are compared to descriptions, line drawings and copperplate etchings, and everything the literature has to offer. However, they will also be compared to already classified animals. In this regard, classification is an established procedure in taxonomy, in which the research specimen is assigned a taxonomical name. With the statement, "this is a mouse," a name (from the English lexicon) assigned unambiguously to a certain rodent species is applied to a certain rodent individual. Even this is an act of classification, although it requires no more than basic prior knowledge of Hickory Dickory Dock. Classification in the scientific context functions in similar fashion, in that the scientific name one deems appropriate is "fastened" to the animal. In practice, this is literally what happens, in that the result of the classification—that is, the name—is written on a tag and carefully affixed to the animal.

Classification can occur on many levels. Even the most professional of museums are in possession of so-called unidentified material. This is a rather casual way of indicating that for these animals, the process of identification—which should ideally proceed to the level of species—got stuck somewhere along the way. It amounts to a collection of animals little is known about, beyond their being long-horned beetles, katydids, or flatworms, for example. Perhaps only the family or genus is identified, but there's usually something known about them. There may even be cases in which the taxonomy pros in a natural history museum don't get further in their classification than "animal," but those exceptions are rare. In 2003, for instance, a thirteen-ton, twelve-meter-wide mass of tissue washed up on the coast of Chile and made international headlines as the "Chilean blob." Similar "blobs" had been discovered on other coastlines, and sensational speculations were stirred up. Was it the enigmatic *Octopus giganteus* or some other mythical creature? In Chile, at least, there was no doubt as to the animal's provenance, but beyond that even marine biologists were baffled. A DNA test finally illuminated the case, and the seaside find could be determined definitively. It was a huge mass of decaying fat tissue of a dead sperm whale.

The most important point of reference in this process is the type specimen. Types or type specimens are the individual creatures that scientists lay out on their desks during the naming process and base their names on. In the case of Father David and the giant panda, in his original description of 1869, he verifiably examined and explicitly named two type specimens. The species name is irreversibly stuck to these type specimens. Strictly speaking, for the sake of clarity, the species name should apply to a single individual alone, but more on that later. In any case, it's inevitable that the original type specimen will be examined if the published description doesn't provide enough information for the species in question to be identified. The sample specimens are often scattered throughout museum collections around the world, which doesn't exactly make it easier to work with them. Type specimens in particular are increasingly being digitally documented, and for some animal groups, it's enough to examine high-resolution digital photos instead of the types themselves.

The second most important resource is the material identified by one of our "world authorities." These individual creatures—which our fictitious booklice expert, for example, has already examined and identified—are of huge significance to every other booklouse taxonomist who might be onto a new species. Although even the booklouse world authorities are not immune to making mistakes, one can expect a high level of reliability from the animals they identify. This is one of the reasons that it's important to write the author's name on the label.

Finally, in addition to everything else, the taxonomist requires as much other unidentified material as possible. The reason for this need is intraspecific variability. No individual is exactly the same as another. Through various processes, genetic information passed to the next generation is randomly modified and mixed in each individual, resulting in mostly small but sometimes bigger differences between organisms within a species. This variability is a significant, if not *the* most serious, disturbance to judging the differences between species. One could say that the art of taxonomy is the ability to discern between intra- and interspecific variability. One can always find differences between any two animals, but how big do these differences need to be for talk of two species to be justified? Or vice versa, how many differences should be tolerated for two animals to be rightly interpreted as elements of a shared species? These questions are probably the most salient and difficult that exist in taxonomy, and they can only be answered when the sample size is large. The more animals one views, the more deviations from the ideal are found, and the better one can judge the scale of variability within the species. Understandably, then, most taxonomists shy away from describing a species based on a single individual because the variability of the species naturally can't be assessed. Exceptional conditions must apply—that is, a unique trait must be evident that cannot possibly be connected by a string of transitions to another species, at least according to the rules of probability. Even if Father David had had only one panda, he wouldn't have wasted a moment in classifying it. The idea that, over a wide spectrum of variability, a bear this unique could be connected to some other known bear—in other words, that it could be an example of extreme intraspecific color variation of another species—appears utterly unlikely, given the panda's undeniable distinctiveness.

Unidentified material in collections is of interest to every taxonomist for yet another different, obvious reason. Undiscovered by past compilers, real treasures can be secreted away here, like as-yet-unknown species or the sorely missed other sex of a species that has already been described.

At this point, the specialist has gathered all relevant species descriptions, has compared his animals to them—along with all (or most) of the type specimens and the bulk of materials culled from museums worldwide—and has now developed a well-founded sense of which species exist and what their diagnostic characteristics are. All of these data, interpretations, and descriptions should ultimately yield a publication for one simple reason. An important taxonomic principle holds that, with regard to species descriptions and other taxonomic processes, only that which is published is considered valid. As a rule, even the information provided on the label of a type specimen is relevant to taxonomic decisions only after its publication. Publication—representing both painstaking scientific work and the legalization of taxonomic decisions—is the be-all and end-all of the taxonomic process. To get a publication on track, relevant information must be put down on paper or rather entered into a computer. Features are documented in the form of drawings, scanning electron microscopic images, and other representations; maps are created, tables written, and DNA sequences compiled in endless columns of letters.

A decision must now be made as to what each species is called (although in practice this typically occurs in tandem with the scientific examination). It's actually quite easy, at least in principle. For each new species, a holotype is selected from the array of individuals at hand. This designated individual will be the eternal name bearer of its species. Regardless of where the holotype ends up—that is, to which species it ultimately belongs—it will always carry its name with it. Should the species be divided, because it actually turns out to be two discrete species, the group the holotype belongs to will retain the old name, while the other species receives a new label. Today, holotypes must be officially determined, otherwise the description is not valid and the name not available. Should the scientist writing the description have a single individual available, this will automatically be the holotype. By contrast, if the type series consists of several specimens, then one will be chosen as the holotype, whereas the others become paratypes. Serving the function of name bearers, holotypes are of great significance to taxonomy and are considered the real treasures of natural history museum collections. They are the yardstick, the absolute benchmark for each respective species name. These species types make the great natural history museums what they are, famous and so critical to the study of biodiversity. It is thus expected that the species description include explicit mention of the types' final repository, and it is advised that this be a collection open to the public.

Availability versus Validity

At this juncture, the difference between the availability and validity of a name bears repeating. A name is valid after thorough scrutiny and the application of nomenclatural nuance show it to be the correct name for a species. To gain access to the testing machinery of the Code in the first place, however, a linguistic element—which we would like to use as a name— must fulfill certain basic conditions. This first hurdle is that of availability.

The most important requirement for a name to be considered available is, as already mentioned, publication. A special paragraph in the nomenclature rules is dedicated to outlining, in some detail, what counts as a publication. First and foremost, the use of the Latin alphabet is mandatory. Whether the description is written in Cyrillic script or Chinese characters, the taxonomic name must be formed entirely of Latin letters.

Another important requirement is that the name be traceable to a specific language, with traditional preference for Latin or Greek. An arbitrary combination of letters may also be allowed, "providing this is formed to be used as a word."[1] For instance, many species names originate in Aboriginal Australian languages, which produce combinations of letters in the Latin alphabet that, from our perspective, may appear unusual. Their linguistic derivation is verifiable, however, and the names are, by their nature, words. In contrast, an artificial combination of letters, such as "cbafgd," cannot be seen as a word or used as a name. Last but not least, in taxonomic work, where taxonomic decisions are being made, the principles of binomial nomenclature—that is, of two-part species names—must be implemented. Moreover, the generic and specific names must each consist of at least two letters. Add to that the many smaller rules that have been introduced over time to various editions of the Code. This means that names published at different times have been formed according to slightly different rules. Thus, somewhat different requirements existed for names published before 1931, after 1930, after 1960, and after 1999. For instance, the fourth edition of the Code (published in 1999) included the requirement that all new taxonomic names clearly be labeled as such. It was suggested that long-established Latin designations—such as "species nova" for "new species" and "genus novum" for "new genus"—be used. The corresponding abbreviations "sp. nov." or "sp. n." are now commonly used. Expressions in other languages, such as "new species," are also allowed. Other important changes first introduced in 1999 include the mandatory designation of holotypes and the explicit mention of type specimens' final homes.

And with that, the requirements regarding availability have essentially been addressed. Not that difficult a hurdle, really. The work thus having been completed, now comes the crowning moment of the process of species description: selecting the fitting name. Imagination is of the essence here because the scientists may now deviate from the strict parameters of pure science and indulge in their own preferences and proclivities. Taxonomists are more or less free to choose whatever name they please. This freedom, however, extends only to the selection of etymological meanings for the new name and the selection of words that best reflect the desired meaning. All other aspects of the formulation of the species name are strictly governed by the Code. No special characters may be used. Special characters include diacritical marks, ligatures—joined letters such as the German ß—along with every form of apostrophe and hyphen. In German, the most common diacritics are the umlauts ä, ö, and ü, as well as the diaereses ë and ï, which serve to split the pronunciation of two adjacent vowels. In other languages, special characters might include letters with dots, lines, hooks, or other glyphs, such as ç, á, ñ, and ø. Umlauts are replaced by their root letter without the umlaut, ligatures are dropped. The initial letters of species and subspecies names are always lowercase, while all other names start with an uppercase letter.

Species names are typically classically derived, and those that aren't are Latinized. This will impact the formation of names. A species name thus usually falls into one of the following word groups:

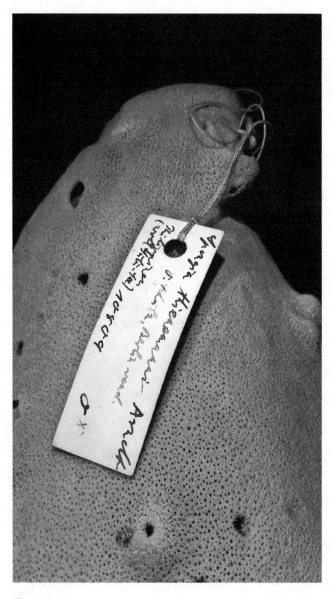

Figure 2.5
The tip of an upside-down "elephant ear" sponge with one of Walther Arndt's hand-written labels. Arndt described this species in 1943 as *Spongia thienemanni*, which is now considered a junior synonym of *Spongia agaricina* Pallas, 1766. Museum für Naturkunde Berlin, M. Ohl photo.

• An adjective or participle in the nominative singular case. Most species names belong to this group: *Echinus esculentus,* the edible sea urchin, and *Somatochlora metallica,* the brilliant emerald, a dragonfly.
• A noun in the nominative singular case that is in apposition to the genus name: *Cercopithecus diana,* or Diana monkey.
• A noun in the genitive case: *Myotis daubentonii,* Daubenton's bat, and *Diplolepis rosae,* the rose bedeguar gall.

This all sounds pretty complicated, and it would seem as though strong knowledge of Latin were crucial. Indeed, many taxonomists are unsure as to whether they really can create correct species names. The public considers scientific names a world of gobbledygook to which the uninitiated have no access. Far from it! The range of required Latin is minimal and simple to understand, and the details can be looked up in the appropriate books and online.

The challenge, then, is to figure out what the name should express. Is there a feature so distinct that the species should be named after it? Is the species' habitat or the type specimen's geographical origins interesting? Would I like to honor a colleague, a person close to me, or a generous donor in the form of a name? Or would I simply like to be unusual and use that to attract attention that classical names wouldn't get me?

First of all, the source word one would like to base the name on must be selected. Even without knowledge of Greek or Latin, it's possible to find the right word for any characteristic feature. Many books are available to search out the desired term and its classical equivalent. A truly extraordinary book intended for the verbalization of morphological forms is *Die Benennung der Organismen und Organe nach Größe, Form, Farbe und anderen Merkmalen* (*The Naming of Organisms and Organs According to Size, Shape, Color and Other Features,* not yet translated), by Leipzig-based zoologist Fritz Clemens Werner, published in 1970 and never reissued. In more than 550 pages, Werner works his way through every imaginable shape and color that could be used to describe morphological structures and provides the corresponding Latin and Greek word elements. Werner thus covers "Quantitative Features" (with chapter headings such as "Number of Organs," "Indefinite Designation of Numbers," "Numbers in Instances of Radial Symmetry," and "The Size of Organs Relative to Body Size"); "Shape Types" (shorter chapters here are named "Egg, Pear, Club" and "Pin, Wedge, Cone, Pyramids," for instance); "Concavity and Convexity of Surfaces" (such as "Convex

Formations" and "Hollow Spaces and Hollow Bodies"); and "Light, Color, Spots, and Markings" (with a four-page chapter dedicated to the color yellow alone). A real trove of descriptive words! Werner had already published *Wortelemente lateinisch-griechischer Fachausdrücke in der Biologie, Zoologie und vergleichenden Anatomie* (*Word Elements of Latin and Greek Specialist Terms in Biology, Zoology, and Comparative Anatomy*, not yet translated) in 1956, the ninth edition of which was released in 2003 and which remains an important reference book for biologists and physicians. In *Word Elements*, Werner starts with the classical word component and then provides its meaning in German with the aid of numerous examples. Should one want to know the meaning of classically formed taxonomical names and biological specialist terms, Werner's *Word Elements* is the book of choice. *The Naming*, meanwhile, is enormously helpful when one wants to create descriptive names based on Greek or Latin word components.

More broadly conceived is Roland Wilbur Brown's *Composition of Scientific Words*, which first appeared in 1927 and is still available in reprints of the updated 1956 edition. It is a lexical list of all the words that seemed important to Brown in the context of scientific nomenclature, whether in English, Latin, or Greek. Every word is followed by a more or less lengthy list of synonyms in Latin and Greek, each coupled with an explanation in English. In contrast to Werner's *Naming*, his word choice includes not only morphological terms, but many contemporary terms, such as "earring," "glass," and "difference," as well. All words that may certainly assume their legitimate spot as building blocks for species names. These and other catalogs of classical terms and their definitions also help in understanding the etymological meaning of already published words.

Thus, with some knowledge of the appropriate vocabulary, fitting names can be cobbled together pretty quickly and without too many problems. To be fair, in moments of doubt, one might have to spend a little time deciphering Latin declension tables, but this truly is rare. Many linguistic anomalies, such as linking elements in some compound words, are even included in the nomenclature rules. A little stamina and the right books are all it takes to solve most problems, and when there's just no hope, professional taxonomists at one of the natural history museums can sometimes help.

Geographical names such as *Blattella germanica*, the German cockroach, are usually self-explanatory, unless, of course, the expressions for place or country have been drawn from the classical Latin and are no longer used in this form. For example, the Portuguese slug is named *Arion lusitanicus*, where the specific name *lusitanicus* refers to Portugal. Species names such as *africanus*, *californicus*, *asiaticus*, and *australiensis* are also easily understood today. In these cases, the names are used adjectivally and must match the gender of the genus name: *canadensis* is masculine and feminine, whereas the neuter is *canadense*.

An important and popular category of species names is that of patronyms, or names in honor of one or more people. More popular than ever today are humorous or otherwise peculiar names that have little or nothing to do with the species named, but more on those later.

Not only have we now wrapped up the description of the new species, we have found an attractive new name formed according to the nomenclature rules and published the lot—making every effort to revisit the nomenclature rules anew to avoid any unexpected problems from surfacing. From the moment the publication appears, one is now the author of a new name and may bask in the glow of fame. The whole process requires thoroughness and persistence in research, robust collections for specimen comparisons, and something of a feel for morphological forms. The naming itself, though, calls for something much different: a feel for language can help, but extensive reference texts, a broad overview of the most important nomenclature rules, and a healthy dose of imagination can help make naming a matter that is more joyful than difficult.

Moreover, even the simplest species descriptions take time—often a surprisingly long time, and that's because of the published names, which represent the real obstacle to taxonomic work. The oldest names from the latter half of the eighteenth and early nineteenth centuries, in particular, are often accompanied by descriptions considered inadequate by today's standards, which often make it incredibly difficult or even impossible to match these names with specific species. Species were often accidentally described multiple times, and as frequently, the same names were used multiple times for different species. In many cases, the original spelling no longer conforms to today's rules and must be changed. These and other problems make it anything but easy to determine the valid name for the many species that have been described and named in the past. As a reminder, an available name, one that abides by certain conditions of the nomenclature rules, is not necessarily also the valid name. What's more, the question of a name's validity can be decided only between those names that have already passed the availability test.

Probably the most important standard governing the validity of scientific names is the principle of priority. Basically, the priority thing is pretty straightforward. A taxon's oldest name is always the valid one. This sounds simpler than it is, though. First and foremost, the species names in question must be clearly dated. In journals today, publication dates are provided automatically to the day, which was not the case in the eighteenth century. As a rule, an indication of the year suffices, although synonyms will sometimes appear within the same year, in which case a more precise date is required. Should it prove impossible to extract the month or even day of publication from the work itself, notices of receipt from libraries can help, at least in determining a date by which the book in question must have been published.

The most common occasions for pondering nomenclatural priority are instances of synonymy, that is, when different names have been given to the same taxon. Speaking of taxon—taxa in the plural. This term, frequently used in biology, is also embedded in the word "taxonomy." Biologists tend to use the term as a general placeholder for any imaginable grouping of organisms, whether known or not. Mammals are a taxon, and the three-toed sloth is a taxon. Even the worms that Linnaeus labeled "Vermes" are a taxon, although biologists today agree that this grouping of animals was rather arbitrary. It unites the basic worm form, but this has emerged independently, and in any number of ways, over the course of the organisms' evolution.

But back to synonyms. On their own merits, synonyms are mistakes that can have many different causes. New research material can provide new information about the extent of intraspecific variability, with the result that what was once considered two discrete species turns out to be extreme outliers of one and the same species. Not infrequently, different life stages or sexes of a species will be described as distinct species. This comes as little surprise if one considers how different the caterpillar and winged stages of a butterfly are, for example. When it comes down to it, though, many species have been described multiple times simply because the one scientist didn't know about another scientist's species description or because there are differing opinions concerning what defines a species. Synonymy of this sort has to be caught, first, by scientists running a taxonomic review of species.

Because it does actually represent the scientific hypothesis taxonomists propose following their own assessment and painstaking substantiation—suggesting the identical nature of taxa hitherto believed to be two separate species—this is known as subjective synonymy. Because subjective synonymy exists, it stands to reason that objective synonymy would, too. This signifies the truly rare cases in which two different species descriptions exist for the same source material. As both descriptions pertain to the same individuals, they undoubtedly and objectively refer to the same biological taxon. Whether the synonym is subjective or objective, the principle of priority applies to both. This means that when in doubt, the older name will also be the valid one.

It's a similar situation for homonyms—that is, the same names for different species. In cases of homonymy, the older name also takes precedence, while the name of the younger species becomes void. Should the junior homonym have served as the valid name for its species, the principle of priority requires that it be replaced by the next junior synonym for the species, but only if such a synonym exists. If this isn't the case, then the revising authors may think up an ersatz name, an entirely new scientific name that becomes available with them as the author. As it happens, this is a remarkably simple way to arrive at one's own species names, without having once set eyes on any of the animals in question. If one were to stumble on an unresolved homonym in a catalog, then one could (if one wanted) publish a new species name as a replacement for the junior homonym, requiring no more action than citing the state of the literature. Some scientists really do this, combing through taxonomic catalogs in the targeted search for such inconsistencies, and they almost always find something. This kind of replacement-name-bricolage—performed by scientists who don't necessarily know much about the respective animal groups beyond the files—is frowned upon in the guild.

Homonyms, like synonyms, can be split into primary and secondary categories. A primary homonym is a name that was originally described in a genus that already contained the given species name. Secondary homonyms, on the other hand, appear when the species in question is later moved into a different genus than it was originally ascribed.

This all sounds quite complicated, and when cases crop up in which synonyms and homonyms bleed together for a single species, it's a struggle to maintain an overview. An example to illustrate:

In 1787, entomologist Johann Christian Fabricius described a digger wasp species he named *Crabro sabulosus*. The same year, however, Johann Friedrich Gmelin, another well-known entomologist, hypothesized that *Crabro sabulosus* would be better placed in the genus *Sphex*. The resultant new name combination *Sphex sabulosus* already existed, however, authored by Linnaeus in 1758. In this instance of secondary homonymy, two substitution names were directly suggested, namely, *Sphex ruficornis* by Charles Joseph de Villers in 1789 and *Sphex crabronea* two years later by Carl Peter Thunberg. In retrospect, both substitutions were superfluous: *Crabro sabulosus* actually belongs to the genus *Mellinus*, meaning there was no secondary homonymy in the first place. These unnecessary replacement names are thus simply ignored, meaning the species should actually be called *Mellinus sabulosus*. According to another rule of the Code, however, junior homonyms introduced before 1961 (in this case, *sabulosus*) are forever invalid and cannot be changed to be made valid. This means that the replacements that Villers and Thunberg suggested for *Crabro sabulosus*, which were unjustifiable in the first place, have led to the eternal and unalterable invalidity of this name. *Mellinus sabulosus* is thus also out of the running as a valid name. In these situations, the string of valid names is reviewed to determine whether the junior name next in line might be viable. That would be *Sphex ruficornis* Villers, 1789, which is a junior primary homonym of a different name, however, namely, *Sphex ruficornis* Fabricius, 1775. Next in line of priority is *Sphex crabronea* Thunberg, 1791, which is not only valid as a replacement name, but also doesn't conflict with any other names. *Sphex crabronea* is clearly the oldest available name for this species and thus the valid option. Because this species definitely belongs to the genus *Mellinus*, however, the ending of the specific epithet must be changed from feminine to male. The correct name for this species, then, is *Mellinus crabroneus* (Thunberg, 1791).

It's easy to see that historical names present potential obstacles to the taxonomic identification process. Problems with homonyms are relatively manageable because in reviewing the literature, one can usually spot and often solve them. By contrast, subjective synonyms present the greatest difficulty because the revising author—that is, the individual taking on the confused history of the correct name—must provide clarity as to what the various authors had in mind with their respective species names. In other words, which species the respective names refer to. The original description of each species is the first source for relevant information, but in most cases nothing can be accomplished without revisiting the type specimen, at least not if one wants to gain 100 percent certainty. This means going on the search for the type specimen in question, which is no simple task, especially when considering historic species descriptions. It's worth erring on the side of safety in these cases and securing the entirety of the type specimen for review. Did the original author really have just the one animal that automatically became the holotype? Or did he actually have access to two or even more animals for reference while writing the species description? And do they really all belong to one species or, in fact, to several? Only once these questions have been resolved and the species ID of the type specimen secured can a scientist substantiate possible subjective synonymy and introduce the appropriate measures for solving it.

The "International Code of Zoological Nomenclature" is not a particularly engaging document. Rules, paragraphs, and formalisms line up and try to catch every potential case of conflict, but one needs it to create new names that comply with the rules. Plenty of nomenclatural moments of doubt abound for names that already exist, and finding the paragraph in the Code that applies to each individual instance is a challenge. The search is fruitless often enough as it is. As a taxonomist, one always bumps up against borderline cases that aren't covered in the Code, whether in total or in part. In these moments, online forum discussions with competent colleagues can help. The responses may be far from unanimous, but it's comforting to see that the nomenclature rules drive others to the brink, too.

Naming Rights for Sale

To the taxonomist, the act of naming is much more than putting one's knowledge of nature into writing and carrying out formal nomenclatural requirements. In naming a species, one adds not only another entry to the catalog of life, but one's own name, as well, which will remain inextricably tied to the coinage for eternity. The taxonomist holds the copyright of the new discovery, given the combination of assigning the species name—the culminating point of a complex hypothesis on nature—and adding one's own name. The new species is "his" or "her" species. There's no question that the fame which comes along with authoring a new species has limited reach. Beyond a handful of close colleagues and maybe an individual

International Commission on Zoological Nomenclature

INTERNATIONAL CODE
OF ZOOLOGICAL NOMENCLATURE

Fourth Edition

adopted by the
International Union of Biological Sciences

The provisions of this Code supersede those of the previous editions
with effect from 1 January 2000

ICZN

ISBN 0 85301 006 4

Figure 2.6
The title page of the fourth edition of the "International Code of Zoological Nomen-
clature." Courtesy of the International Commission of Zoological Nomenclature,
Thomas Pape. Library of the Museum für Naturkunde Berlin.

honored with a patronym, few will take note of it. Given the multitude of
taxonomic descriptions, it's the nature of the beast that authors will eventually become eclipsed by their own name.

And yet. Few other expressions of scientific effort point so clearly, and
in so few words, to their creators. These authors command an open space
that they may shape linguistically, independent of external forces, which is
generally so rare within the natural sciences. Time and again, the choice of
a name represents the emotional apogee of taxonomic work.

It is therefore all the more remarkable that in some instances the choice and creation of scientific names can be separated from their formal description and publication. Years ago, taxonomists came up with the idea to relinquish naming rights to other people, although they would remain the formal authors of the name. They naturally don't do this without something in return, and this something in return is typically—and despicably—money.

More than twenty years ago, the first taxonomists realized that the basic idea of patronyms was something they could develop in a strategic way: a patron donates money toward an expedition or research proposal, and in return, a species is named after him or her. Given the massive backlog of undescribed species in the world's museums, taxonomists are in the favorable position of having undescribed species to offer up front. The sponsors pick out their favorite and choose the species name. The discovering scientists then make it compatible with nomenclature rules and official through publication. The taxonomists hold onto the fame of the discovery and description, and the donors bask in the awareness and permanence of the scientific name they've chosen: a win-win arrangement.

Any taxonomist could organize one of these "naming rights auctions" on their own. By 1999, however, the German organization BIOPAT had been founded, which makes undescribed species available to donors. Rates start at 2,600 euros per species, and the price tag increases sharply for popular animal and plant groups like mammals or orchids. In exchange, the sponsors receive the naming right, a certificate, and a receipt of charitable giving for the tax authority. The collected donations are used in part to aid in the taxonomic research performed by the scientists involved, and the other half goes to protecting biodiversity in the new species' native lands. By its own account, BIOPAT had raised 620,000 euros by 2013 following this model.

On the BIOPAT homepage, visitors can surf through a catalog of undescribed species as well as a list of species that have already found sponsors. Charismatic organisms like orchids and hummingbirds are naturally among the most popular, and donors tend to choose personal names, dedicated to someone close to them. For instance, there's a Malagasy frog named *Mantidactylus charlotteae*, a Turkmen mining bee called *Andrena lehmannii*, an Indonesian diving beetle *Neptosternus viktordulgeri*, and a Brazilian scorpion *Tityus martinpaechii*.

Among the ranks of name sponsors are also a few celebrities. Stan Vlasimsky, a successful businessman, saw to the naming of an orchid, two frog species, a butterfly, and a weevil for his wife and children. A small financial investment for him but presumably accompanied by the satisfaction of being included in the honorable register of conservationists. There's an African orchid species called *Polystachia anastacialynae* in honor of the American musician Anastacia Lyn Newkirk. A former Soviet head of state was similarly honored with a patronym. For his seventieth birthday, a close family friend presented him with *Maxillaria gorbatschowii*, a Bolivian orchid.

A whole other category of name sponsors are companies that like to put their dedication to conservation efforts on display. The Danfoss Group, a corporation active in the area of heat engineering, adopted a mouse lemur from Madagascar—barely the size of a hamster—that is now called *Microcebus danfossi*. The organic food company Vitaquell sponsored a Colombian hummingbird named *Thalurania vitaquelli*. A Vietnamese gecko, whose discovery was documented by the German TV program *Abenteuer Wissen* ("Science Adventure"), received the name *Gekko scientiadventura*.

BIOPAT is a success story and the only organization worldwide that manages the "sale" of species names in such a professional manner. Around 150 sponsorships have been brokered since the site's launch in 1999, and the rate of sale currently swings between five and ten names per year. The two key players at BIOPAT, Claus Bätke and Jörn Köhler, both have other careers and manage the sponsorship program on the side. As such, their resources are limited in public relations and spreading the word. Times were different in 2000, a year after BIOPAT's founding, when everyone was talking about it and the media couldn't get enough. Fifty species changed hands that year. Those days are gone.

Since then, many natural history museums, universities, and conservation organizations worldwide have conceived similar models. They tend to focus on marketing the taxonomic treasures their own scientists have discovered. Between insect posters and t-shirts, the Bohart Museum of Entomology at the University of California, Davis offers the opportunity to acquire a new insect species—that is, to name it. Under the product description, background information on the principles and value of species naming is provided, and if the product and $2,000 price tag are agreeable, the buyer clicks "Add to Cart" and pays the balance via PayPal. The Bohart Museum scientists and the buyer then discuss the rest privately.

A number of exceptional purchases or auctions of species have found their way into the press, whether because of an exorbitant price or because celebrities were involved. In 2005, a new shrimp species was discovered off the southwestern coast of Australia, the naming rights for which were sold through the online auction site eBay. The former pro basketball player Luc Longley won with his bid of $2,900 and named the new species *Lebbeus clarehanna*, after his daughter Clare Hanna Longley. Clare received this name sponsorship as a gift for her fifteenth birthday. The initiative had been spearheaded by an Australian student at the University of Melbourne, who was looking to use the eBay auction to acquire financial support for the Australian Marine Conservation Society.

In 2007, entomologists discovered an unusual, undescribed Mexican butterfly species in the collection at the Florida Museum of Natural History. It sold at auction to an anonymous bidder for $40,800 and was named after Margery Minerva Blythe Kitzmiller of Ohio on behalf of her five grandchildren.[2] Its scientific name is *Opsiphanes blythekitzmillerae*.

The most spectacular naming deal to date, however, remains the naming of a new Bolivian titi monkey species in 2005. A number of years earlier, two biologists had discovered the unknown monkey species in Bolivia's Madidi National Park. Like many other parks, Madidi National Park is under the constant threat of illegal logging. To maintain its current condition, the park administration requires about $550,000 per year. In cooperation with the Wildlife Conservation Society, British biologist Robert Wallace decided to auction off the naming rights for the new monkey to secure a significant sum in support of the park. The anonymous auction led to much publicity, and many Fortune 500 companies—that is, the 500 highest-selling companies in the United States—were in the bidding. The winner was the online casino GoldenPalace.com, which acquired the naming rights for $650,000. The people in power at the casino chose the scientific name *Callicebus aureipalatii*, in which the specific name means "of the Golden Palace," and the animal is commonly known as the GoldenPalace.com monkey.

Not surprisingly, this auction in particular sparked an international discussion among taxonomists and conservationists, not least because of all things an online casino had the winning bid. There was talk of scientific ideals selling out and the purchasability of taxonomy. Protest was mild, however, and its effects short-lived. Many institutions and museums worldwide now offer the sale or auction of naming rights, but these play a minimal role in financing taxonomic research and conservation projects.

Spectacular events like the GoldenPalace.com monkey auction are rare occurrences but do reach a lot of people through their enormous publicity, attracting attention to both conservancy issues and the fact that new animal species are still being discovered today. For all the criticism surrounding it, this form of species naming is still accepted doubtless because of the inherent quality control given the requirement of scientific publication to make the name officially available. Many critics fear that scientists could become tempted, out of commercial interests, to start seeing species where there aren't any, and to offer up species that wouldn't pass a scientific review. This isn't beyond the realm of possibility, but even without this aspect, the quality of a species description hinges on many factors, such as the publication organ.

Fame from the Shadows of the Species

Many questions still remain unanswered. Winning an auction or making a donation may secure the winner or donor the right to decide on a species name. But does this include the responsibility that the new species name be valid? What happens if the expensive and personally named species turns out to be a synonym for another, already known species? The name bought at auction would of course remain available, but it would no longer be valid, thus receding into the shadow of the valid name. Is there a return policy for cases like this? It's unclear how dissatisfied buyers would react. Providers of undescribed species would do well to select only those that are likely to be truly undescribed and ultimately able to keep their status as a "good" name.

It is honorable to be the author of a new species, although this fame is usually contained within small circles. Although the wider public hardly recognizes scientific names—even those of well-known animal species—the authors of the same go utterly unnoticed. Some might know what's hidden behind *Canis lupus*, *Corvus corax*, *Mus musculus*, *Gorilla gorilla*, and *Rattus norvegius*, but who were the authors? Answer key: wolf, raven, and house mouse first appeared in Carl Linnaeus's 1758 *Systema Naturae*, the gorilla was described by Thomas Staughton Savage and Jeffries Wyman in 1847, and John Berkenhout named the common rat in 1769.

Yet—at least for those in the know and the authors—a little bit of their fame radiates from their place in the shadow of the species. Not only did they succeed in recognizing a natural species—the product of millions of years of evolutionary development existing entirely without human involvement—but they also managed to wrest it from the darkness of disregard through the act of naming. A species first takes on the form of existence after its name is published and it is introduced to human perception, albeit usually in the form of scientific attention. The name allows the multitudes to be shaped into digestible pieces. This is truly something to be proud of, at least a little bit.

Father Armand David was proud of his discovery, truly proud. Relinquishing the fame of having named the giant panda to someone else, even if that someone else was Alphonse Milne-Edwards, was out of the question. With only slight effort and in compliance with the most necessary nomenclatural criteria, David irrevocably secured ownership of this unique animal's name.

The giant panda was not the only zoological anomaly attributed to David, although he didn't describe it himself. *Elaphurus davidianus*, the well-known Père David's deer or milu, is named after David; the tale of its discovery is certainly gripping. By the second century AD, the handsome Père David's deer, which was originally found in China, Korea, and Japan, is believed to have been decimated in the wild through overhunting. The last of these animals living in the wild were likely wiped out in the seventeenth or eighteenth century. Over the course of several centuries, however, a herd more than 100 strong had been kept for meat and the emperor's

Figure 2.7
A starfish specimen (*Paulia horrida* Gray, 1840). Museum für Naturkunde Berlin, M. Ohl photo.

hunting pleasure in Nan Hai-tsu, the imperial game reserve outside Peking. The park, surrounded by a perimeter wall seventy-two kilometers in length, was heavily guarded by Tartars, and no one was permitted to so much as look into the park. Four years before the discovery of the panda, David bribed the Tartar guards and climbed onto the wall of Nan Hai-tsu, and there he saw them, an impressive herd of 120 large stags and does. Given their unusual antlers, David first thought them to be an unknown reindeer species. He learned their Chinese name, *Sze-pu-hsiang*, from the guards, along with the information that killing one of the deer was punishable by death. But David knew that Chinese bone carvers traded in small carvings of *Sze-pu-hsiang* antlers. Perhaps the Tartar guards were secretly hunting the deer and selling their antlers to the carvers. In late 1865, at David's insistence, the French delegation staged an appeal to the appropriate imperial offices for the acquisition of a *Sze-pu-hsiang*. In vain. David decided to take things into his own hands. He bribed the guards at Nan Hai-tsu again, and in January of 1866, he walked away with two complete Père David's deerskins in his possession. He sent both skins, along with a detailed letter, to Henri Milne Edwards, Alphonse's father. Before the skins even reached Paris, France's plea was granted. By order of the Chinese emperor, Imperial Minister Hen-Chi presented the French embassy with three living deer. These died on the sea voyage to France, nevertheless contributing to the five animals Milne Edwards received overall and that served as the basis for his 1866 description of Père David's deer, or *Elaphurus davidianus*. A small error slipped through, however. Although David had mentioned in his letter that the Chinese name was *Sze-pu-hsiang*, Milne Edwards claimed in his piece that the Père David's deer was known in China as the milu. This detail was presumably based on other sources regarding Chinese deer names. In doing so, Milne Edwards overlooked the fact that "milu" referred to the much smaller and common sika deer, which had been discovered and described by Dutch naturalist Coenraad Jacob Temminck in 1838. Milne Edwards's description sparked huge international interest in the Père David's deer, and Imperial Minister Hen-Chi received requests for living animals from all over the world. In next to no time, Milne Edwards's erroneous use of "milu" had become so popular that it is still in use today. By 1869, the London zoo had two living Père David's deer to show the public, and a few years later, the Berlin and Paris zoos had several of their own, and merrily they bred, such that many zoos soon had baby animals to admire.

It initially appeared as though David's adventurous discovery would ultimately lead to the survival of the endangered deer species through the many groups breeding in zoos worldwide, but that's not what happened. In 1895, the region south of Peking was visited by a devastating flood that also partially destroyed Nan Hai-tsu park. Many deer died in the flood or escaped the park, whereupon they were killed by the starving population. About twenty to thirty deer survived the catastrophe, only to be slaughtered and eaten by troops in the "international expeditionary corps" sent to fight the Chinese in the Boxer Rebellion of 1900–1901. A single doe survived the Boxer Rebellion and died of natural causes in 1920. The Père David's deer could thus be considered extinct in its original habitat. And the European deer? None of the zoos' breeding groups, which had grown far too old, survived the First World War. The fate of the species appeared sealed.

However, thanks to Duke of Bedford, considered one of the great English conservationists, among other environmental feats, large populations of European bison still exist today, but that's another story. The Duke had the impression that the Père David's deer was not doing well in either the Peking or European zoos. He therefore purchased eighteen young animals from different zoos over time and relocated them to his park at Woburn Abbey. Because the animal was originally at home in swampland, which many zoos either didn't know or simply ignored, the deer flourished in the marshy hollows surrounding the estate, and the group grew to an impressive seventy animals. After the Père David's deer had been considered extinct, following the debacle in China and the collapse of the European breeding groups, the Duke presented his herd to some incredulous zoologists. He sold animals to various zoos, including the Hagenbeck animal park in Hamburg. Despite several setbacks during World War II, Père David's deer that stem from Woburn Abbey can be found around the world today. Some of these British animals were even brought to Beijing, where they formed the foundation for later reintroduction initiatives. In 2005, after the international studbook registered 1,300 Père David's deer globally, 1,000 of which were living in their original Chinese habitat, the survival of *Elaphurus davidianus* was considered secured.

Between the giant panda and the Père David's deer, Father Armand David, the enterprising explorer of China, thus counts as having discovered two large mammals that humans first drove to the verge of extinction but whose rescue was then made possible through human intervention.

3 Words, Proper Names, Individuals

Henry Fairfield Osborn, renowned paleontologist and proponent of evolution, was born in 1857, two years before the publication of Charles Darwin's *Origin of Species* elevated the study of fossils as a key to unraveling the mystery of evolution. He began his scientific career in the heady 1870s, studying under Edward Drinker Cope, whom we will encounter in chapter 4. In the following decades, Osborn made a name for himself through his discoveries of several charismatic dinosaur species, including *Tyrannosaurus rex* and *Velociraptor mongoliensis*. By 1908 he was appointed president of the American Museum of Natural History in New York.

Around that time, an enterprising young fellow named Roy Chapman Andrews entered the employ of the museum. An autodidact, he had trained himself in the art of taxidermy with the dream of a career at the august institution. However, with no vacancies at that time for someone of his qualifications, he instead took a job there as a janitor, in his spare time studying zoology at Columbia University and preserving animal specimens for the museum.

Andrews, however, always aspired for glory beyond the toil of the dusty laboratory. In fact, Andrews had already planned and led a research trip to Asia himself: from 1916 to 1917, he had conducted a zoological expedition with his wife to Yunnan and other Chinese provinces. Mongolia seemed a promising destination for a major undertaking—it just hadn't been explored enough yet.

Meanwhile, President Osborn, taking stock of accumulated fossils and paleontological reports, trying to make sense of it all, had formulated a grand theory of his own: dinosaurs, mammals, and even humans all had their origins in a single geographic region—Central Asia, particularly Mongolia—and had spread out over the earth from there. So far there was a

Figure 3.1
The type specimen of *Scomber minutus*, a species of toothpony described in 1795 by Marcus Élieser Bloch, which today belongs to the genus *Gazza*. Museum für Naturkunde Berlin, M. Ohl photo.

Figure 3.2
Roy Chapman Andrews in the Mongolian desert during one of his expeditions. Courtesy of the Library of the American Museum of Natural History, New York, image #411083.

dearth of relevant fossils Osborn could have used to prove his "Central Asia theory." Beyond a single rhinoceros tooth, there were no known vertebrate fossils from this region.

No surprise, then, that when Andrews approached him one spring day in 1920 with a proposal to lead an expedition to Outer Mongolia, Osborn leapt at the chance to finally substantiate his theory through extensive field research. Over lunch, Andrews detailed his plans for a large-scale, systematic expedition. In addition to interesting dinosaur and mammal fossils, he hoped to find evidence of human life to support the "Out of Asia" theory. At that time, Outer Mongolia remained largely unexplored by Westerners, given the harsh conditions of the Gobi Desert as well as dangerous political instability. Sending a big scientific expedition there was a daring endeavor, a risk Osborn was willing to take.

Andrews began the laborious preparations, and on April 22, 1921, a caravan of Dodge automobiles, horses, and camels set out from the Chinese city of Kalgan—Zhangjiakou today—passing through the gate in the Great Wall. This was the first in a series of outrageously successful research expeditions the American Museum of Natural History led into Outer Mongolia, the last of which took place in 1930. In several popular accounts of his adventures through Asia, Andrews stole the show. In his trademark distressed brimmed hat, usually in combination with a rifle, ammunition belt, and 0.38 Colt, he certainly cut a dashing figure, and there is much to suggest that he served as the inspiration for Indiana Jones.

Egg Thief Exonerated

A personal success for Andrews (who was appointed director of the museum in 1934), in scientific terms the five total expeditions to the Gobi Desert led to the large-scale discovery of mammal and dinosaur fossils, as well as a great many dinosaur eggs. All of the fossils dated back to the Late Cretaceous, the last period of the Mesozoic that began about 145 million years ago and ended 65 million years ago with the mass extinction event to which the dinosaurs also fell victim. One of the most spectacular finds was the partial skeleton of a dinosaur with a damaged skull, discovered directly beside a nest of about fifteen eggs. In 1924, Osborn described this dinosaur as part of a new genus, *Oviraptor*, the new species receiving the name *Oviraptor philoceratops*. The new genus name was a combination of the Latin words "ovum" (egg) and "raptor" (thief) because Osborn concluded that he had an egg thief on his hands given the saurian's proximity to the nesting place. He further concluded that the eggs belonged to *Protoceratops*, a member of Ceratopsia, the group that also includes the well-known three-horned *Triceratops*. Through its Greek prefix philo-, the species name was meant to express "*Ceratops*-loving." The meddlesome egg thief was thought to have met his end at the intervention of the selfless *Protoceratops* parents striving to protect their clutch. This discovery made great waves in New York. Hokey representations popped up all over the city, depicting the domestic bliss of *Protoceratops* couples forced to defend their brood from the predatory egg thief. A representative diorama was constructed in the American Museum of Natural History, the press releases kept rolling out, and even movie theater news reels reported on the valiant battle of *Protoceratops* versus *Oviraptor*, prehistoric good versus prehistoric evil.

Figure 3.3

A furious *Segnosaurus* mother is chasing an *Oviraptor* with a stolen egg from her nest. Postal stamp from Azerbaijan. Personal library M. Ohl.

It wasn't just the noteworthy physical proximity of *Oviraptor* to the eggs that suggested egg theft. The admittedly poorly preserved skull has a mighty beak that appears well suited to cracking hard egg shells. Even in the original description, however, Osborn expressed some doubt regarding the egg-thief hypothesis: it could very well be, he wrote, that the *Oviraptor's* unique skull shape was misleading and had nothing to do with eggs.

It wasn't until the 1990s that Osborn's doubts were confirmed. On an excursion to the Gobi Desert, again under the auspices of the American Museum of Natural History, one of the expedition vehicles broke down. While stranded about 300 kilometers away from where the first *Oviraptor* had been found, American paleontologist Mark Norell and his team discovered a dinosaur nest similar to the original find. One of the fossils preserved a young hatchling, which to their surprise could easily be identified as an *Oviraptor*. Suspicions were confirmed when another nest was discovered, on which a grown *Oviraptor* had been roosting like a modern-day bird. It was thus clear that the *Oviraptor* was by no means an egg thief; instead it had perished while caring for its own clutch.

Oviraptor, that repugnant egg thief, clearly has the wrong name. This theme has been picked up occasionally by popular media. In James Gurney's best-selling picture book *Dinotopia: The Land Apart from Time*, the *Oviraptor* is thus renamed *Ovinutrix*, which essentially means "caregiver of eggs." In the weekly German newspaper *Die Zeit*, science editor Andreas Sentker posed the question: "After honor restored, will infamous name be wiped from register of evolution?"

Of course not, systematic biologists and taxonomists would reply. Gurney may well have the freedom to name the falsely accused as he chooses in *Dinotopia*. The name *Oviraptor*, however, was given in the context of the scientific description of a biological unit through a formal and binding act of naming, much like children being named at birth. Human names usually have a definition and linguistic history, too, and these don't necessarily have anything to do with their carrier. The name Felix, for example, means "lucky," even if the fellow bearing the name is jinxed. The same applies to unwise women named Sophia or flighty men named Peter. The dissonance is even greater with surnames. Someone named Baker needn't be involved with baking, and Mr. Fisher may not have caught a single fish in his life. Clearly, then, human names are not to be understood as descriptors of the people they identify.

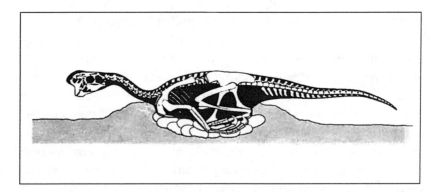

Figure 3.4
According to the authors of the publication titled "A nesting dinosaur," this image shows a nest-caring *Oviraptor* mother "shortly before death." Reprinted by permission from Macmillan Publishers Ltd: NATURE (vol. 379, Norell, M. A., Clark, J. M., Chiappe, L. M. Dashzeveg, D. A nesting dinosaur), copyright 1995.

Yet how does this play out in biology? The name *Oviraptor* was assigned with the explicit intent to reflect a certain characteristic of the creature named. Could this be considered flawed naming that must be corrected? In other words, is the correlation between name and named in biology different from what it is for humans? Or do names function in both contexts as simple labels that refer to the object named in arbitrary linguistic units? These questions lead to the general problem of what names in biology actually are from a linguistic standpoint. Do they even qualify as names? If not, what part of speech are they? What consequences does this have for usage, whether from a linguistic or biological stance?

Once an *Oviraptor*, Always an *Oviraptor*

Data gathered through empirical research and observation usually stands at the forefront in biology. Biologists can therefore often overlook the central role that language actually plays in scientific practices. In the context of scientific language usage, the central question for scientists—in this case, the speakers—is how clear they can make themselves through language. How can they relay their data, results, and interpretations to others? Names are a linguistic element that carry more weight in biology than in any other natural science. Species—as the products of evolution and extremely important units of generalization in biology—play a central role in the study of nature. Statements about species can be presented with the help of scientific language, and a significant part of this verbal scientific practice is the unambiguous linguistic identification of the objects observed. Millions of these objects are already known and named. Other scientists also name their research objects in a manner similar to biologists. What's special about biology, however, is the fact that the majority of entities that exist in nature and are of interest to biological study are not yet known. Every year around 20,000 animal and plant species are discovered, which then means that the catalog of life—the dictionary of nature—expands yearly by the same number of words, most of which are actually neologisms. No one knows for certain how many species remain to be discovered, but even conservative estimates—based on yearly rates of discovery for various organism groups—raise no doubt that it's still a couple million. By current scientific practices, this means that millions of names will still be needed to manage this myriad linguistically.

And not just linguistically. In biology, as in common speech, one of the central communicative problems lies in the tendency to treat words as if they were real things. In other words, in speech we often like to mistake concrete objects for their linguistic labels. It's perfectly obvious that no identity exists between a species name and the species with that name, yet we use the names as self-evidently as if they were the actual focus of biological study. This isn't a big issue in everyday life, and the somewhat careless use of names and named individuals doesn't do much harm to the content of these statements. But if one wants to understand why we treat linguistic elements like names the way we do, and what consequences this has on the way we think about the concrete things we name, then one must dig a little deeper. It is a worthwhile endeavor, even as a nonlinguist, to wander down the road (though it may be rocky at times) to the linguistic background of names—and in our context, of species names, in particular.

An analysis of this sort, however, remains incomplete without a critical look at the objects being named. Names are a particular part of speech with a specific function and grammatical behavior. For them to qualify as names, they must refer to objects that demonstrate certain traits. Although referents (the linguistic term for these reference objects) that do not fulfill these conditions will still receive a linguistic label, these labels cannot be considered proper names. To determine the part of speech of a linguistic term applied to a certain referent, one must know and assess whether the referent fulfills the necessary requirements. More simply, if one wants to understand a name, then one must know what it's actually naming.

In what follows here, these questions should be answered: what are names, from a linguistic viewpoint? From a biological one? In what way does our perception of species influence the linguistic practice of name use? Conversely, how does the way we use names influence our view of biological species as objects of the naming process?

We constantly encounter names in everyday life, especially in the form of personal names. From a young age, children learn to connect their own name with themselves, and they also quickly learn how to say it. Just as early, we start associating names with certain people, usually imbuing them with emotion, depending on the individuals named. Notably, names aren't included in dictionaries, and it also isn't common to translate them, although it would inherently be possible.

Let's return once more to the fact that one does not usually expect a name to reveal something about the individual named. We have thus described one of the fundamental characteristics of names that distinguishes them from other parts of speech. Linguists say that names do not have lexical, intrinsic meaning. A name is primarily a label whose function consists of referring to a specific thing. This applies as readily to biological scientific names as it does to everyday personal names.

In most cases, however, names do have meaning as words, and this meaning isn't lexical but etymological. Most names developed out of words or word components that don't represent names. The reasons behind them are usually buried in the depths of linguistic history, while when it comes to scientific names, finding a name is often a deliberate act of linguistically labeling certain traits. Thus, many tiny animal species are *minimus*, which means "smallest or least significant" in Latin, like *Tamias minimus*, the least chipmunk. While the name *minimus* doesn't have any lexical meaning— functioning instead as a simple label referring to a specific biological trait— characteristics of the object (the smallest species of chipmunk) do coincide with the etymological meaning of the name (tiny). And this is exactly what the scientific author intended when selecting this name. Agreement between a name's etymological meaning and traits possessed by the individual named doesn't just help establish the referential connection between species and name; a species' traits are also a welcome source of new names.

What happens, though, when the etymological meaning of a name does not agree with the species' traits? In such an instance, only within popular context would one want to suggest a name were "false" because it implied a characteristic the species did not demonstrate. Biologists might find the discrepancy regrettable but would otherwise accept the name. Because semantics do not apply to names, the debate over correct or incorrect makes sense only within the context of the appropriate nomenclature rules. As long as a species name has been formed and assigned correctly, according to the nomenclature rules, then its etymological meaning doesn't matter; at most it will be of historical or emotional interest, as we saw with *Oviraptor*. Once an *Oviraptor*, always an *Oviraptor*.

Let's take it one step further. Up to this point, I have spoken primarily of "names." More precisely, what we're really considering here is that linguistic unit known as the "proper name." Linguistically speaking, proper names are grouped with appellatives (common nouns like "tree") and mass nouns (like "milk") as names (singular *nomen*, plural *nomina*) in a broader sense. In the context of researching names, because proper names are the most common name type by far, the terms "name" and "proper name" are often used interchangeably for the sake of simplicity.

As speakers, we all have an intuitive sense of what proper names are. Proper names refer to specific people (Charles Darwin), geographical locations (the Atlantic Ocean), or things (the Eiffel Tower). To approach proper names from a linguistic perspective, it is especially useful to emphasize the difference between them and common nouns. Let's imagine that only a single donkey existed in the entire world, even if the notion invites objection from the biological perspective. To refer to this donkey, one would say, "That's the Donkey." In this case, "Donkey" would be the proper name because it serves as the linguistic label for this unique individual we see before us. Although animal individuals do exist that are the sole representatives of their species, this is a fictitious scenario for the Donkey because it is by no means alone on the planet, which is in fact populated by many millions of donkeys. Therefore, the identical phrase as earlier ("That's the donkey") doesn't lend itself to quick comprehension because without a shared context (such as the single donkey in the neighbor's yard), it remains uncertain which donkey is meant. One would then switch to using an indefinite article and say, "That's a donkey."

This example reveals the difference between proper names and appellatives (or generic or class names). A proper name refers unambiguously to a specific object—in this case, the fictitious single Donkey in the whole universe. Appellatives, on the other hand, can apply to many objects at once because the statement "That's a donkey" could be used to indicate any one of the countless donkeys out there.

Not all individuals have names that truly apply only to them. Instead, lots of personal names are used for different people. For example, many people share my first name, Michael, and the question arises as to how clarity can be maintained. In everyday speech, the requisite clarity is secured through conversational context as already mentioned. In the context of my (closer) family, the term "Michael" is totally unmistakable as a rule. Of course my family will also speak about other Michaels at times, but here, too, the speakers will typically ensure that the context allows for the named object to be clearly identified. In formal speech patterns in our society, a surname will also be attached to the first name, which may help with clarity but doesn't ensure it. Plenty of other men are named Michael Ohl, even.

It's similar in biology. It is also expected that each zoological name will refer unambiguously and unmistakably to exactly one taxon—that is, one named group of individuals, such as a species. Unrelated animals may bear the same species name, provided they belong to different genera. Thus, many animal species bear simple and easily formulated names such as *similis*, *minor*, or *americanus*. The context here is each animal's membership in a classification system of increasingly broad groupings nested within each other, and of these levels, the genus is reflected in the name. One reaches the necessary clarity through the resultant binomen of genus name and specific epithet.

We have thus outlined the most important function of proper names. They refer linguistically to a single object, and this connection is known to linguists as a direct reference. The term signifies the reference to a single object but also to the fact that names perform their referential function immediately—that is, directly and without a "detour" through semantic meaning.

It's different for appellatives. Appellatives help make reference, not to a single thing, but to a whole class of things. Various things' affiliation with this class is defined by certain class-specific properties. Thus, it is possible to infer certain characteristics of an object through an appellative. To a speaker with the required background knowledge, the statement "That's a raven" therefore implies that it possesses the traits "black, with large beak and croaking call." All members of this class possess these traits and can be categorized as part of this class because of them.

Let's hold onto this idea: linguistically speaking, names refer to a single, individual, and extralinguistic object. Objects labeled with a proper name are individuals, usually those with a temporally limited existence, that can be historical or contemporary figures (Barack Obama) or imaginary constructs (Captain James T. Kirk). Proper names perform this referential function directly and not by means of semantic sense. In this one-to-one relationship between name and object, proper names differ fundamentally from appellatives, which refer to a class of objects. Thus, the use of a name allows one to refer to a clearly defined individual object. This doesn't work with an appellative. Instead, the meaning of the expression must be known to group individuals into a certain class.

We can see that from a linguistic perspective that fundamental differences exist between proper names and appellatives, but in practice the lines between the two sometimes blur, making it difficult to decide whether one is dealing with one or the other. In the sentence "The sun is positioned over the mountaintop," for example, the word "sun" is unquestionably an appellative, and yet to anyone on earth who hears it, it's still obvious that what is meant is the one specific sun located at the center of our solar system. Another example might be a sentence like, "As an evolutionary biologist, he's no Charles Darwin." The proper name Charles Darwin, which has no meaning, is thus "loaded" with a secondary connotation of the knowledgeable evolutionary biologist, thereby functioning as an appellative.

So far, so good. Linguistically speaking, then, the central criterion for a proper name is that it allows for individualization. To ascertain whether species and other biological names qualify linguistically as proper names, we must examine whether they refer to species and higher taxa as individual objects in a sensible manner. At this juncture, we are leaving the domain of linguistics. The discipline responsible for answering these questions is biophilosophy, a branch of scientific theory that bridges philosophy and biology. Its focus is on the premises, conditions, and consequences of biological theories, as well as on experimental and other applications and the historical scientific foundations of biology. This also includes an analysis of word formation and usage in biology.

Birds of a Feather ...

Getting at the essence of a species is one of the most difficult, controversial, and yet most important questions in biology: what are biological species anyway? We talk about species, loss of species, species conservation, numbers of species, and—when things turn scientific—speciation, species splitting, species definitions. The books and scientific journal articles written on the topic of species are countless, and every year the number grows. Well before the birth of modern biology, natural scientists recognized that the diversity of organismic forms surrounding us does not represent a continuum of blending polymorphism. Instead, discontinuity exists between groups of individuals of similar appearance. The distinct groups and the gaps between them appear to be stable and continually passed on from generation to generation. Among biologists, it is generally agreed that beyond human perception, real units exist in nature that we label with the term "species."

Undoubtedly, the elements that constitute a species—that is, individuals and populations—have a material existence beyond our perception. In other words, they exist in our minds and also completely independently of whether we're thinking about nature. The situation is trickier when it comes to species. Our everyday experiences already show us that organisms are typically bound together by sexual procreation, and that they form systems isolated from other systems by the fact that they do not reproduce with one another. In other words, "Those that congregate and copulate, a species do populate," or as the saying goes, "Birds of a feather flock together." In practice, this reproductive isolation between species often cannot be observed directly. Consistent similarities between individuals of the same species and consistent differences between individuals of different species are therefore usually interpreted as an indication of reproductive barriers. The underlying idea of the reproductive isolation of various procreative communities informs the species definition known as the biological species concept, developed by German-born evolutionary biologist Ernst Mayr.

Figure 3.5
Orthetrum nitidinerve (Selys Longchamps, 1841), a dragonfly species from the zoological collection of Count Johann Centurius von Hoffmannsegg. This collection, together with the Royal *Kunstkammer* collection, provided the basis for the Zoological Museum's founding in Berlin in 1810. Museum für Naturkunde Berlin, M. Ohl photo.

One of the problems with the biospecies concept is that it applies only to bisexual organisms—that is, to those that reproduce sexually between two partners. For the large majority of higher animals, this is the typical mode of reproduction. However, some species—such as cnidarians with their polyps—multiply through budding, and for others—such as walking sticks—one gender suffices to produce offspring by means of so-called parthenogenesis, or "virgin" reproduction. Only bisexual organisms are capable of building reproductive communities, however. This and other problems—some theoretical, others practical—have led in the past to many species definitions being suggested, each of which solved some problems while usually creating new ones. Biologists are still nowhere near a widely accepted and consistent species definition, and a solution is not in sight.

A critical discussion of the existing species concepts alone would surpass the scope of this book and is mostly irrelevant to an understanding of how species are named. Although convincing evidence supports the existence of hypothetically real entities in nature that would continue to exist, even if humans didn't study them, that isn't a necessary prerequisite for naming species either. Even if we took the stance that all identified species were projections of our minds, mental constructions that have no concrete parallel in nature, it wouldn't change anything. As discussed, mental structures can be named or labeled, too.

The linguistic observations made earlier demonstrated that proper names are reserved for singular things. The question as to whether species names are proper names is reflected in the question of whether species are individuals—that is, singular things. The shorthand for this problem in biology is "species as individuals or species as classes." Intuitively, it seems absurd to see species as singular things. Organisms—at least those that reproduce through sex—may appear to create reproductive communities, but these are of a looser nature, and it's tough to view such a group as an individual. Take, for instance, a common species like the red fox, which ranges across Europe and most of North America, from the Arctic Circle to the subtropics. It was even brought into Australia by humans and can now be found almost everywhere on the continent. All of these many thousand individuals undoubtedly belong to a biological unit, the members of which can mate fruitfully with one another. Those foxes that live in a certain geographical area will do just that, while the red foxes of Sacramento are unlikely ever to have the opportunity to couple up with a fellow species member in Berlin. But they could, at least potentially. Somewhere along the path of predator evolution, foxes emerged from other predatory ancestors. From their place of origin, which is believed to be in Eurasia, the red foxes launched their triumphal march across the Northern Hemisphere. Their spread took hundreds of generations, and they're all bound together by the (historical) reproductive connection and the passing on and mixing of genetic material.

One can recognize genetic ties between individuals of a widespread species when genetic changes emerge in one area of the population. In the rare instances that these changes have a positive effect on their carrier, they will spread throughout the whole population. Significant geographical barriers such as the Atlantic effectively hinder genetic contact between Eurasian and North American populations. However, the genetic connection remains, at least historically, although there's potential for more should the geographical barriers ever be overcome.

With regard to biological species, we're clearly dealing with systems whose members are linked through historic, potential, or active reproductive ties. Can we therefore say that species are individuals? Unfortunately, the term "individual" has a specific meaning in biology, namely, an organismic individual being in everyday terms. Charles Darwin is unquestionably an individual and the goldfinch sitting in that tree over there is another, as is the wasp that just landed on your piece of apple pie. The fact should be disregarded for now that all sorts of issues emerge when distinguishing individuals, such as coral, where it's not easy to say where one animal ends and the other begins. If a species is to be considered an individual, then the definition will obviously be understood differently than for an individual organism. A species cannot be touched, and one cannot see it. Its existence can only be inferred indirectly by means of observations and studies of selected members of its population. The term "individual" thus appears amiss in this instance, even if biologists still tend to use it.

The "Thing Test"

Linguists are naturally less interested in this kind of biological hair-splitting. When they say that a proper name signifies an individual, what they mean is a single thing or, as one says in philosophy, an entity (although in philosophy, in addition to concrete and abstract matter, an entity also constitutes circumstance, events, and much more). Therefore, to define the linguistic status of species names, we don't need the biological term "individual" at all. The field of linguistics cannot help here because it simply states that proper names refer to individual things and outlines how proper names behave as a part of speech. Beyond that it cannot provide any insight as to what an individual thing actually is.

This important and basic question is addressed in philosophy, specifically by the philosophical branch concerned with the fundamental determination of being, known as categorical ontology. Generally speaking in philosophy, ontology seeks to answer the question of what really or only potentially exists, and what it means to exist. The idea of existence is thus one of the big philosophical questions in general ontology. Categorical ontology, in contrast, is concerned with the fundamental determination and underlying categories of being. It is thus interested in the concepts of things, properties, events, and circumstance. Because categorical ontology is responsible for defining what a thing is, it should be able to help us determine whether a species can be seen as a thing in a meaningful way.

To understand what the alternative is to "species are individuals," it appears necessary to first introduce the standard ontological view of species. The classic interpretation, which extends back into the early days of taxonomy, is that of species as "classes." Classes are defined by the fact that all of their constituents correspond in certain properties. Therefore, to belong to a certain class, an object must possess the same class-specific property as those objects that are already elements of the class. The class designation is especially applicable to inanimate objects. One example is the class of doors. Doors can be large or small, angular or rounded, made of metal or wood. All doors are alike in that they are more or less flat, hung to swing from hinges, and intended for closing and opening. Any object equipped in this manner would belong to the class of doors. One important quality of such a class is also its consistency, which can be attributed to the fact that a specific, unalterable quality—a so-called essence—is unique to it. A special relationship between the doors of this world (and the possible doors of other worlds) obviously doesn't exist.

Based on the general observation that the organisms constituting a species often demonstrate a high level of similarity, the conclusion was drawn that the presence of certain common qualities determined inclusion in a species. Therefore, species would be logical classes out of a multitude of elements that correspond in certain class-specific properties. Every individual that possesses these qualities belongs to the class, whereas any individual that doesn't have them does not belong. Linnaeus and his contemporaries employed this so-called typological species concept, which formed the basis of the most prevalent species definition into the nineteenth century. The notion of species as classes with constant, class-specific qualities represents a monumental contradiction to the notion of a dynamic evolutionary process and changing species. The insistence on a typological species concept was thus one of the greatest hindrances to a general acceptance of modern evolutionary theory.

By the nineteenth century at the latest, through the growing understanding of species, the idea that species were considered classes—in a philosophical sense—led increasingly to internal objections. An alternative view of species as individuals was first explicitly published in 1966 by the American biologist Michael T. Ghiselin, but it was subsequently largely ignored. His 1974 work, "A Radical Solution to the Species Problem," and several other publications were the first to make philosophers and biologists aware of this problem and to introduce a new way of thinking.

What does it mean, then, to see a biological species as an individual, in the sense of a thing? According to categorical ontology, things have the following properties (among others): they are concrete—that is, they are spatial and temporally locatable. They are accessible to the senses. They're particular. They change. And finally, their existence is contingent.

Let's take a closer look at these different points. According to most biologists, species are truly spatial, and they're certainly temporally locatable, which makes them unquestionably tangible. Species are found in certain geographical parts of the world, which gives them a fairly good spatial framework. Problems arise with discontinuous distribution areas of common species, whose various territories are not in contact with one another, such as the red foxes in California and Germany mentioned earlier. In cases like these, additional knowledge is required, such as historical distribution processes or geological changes that render it likely that populations were connected with each other at an earlier point in history. The discontinuity of an "individual" that exists in areas distant from one another definitely poses a problem to the "species as individuals" concept.

Are species temporally definable? Species typically emerge when a stem species splits into two daughter species. The splitting of a species—which consists of countless individuals, usually in many subpopulations—is a process that presumably takes a fair amount of time. Measured in geological eras, however, there comes a certain point in time when the two newly emerged daughter species become completely genetically isolated from one another. To put it bluntly, this is the moment, up to which the last individuals of both species were able to mate successfully, and after which there were no more fruitful pairings. This moment marks the beginning of a new species and its simultaneously newly established sister species. This species, too, will one day cease to exist, usually through extinction or through a new splitting into daughter species. Every species is thus precisely limited and defined in temporal terms. The fact that it can be difficult in most cases to determine the date a new species pair emerged, because it's often buried deep within evolutionary history, is no more than a methodological problem.

Are species accessible to the senses? That doesn't look so good. The individual organisms of a species can be seen, heard, and touched. With acutely endangered species, of which only a few individuals remain, it may even be possible to do this with the species' every last individual. It is not possible, however, to do this with the species as a higher system. That is possible only indirectly through scientific studies.

Are species particular? "Particular" means that a statement can be applied only to certain objects. For example, while hornets—or rather the individual creatures known as hornets—are large, are four-winged, and have yellow-brown coloration and an unpleasant sting, there's no one thing that's "hornetty."

Do species change? Yes. Over the course of their existence, species can adapt to changing environmental conditions. This kind of change, which doesn't lead to splitting in a species, is known in biology as anagenesis.

And finally, contingency. This is a philosophical term, and "contingent being" is the random, ungovernable existence of a thing. Thus, if something has a contingent existence, its existence is not destined to be necessary. As products of evolution, this is definitely the case for species, which could just as easily not exist as exist.

We can see, then, that species fulfill most of the ontological criteria for thingness. We come up against some trouble with sensory accessibility, but there are many other things whose properties or existence can be proved only by means of scientific methods. Venus, for instance, similarly to planet

Earth, has a core of nickel and iron with a diameter of about 3,000 kilometers, the existence of which can be found through scientific observations and data but is as inaccessible to the senses as a species.

We can thus hang onto the conclusion that the categorical ontological "thing test" doesn't lead to serious contradictions with the species-as-individual supposition. This test is purely philosophical, however, and Ernst Mayr was among the first to argue that a purely philosophical solution to the species problem isn't possible. A clear determination of the factual—that is, empirical—background of a species' biological nature is indispensable because biology lays claim to making statements on hypothetically real nature.

In the past few decades, biologists and philosophers have formulated a variety of further properties typical to individuals that aren't necessarily connected to classes. One example would be inner organization. For an individual, which naturally consists of various parts—namely, organs, cells, molecules, and even smaller building blocks—a narrower and more specific relationship should exist between these parts than between the objects of some class. For organisms that reproduce sexually, at least, fruitful reproduction with other organisms of the same species is the glue that holds the species together. As reproductive communities, however, every species isolates itself genetically from other species through the construction of certain mechanisms, and they must especially do this toward their sister species, with which they emerged from the shared stem species and with which they have had genetic exchange until recently. A closer relationship thus truly exists between the individual organisms of a species than would be possible in any given class of objects. Given this background, it's advisable to see individual organisms as parts of their species, and not as elements, as one would consider objects of a class.

Another powerful argument that biologists make for species as individuals is their ability to evolve. In addition to anagenesis, evolution includes the capacity for speciation (the creation of new species through splitting) and hybridization (blending), as well as the possibility of extinction. One would not expect any given class to change as a whole, comprised as it is of objects similar in certain properties but not otherwise connected.

At this point, we can stop and summarize. From both philosophical and biological perspectives, species clearly demonstrate the qualities of an individual more than those of a class. Admittedly, for some properties, one must bend the argument a bit to reconcile empirical observations and theoretical consequences. The geographical discontinuity of widespread species with subpopulations that no longer engage in genetic exchange is difficult to align with our notion of the individual. For this reason, Ernst Mayr also pointed out that, in his opinion, the term "individual" should apply to the *population* because it's the object of evolutionary processes.

To be fair, most biologists don't often engage in philosophical discussions such as this one. For our original question, as to which part of speech species names belong to, however, it's far from insignificant. The current biophilosophical stance seems to convincingly show that species are individuals. It should be noted, however, that other opinions do exist that latch onto the contradictions inherent to the concept of the individual. One example is the concept of species as "natural kinds." As opposed to the "species-as-individuals" concept, "natural kinds" are neither individuals nor individual things but rather classes. They are not the objects that humans arbitrarily established as collections, as with the class of doors. Instead, "natural kinds" are classes comprised of real natural objects that share certain properties and have emerged through processes of natural law. In terms of species, the actual physical organisms are the members of the "natural kinds." Generally speaking, "natural kinds" are thus objects conceptualized by humans that nonetheless have objective commonalities. One of these classes is therefore a mental equivalent of the natural situation, which explains the derivation of the expression "natural equivalence class."

We can see, then, that species can be things or classes, and they can also be "natural kinds." Admittedly, this notion is fairly confusing, even for biologists, and it is therefore not surprising that the species question has evaded a clear-cut solution to this day.

Taxonomic Misnomers

Let's come back now to the starting point of our discussion and pose the question anew, as to whether species names are proper names or appellatives. If one takes the stance that species are individuals, then species names are clearly proper names. If one considers species to be classes (which practically no one does these days) or "natural kinds" (which indeed many biologists and biophilosophers do), then they would have to be appellatives.

So, the answer is: it all depends. When speaking about species, the stance one takes plays only a marginal role. The central criterion for linguists in this debate is the direct reference—that is, the definitive one-to-one reference of a name to an individuated single thing. Those properties of species that speak to their thingness appear (from the stance favored here) to be responsible for species names to be treated intuitively like proper names.

Yet how exact is our language usage here really? For example, do species really die out? The act of dying requires life to have existed, and species definitely do not satisfy our notion of what living is. The individuals of a species live, but a species does not. If species have never lived, then they also cannot die. This is metaphorical language usage for the phenomenon that at some point all organisms of a species will die without offspring, so that the species they once constituted no longer exists, either tangibly or conceptually. The same applies on a more abstract level. We use a variety of phrases, such as "species evolve" or "species develop," implying linguistically that species are agents of events and processes. If species are agents, then there would be a serious argument for viewing them as individuals. All of these statements are metaphorical expressions for biological phenomena, in which the species-as-thing doesn't play an active role. It thus

Figure 3.6
Boxes containing paraffin blocks with reproductive organs of monotremes (platypus and echidnas) and marsupials (kangaroos, possums, and related) for histological sectioning. Museum für Naturkunde Berlin, M. Ohl photo.

appears vital to distinguish clearly between the actual properties of a species and the metaphorical ways of speaking about them.

In the field of biology, one can therefore consider (with clear conscience) species names to be proper names, but in doing so one must also be aware that this implies certain fundamental assumptions about the nature of species. If species names are seen as appellatives, then the species are understood to be classes or natural kinds, which represent the perspective of most linguists.

Grammatically speaking, species names are de facto treated as if they were proper names, and certain inconsistencies are deliberately ignored in everyday biological speech. Thus, there is no arguing the fact that "raven" is an appellative. A sentence may be in reference to a certain individual raven the casual observer is currently looking at, but it's ultimately interchangeable with any other raven. The scientific species name, however, is treated differently in speech. A statement like, "This is a *Corvus corax*" may be possible but isn't used in the scientific vernacular. The sentence "This is *Corvus corax*" is more common, but it can be understood in two different ways. For one, it can mean the identification of an individual belonging to the corvids. The individual is present, and one makes an informative statement regarding its species membership. This statement is thus an abbreviated form—adapted for practical usage—of, "This is an individual of the species bearing the name *Corvus corax*."

The other possible meaning is a reference to the species. As a product of the evolutionary process, statements about an entire species are possible without further ado, and in this sense one could refer to the geographic range of *Corvus corax*. This example clearly demonstrates that in linguistic usage, colloquial animal names are often used as appellatives, whereas scientific species names are more commonly used as proper names.

The Code

Let's come back one more time to the connection between names and meaning. As mentioned, proper names have no semantic meaning. Therefore, a species name is not expected to relay information about the species. It's irrelevant to the function of species names as basic linguistic labels, then, how a species is recognized, where it can be found, how it lives, and even whether the majority of researchers agree it's actually a species. This biological information plays no part in the naming process. For this reason, it's also said that species naming is "biologically neutral."

This is also reflected in an important terminological differentiation among the different lenses used to view species. The discipline within biological systematics concerned with the naming of species and higher taxa is known as nomenclature. The guidelines—which have been mentioned several times already and organize the creation of names and establish conditions for their formal validity in zoology—are accordingly titled the "International Code of Zoological Nomenclature"—"zoological nomenclature rules" for short, or "the Code," for even shorter. Standing opposite is the discipline of taxonomy, which may incorporate the nomenclature in everyday speech but is primarily responsible for clarifying which species exist, how they're recognized, and how they're distinguished from one another. Taxonomy thus makes statements with biologically relevant content, whereas nomenclature does not. This fundamental difference is often overlooked in biology and can frequently lead to confusion.

The difficulty of differentiating between these two lenses is furthered by the fact that oftentimes—and understandably—species names are created in such a way that reflects observable traits in the species. For one, species' features are a welcome source of species names. In many instances, it can also help with establishing and sometimes verifying individuals' association with existing names. As a rule, a pitch-black insect assigned to a species named *viridis* (green) will awaken certain misgivings regarding its assignment.

The zoological nomenclature rules take the important tenet of separation between nomenclature and taxonomy into account, the guidelines opening with a rather prosaic-sounding preamble, which includes the following sentence:

The objects of the Code are to promote stability and universality in the scientific names of animals and to ensure that the name of each taxon is unique and distinct. All its provisions and recommendations are subservient to those ends and none restricts the freedom of taxonomic thought or actions.[1]

"[The] freedom of taxonomic thought or actions." Again, the point is made abundantly clear: biologically speaking, the hypothetical existence of species and higher taxa can be established however one wants and however seems to make sense. The way that names are created and used is utterly untouched by this process. The only names in need of correction, then, are those formed incorrectly—that is, those that are in conflict with the nomenclature rules. That said, taxonomists must tolerate false etymological derivations. For this reason, there are actually many examples of etymologically incorrect names. For instance, the digger wasp species *Podium sexdentatum*, named by Ernst Ludwig Taschenberg for the six teeth on the edge of its facial plate, in fact has seven teeth. Maybe he simply miscounted, but that would be unexpected because even-numbered structures that straddle the long axis on bilaterally symmetrical organisms have a different and more recognizable pattern than those in odd numbers.

A further example is *Apus apus*, the swift. Both words mean "footless" and reflect the bird's extremely short (albeit decidedly present) pedal apparatus. The scientific name of the greater bird-of-paradise, *Paradisaea apoda* (*apoda* also means "footless"), an extraordinary bird native to New Guinea, has a different backstory. The first two specimens brought to Europe from New Guinea in the sixteenth century had their legs cut off in the preserving process, which led European scientists to conclude that birds-of-paradise were legless and spent their life in flight.

The Eastern mole is named *Scalopus aquaticus*, but like its European counterpart, it lives underground and not in water.

The giant anteater, whose scientific name is *Myrmecophaga tridactyla*, doesn't have just three fingers, as its specific epithet suggests, but five. The middle three fingers of the front feet are, however, greatly elongated and equipped with huge crescent-shaped claws. Perhaps these enlarged digits were the reason behind the species name.

This list of names with "incorrect" definitions could go on, but only so far; such "mistakes" rarely occur, despite the large number of names that refer to a species' particular features. When they do, taxonomists needn't fret. These names will endure as proper names as long as there are humans who name species.

Now what about our *Oviraptor philoceratops*, so wrongly accused of egg theft? This, too, is a purely nomenclatural problem that has nothing to do with the dinosaur's taxonomy or biological features. As a proper name, *Oviraptor* has no semantic meaning and performs its function as a label for this species without difficulty and without consideration for its etymological origins. It does so even when the definition has proved to be inaccurate, implying a trait not demonstrated by the saurian. Should there be no nomenclatural objections to its name, then the rule stands: once an *Oviraptor*, always an *Oviraptor*.

4 Types and the Materiality of Names

On a mild summer's eve in 1876, the paleontologist Edward Drinker Cope led a group of men armed with shovels and pickaxes to set up camp on the banks of the Judith River, a tributary of the Missouri in central Montana. Almost directly across from them, on the other side of the river, was a Native American village comprising several hundred richly ornamented tipis, home to about 2,000 Apsaalooké, also known as the Crow. These were dangerous times. Just 200 miles away, the discovery of gold in Montana's Black Hills was drawing white settlers into conflict with the Sioux, and earlier that year the US army had launched a campaign against the Sioux to drive them onto reservations, in what became known as the Great Sioux War of 1876. In June of that summer, under the leadership of Sitting Bull, the Lakota Sioux and Northern Cheyenne routed General Custer's 7th Cavalry Regiment in the Battle of the Little Bighorn.

Although the Crow were allied with the US government against their traditional Sioux enemies, tensions ran high. Cope, a slim man with a contemporary Buffalo Bill-style beard, who was known as a fanatical "bone hunter," therefore left no doubt that he was prepared to expose the expedition to danger in pursuit of fossils. The Judith River Group, a series of geological formations from the late Cretaceous located in Montana, was famous among specialists for its wealth of dinosaur remains.

Cope had the good sense to make overtures to the Crow that the fossil diggers posed no threat. From time to time, Crow chieftains crossed the Judith River and rode into the paleontologist camp to visit. One morning, as legend has it, they came upon Cope in the middle of his morning routine, cleaning his false teeth. In this awkward moment, Cope had no choice but to insert the dentures as the chieftains watched and welcome them with a broad smile of artificial teeth. They were astounded and requested

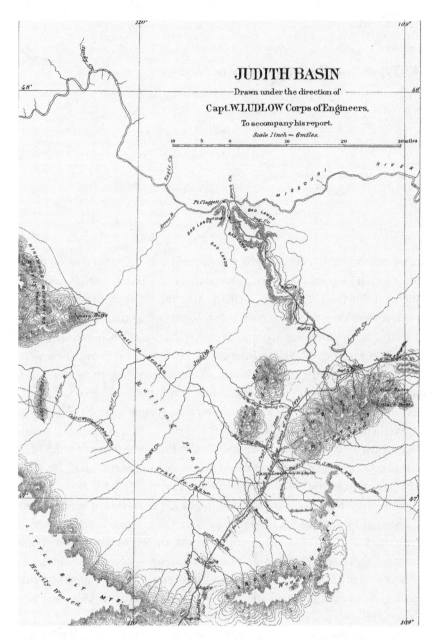

Figure 4.1

Judith Basin, Montana Territory, as surveyed in 1875. One year later, Cope's expedition pitched camp in the vicinity of the confluence of the Judith and Missouri rivers, near the spot labeled "Ft. Claggett" on the map. N. Peters, "Judith Basin: Drawn under the direction of Capt. W. Ludlow Corps of Engineers," from William Ludlow, Report of a Reconnaissance From Carroll, Montana Territory, on the Upper Missouri, to the Yellowstone National Park, and Return Made in the Summer of 1875 (Washington, DC: Government Printing Office, 1876). Image courtesy David Rumsey Map Collection, http://www.davidrumsey.com.

repeat performances of this incredible feat. Word spread quickly about "Magic Tooth," as the Crow dubbed Cope, and his extraordinary abilities. True or not, the story suggests that the Crow regarded the paleontologist as an innocuous if curious presence.

Indeed, in 1876, another struggle was raging across the American West and the pages of scientific journals: the Bone Wars, a heated feud between the two most important American vertebrate paleontologists of the nineteenth century, Edward Drinker Cope and Othniel Charles Marsh. Both extraordinary experts on fossil vertebrates and formerly close friends, the men also shared pronounced traits of vanity and competitiveness. As is so often the case with personal conflicts, one can only guess at the actual

Figure 4.2
The late Edward Drinker Cope. From the Collections of the University of Pennsylvania Archives, Digital Image Number: UARC20041111003.

Figure 4.3
The late Othniel Charles Marsh. Courtesy of the Library of the American Museum of
Natural History, New York, image #37641.

cause of the strife between Cope and Marsh. Cope was the first to experience publicly recorded defeat, which coincided with a personal betrayal,
a combination of injuries that likely triggered the conflict. In 1868, Cope
invited his friend Marsh to explore a rich fossil quarry in New Jersey; behind
Cope's back, Marsh struck a deal with the quarry owner that any new fossils
be sent directly to his offices at Yale. The same year, Cope had described the
new genus and species *Elasmosaurus platyurus*, misconstruing its unusual
spinal anatomy. His incorrect interpretation of the vertebrae led him to
confuse head and tail and mount the skull on the tip of the tail. Cope's

reconstruction of *Elasmosaurus* thus had an extremely long tail and very short neck. Of all people, Marsh was the one who detected this humiliating error; his response is said to have been "caustic, perhaps even gloating." Cope was deeply affected. He corrected the embarrassing mistake in a new publication and even tried to buy back the entire first print run. Although the scientific public barely took notice of his gaffe, Cope resolved to even the score with Marsh. As Marsh later acknowledged, "When I informed Professor Cope of it, his wounded vanity received a shock from which it has never recovered, and he has since been my bitter enemy."[1]

The Bone Wars were ultimately more of a "Dinosaur Rush," although neither party shied away from aggressive tactics. Cope and Marsh each attempted to outdo the other in significant fossil discoveries. Marsh unearths a pterosaur along the Smoky Hill River in Kansas, whose size outstrips all pterosaurs discovered to date in Europe. Enter Cope, who digs further at the same site upon Marsh's departure, and successfully. Cope finds a pterosaur even bigger than Marsh's, along with a mosasaurus and many other spectacular fossils. Cope triumphs. In the ensuing years, the rivals dug and published like there was no tomorrow, each hoping to find an even bigger skeleton of an even more impressive dinosaur. In total, Marsh and Cope described more than 130 fossil vertebrate species, whose discovery and publication trace directly back to the competitive pressure of the Bone Wars.

Wars universally wreak destruction and suffering. Although the competition between Cope and Marsh ruined their reputations and ultimately their careers, it also helped lay the foundations of paleontology, providing evidence for the theory of evolution and filling natural history museums

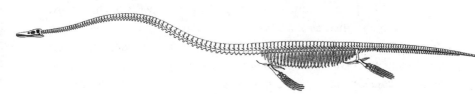

Figure 4.4
Cope's incorrect reconstruction of *Elasmosaurus platyurus*, with the head mistakenly mounted on the actual tale. Cope, E. D., *Synopsis of the extinct Batrachia and Reptilia of North America*. Part I. Tafel II, Fig. 1 (Philadelphia: McCalla and Stavely, 1869). Staatsbibliothek Berlin.

Figure 4.5
A drawing by Cope with two incorrectly reconstructed *Elasmosaurus* in the lower foreground and the right background. Cope, E. D., The fossil reptiles of New Jersey, *The American Naturalist* 3: 84–91, 1869. Library of the Museum für Naturkunde Berlin.

with fossils that draw curious crowds to this day. The Bone Wars wouldn't end until the deaths of Cope and Marsh in 1897 and 1899. Who was the victor? The question remains open for debate to this day. Cope was considered the more brilliant scientist; Marsh, the better organizer and politician. Cope lacked the financial means to keep up with Marsh, who had government connections and discovered about twenty more new dinosaur species than Cope. On the other hand, Cope was the master of publication: 1,400 scientific publications, often of significant scope, is an impressive accomplishment, then as now. What have endured above all the rest are the countless scientific names of special, charismatic dinosaurs that every dino-loving child knows. Marsh described *Triceratops*, *Diplodocus*, *Stegosaurus*, and *Allosaurus*, among others, while Cope's descriptions included *Elasmosaurus* and *Coelophysis*.

It's not just these names, though, that prompt us to follow the trail of Cope, Marsh, and the Bone Wars. For the most part, we're able to accept that after our inevitable death, we cease to exercise a physical presence and personal influence on earth. Although scientists are not fundamentally different from us in this regard, it's not surprising that after a fulfilling life of research, they might hope for their results, books, and journal articles to represent a lasting legacy of influence after their passing. Cope, unquestionably one of the most influential American paleontologists of the early twentieth century, wanted to make absolutely sure that it wasn't just his 1,400-plus publications and the 1,000-plus vertebrate fossils he'd described that remained unforgotten. *He* wanted to be remembered. Thus, during his lifetime, he ordered that his skull and bones be made available to science, and not just for some medical student to practice dissection. Instead (as some of the literature claims, at least), Cope aimed for a specific, unique purpose that would differentiate him from all other humans, even posthumously. His last will and unquestionably most serious testament was to become the type specimen for a special and unique animal species. Cope wanted to become the type specimen for *Homo sapiens*—humans. What Cope could not have anticipated beyond this absurdly megalomaniacal conceit, however, was that almost 100 years after his death, his skull would undertake a great journey back to North America's most famous bone beds, the key battlegrounds of the Bone Wars.

As Cope's life neared its end, he had to accept that he could not claim triumph in the Bone Wars. But that does not mean he accepted defeat. According to legend, to put one more over on Marsh, beyond the grave, Cope declared that his skeleton should find use retroactively as the central reference point for our own species. If Cope truly did have Marsh in mind when he did this, it was a genius play to ultimately triumph over his adversary. Dinosaurs be damned! He would become the most important individual of all humankind (in the eye of systematic biologists, at least), and what's more, he, Cope, would have formally designated the type specimen, not Marsh, whose *Stegosaurus* specimen would pale miserably in comparison. Cope as the benchmark for *Homo sapiens*? The victor of the Bone Wars would be obvious.

In doing so, Cope made use of common procedures in the early days of taxonomy, which are comparatively loose by today's standards. For today's species descriptions, the clear designation of one or more type specimens is absolutely required. In the eighteenth century, however, at which point today's formalized nomenclature was still in its infancy, this requirement did not exist, especially not for species whose taxonomic status was totally obvious. The human species, which Linnaeus formally named *Homo sapiens* in 1758, was unquestionably part of this category. Linnaeus hadn't designated a type specimen, though—and why should he have?

Ultimately, Cope's plan was not realized for a number of reasons. He may have bequeathed his skeleton to science, but science didn't want it. Although type specimens don't necessarily have to be especially typical representatives of their species, for our own species, of all things, one would set certain requirements. Cope's deformed remains didn't make the cut, and his skeleton ultimately landed in a large natural history collection, first at the Wistar Institute in Philadelphia and later in the University of Pennsylvania's anatomy collection, cataloged under the Wistar inventory number 4989.

Why didn't he make the cut? His bones were highly decalcified, which suggested the onset of syphilis. And it wasn't just the syphilis. To understand why Cope's skeleton couldn't have become the type specimen for *Homo sapiens*, even if he'd been a world-class athlete who died in his prime,

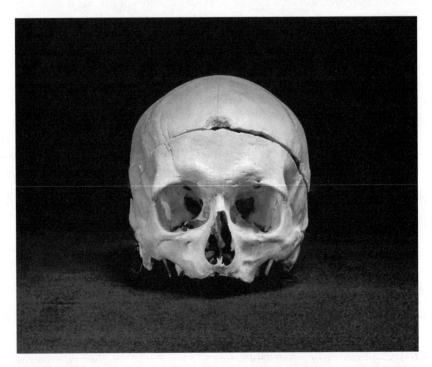

Figure 4.6
The skull of Edward Drinker Cope. Courtesy of Penn Museum, image #298584.

one must examine how the so-called type procedure operates in the naming of organisms.

Judging a Species by Its Traits

Taxonomists—who describe in meticulous detail which species of flies, wasps, mosquitos, bats, or other animals exist on earth—are commonly faced with a critical problem. After having studied a large number of individuals, taking note of various features, they will then begin to sort the individuals into groups based on their differences: prominent abdominal markings or not, head black or red, lateral section of thoracic segment exhibiting lengthwise grooves or smooth, with trunk or without, fin with three spikes or more. These and similar differences can be used to sort, and not according to some arbitrary bookkeeping principle, but with the thought in the back of one's mind that every one of these groups represents a biological species that emerged in nature as the historical product of evolution. The result of such studies is a certain number of species that can be recognized by certain traits or combinations of traits and, most important, can later be used to categorize newly discovered individuals.

At this point in the process of discovering animal species, the scientist does not necessarily need to know which species have already been named and which are new finds. In the process of species discovery, one can easily do without names at first, devising a free-form labeling system for the supposed new species. Letters, numbers, or a combination of the two—anything goes. Taxonomists truly do fall back on this, but as soon as they're convinced they know which species exist in the animal group they've prepared, it's time to take a stand. They must decide which of the species they've differentiated have been described in the past and which are new discoveries that they may name.

To compare the species one has found with those that have already been described, one must first read the original description, in which the name in question was published and the new species established. With any luck, the description (which ideally includes images of key features) and the organism in question match perfectly. One can then assume that the animal one hopes to identify belongs to the species described. It is not uncommon, though, for this path not to lead to the desired result, and an example from the world of wasps can help illustrate why.

In 1758, in the tenth edition of *Systema Naturae*, Linnaeus described a species of wasp he named *Crabro arenaria*. The species—a type of digger wasp—is now known scientifically as *Cerceris arenaria*, so its genus was changed. But that's another story.

Linnaeus described the species with the following Latin words: "Abdominis fasciis quatuor flavis, primo segmento duobus punctis flavis," or "abdomen with four yellow stripes, first segment with two yellow markings." That was it: he didn't need any more information to designate this species. Basically, within the context of the diversity known by 1758, Linnaeus was right. In the mid-eighteenth century, this paltry description was enough to help identify *Cerceris arenaria* based on its typical color pattern. We know more today, though. The genus *Cerceris*, which this digger wasp belongs to, comprised 863 species worldwide at last count and is thus one of the most species-rich genera in the entire animal kingdom. The United States is home to almost ninety *Cerceris* species, Western Europe to about forty, and many of these species have a color pattern similar to what Linnaeus used to describe *Cerceris arenaria*. Looking at the various species of digger wasps, it's clear that the yellow markings on the first abdominal segment and the yellow stripes on the second through fourth abdominal segments present differently. On some species, the markings are so large that they touch and sometimes even appear to blend into a large patch. On others, the abdominal stripes are broken in the middle and look more like patches than stripes. Linnaeus's description doesn't help with distinguishing between *Cerceris arenaria* and other digger wasps in this genus.

Today's specialists use much different traits to differentiate species in *Cerceris*. One specific trait divides all species directly into two groups: "lower plate of second abdominal segment, on the base, with clearly delimited raised area" versus "without raised area." The European *Cerceris arenaria* doesn't have this raised area, but Linnaeus doesn't make note of that. Among the species that don't have this raised area, *Cerceris arenaria* can be distinguished clearly from the others by the particular shape of its facial plate. This means that there's a simple combination of traits—missing raised area, uniquely shaped facial plate—that one can use to recognize digger wasps with certainty.

Yet how can we know whether Linnaeus had this exact "missing-raised-area-but-featuring-uniquely-shaped-facial-plate" species in his sights when he described his *Cerceris arenaria* with the aforementioned color pattern? Comparing today's animals to Linnaeus's description isn't helpful because different (structural) traits are now used, unlike in Linnaeus's day when colors still sufficed.

This is where the types come into play. Like any other scientist, Linnaeus had a certain number of individuals at his disposal while compiling *Systema Naturae*. For *Cerceris arenaria*, it was a single female wasp. In species descriptions, this original material is known as the type material.

Since Linnaeus doesn't name the traits relevant to modern descriptions, if scientists today want to clarify which species his original description of *Cerceris arenaria* refers to, they must examine the abdomen and cephalic shield of the type material. And what is the result of such a study? Let's imagine we have representatives from five different digger wasp species laid out on the desk before us, bearing provisional names *Cerceris* A through *Cerceris* E, all of which share the color pattern Linnaeus described. Upon studying the type with regard to the structural traits needed to differentiate our five species, we know that the type for *Cerceris arenaria* matches *Cerceris* B. Based on this match, we can reason that, according to today's standards, this one Linnaean individual belongs to the species with the provisional name *Cerceris* B. So there's the biologically relevant reasoning. In nomenclatural terms, this means that by assigning the *Cerceris arenaria* type to *Cerceris* B, the Linnaean name carries over, and the nomenclaturally correct name for *Cerceris* B is thus *Cerceris arenaria*.

One could say that the name being discussed here clings to the type specimen. For this reason, a type is also referred to as a "name bearer." The primary function of a type specimen is to be a name bearer.

To fully understand how important one of these type specimens can be, it's best to consider a different scenario. Since Linnaeus's description of *Cerceris arenaria*, taxonomists have been assigning individuals to this species. In scientific lingo, one says they've identified these animals as *Cerceris arenaria*. Now, imagine that one of these taxonomists discovered differences between two wasps identified as *Cerceris arenaria* and concluded that they were actually two different species that had been operating under the same name. The next step would be to describe both species in great detail, working out their differences and similarities and, finally, naming them. Which of these two species should keep the old name *Cerceris arenaria* and which should receive a new name? This question is answered by the type because in its function as name bearer, it "carries" the name applied to it over to

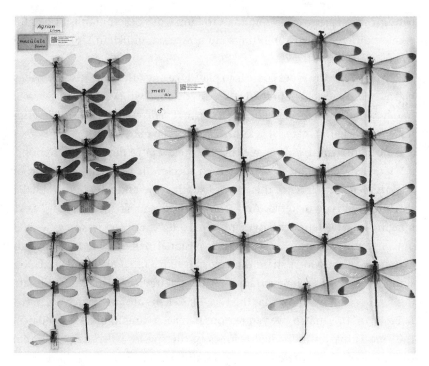

Figure 4.7
An insect drawer containing damselflies of the genus *Calopteryx*, but here still bearing the older name *Agrion*. Museum für Naturkunde Berlin, M. Ohl photo.

the species to which it belongs. The other species, which the type doesn't belong to, gets the new name.

Atypical Types

Type specimens—and this is something overlooked at times in biology—are thus not representatives of biological species but representatives of *names* of biological species. Their function is purely nomenclatural. They establish the name of the species they belong to, no more, and no less. Admittedly, the term "type" can be misleading. "Type" implies that the individual in question must be "typical" of the species it's connected with. This is by no means the case. Every biological species demonstrates a degree of variability in its features, however small these differences may be. The easiest example for this biological phenomenon is humans. All it takes is a quick glance at our own relatives, with whom we share an incredibly high level of genetic correspondence. Yet we don't all look the same, like peas in a pod. Each individual is different from all the rest. The same holds for every other biological species, even if the differences are usually less noticeable. One may need a microscope whose measuring scale reaches into the micrometers to tell the difference between individuals in a population of common green bottle flies. But there really are differences. Normally, variations of a given feature are divided among the population in such a way that certain characteristics and slight deviations appear frequently, whereas greater or even serious deviations are rare. Among *Homo sapiens*, for instance, about half of all women in the United States are between 5-foot-2 and 5-foot-6, while only five percent fall in the range of 4-foot-11 and shorter or 5-foot-8 and taller, respectively.[2] This trend is reflected quite well in our everyday observations: a middle range occurs frequently, while extreme deviations are rare.

In mathematics, this kind of distribution of features is known as normal (or Gaussian) distribution, which is visually represented by the familiar bell curve. The middle of the bell represents those features that appear most frequently in the population. The more the features deviate from this value, the more the curve drops, and the more rarely these traits appear. What does this mean for the type? If a type specimen were expected to show its species' "typical" features, then the given individual would have to fall within a particular, ideally narrow area under the middle part of the Gaussian bell curve. In the literal sense of the word, its features should be "typical" of its species. This is impossible for various reasons; in fact, it doesn't even make sense. This kind of distribution curve of a population's features can only be established when a large enough number of individuals is available—in other words, when the variability within a population can be assessed. As a rule, this isn't possible with a limited number of available individuals. In many cases with newly discovered animal, there's only one specimen, which appears to be different enough as to justify the description of a new species. No one can really say whether a single animal like this is "typical" of its species, and for this reason many systematic biologists advise that new species descriptions based on a single individual occur only as extraordinarily well-founded exceptions. A large number of animals is rarely available for the description of a species, and even then the criterion of what's "typical" doesn't help much. Because everything depends on the statistical sample size, newly discovered individuals later on can change the distribution curve of features so drastically that what was once seen as a typical animal suddenly doesn't appear so typical anymore.

On a much more general level, nothing typical can be expected of a type. The concept of types is a nomenclatural tool that serves to secure the unambiguous assignment of a name to a species. Here, too, the central difference between biological nomenclature and biological taxonomy, which always causes confusion, is brought to bear: nomenclature is concerned with names only and has no influence on taxonomical interpretations. Types thus determine what a species must be named but not how the species is distinguished.

Whether by chance or intentionally, a type specimen can thus fall at any point of a Gaussian distribution of a population. Even if the type falls at the tip of the left or right tail, demonstrating the most extreme deviation from the mean, it can still fulfill its function as name bearer.

There, at least, is the rationale behind types and why they don't need to be "typical," however counterintuitive this may seem. In the reality of today's species descriptions, more effort is made to select individuals that appear highly representative of the species. A selection can naturally only be made when there's something to select—in other words, when multiple individuals are available. Taxonomists will then typically move forward in the following way: using all of the type specimens available, they'll try to work out which features can justifiably be said to define the underlying species. In a species description, it's thus not the type or types being described; rather, it describes the features of the (hypothetical) species to which the type belongs. To what extent the individual type specimens then deviate from the "ideal" established in the species description is summarized in a short paragraph, usually named "Variability" or similar. To ensure that a type can fulfill its function as a name bearer, it makes sense to select one from the lineup that has a lot (and ideally, all) of the features the species is assumed to have. This kind of "typical" individual specimen then serves as something of a model for the entire species.

The requirement to designate a holotype to make a new species description valid was incorporated into the nomenclature rules in 2000. In the past, publications would often include the basic statement that a species description was based on, say, three male specimens from Sudan. These individuals, uniformly labeled as types, are called "syntypes" and, as a group, count as a name bearer. Which is actually nonsensical, because in series such as these, the problem can arise that the syntypes belong to different species. New research results, previously overlooked features, and updated views on the range of variability within a species can provide evidence to show that the specimens in a type series actually belong to different species. This problem occurs frequently. This kind of type series clearly can't fulfill the function of a name bearer. For instance, if a type series consists of two equally ranked individuals that actually belong to two different species, which of the two species should then bear the previously shared species name? In these cases, a "revising author"—that is, a scientist who is concerned with the taxonomy of these species—will retroactively appoint an individual animal from the syntype series as the single name bearer. This kind of retroactively designated individual is called a "lectotype" to distinguish it from a holotype, which is selected directly from the first. Following the selection of the lectotype, the remaining syntypes are consequently named "paralectotypes." They have as little claim to being name bearers as paratypes do.

Yet another "type" of nomenclatural types is permitted in zoological taxonomy today. Not at all infrequently, a species' original type material will be lost to the chaos of time, destruction of war, or improper handling and destructive infestation. This doesn't pose a problem, provided the species' taxonomic status can be confirmed without examining the type. But what to do when this isn't possible—that is, when the identity of the species, based on the original description, remains unclear? In such cases, it is sometimes advisable to designate a "neotype," or a "new type." To do so, a new (and, if possible, newly captured) individual is selected, which can be assumed—with a degree of likelihood bordering on certainty—to belong to the same species as the original type material. For example, neotypes should come from the same habitat and a location as close to the original place of discovery as possible, and they should usually be the same sex and at the same developmental stage. Still, one can never be entirely sure that the animal that has been caught truly belongs to the originally named species. For this reason, the nomenclature rules state repeatedly, and with considerable emphasis, that the designation of a neotype is allowed only under certain conditions. An important one is that the original type can be proven to be truly, irretrievably lost. What's more, it's even required that the author explain the steps taken to retrieve the original material and why the attempt failed.

The second fundamental condition seems trivial but isn't. Designating a neotype is permitted only if it serves to improve nomenclatural stability. In other words, a neotype may only be selected by necessity—that is, when it's needed to solve a taxonomical problem. There are practical considerations behind this rule: neotypes—just like holotypes, lectotypes, and syntypes— are primary types, meaning that as compared to paratypes and paralectotypes (also known as secondary types), they are actual name bearers. Primary types vastly increase the value of a collection, and every museum prides itself on the number of primary types it can call its own, particularly those of popular species. What kind of museum director wouldn't be happy, then, to see the number of types in the collection increase? The entomological collections of the National Museum of Natural History of the Smithsonian in Washington, DC, holds 33 million insect specimens in total, with 125,000 type records in the their online database. Holotypes, syntypes, and lectotypes were named in the original description, meaning they were available to the original author. For a museum, this means they either have them or they don't. Literally speaking, these types of types are historical and can't be newly "made." Not so with neotypes. Basically, any old animal can be made a neotype, and any old scientist can establish it as such. There are plenty of alleged losses of types among the millions of already published names, with their millions of type specimens behind them. So why not designate a couple of neotypes to boost the number of primary types in a collection? At this point, the nomenclature rules are unambiguous. They forbid the designation of a neotype "as a matter of curatorial routine."[3]

The fact that type specimens are linked to names, and not to certain biologically based ideas about the species, is in direct evidence when species are described multiple times. The principle of priority stipulates that the oldest name be given precedence. Yet what happens to the types and the name of junior synonyms when it turns out they refer to an already described species? Nothing, actually. They were chosen by the original author to represent this (now synonymous) name, and that's what they'll continue doing. There's a rather well-known example for this sort of situation.

On display in the Berlin Museum für Naturkunde is one of the most important and well-known icons of evolutionary research, the so-called Berlin specimen of the "Urvogel"—or primordial bird—*Archaeopteryx lithographica*. After collecting dust in the back rooms of the museum for some time, in recent years, this truly magnificent skeleton has been displayed behind bulletproof glass for visitors to admire as part of a newly designed exhibition. In 1861, when Hermann von Meyer—a prominent financier in Frankfurt and active amateur paleontologist—described *Archaeopteryx lithographica*, the species' complete fossil now on display in Berlin hadn't even been unearthed yet. Instead, Meyer based the original Urvogel image on two other specimens: a single fossilized feather also housed in the Berlin collection and the so-called London specimen, a feathered skeleton discovered in the same region of the Solnhofen Limestone in southeastern Germany. There was a long-standing dispute surrounding whether Meyer's isolated feather should count as the holotype of *Archaeopteryx lithographica*, or whether the London specimen should instead, which Meyer mentions as an aside in his original description of the feather. There is, however, evidence that Meyer attributed the new name to the feather alone and only personally studied the skeleton after the fact. To this day, the feather cannot be proven to belong to the same species as the *Archaeopteryx lithographica* specimen found later: between 1874 and 1876, almost fifteen years after Meyer's original description and naming of the Urvogel, the miraculously intact specimen was found near the Bavarian town of Eichstätt and traded in for a cow by its finder. Several episodes later, it was ultimately acquired by the Museum für Naturkunde in Berlin through the financial support of Werner von Siemens. After comparing this specimen to its London counterpart, the Berlin curator Wilhelm Dames concluded that they were two different species. In 1897, he then described a new species based on the Berlin specimen, which he named *Archaeopteryx siemensii*, in honor of its patron, Werner von Siemens. The original description of *Archaeopteryx siemensii* is based unquestionably on only one specimen, which means that the Berlin specimen is the holotype of *Archaeopteryx siemensii*.

So far, so good. To this day, the question goes unresolved as to how many species are represented by the ten Urvogel specimens found since the nineteenth century. Even the Berlin specimen's species assignment remains contentious among specialists in the evolution and systematics of birds and their dinosaurian relatives. There's a lot to suggest that the specimen is a smaller representative of *Archaeopteryx lithographica*—in other words, that *Archaeopteryx siemensii*, described thirty-eight years after Hermann von Meyers's original description, is a junior synonym of *Archaeopteryx lithographica*. Museum für Naturkunde in Berlin also presents its specimen in this way: on the plaque next to the display case, the species name *Archaeopteryx*

Figure 4.8
The type specimen of *Archaeopteryx siemensii* Dames, 1897, known as the Berlin specimen of *Archaeopteryx*. Museum für Naturkunde Berlin, C. Radke photo.

lithographica is given. What's important to note, however, is that the Berlin specimen still serves its original function as name bearer for the (junior and thus no longer valid) name *Archaeopteryx siemensii*. It will forever remain the holotype of *Archaeopteryx siemensii*, independent of its current or future taxonomical status. This makes sense. Should one assume, as many avian paleontologists do, that the isolated Berlin feather and the famous Berlin specimen belong to different species, their respective names remain fixed. The species the feather belongs to is thus *Archaeopteryx lithographica*; the other, which the Berlin specimen belongs to, is *Archaeopteryx siemensii*.

Sustainable Taxonomy

For the vast majority of zoological names, their type specimens are present in museum collections, available for examination by scientists. There are many possible reasons for the fact that occasional discussions or even arguments may arise regarding which individuals are the actual and true types. The root of these problems is usually that the initial publication did not provide a detailed discussion of which specimens the original description was really based on, which collection houses them, and how they may be recognized even centuries later. The respective specimens may be clearly tagged with an actual label, and they're often depicted in publications. An important rule is often overlooked, however, even by biologists. In biological nomenclature, information is considered valid only once it has been published. Labels or collection catalogs may provide important additional information that helps in judging an individual's taxonomical status. If the published data and unpublished labels or catalog content conflict with each other, then the published word takes precedence. Usually, one can safely assume that an animal labeled as the holotype is actually the holotype, as long as there isn't important outside information that speaks against it. For example, the original description may state that the holotype is female, but the animal in question turns out to be male. The situation is then examined more closely in hopes of discovering the reason for the discrepancy, and typically the animal labeled as the holotype will continue to be accepted as such, discrepancy notwithstanding.

Taxonomists work empirically, and they want to make concrete scientific statements about concrete natural phenomena. Types are distinct objects, so it seems obvious that they should be fundamentally, tangibly available. However, this needn't always be the case, at least according to many taxonomists. In recent years, several newly discovered vertebrates have been described whose type specimens may have been captured, measured, examined, and photographed but then intentionally released back into the wild by the authors. In 1995, for instance, the Indian astronomer Ramana Athreya was in Eaglenest Wildlife Sanctuary in Arunachal Pradesh, in the northeastern corner of India, where he observed two brightly colored, thrush-sized birds that he couldn't find in any field guide. Based on Athreya's field sketches, one of his colleagues suspected the bird was *Liocichla omeiensis*, a species belonging to the large bird family Timaliidae. The family is sometimes referred to as Old World babblers, or simply timaliids, and *Liocichla omeiensis* is known colloquially as Emei Shan liocichla. As the name implies, this species comes from the area surrounding Mount Emei in southwestern China. Eaglenest Wildlife Sanctuary, where Athreya made his bird observations, is about 1,000 kilometers away from the closest known place these birds had been seen. Athreya was skeptical and kept digging. In 2006, he managed to net one of these birds, which he'd first observed more than 10 years earlier. Athreya examined the living bird, measured and photographed it as precisely as possible, and then released it back into the wild. It was clearly a species of the Timaliidae family that was highly similar to the Emei Shan liocichla. Differences in plumage and especially in song indicated that this species evidently hadn't yet been described. In 2006, Athreya published the formal species description in an Indian bird magazine, naming the species *Liocichla bugunorum*, or Bugun liocichla. The name is in reference to the local Bugun ethnic group.

Why didn't Athreya kill the bird and preserve it permanently for future use, as most taxonomists would likely have done? Based on how few observations had been made, Athreya assumed that the entire population of the Bugun liocichla was extremely small, with maybe only three breeding pairs. Removing a grown animal from so small a population would have led to a significant weakening of the overall group, which Athreya decided against, for the preservation of the species. Additionally, the construction of a highway was planned for the area, which posed a direct threat to the survival of the species.

Where do things stand, then, with the holotype of *Liocichla bugunorum*, when the nomenclature rules so stringently require the explicit designation of a name-bearing individual? What's more, species descriptions of recent—that is, currently existent—species must include a statement of intent, outlining that a primary type will be housed in a specific collection. Given the photos, Athreya had unquestionably designated a certain Bugun liocichla as the holotype, meaning that this condition within the nomenclature rules was met. What's important here—and this can sometimes cause confusion—is that the holotype is not the photo but rather the bird pictured in the photo. Given intraspecific variability, it should be possible to recognize the photographed type in later catches of *Liocichla bugunorum*, even if this is no more than a theoretical possibility. But it doesn't matter; the nomenclature rules do not fundamentally prohibit designating a holotype through a photo without the animal remaining physically available. The second condition—an explanation or at least a statement of intent regarding the holotype's safekeeping in a collection—is problematic, however. Athreya states unambiguously that the bird in the photos is the type specimen, which—because it was freed—cannot be deposited in a collection. Several feathers left behind in the net after the catch have been properly inventoried and entered into the collection of the Bombay Natural History Society. At a different spot in his publication, Athreya writes that these feathers were gathered as type material, which is entirely possible, as the holotype of *Archaeopteryx lithographica*, a single feather, demonstrates. In our case here, though, Athreya had already explicitly designated the entire bird as the holotype.

Taxonomists largely agree that the nomenclature rules are not clear here and perhaps should be changed in the future. In the instance of the Bugun liocichla, it appears beyond debate that Athreya truly did detect an unknown and rather unusual bird species. Despite the minor issues with the required explanation of the type specimen's placement in a collection, ornithologists accept his species description and species name.

As part of other species descriptions, attempts have been made to solve this problem. In 2009, the Galápagos pink land iguana *Conolophus marthae* was formally described. Here, too, a careful examination was performed on the living holotype, with all relevant data documented. It was then released, with one special catch. Before its release, the researchers had implanted a tracking device under the skin of one of its hind legs. Upon the holotype's death, the team will thus be able to find its body, preserve it, and deposit it in a collection. With the explanation that the tracker will be employed to ensure that the holotype finds its way into a collection at the end of its life

Figure 4.9
The holotype of *Stromateus niger*, a fish species described by Marcus Élieser Bloch in 1795. Today, the species belongs to the genus *Parastromateus*. Museum für Naturkunde Berlin, M. Ohl photo.

(at the Charles Darwin Research Station on the Galápagos Islands, no less), all conditions of the nomenclature rules appear to be met.

This all demonstrates that it really is possible to publish a valid species description without making the holotype available in physical form. From the perspective of sustainable taxonomy, which will be implementing as yet unforeseeable methods and potentially discovering new features in the process, it is certainly desirable to have a holotype for every published species name permanently housed in a public collection and available for general use. To risk the extinction of a rare species to accomplish this, however, is too high a price.

Homo nosce te ipsum

As just one of many animal species, our own species, *Homo sapiens*, was also formally described and named, meaning the zoological nomenclature rules also apply to it. Here, too, the question arises as to what the type specimen for *Homo sapiens* is. One could also ask "who" the type for *Homo sapiens* is, which highlights the fact that in asking about the type specimen for humans, it's not just a question about a zoological object. Ultimately, it's about a person who is slated to serve as the reference point for the name of all humanity. Quite the responsibility! When Linnaeus published *Homo sapiens* in 1758, he didn't designate any individual as the type. Because the requirement to designate a name bearer was instituted in more recent years, its missing from Linnaeus's *Systema Naturae* comes as no surprise. What's more, Linnaeus probably had no intention of selecting examples of *Homo sapiens*, considering how little he practiced the habit with any of his other species descriptions for want of formal regulations. We are only able to verify type specimens today that belong to the names Linnaeus published because large portions of his reference collection are still intact, and one can look into what animals he had available. He doesn't mention any of them in his descriptions.

Linnaeus describes the human species in a level of detail unusual for him: five pages of text, including a multipage footnote, cover several sub-species of humans, along with all manner of cultural features. Then, as now, the zoological identity of *Homo sapiens* can count as secured so that its lacking a holotype as a name bearer is painless enough to tolerate. Yet scientists always come back to the question of how this formal nomenclatural gap should be filled.

Preceding the description of *Homo sapiens* is a well-known aphorism: "Homo nosce te ipsum," or "Know thyself." These four Latin words are generally interpreted in two different ways. First, and most obvious, Linnaeus is proclaiming that humans are capable of recognizing their being through self-reflection—that is, through the examination of the self. In the context of Linnaean classification, this means that they can recognize their own position in the system of animals. Linnaeus is thus echoing a widespread call for self-awareness in humans; the Greek form of this adage, "Gnothi seauton," has its origins in ancient Greek philosophy.

Second, some systematic biologists do not see "Homo nosce te ipsum" as a general philosophical statement, so much as they see it as an intentional reference Linnaeus is making to himself. With what we now know about Linnaeus, it cannot be ruled out that he used himself as the reference for the human species. Linnaeus was well aware of his significance in systematics, if not in science, at large. In other words, during his lifetime and beyond, Linnaeus was known for his highly cultivated ego and vanity. He wrote five autobiographies, and what he writes about himself there speaks volumes: "None have written more works, nor better, more ordered, or from personal experience"; "None were better known in all the world"; and "Not one was a greater botanist or zoologist." In that case, why not serve directly as the reference point, the type for *Homo sapiens*? No convincing arguments, however, prove that the self-infatuated Linnaeus had something like this in mind. Considering that he didn't explicitly designate types for any of the thousands of invertebrates he described, it's highly unlikely that he would have based his description of humans—the most familiar of all species to him—on specific individuals. Therefore, most scientists who have spent time on this question agree that the description of *Homo sapiens* is not based on a specific individual Linnaeus selected for the job. Given these circumstances, taxonomists will ask which individuals the author did have on hand while penning his description. Every species description is based on a finite and an enumerable group of concrete individuals physically present at the time of the original description, and thus available for examination. In terms of *Homo sapiens*, this means that the only individuals who come into question as types are those whose features somehow found their way into the species description. In zoology, the general assumption is not that every animal known to the describer will serve as types. In most cases, taxonomists will attempt to declare all known animals in the newly discovered species as types, thus creating the largest possible type series, but it's not required. The species describer has the license to include or exclude particular organisms at will.

Although it may seem like the nit-picking antics of overly fastidious, unworldly taxonomists to search for this type specimen—itself utterly superfluous to an understanding of human identity—it's only consistent with today's nomenclature rules. In the context of Linnaeus's historic description, it must be possible, at least hypothetically, to designate people who would come into question as type specimens for *Homo sapiens*. Admittedly, this is more an amusing intellectual game than scientific process leading to knowledge, but the framework of modern taxonomy certainly allows for this question, and that's also why it's posed.

To narrow down which human individuals could be considered as types, in terms of the nomenclature rules, the search must be limited to the humans existing in 1758 and who—knowingly or unknowingly—made their way into Linnaeus's description. "Existing in 1758" doesn't necessarily mean living humans because the store of mortal remains available at this time also could have been mined. In any case, the human type series can't be all of humankind—past or future, from that point in time—as sometimes discussed in the literature, because an animal that doesn't yet exist at the time of the original description can't yet fulfill its function as name bearer and reference object for the species description.

One could also take the stance, of course, that Linnaeus's description of *Homo sapiens* represents a summary of his knowledge about the human species based on his personal experience with anatomy, society, art, and culture—that is, with every source of knowledge available to an educated scientist in the eighteenth century. As intangible as it may seem, humans as a whole—those who had lived up to 1758, whose properties merged in Linnaeus's mind to form a collective image of humankind as a biological unit—would thus represent the type series for *Homo sapiens*. A notion of this sort leads to all manner of problems. It is not difficult to determine, in any case, who would have to be included in the syntype series. Linnaeus, for one; his parents and family, colleagues, and neighbors—that is, all of the humans who had influenced his perception of humans over the course of his life, whether consciously or unconsciously. His perception of *Homo sapiens* must also have been shaped by historical figures he'd read about or perhaps seen in paintings but never experienced in person. Direct ancestors of his own family also seem quite plausible, but what about the long-deceased kings of Sweden? Going back even further, is Aristotle—whom Linnaeus is certain to have read—a likely member of the syntype series? It's clearly unhelpful to view as syntypes all of the humans who may have influenced Linnaeus's notion of humans. At the least, it's impossible to set limits on this multitude.

We don't necessarily need to do so to take this idea further. We could tentatively limit ourselves to the people Linnaeus knew personally. If it makes any sense to construct a type series in the first place, then certainly we should draw on Linnaeus's contemporaries. We would then have identified a whole group of people, all of whom could be name bearers as a zoological series but would conflict with the actual purpose of a name bearer. In this case, a taxonomist would select an individual from the syntype series to serve as a lectotype or the retroactively appointed name bearer. This would be possible, and it has also been done, but more on that later.

Where things stand with Linnaeus's human type specimen can be considered from a different angle. Maybe it's better to assume that there truly weren't any types because neither a single type nor type series can be derived from Linnaeus's description. Then a taxonomist could select a neotype—that is, designate an individual as the type specimen who couldn't possibly have been part of the original type series but who now assumes the function of name bearer. As discussed earlier in extensive detail, the designation of a neotype is permitted only under strict conditions, the most important and obvious of which is this: a determination of this sort is deemed legitimate only when absolutely required to resolve a burning nomenclatural problem. This is where any attempt to designate a neotype will fail. It's safe to say that the taxonomical identity of *Homo sapiens* is fairly uncontentious. We have a pretty clear picture of what characterizes our species. Another living species of the genus *Homo* doesn't currently exist, and we can also assume that one won't ever be discovered. Other species belonging to *Homo* have died out, and it isn't difficult to distinguish them from *Homo sapiens*. Thus, there isn't a burning nomenclatural problem with humans that can only be solved by a neotype, and for this reason neotype designations for *Homo sapiens* are unnecessary and invalid.

At this juncture, our old friend Edward Drinker Cope comes back into play. Cope belonged to the American Anthropometric Society, founded in 1889, which brought researchers together for the preservation and scientific study of their brains. At the end of the nineteenth century, the study of the cranium was a blossoming and tremendously popular science. Up until that time, character and mental traits of humans were not considered objectively ascertainable. Nascent evolutionary theory suggested that all organisms were linked by genealogical connections from ancestor to descendent in the "tree of life." The passing on of traits from one generation to the next became the focal point of natural sciences. Human traits, whether physical or mental, were now no longer God-given or random attributes but the result of scientifically definable processes. This was the birth of anthropometry, whose disciples believed it possible to objectively ascertain character traits through the exact measurement of the human body, in particular the skull and brain. The desire to possess intangible criteria—for instance, for recognizing and thus predicting criminality and genius—led to a veritable flood of standardized measurement procedures in the nineteenth century. Cope, too, fell prey to the "allure of numbers," as Stephen J. Gould termed the measuring obsession of the time, which has since come to be seen as quackery.

The skull and brain researchers didn't only assume that race and gender could be determined by an individual's skull; they also believed that mental capability was mirrored in anatomical features. It would follow, then, that the brain size and brain weight of the big thinkers would be significantly greater than those of the mentally less capable. In the United States, the anatomist Edward A. Spitzka urged the intellectual elite to give their brains to science after their death for a craniometrical autopsy. Spitzka was one of the five founding fathers of the American Anthropometric Society, which he linked to the pursuit of hard science as well as the belief that he was onto the "objective ascertainment" of genius—his own, included.

In 1907, Spitzka published a comprehensive work on the anatomy of eight "elite brains" he had dissected, which he then compared to the known brain measurements of such great thinkers as Georges Cuvier and Carl Friedrich Gauss. Two of the eight brains belonged to fellow founding fathers of the society, whereas the others were added later. Among them was the brain of poet Walt Whitman. A careless assistant at the society dropped the jar of alcohol containing Whitman's brain to the floor, which damaged it so badly that not even the remains could be salvaged. Another brain Spitzka examined, finally, was Cope's. It was in perfect condition in 1907, and it was weighed, measured, and described in detail. Fresh on the scale, it weighed 1,545 grams, which exceeded the average brain weight Spitzka expected for white males by 150 grams.[4]

A result Cope would assuredly have been pleased to receive. Whether it truly was Cope's goal to posthumously become the type specimen for *Homo sapiens*, though, can no longer be stated with certainty. Although it has always been circulated, Jane Pierce Davidson, one of his biographers, was unable to find definitive evidence for this theory. It's a fact, however, that he ordered his skeleton to be stored in a scientific collection to remain available to posterity. What's also true is that after Cope's death, his skeleton was properly inventoried, archived, and then largely forgotten. Regardless of whether this story is true, this tale of ego and eccentricity in science is too appealing and captivating for it to ever be erased from the annals of systematics. It also fits all too well with the image that Cope created for himself as one of the adversaries of the Bone Wars. The idea that Cope would want to put just one last one over Marsh after his death is so absurd that we can't help but want to believe it.

The Ultimate Man

The story would probably have been forgotten, though, had the author, photographer, and film-maker Louis Psihoyos not come up with the idea to take a trip with Cope. Psihoyos—a multiple first-place winner of the World Press Contest—is recognized as one of the world's most prominent and accomplished photographers. Psihoyos became known through his documentary *The Cove*, which details the yearly mass killings of dolphins in Japan and won the 2010 Oscar for Best Documentary Feature. The "encounter" with Cope came on the heels of a *National Geographic* report about dinosaurs, which sent Psihoyos to the world's most important fossil digging sites alongside paleontologist John Knoebber. There, he photographed dinosaur bones, dinosaur eggs, and dinosaur tracks. The results were cover story material, and the impressive, aesthetic images sparked a lot of attention. At this point, Psihoyos had been bitten by the dinosaur bug, and the dinosaur story—which he had begrudgingly taken on at first—had become much more than a piece of contract work. Together with Knoebber, Psihoyos extended the dinosaur expedition throughout the world, and in the following months they traveled to further locations—from Patagonia to the Gobi Desert—to photograph dinosaurs and interview paleontologists. In 1994, Psihoyos's book *Hunting Dinosaurs* was published, an illustrated popular science book about dinosaur discovery and discoverers.

A whole chapter of Psihoyos's book was dedicated to the early dinosaur researchers. To illustrate Cope and Marsh's Bone Wars, Psihoyos created a photo collage of their maps of the United States, recorded accounts, tools, and original drawings borrowed from various museums. On the search for these historical objects, Psihoyos and Knoebber were surprised to stumble across Cope. Under inventory number 4989, his skull was being kept in a plain cardboard box in the collections of the University of Pennsylvania Museum for Archaeology and Anthropology. With his experienced eye for a special story, Psihoyos recognized that Cope's remains would be the perfect object for his photo documentation of the Bone Wars. On a whim, he asked the curator responsible whether he could borrow Cope's skull. Psihoyos received permission, and for the next three years, Cope's skull accompanied Knoebber and him on a journey around the world to the most important sites of dinosaur discovery. Psihoyos staged many photos with Cope's skull, including several with contemporary paleontologists he'd surprised with it. On one occasion in Utah, paleontologist Jim Kirkland was telling him that Cope was one of his personal heroes. "Really," Psihoyos asked. "Would you like to meet him? He's in the van."[5] Thus, *Hunting Dinosaurs* features one staged photo after the other: Cope's skull with this or that dinosaur researcher; in the desert or someone's yard; in a coffee shop in Boulder, Colorado; with paleontologist Bob Bakker; or on Georgia O'Keeffe's famous Ghost Ranch, which is not far from where the skeleton of *Coelophysis* was found. The photographic highpoint of the series is the "postmortem reunion" of the archrivals that Psihoyos staged in the Peabody Museum at Yale University.[6] Two hands hold Cope's glowing white skull before a dark oil painting of Marsh. They probably hadn't been this close to each other since their battle began.

Psihoyos's travels to the key sites and actors of North American dinosaur research, along with Cope—who always "seemed to be smiling, as skeletons do"[7]—received mixed responses from the public and colleagues in the field. No small number of people view the staging of Cope's mortal remains in this sort of historical collage of dinosaur research irreverent—or at least questionable in taste.

Psihoyos had even bigger plans for the skull, however. He called in professional paleontologist and taxonomist Bob Bakker, who helped elucidate the meaning of type specimens in biology for the journalist, himself hardly a specialist in systematics. Psihoyos also learned from Bakker that Cope's last will and testament had been to become the type specimen for *Homo sapiens*. This information inspired Psihoyos to roll out an even bigger production, namely, the presentation of Cope's skull as the type for humankind. Above all else, Psihoyos's texts bespeak a significant lack of specialist knowledge in this area. It's neither correct that the description of *Homo sapiens* is invalid without a designated type specimen nor could Bakker and Psihoyos change Linnaeus's published name, *Homo sapiens*, to "anything we wanted."[8] What is correct is that this kind of retroactive designation of a type must be published in a scientific journal to be considered valid. Psihoyos claims Bakker submitted a paper that was approved and accepted by—he implies vaguely—a "dignified but amused review board."[9] Thus, in 1994, Psihoyos asserts that almost 100 years after Cope's death, his dying wish was finally granted, and Cope was allegedly entered into the scientific literature as the type specimen for *Homo sapiens*. To underscore this formal act of making Cope the "ultimate man," Bakker crafted a fancy mahogany box, lined with red velvet, which was meant to be Cope's future home. A brass plate on the outside of the box identifies Edward Drinker Cope as the "Type Specimen for *Homo sapiens* / Described by Robert T. Bakker 1993." Typically for Psihoyos, everything was carefully arranged and photographed.

To some degree it was a publicity stunt, but the story of Cope as the human type specimen still managed to make the *Wall Street Journal*.[10] Yet an appropriate scientific publication, in which Cope is formally designated as the lectotype for humans, was never written, let alone published. Had it been, Cope would come no closer to achieving his dying wish, the requirements for nomenclatural validity remaining eternally out of reach.

So where do things stand today regarding the nomenclatural reference point of our own species? As hard as we try to tease hints out of Linnaeus's original Latin description, this question will continue to confound. It's hard for taxonomists to take this lying down because the type ensures stability—clarity in the chaos, reference in the continuum. Ultimately, even taxonomists can agree that we don't need a type specimen for the zoological nomenclature of humans. Yet taxonomists will regularly chime in about how nice and comforting it would be if we were to select someone from our ranks—or the ranks of our fathers or forefathers—and confer on them the title of name bearer. Who should be given this honor? Adam? Kings or princes? The great minds of the sciences? If one gives in to the joys of speculative thinking and takes this thought a little further, then one unavoidably comes back to one specific person: Linnaeus. In this case, the type locality would be Uppsala, Sweden, where he lived when *Systema Naturae* was published and when he gave up the ghost. His body still exists, even, because his mortal remains are kept in Uppsala Cathedral, where they are neatly labeled "Ossa Caroli a Linné," or "The Bones of Carl von Linné." Considering Linnaeus's outsized ego, it's easy to imagine him feeling perfectly content as the representative "wise person," as *Homo sapiens* translates into English. Linnaeus can at least be counted as one of the individuals on which *Homo sapiens* was based, not least given that he's the author of the name. William T. Stearn—a botanist and author of *Botanical Latin*, a popular book in the field—thought as much. In 1959, one year after the two hundredth anniversary of the tenth edition of Linnaeus's *Systema Naturae*, which can hardly have been coincidence, Stearn published a scientific article in the renowned journal *Systematic Zoology*. In it, he discusses Linnaeus's contributions to the nomenclature of organisms and his services to systematic biology. Stearn points out that it is common practice in taxonomy to select an especially good and carefully examined individual as the type, and Linnaeus should be considered for the designation. Really, if we disregard the uncontested fact that there are no objective reasons a name bearer for the human species should ever be selected, then Linnaeus would be an obvious candidate. Stearn took his own recommendation literally and unceremoniously appointed Linnaeus the lectotype of humans. As Stearn proclaimed, "This conclusion he would have regarded as satisfactory and just. As he himself said, *'Home nosce Te ipsum.'*"[11]

It may seem odd to take humankind—the species we know the best, the most personally, the most intimately of all organisms on earth—and treat and discuss its nomenclature in such a dry manner. It doesn't ultimately matter whether a historically plausible name bearer exists (and is widely accepted) for *Homo sapiens*. Humans are just one of millions of species on earth, and we have borne our name for more than a quarter millennium. Either way, questions regarding humans as biological entities are different than those regarding an objective reference point in the naming process. Stearn—a professional botanist and systematic biologist—was unquestionably aware of this. His official and therefore formally valid designation of Linnaeus as the lectotype is thus something of a bow before Linnaeus, who established the framework for the standardized naming of organisms more than 250 years ago: a framework we may have expanded but haven't abandoned to this day. And why not make Linnaeus the reference point for the name of our species? Are we resisting the thought of accepting this conceited eighteenth-century egomaniac as the "ultimate man"? The function of the type in biological nomenclature presents itself here once more. Selecting Linnaeus as a possible lectotype doesn't imply he's being honored as an exceptional human being. Instead, it simply means that Linnaeus bears the name as a representative for all other individuals of our species. Because he belongs to our species, the name would then carry over to all of us. Linnaeus would have thus fulfilled his function as a name bearer, and whether he was an organizational fanatic, genius, or egomaniac shouldn't really matter to any other humans who don't share the name bearer's strange burden.

5 The Curio Collection of Animal Names

When winter temperatures fall to negative 40 degrees and storms batter the
land, life on Lake Baikal in southern Siberia is anything but easy. Even with
today's high-tech equipment and performance apparel, scientific activities under these conditions can be quite the adventure. It stands to reason,
then, that conditions in the mid-nineteenth century were nothing short
of life-threatening, not least for two deportees whose Siberian imprisonment was hardly characterized by the creature comforts, as it was. One of
the men, Benedykt Dybowski, came from today's Belarus and had studied
medicine at the University of Dorpat (today's Tartu). Following an illegal
duel, he had transferred to the University of Wrocław in the more liberal
state of Prussia; after completing his doctorate at the Friedrich-Wilhelms-
University in Berlin, which is now the Humboldt-University, he accepted a
professorship in zoology at the University of Warsaw in 1862.

The political situation in Poland at that time was incredibly tense. After
the Napoleonic Wars, the country had been divided among Russia, Austria, and Prussia, yet an active independence movement still yearned for
an autonomous Poland. In the Russian-held part of Poland in 1863, a huge
uprising was staged, in which more than 80,000 Poles took up arms against
the Russian regime under Alexander II. The uprising was crushed, with tens
of thousands of casualties. Nearly 20,000 Poles were detained, sentenced
to forced labor, and deported to Siberia. The 1863 uprising was essentially
spearheaded by Poland's social elite, for whom the retribution of the Russian regime was particularly painful. They represented the largest group of
those insurgents imprisoned for political reasons.

Among them was Dybowski, who had joined a conspiratorial group
in Warsaw and become a leading figure of the resistance. In 1864, he was
arrested in Warsaw and sentenced to death. Most likely because of an appeal

Figure 5.1
A bullfinch (*Pyrrhula pyrrhula*) specimen prepared by Benedykt Dybowski with the label he handwrote in Siberia in 1873. Museum für Naturkunde Berlin, M. Ohl photo.

Figure 5.2
The late Benedykt Dybowski. Narodowe Archiwum Cyfrowe (National Digital Archive), Poland. Signature 1-N-146.

for clemency made by his academic mentors, his sentence was ultimately reduced to twelve years' forced labor in the infamous mines of Nerchinsk in eastern Siberia. His deportation ensued within the year. Because of his social class and financial resources, but also because of the network of acquaintances, friends, and colleagues he had built over the course of his studies, Dybowski could make a slightly more comfortable life for himself in captivity, conducting scientific studies in his free time. Despite his imprisonment, he managed to maintain and expand his contacts in the scientific community; through the help of the Russian Geological Society, he was able to send zoological research materials to various museums for further processing. Dybowski did not live directly in the camp; instead, he and a number of Polish compatriots were housed in a clay hut outside the penal colony. It was often simpler for the administration to place the deportees in neighboring villages, leaving them to fend for themselves. Eventually, Dybowski and his compatriot Wiktor Godlewski managed to receive permission to move to the small fishing village of Kultuk on the southern shore of Lake Baikal. From there, they began to undertake a systematic study of the freshwater fauna of the lake.

On a winter morning in 1868, Dybowski and Godlewski witnessed an impressive natural display: after a quiet, windless night, the two exiles ventured out from the shore onto the frozen surface of Baikal. In Dybowski's account, the ice resembled a crystal platter; the lakebed "appeared with such clarity, it was as though illuminated from below. For a moment, it seemed as if by miracle, we were walking on the surface of water that had not frozen over." In the translucent liquid beneath them, they beheld a flurry of crabs and fish. They had found fish skeletons on shore that had been gnawed clean by gammarids (crustaceans known as "scuds," in North American parlance), which they decided to catch. They drilled many holes in the ice, lowering baited traps to various depths. This proved a highly successful strategy for gathering huge quantities of gammarid specimens; Lake Baikal proved to be home to a startling diversity of endemic gammarids, some of them relatively large in size and brilliant in color.

Over the course of his exile—both while working as the personal physician to a Russian general in 1872 and in collaboration with Godlewski from 1872 to 1875—Dybowski surveyed the biology of the Amur-Ussuri region in Russia's Far East. He remained there until 1877 and continued sending collection materials back to Europe from the newly established seaport of Vladivostok. In recognition of his scientific achievements, he was granted permission to return to Poland at the end of his term of exile. He was even offered the honorific of "Dybowski-Baikalski," which he understandably declined in light of the compulsory nature of his tenure in Siberia. In 1879, he voluntarily returned to Siberia and worked as a regional doctor on Kamchatka, ministering to the health of various indigenous communities of the Russian Far East. With the continued financial support of the Russian Geological Society, he dedicated himself to the intense study of the peninsula's fauna and flora.

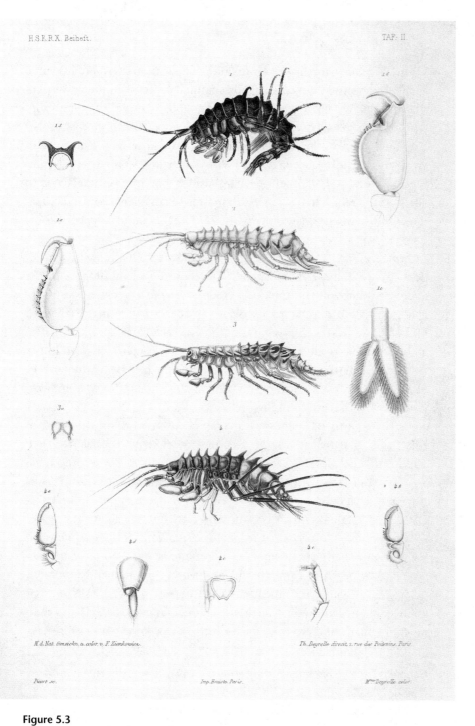

N. d. Nat. Gezeichn, u. color. v. F. Zienkowicz.   Th. Deyrolle dirext, 2. rue des Poitevins, Paris.

Deart. sc.   Imp. Henisto. Paris.   Mme Deyrolle color.

Figure 5.3

Color plate of gammarids from Lake Baikal in one of Dybowski's major monographs.
Dybowski, B., Beiträge zur näheren Kenntnis der in dem Baikalsee vorkommenden
niederen Krebse aus der Gruppe der Gammariden. Horae Soc. Ent. Rossica 10, Beiheft
(1874). Library of the Museum für Naturkunde Berlin.

In 1883, following his return to Europe, he was offered a professorship at the University of Lemberg, a Polish cultural center then under Austrian rule. In 1906, Dybowski was forced into retirement (at age 70) over his support for Darwin's theory of evolution. He emigrated back into the Russian Empire to live with his sister near the western border. At the outbreak of World War I, he was again sent to Siberia, but due to his scientific stature and previous work, the Petersburg Academy of Sciences intervened to allow him to return to his home, just in time to fall under German occupation. However, a German officer, who by some accounts happened to be the grandson of Alexander von Humboldt, permitted Dybowski to return to Lemberg. After Armistice, Polish independence was restored, Lemberg became Lwów, and Dybowski gradually rebuilt his connections with the scientific community. In the final decade of his life, Dybowski was finally able to focus on researching his Siberian collections. He had established himself as a world authority on the fauna of Lake Baikal and Kamchatka, and researchers began sending him their own specimens gathered in the field there. In 1928, Dybowski was elected as a member-correspondent of the Academy of Sciences of the USSR, a great honor. He died in Lwów (today's Lviv, Ukraine) at the age of 97.

In 1926, Dybowski published a comprehensive work on the fauna of Lake Baikal that created a furor, even outside the field of Baikal research. The work is entitled *Synoptic Register with Short Description of Genera and Species of This Group of Baikal Gammarids* and reads about as stiffly as its title. In it, Dybowski describes many crustacean species found in Lake Baikal, embedded in a complex classification system of the gammarid species familiar to him.[1] A specialized report for crustacean specialists, published without introduction or discussion. Almost immediately, however, the *Synoptic Register* began to garner notoriety beyond the gammarid scene, not because of the gammarids themselves, but because of Dybowski's new scientific names. Many of them are nearly endless, tongue-twisting letter combinations that can scarcely be parsed into word components and remain popular examples of bizarre naming. Here, a small sampling:

Cancelloidokytodermogammarus (Loveninsuskytodermogammarus) loveni
Crassocornoechinogammarus crassicornis
Parapallaseakytodermogammarus abyssalis
Zienkowiczikytodermogammarus zienkowiczi
Toxophthalmoechinogammarus toxophthalmus

Siemienkiewicziechinogammarus siemenkiewitschii
Rhodophthalmokytodermogammarus cinnamomeus
Gammaracanthuskytodermogammarus loricatobaicalensis

Not only are the names unusually long, some contain components of Russian or Polish origin, which make things considerably more difficult for the unpracticed reader. Dybowski was attempting to connect several word elements with different meanings in a single word. For example, by honoring his colleague Zienkowicz in both the specific epithet and the genus name and tying it to the name of a similar genus (*Dermo-gammarus*), he produced the unwieldy *Zienkowiczikytodermogammarus zienkowiczi*.

Dybowski's names did not find much favor in the gammarid scene. The same year, Mary J. Rathbun, a specialist in crustaceans at the Smithsonian Institution in Washington, DC, questioned the *Synoptic Register* in its entirety and submitted a case with the International Commission on Zoological Nomenclature, requesting that the validity of the names be assessed. Should the evaluation deem the names in conflict with the nomenclature rules, the request followed, the Commission should consider whether it be advisable to suppress all Dybowskian names from 1927—that is, to declare them invalid across the board. The Secretary of the Commission turned to Dybowski and requested comment. In his response, Dybowski explained that he "intended the designations in question only as provisional names and that the time [was] not yet ripe for the definite naming of these animals." The idea of publishing provisional names, only to change them later, stood in direct conflict with the nomenclature rules, the Commission countered. The board held that the Dybowskian names fulfilled the criteria for availability, meaning that the problem could not be solved by simply denying this fact. All that remained was the retroactive suppression, and indeed the Commission decided unanimously to revoke the validity of the *Synoptic Register* and all of the new names it contained, suppressing the work overall. The reason cited was that the names it introduced were in conflict with the requirement of linguistic harmony and manageability: should they be accepted, they would likely pose the risk of "greater confusion than uniformity."[2] Thus, the resolution entitled "Opinion 105," in which the problem is presented and the decision substantiated, marked the end of Dybowski's names. Definitively.

Cracking the Code: Nomenclators at Play

Without a doubt, the privilege of picking out the name of a newly discovered species is one of the most pleasing parts of biological nomenclature and represents far more than just the final flourish to a scientific species description. The result of this process of scientific recognition is made official—and enters the radar of the scientific community—only once the naming and subsequent publication have occurred. This "baptism" thus transmits many levels of information through the name. If possible, primarily information about the thing named—that is, the species or higher ranked group: appearance, behavior, habitat, and geographical origins have always been popular and frequently used name components. Looking at the scientific animal names published in the eighteenth and nineteenth centuries, it seems the vast majority of names were created in this fashion. This form of naming—in which an effort is made to incorporate essential features of the animal in the name, thus giving the name a linguistically meaningful definition—are considered serious and reliable but are also seen today as unimaginative and boring. Species names such as *viridis* (green), *africanus* (African), *albispinosus* (white-spined), and *silvestris* (forest-dwelling) are possibilities allowed to this day, but they tend to join the seemingly endless catalog of life without making much of a splash.

By the eighteenth century, scientists like Linnaeus already knew that cleverly crafted names would lead to greater attention. Creative names also provided an opportunity to convey information beyond what was included in the formal naming. These names can be indicators of one's own (high) level of education by containing allusions understood only by those with similarly vast stores of knowledge. As we have seen, it also gives scientists the opportunity to disparage unpleasant associates or elevate beloved colleagues. Humor is also a feature that many a systematic biologist has tried (and still tries) to express through the appropriate name. By Linnaeus's day, scientists could already count on attracting attention with an unusual name that deviated from the standard, classical linguistic context. Certainly among colleagues, who were typically the first—and often the only—to read the original publication. A particularly catchy name would spread quickly beyond the scientific circles, and one could count on widespread attention.

This hasn't changed, even in taxonomy today. Personal sensibilities and inclinations have a noticeable influence on every scientist's way of naming. The situation today has intensified in two ways: we're up to almost two million described and named animal species at this point, and we have reason to believe that millions more remain. According to his modest calculations, New Zealand biologist Mark Costello suspects another 5 million species remain to be discovered. Now, this doesn't mean we'll need another 5 million new species names because the same names may be used multiple times in various genera. This, however, still leaves the need for creating several hundred thousand names for the earth's diversity. This isn't an entirely new situation because there has almost always been a need for lots of names. However, publications are currently exploding, giving rise to so-called "fast-track" or "turbo" taxonomy. This means nothing other than that automating a certain part of the complex species-recognition process—usually the genetics—and minimizing the remaining steps has significantly accelerated the overall taxonomic process. It can thus come to pass that a hundred weevils of the same genus will be described in a single publication. In one fell swoop, one hundred new names are needed, which—since they're all within the same genus—must each be clear and unique. A little ingenuity goes a long way here.

Today, greater significance than ever awaits those taxonomists who emerge from the ranks and attract attention through their name choice. The results of taxonomic research are seldom spectacular enough to make the cover of scientific journals or the front page of newspapers. Attracting attention and appearing in public are modern marketing strategies that make sense on two fronts. This approach helps to shed some light on taxonomy and its findings, but it also lends visibility to the scientists and their work. Today, in the climate of stiff competition for research funding and tenure-track positions, this is an understandable motivation for using unusual names.

Thus, there are many reasons a taxonomist might decide to name a species after a person of public interest, such as Johnny Cash (honored in the tarantula species name *Aphonopelma johnnycashi*), and not *minor* (small). Although this kind of VIP name may exist only once in the zoological register, *minor* must exist hundreds—if not several thousands—of times. For this reason today, a battle for the most creative names seems to have broken out. Often the results don't lack a certain comic edge. The joke isn't usually contained in the name itself, though; instead, it's found in the original publication, which typically provides the etymological meaning or origins. And for some taxonomists, creating a name whose meaning does not immediately reveal itself can be their actual motivation. In his book on the meaning and origins of British butterfly names, lepidopterist Arthur Maitland Emmet writes, "Scientific names have much in common with crossword puzzles. The nomenclator is the setter; [...] and if he can mystify his fellow entomologists, he will derive sadistic pleasure in so doing."[3]

Humor in naming is always a balancing act of good taste because what's funny to one person can be considered downright appalling to another. This also applies to names with sexual connotations, where it's advisable to select the right name deliberately to be understood and respected beyond one's own cultural borders.

Some names are neither enigmatic nor absurd themselves but become so in combination with others. In 1907, the butterfly researcher William Dunham Kearfott described a whole series of new species within the genus *Eucosma*. The genus belongs to the moth family Tortricidae or leafroller moths, which include codling moths and other fruit pests. *Eucosma bobana* is one of Kearfott's names, but only once it's placed in concert with the other names, which run through nearly all the consonants in the alphabet, does the appeal of his creations manifest itself: *bobana, cocana, dodana, fofana, hohana, kokana, lolana, momana, popana, rorana, sosana, totana, vovana, fandana, gandana, handana, kandana, mandana, nandana, randana, sandana, tandana, vandana, wandana, xandana, yandana, zandana, nomana, sonomana, vomonana, womonana, boxeana, canariana, foridana, idahoana,* and *miscana.*

The zoological nomenclature rules don't play much of a role in making a name special, with one exception: they require that both the genus and species names be one word, each consisting of at least two letters. These letters must be selected from the twenty-six letters of the Latin alphabet. Special characters—such as hyphens, apostrophes, and others—may be verboten, but they do not invalidate a name if used in the original description. Typically, these special characters are then simply dropped to arrive at a Code-compatible version of the name.

A scientific name must therefore be a "word" or a letter combination that can be construed as such. Although it's preferable to derive scientific names from other words (like those of classical origin, for example), random combinations of letters are not necessarily barred, nor are those that could be considered unusual for the "feel" of Western languages, stemming from exotic tongues. As discussed in chapter 2, it should be possible to regard them as "words." However, the nomenclature rules don't define what exactly a word should be. If we take the basic definition of "word" as an independent linguistic unit with its own meaning, the difficulty of the definition quickly becomes clear. For example, the Code sees "cbafdg" as an artificial letter combination that doesn't represent a word and therefore isn't acceptable as a name. A word being speakable (and thus manageable) is often used as a criterion for determining whether a letter combination may be characterized as a word, and indeed "cbafdg" doesn't exactly roll off the tongue. It would be different, however, if "cbafdg" were a foreign term in active use. "Cbafdg" would then have the ennobling qualities of a word and would need to be accepted as such, despite its challenging pronunciation. The popular example of the South American wasp genus *Zyzzyx* illustrates how small a role this latter factor plays.

The darkling beetle genus name *Csiro* is at least pronounceable (with a little effort), while not an actual word but an acronym—that is, an abbreviation formed by the first letters of several words. It's based on CSIRO, the Australian research institution, Commonwealth Scientific and Industrial Research Organisation. Similar examples are the bacteria genera *Deefgea*, named after the DFG (Deutsche Forschungsgemeinschaft, or German Research Foundation), and *Basfia*, named after the German chemical company BASF (Badische Anilin- & Soda-Fabrik, the Baden Aniline and Soda Factory). A further example from the Anglo-American world is the beetle species *Foadia*, derived from the acronym FOAD, which stands for "fuck off and die." Although the starting points for these names aren't words in the literal sense, the zoological nomenclature rules prove generous and accept them, given the specific formation, or rather, use of these names.

As noted, at least two letters are needed for a valid genus and species name. This fundamental rule is undercut by *Plesiothrips o*, a thrips species published by Alexandre Arsène Girault, one of the most prolific authors ever among wasp researchers. However, because *Plesiothrips o* is a junior synonym of a species described in 1913 (*Stenchaetothrips biformis*, to be precise), thrips researchers don't have to spend much time deciding what to do with the name that came up short.

Things worked out differently for the South American digger wasp species *Podium T*. Its author, French baron Ambroise Palisot de Beauvois, described the species in 1811. Palisot used a "T" as the specific epithet in the original description, which was then adopted by later wasp taxonomists. In 1897, however, the Austrian entomologist Karl Wilhelm von Dalla Torre realized what the problem was with the overly short species name while working with digger wasps for his monumental catalog of hymenopterous insects, *Catalogus hymenopterorum hucusque descriptorum systematicus et synonymicus*. He interpreted the letter "T" as the Greek capital letter "Tau" and suggested *tau* as a replacement name for Palisot's "T." The nomenclature rules state that the individual responsible for publishing a replacement for an unavailable name is then considered the official author of the new name. So, while Dalla Torre may never have seen this species himself, and knew it only from Palisot's original description, he is forever the author of *Podium tau*.

Plenty of examples of genus and species names consist of only two or three letters and are Code-compliant (e.g., the Southeast Asian digger wasp *Aha ha*, described in 1988 by American wasp researcher Arnold S. Menke). Menke's reasoning, however, is fairly uninspired: *Aha* was a random letter combination chosen for its length. He doesn't write anything about the species name *ha*, but one can assume that the reason wasn't anything more profound than the name's overall compactness. For a long time, Arnold Menke's vanity plates read *"Aha ha."*

Because comprehensive lists of taxonomic names are not presented at random—but rather in a list or catalog form—alphabetical order plays an undeniable part in name choice. The mollusk species *Aa* Baker, 1940 isn't likely to be bumped from first place in the alphabetical list of genus names. Similarly situated—albeit at the other end of the alphabet—is the mollusk species *Zyzzyzus* Stechow, 1921. The wasp genus *Zyzzyx*, mentioned earlier, follows it narrowly. Then there's *Zyzzyva* Casey, 1922, a tropical weevil genus that brings up the caboose in some English dictionaries.

The number of letters used isn't capped, giving taxonomists carte blanche to do what they will in this regard. There are several candidates in the running for longest name depending on whether one is looking for the longest genus name ever published or the longest valid genus name, the longest binomial name, or any other superlative. The lengthiest name, albeit consisting of four parts, was bestowed on the longhorn beetle *Brachyta interrogationis interrogationis* var. *nigrohumeralisscutello-humeroconjuncta* Plavilstshikov, 1936. It's not available, though, because *nigrohumeralisscutellohumeroconjuncta* is placed under the subspecies, which the nomenclature rules prohibit. *Kimmeridgebrachypteraeschnidium* Fleck & Nel, 2003 appears to be the longest valid genus name.

Some taxonomists get a kick out of searching for other superlatives. For instance, Cicadellidae—or leaf hoppers—have the longest scientific name in which each letter appears twice; and *Aegilops* Hall, 1850—a mussel—is the longest name in which all letters appear in alphabetical order.

Sound Practice

Wordplay based on the sound of a name can be problematic because it may not be understood depending on a reader's linguistic origins. One famous example is the stick insect species *Denhama aussa*, described in 1912 by the Austrian zoologist Franz Werner. The name has echoes of the expression *"den haben wir raus"* (something along the lines of "we identified it!") in Viennese dialect, which resounds with the relief felt on wrapping up the arduous process of studying the species. The etymological meaning of the name is actually doubled. The type material of the species originated in Denham, a small town in Western Australia, which is reflected in the genus name. There is no record as to whether the specific epithet *aussa* is in reference to Australia. According to one obituary, however, Franz Werner—a professor at the University of Vienna—had a notorious sense of humor, which manifested itself in several unusual species names.

Other taxonomists in Austria allow their own regional linguistic flair to color the scientific names they author. The married couple Ulrike and Horst Aspöck, world experts in snakeflies and other lacewings, published a whole series of species names with Viennese inflection. Research into the etymology of these names is greatly facilitated by the 150-page comprehensive etymological directory the couple published in 2013 with the catchy title, *Woher kommen die Namen? (Where Do the Names Come From?)*, which contains all of the names of snakeflies and their linguistic origins. Unfortunately, few monographs like this one exist, in which specialists explore the magic of the names found in their respective areas of expertise. Here are a number of Aspöckian name creations:

Phaeostigma noane: The standard German *"noch eine"* (one more, another) is expressed in Austrian dialect as *"no ane"* and is used in this name to signify another as yet undescribed species of snakefly. The Aspöcks write that, on later questioning, they claimed the species had been named after Noane, goddess of repetition.

Agulla modesta adryte, *Agulla modesta aphyrte*, and *Agulla modesta aphynphte*: However ostensibly Greek in origin, these three names simply signify "*a dritte*" (a third), "*a vierte*" (a fourth), and "*a fünfte*" (a fifth) subspecies of the snakefly *Agulla modesta*.

Parvoraphidia aphaphlyxte: According to the original description, the species was named after Aphaphlyxte, an Aspöckian invention and purported daughter of Hermes, the god of merchants known for his slyness. In *Where Do the Names Come From?*, the Aspöcks note that this derivation would be acceptable; equally acceptable, however, would be the use of Aphaphlyxte to represent the Austrian term, "*a Verflixte*" (a damned or tricky thing) because this species had proven particularly challenging to place within the snakefly system.

Finally, an Aspöckian creation from the Mantispidae family (mantidflies), which are included among the lacewings. In 1994, the Aspöcks described a new central European species named *Mantispa aphavexelte*, which had long been placed incorrectly within the most common central European species, namely, *Mantispa styriaca*. The description of *Mantispa aphavexelte* solved this taxonomic problem. The name was derived from the Greek goddess of confusion, the description claimed, but it is all too obvious that the Austrian dialect is at play yet again, and the name really means "*a Verwechselte*" (a mistaken or confused thing).

In light of these inspired double meanings, the names that Jochen Gerber created in 1996 for the snail species *Vallonia eiapopeia*, *Vallonia hoppla hoppla*, and *Vallonia patens tralala* come across as rather mundane, however melodic.

In the Anglo-American sphere, classical animal names are pronounced in an unusual way, at least to the ear untrained in Anglophonic elocution—namely, they're spoken as if they were English words. English-speaking taxonomists have often used this for wordplay.

The syllable "eu" is thus pronounced "you"—instead of "oi"—which led Arnold Menke to name a digger wasp *Pison eu* ("piss on you") in 1988. A similar but potentially unintentional connotation applies to *Eremobates inyoanus* Muma & Brookhart, 1988, a camel spider found in Inyo County,

Arizona; those readers who feel so inclined may choose to read the species name aloud to work out the double meaning.

English entomologist George Willis Kirkaldy took advantage of the fact that the consonant digraph "ch" can also be pronounced as a "k" in English when he described a number of wasp species in 1904 built around the suffix -chisme, pronounced "kiss me." Preceding the suffix, he placed the names of various women with whom he'd supposedly been involved. In addition to a general *Ochisme* ("oh, kiss me"), there was *Dolichisme* ("Dolly, kiss me") and *Peggichisme* ("Peggy, kiss me"), along with *Florichisme*, *Marichisme*, *Nanichisme*, and *Polychisme*. It's said that the venerable London Zoological Society censured him for his frivolous name choices.

The braconid wasp *Verae peculya* Marsh, 1993 has a "very peculiar" name, and with *Heerz lukenatcha*, another braconid described by Paul Marsh in 1993, he chose to phonetically imitate one of the most famous lines in film. In the final scene of *Casablanca*, as Rick Blaine—played by Humphrey Bogart in the lead role—parts from his estranged lover Ilsa Lund (Ingrid Bergman), he says to her, "Here's looking at you, kid."

Although the genus name *Ytu* refers to the local Brazilian word for "waterfall," where this species of water scavenger beetle was discovered, it's pronounced "you too" in English. This inspired entomologist Paul J. Spangler to choose the specific epithet *brutus*, in imitation of the famous line attributed to Julius Caesar, "Et tu, Brute?"

The fungus beetle genus *Gelae* should also be spoken out loud to fully capture the joke behind it. The resulting names cover all manner of sweets, a marine animal, and a brand of candy: *Gelae baen* ("jelly bean"), *Gelae donut*, *Gelae rol*, *Gelae fish*, and *Gelae belae*. Similar culinary wordplay can be found in the Mythicomyiidae family of flies. The genus *Pieza* includes such species as *Pieza kake*, *Pieza pi*, and *Pieza rhea*.

Sound is important to another group of names—onomatopoeic names. These are especially common for birds and applied to few other vertebrates. Examples of onomatopoeic genus or species names are the Eurasian teal *Anas crecca*, the corn crake *Crex crex*, the cuckoo *Cuculus canorus*, the wood lark *Lullula arborea*, the turtle dove *Streptopelia turtur*, and the northern hawk owl *Surnia ulula*.

Upupa epops, the hoopoe, one of the most melodic names in zoology, has a slightly more complicated derivation. *Upupa* is unquestionably an onomatopoeic word, mimicking the bird's characteristic call, "hu-pu-pu." The specific epithet *epops*, meanwhile, is the Greek word for hoopoe, first used in the comedy *The Birds* by ancient Greek playwright Aristophanes. *Equus quagga quagga*, the plains zebra driven to extinction by humans in the late nineteenth century—which is considered a subspecies of plains zebra *Equus quagga*—also has an onomatopoeic specific epithet. The word was borrowed from the language of the Khoikhoi, a group indigenous to southern Africa, and was originally pronounced "kwa-ha." When repeated rapidly, the name echoes the zebra's call, "kwa-ha kwa-ha kwa-ha."

Naming species after things that are neither direct nor indirect biological entities, and whose essence or purpose also has nothing to do with the taxon being named, is more of an exception to the rule. For instance, the masked bee *Hylaeus tetris* Dathe, 2000 is named after the legendary computer game, in which the player must arrange shapes formed of four squares, falling from the top of the screen, into (ideally) uninterrupted rows at the bottom of the screen. The name is in reference to the four characteristic marks on the back of the thorax. Compared with its close relatives, the scarab beetle *Orizabus botox* Ratcliffe & Cave, 2006 is unusually smooth on top. The type material for the window fly species *Pseudatrichia atombomba* Kelsey, 1969 was gathered in Alamogordo, New Mexico, not far from the Trinity Site, where the world's first atomic weapon was detonated. Adam Striegel, a college student at the time, discovered the holotype of a fossilized carnivorous amphibian on land owned by FedEx; in 2010, it was described as *Fedexia striegeli*. For decades, "Bärenschenke" in the Berlin neighborhood of Mitte was a bar frequented by the entomologists at the Berlin Museum für Naturkunde for their regular drinks after work (*"Umtrunk"*). After the Bärenschenke closed in 2011, Wolfram Mey, the museum's lepidopterist, named a smaller moth species from Namibia *Baerenschenkia umtrunkala*, in memory of those regular get-togethers. A new species in the African parasitoid wasp family Figitidae, *Stenorceps vuvuzela* Nielsen & Buffington, 2011, got its name from the vuvuzela, the plastic trumpet that became known worldwide during the 2010 FIFA World Cup in South Africa. The name is in reference to the wasp's vuvuzela-shaped head. The genus name, *Stentorceps*, is composed of "Stentor," a warrior in Greek mythology whose voice was as loud as fifty men, and -ceps, a suffix derived from "caput" or "head." *Stentorceps vuvuzela* thus means something along the lines of "vuvuzela head." In biology, *Stentor* is also well known as the genus name for trumpet animalcules, a group of unicellular organisms that typically live attached to a substrate and can reach an unusually large two millimeters in length. *Oxybelus cocacolae* Verhoeff, 1968 is a digger wasp native to northwestern Africa and the Canary Islands. In his original description, the author wrote that he was about to drink a Coke when he spotted the wasp—and managed to catch it, too.

Acronyms are abbreviations formed from the first letters or syllables of other words. They're either pronounced as individual letters (UN for United Nations) or as new words created out of syllables or letters (NATO, AIDS). Acronyms play a small part in taxonomy because they tend to conflict with the zoological nomenclature rules, which will only recognize an arbitrary letter combination as a valid name, "providing this is formed to be used as a word."[4] This definitely isn't the case for all of the known names based on acronyms, such as the chigger *Afropolonia tgifi* Goff, 1983, whose specific epithet is derived from "Thank God It's Friday." The roundworm *Atalodera ucri*, named after the acronym for the University of California, Riverside (UCR), can certainly pass as a word. The names based on CSIRO, the Commonwealth Scientific and Industrial Research Organisation in Australia, however, pose some difficulties. Examples include the darkling beetle genus *Csiro* Medvedev & Lawrence, 1984 and the jellyfish genus *Csiromedusa* Gershwin & Zeidler, 2010. The spider *Habronestes boq* Baehr, 2008 was named after the Bank of Queensland. *Lasioglossum gattaca* Danforth & Wcislo, 1999, a sweat bee, was named after the four bases comprising the genetic code: A, T, C, and G. It's certainly possible, though, that the science fiction film of the same name, released just two years earlier, also played a part. The frog *Physalaemus enesefae* Heatwole, Solano & Heatwole, 1965 was named after NSF, the National Science Foundation—one of the most important institutions supporting scientific research in the United States.

When a new word is generated by rearranging the letters of another, it's called an anagram. These appear to be hugely popular in zoology, especially when separating the new species or genus from a species or genus that has already been described. The linguistic proximity of the two names can help symbolize striking similarities or close relatedness. In the 1860s, the French entomologist Victor Antoine Signoret (1816–1889) achieved a singular degree of perfection when he named various insect species by rearranging letters, thus yielding the genera *Acledra*, *Clerada*, *Eldarca*, *Erlacda*, *Racelda*, and *Dalcera*. Further examples include the mantispid genera *Mantispa* and *Nampista*, as well as the beetle genera *Ptinus*, *Niptus*, and *Tipnus*.

Words that read the same front to back as back to front are palindromes. Short words are especially well suited to this feat, and the longer the names are, the more difficult it becomes. The easiest examples are those names comprised of two identical letters, such as the mollusk genus that came up earlier, *Aa* Baker, 1940. Three letters are even more common: *Aia* Eyton, 1838, a bird; *Aka* White, 1879, an insect; *Aoa* de Nicéville, 1898, a butterfly; and particularly elegant, the digger wasp *Aha ha* mentioned earlier—not only is its genus name palindromic, both name components of the complete binomial are, too. Few other examples exist in this latter category: the rhinoceros beetle *Orizabus subaziro* Ratcliffe, 1994 and the hoverfly *Xela alex* Thompson, 1999. The genus name *Xela* is a letter combination derived from the specific epithet *alex*, and it refers to the nickname of Charles P. Alexander, one of the most prolific species authors ever to have lived. Because Alexander never tired of pointing out that his extraordinary productivity would have been unthinkable, were it not for his wife Mabel Margarita, entomologist Chris Thompson dedicated his new genus *Xela* to Charles P. Alexander, and its two new species to either of the Alexanders, namely, *Xela alex* and *Xela margarita*. The reason behind the name *Aidemedia*, a Hawaiian bird genus, is peculiar, however understandable. The name was dedicated to Hawaiian naturalist Joan Aidem, and the authors state that the genus name's unusual ending was selected solely because they couldn't resist the temptation of creating a palindrome.

Naughty by Nomenclature

Sex is a popular topic, even in taxonomy, and since its beginnings no less. Linnaeus, whose system of flora was based on the similarities and differences between sexual organs, created a range of provocative names with direct or insinuated sexual meanings. Since then, erotic connotations have been a common part of scientific naming, whether it be to reflect features of genital structures—which are often significant to taxonomic determinations—or simply to weave in sexual innuendo. It isn't easy to narrow down the examples in this category.

Let's start with the snakeflies described by Ulrike and Horst Aspöck, the married couple profiled earlier with the Austrian dialect-infused names. In 1974, the pair described *Phaeostigma mammaphila* (literally, "breast-loving"). This name was chosen because one of these insects—while still

Figure 5.4

The type specimen of *Papuogryllacris adoxa* Karny, 1928, with the genus and species labels typical of the Berlin collections. The new label with the QR code was added as part of the digitization of the locust collection. Museum für Naturkunde Berlin, M. Ohl photo.

an undiscovered species in Greece—landed on Ulrike Aspöck's chest, where it was then also captured. The Aspöcks also described *Ohmella libidinosa* together, in which the specific epithet derives from the Latin adjective *libidinosus*—quite clearly, "libidinous" in English. This is a nod to "the noticeable male genital segments with endophallus frequently turned outward." In the same genus three years earlier, they had described *Ohmella casta*, which derives from *castus* for "chaste" and refers to the especially small genitalia of the species' male population. In reference to the monstrous male genitalia of the snakefly species *Subilla priapella*, by contrast, the Aspöcks were reminded of Priapos, the god of fertility, who is often depicted with an outsized phallus.

Things get a little raunchier in the family of round fungus beetles or Leiodidae. Beetle taxonomists Quentin Wheeler and Kelly Miller described a new species named *Agathidium gallititillo* in 2005. Translated literally, the specific epithet means "French tickle," a certain sexual practice the reader may choose to research independently if curious. The name is in reference to a "long, ribbed section of the ventral part of the male genitalia." Quentin Wheeler, who is well known outside the beetle scene as a systematic biologist and biodiversity researcher, admits that this is his favorite of all the names he has ever described.

Two Southeast Asian fish species in the carp family (Cyprinidae) have the names *Probarbus labeamajor* and *Probarbus labeaminor*, both described in 1992 by the ichthyologist Tyson Roberts. The medical names labia majora and minora (dropping the suffix –a in English usage) are common terms beyond medicine as well. There are actually differences in lip size between these two fish species, although it isn't clear from the species descriptions whether the author had intended this obviously sexual connotation. However obvious it seems to be, it must ultimately remain unconfirmed. A side note regarding these names: in comparing the species names (*labeamajor* and *labeaminor*) and the anatomical labels (labia majora and minora), linguistic differences are revealed to suggest that the zoological names were not formulated correctly. At the least, the vowel "e" in the specific epithet is definitely wrong because the name is based on *labium*—Latin for "lip"—meaning the root for the first name component is labi–. The –a at the end of "labea" indicates the plural, which conflicts with the singular forms, major and minor. Unless Tyson Roberts had something totally different in mind, the name was not formed correctly.

There are quite a lot of name combinations with "phallus." *Brachyphallus*, "short phallus," is a parasitic flatworm in fish. The specific epithet *pachyphallus*, "thick phallus," is used in various families of flies and beetles. In 2003, French entomologists Marie-Thérèse Chassagnard and Léonidas Tsacas named a fruit fly species *Cacoxenus pachyphallus*, and in the same work, they also described *Cacoxenus campsiphallus* ("little box phallus") and *Cacoxenus oxyphallus* ("pointy phallus").

Colymbosathon ecplecticos is a fossil ostracode described in 2003 by David J. Siveter and his colleagues in the journal *Science*. The crustacean is from the Silurian Period in the United Kingdom, making it about 425 million years old. What's remarkable about the fossil is how well the soft tissues are preserved and how similar the creature is to species living today. The name is derived from the Greek words *kolymbos*, for swimmer, *sathon* for someone with a large penis, and *ekplektikos* for amazing. The ostracode is thus the amazing swimmer with a large penis. Following the publication, popular media touted the discovery as the "oldest penis in the world."

For all the creative freedom taxonomists enjoy, some have taken things too far from the perspective of the International Commission on Zoological Nomenclature. Although the panel demonstrated some flexibility with other names, when it came to Dybowski and his mile-long Siberian crustacean names, they were intractable and passed the harshest verdict that could befall a dedicated and well-respected species author. One of his most important works, which was intended to summarize his ideas on gammarid taxonomy at the end of his life, was suppressed in its entirety by the Commission. Not individual names—the whole thing. This was a terrible blow for the 93-year-old without a doubt. As a deportee in Siberia, he had painstakingly researched the Baikal crustaceans under the harsh conditions of exile. The Commission's suppression of the entire *Synoptic Register* discredited his decades of scientific work, cementing his reputation as a recklessly deviant taxonomist. Whether the names truly were meant to be provisional was irrelevant, although Dybowski was experienced enough to know that the nomenclature rules don't allow for stopgaps. To be fair, the influence of Russian and Polish in Dybowski's names was a challenge to his Anglophone colleagues, and it bears mentioning that the suggestion for suppression came from the United States. Put bluntly, it was pure bad luck. Although it's easy to see that Dybowski failed to meet the Code's requirement for easy communicability narrowly defined, subsequent examples of names that are scarcely less linguistically challenging have passed without complaint. Had Mary Rathbun, in her capacity of voluntary representative of the international gammarid-researcher community, shown the slightest indulgence, Dybowski might have savored the crowning moment of his life's work, rather than suffering deep disgrace in his twilight years. And the crustacean collections in today's natural history museums would elicit higher demand for extra-long labels.

6 "I Shall Name This Beetle After My Beloved Wife ..."

In the first half of the nineteenth century, telegraph technology—which enabled the electrical transmission of encoded letters and other characters— had developed to the point where information could be securely sent over increasingly long distances. While Carl August von Steinhall was still experimenting with distances of five kilometers in 1836 Germany, by 1850, English engineers and scientists had begun with the systematic development of a cable connection between Great Britain and the United States. Laying a 4,500-kilometer-long cable was one of the greatest technological challenges of the day: not only was the process incredibly expensive and involved, but no one knew whether electrical signals could even *be* transmitted such great distances. After two failed attempts, a cable was successfully laid between Ireland and Newfoundland in 1858. A global sensation! In August 1858, despite several hiccups, Queen Victoria of Britain and U.S. President James Buchanan were able to send each other congratulatory telegrams.

Initially, the transatlantic cable didn't quite live up to its promise. The message from Queen Victoria, which contained only 103 words, took almost sixteen hours from the Irish telegraph station to reach its destination in Newfoundland. Only a month after its inauguration, the cable failed terminally probably because of its damaged casing, which left the core of the cable vulnerable to the destructive force of seawater. It wasn't until 1866, after great cost and effort, that a permanent telegraph connection would be established between Ireland and Newfoundland.

The success of such an ambitious undertaking was contingent on countless factors, many of which were not fully understood at the time. For instance, the chemical and physical conditions at great depths, including the features of the ocean floor, remained largely unknown. To remedy this, in 1857, the British Admiralty deployed the H.M.S. *Cyclops* under the

Figure 6.1
Part of the skeletonized holotype of *Serranus goliath* Peters, 1855. The name is a synonym of *Epinephelus lanceolatus* (Bloch, 1790), the giant grouper native to the Indo-Pacific region. Museum für Naturkunde Berlin, M. Ohl photo.

command of Joseph Dayman with the aim of researching and measuring the seabed along the planned cable route—the so-called "telegraphic plateau." The *Cyclops* collected sediment samples, which were subsequently sent to the zoologist Thomas Henry Huxley to identify and describe possible animal life. Dayman monitored the study of the samples. In his 1868 report outlining the results of the exploration, he noted a remarkable observation: almost all of the sediment samples contained microscopic, distinctively round platelets that dissolved in acid and were unquestionably inorganic in makeup. Dayman named these tiny bodies "coccoliths." This provided the backdrop for Huxley as he took on the North Atlantic mud.

Figure 6.2
The late Thomas Henry Huxley. Courtesy of Wellcome Library, image #12958i.

Thomas Henry Huxley was one of the leading biologists of the nine-teenth century. In 1846, at age 21, Huxley joined the H.M.S. *Rattlesnake* as the ship's doctor on a four-year research expedition to New Guinea and Australia, during which he conducted extensive oceanographic studies. He was a talented orator and writer as well as a proponent of Darwin's theory of evolution. His strong advocacy, including his 1863 book *Evidence as to Man's Place in Nature*—not to mention a public feud with Samuel Wilber-force, the Bishop of Oxford—earned him the moniker "Darwin's Bulldog." Huxley was the grandfather of biologist and first UNESCO Secretary-General Julian Huxley, as well as *Brave New World* author Aldous Huxley.

One of the most challenging scientific problems of the time was the ques-tion of how life could have emerged from inorganic matter. Ernst Haeckel—Darwin's foremost defender in Germany and a close correspondent of

Huxley's—postulated that the most primordial living things were entirely homogenous, structureless organisms comprised of protoplasm, an undifferentiated cellular material. These primordial organisms, which Haeckel named "monera," promised to close a gap so painful to evolutionary theory—the gap between inorganic matter and the simplest known life forms. Proving the existence of monera was therefore one of the Darwinians' greatest dreams from the mid-nineteenth century onward.

Figure 6.3
Ernst Haeckel in 1908. Museum für Naturkunde Berlin, Historische Bild- u. Schriftgutsammlungen (MfN, HBSB) Bestand: Zool. Mus., Signatur: B I/60.

With the sediment samples from the *Cyclops*, Huxley struck gold. In nearly every sample, he discovered gelatinous matter in which Dayman's coccoliths were suspended like sliced fruit in Jell-O. Huxley thought he had successfully ended the global search for monera. He described his discovery in extensive detail in an 1868 publication. In honor of Haeckel's prediction, Huxley named the monera he'd discovered *Bathybius haeckelii*. His first thought was to send the namesake his publication, accompanied by a letter expressing his hope that Haeckel not be ashamed of his new godchild. In reply, Haeckel assured Huxley that he was "very proud" and concluded with gusto, "Long live the Monera!"

In the following years, the existence of *Bathybius haeckelii* was proven repeatedly in different locations by different scientists. Haeckel developed his monera concept further and suggested that, starting at depths around

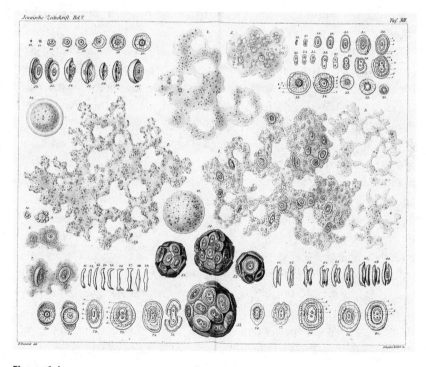

Figure 6.4
A plate depicting the gelatinous *Bathybius haeckelii* Huxley, 1868, and the coccoliths. Haeckel, E., Beiträge zur Plastidentheorie, Jena. Z Med Naturw. 5, Tafel XVII (1870). Staatsbibliothek Berlin.

1,500 meters below sea level, the entire ocean floor was covered in *Bathy-bius* goop. Huxley also proposed the existence of "living scum or film on the seabed, extending over thousands upon thousands of square miles," which represented the simplest and thus oldest form of life on earth.

Dubious Parentage

Haeckel relished the limelight of public presentations and pop science polemics, and he undoubtedly welcomed the flattery of this open tribute. Who wouldn't? This wasn't one of those ordinary biological discoveries, known only to scientists and barely noticed by the public. This was the primordial soup itself, the origins of all life, the protoplasm predicted by the famous Haeckel, the discovery of which the whole world had been waiting for. Who other than Haeckel should derive credit from the honorable discovery and confirmation of his theory? Suddenly, everyone was talking about *Bathybius haeckelii* and its namesake.

Many are surprised to learn that millions of plant and animal species remain undiscovered to this day, and that thousands of new species around the world are described every year. Most people also consider the naming of species in terms of human names: the misconception is widespread that the scientists writing the descriptions get to simply name the species after themselves. Although not explicitly prohibited by the nomenclature rules, this is seen as inappropriate (if not unethical) grandstanding, and it's highly uncommon. Instead, species names derived from human names are almost always dedicated to a person other than the author of the species description, although the motivation and intentions behind the dedication can vary. Another word for such names is "patronym," which isn't entirely accurate because as a "father-name," a patronym denotes those names in which the father's name—usually his first name—can be identified. This is expressed in some languages through the use of certain pre- or suffixes, such as "Klaus Johansson," which means "Klaus, son of Johann." As far as patronymic species names go, the model can be found in German surnames such as Pauli, Wilhelmi, and Caspari, many of which originated in the Middle Ages. By tacking on the Latin suffix—us, for instance, the name "Paul" takes on the Latinized form "Paulus." In the genitive case, "Paulus" becomes "Pauli" and expresses ownership or membership, as the genitive does. "Andreas Pauli" thus literally means "the Andreas of Paul" or

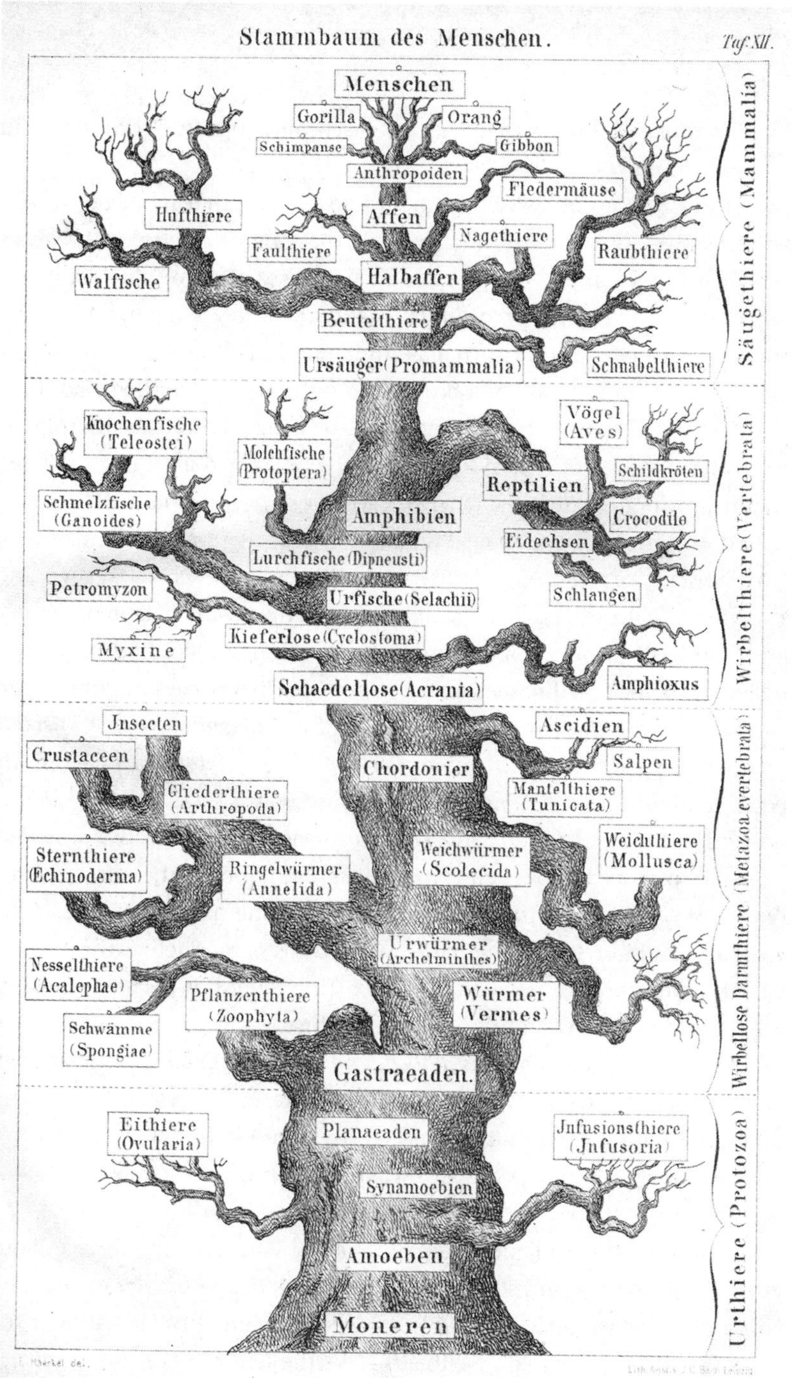

Figure 6.5

Haeckel's "Genealogical Tree of Humans" from 1874, showing the linear development from the monera at the base of the tree to all other animals and ultimately to humans (*Menschen*) at the top of the tree. Haeckel, E., Anthropogenie; oder, Entwickelungsgeschichte des Menschen (Leipzig: Wilhelm Engelmann, 1874). Library of the Museum für Naturkunde Berlin.

"Paul's Andreas." Many species names based on people are formulated in this fashion.

Creating zoological species names based on personal names follows a few easy rules. As just illustrated, most of these names are substantives in the genitive case, expressing possession such as the patronyms Pauli and Caspari. They are formed according to standard Latin grammar, adding the suffix –us for male and –a for female individuals. Following Latin declension rules, the endings are then brought into the genitive, which leads to –i (singular) and –orum (plural) for men and –ae (singular) and –arum (plural) for women. The lesser kestral *Falco naumanni* is named after ornithologist Johann Friedrich Naumann, whereas Eleonora's falcon—named after Eleonora d'Arborea, a Sardinian regent and folk hero—is named *Falco eleonorae*.

As substantives in the genitive, these names have the same meaning as linguistic patronyms. *Falco naumanni* literally means "Naumann's falcon." This basic principle of creating names dedicated to individuals can be applied to the personal names in one's own life. First names might include *johni* for John, *matthewi* for Matthew, *dorisae* for Doris, *miriamae* for Miriam, and *elizabethae* for Elizabeth. Last names are no different: a male Smith becomes *smithi*, a female *smithae*, Schmidt becomes *schmidti* and *schmidtae*, and Bohart becomes *boharti* and *bohartae*. This works perfectly, provided the name forming the base ends in a consonant. Should the name end in a vowel, several peculiarities should be noted. If the names are classical in origin and end in a Latinate syllable, such as –us or –a, they're also treated as Latin endings. This means that the existing ending is declined directly without adding a new ending. In terms of first names, Lisa thus becomes *lisae*, Nikolaus *nikolai*, Fabricius *fabricii*, and Linnaeus *linnaei*. Alternatively, the Code also allows names that seem Latinate to be treated as modern names: a Latin-seeming ending first receives an additional Latin ending, which is then put into the genitive. Fabricius can thus become *fabriciusi*— it's possible but uncommon.

Two options are available for name creation when dealing with a name whose grammatical gender does not correspond to the gender of the person named. For instance, several insect species named *podae*—after entomologist Nicolaus Poda von Neuhaus—take the feminine genitive ending, despite its being a man's name, because Poda is treated as a classical name. Alternatively, Poda can also be treated as a modern name, in which case it would become *podai*.

As with all organism names, those dedicated to individual people may not contain special characters, such as the accents and apostrophes fairly common to personal names. Because special characters are modifications of standard letters, the simple rule applies to nearly all cases—that the special character be removed, leaving the unchanged standard letter. Thus, O'Neill becomes *oneilli*, Sjöberg *sjobergi*, D'Urville *durvillei*, and Méneville *menevillei*. A special rule applies to German umlauts, which have only been replaced by the umlaut-less base letter since 1985, the year the third edition of the nomenclature rules was published. Names published before this year replaced umlauts with the base letter, followed by the letter –e. Up to 1985, Müller was thus *muelleri*, and since 1985, it has been *mulleri*. These mandatory retroactive changes are without nomenclatural effect.

However, plenty of special cases exist. For example, Dr. and other honorific titles are generally dropped, whereas abbreviated saints' names are written out in Latin. St. John would thus become *sanctijohanni*, and St. Catherine would be *sanctacatherinae*. Mc, Mac, or M' are standardized as "Mac" and added to names in the form *macdonaldi*. Prepositions such as von, van, von der, van der, de, la, and so on are usually included only if the actual name appears as a single word that incorporates the preposition: Vanderbilt, for instance, becomes *vanderbilti*. The choice is still left to the author—species named after the wasp researchers van der Vecht and de Beaumont could be *vandervechti* or *vechti*, *debeaumonti* or *beaumonti*.

Last, personal names can also be used as appositions. In these cases, they're treated as substantives that are neither declined nor adjusted to match the grammatical gender of the genus name. They're simply "added" to the genus name unaltered, which aligns with the general function of apposition. One example is *Platygobiopsis akihito*, a fish species named after Japanese emperor and prominent ichthyologist Akihito. Such names are actually fairly common, and although the nomenclature rules explicitly allow them, their use is discouraged. That's because when genus names are created without an associated species name, the author name is typically used. In the case of *Platygobiopsis*, authors Victor G. Springer and John E. Randall described the genus together in 1992, and in a list of genus names, their work would show up as *Platygobiopsis* Springer and Randall, 1992. From the combination with the appositive species name *Platygobiopsis akihito*, one might get the impression that Akihito had described the genus, especially if the combination were accidentally not italicized and *akihito* were capitalized. In a museum collection's daily grind, it can easily come to pass that italics can't be displayed, whether in handwritten records or electronic databases. To preclude any possible confusion, the Code therefore recommends against using appositional names that derive from personal names. Following this recommendation, the better form would have been *akihitoi*, but this wasn't the name that was published. *Platygobiopsis akihito* therefore remains the correct original notation.

There are many reasons for naming species after people. The classic motivation is to honor or thank someone, and it's safe to assume that most of these names are created for people the author wants to thank for supporting the project, providing materials, or similar.

Beyond expressing gratitude, these names often convey additional information. For instance, a name might be chosen to suggest a close relationship—or really any degree of acquaintance—with a prominent colleague or sponsor, which might be viewed with awe or even envy by one's associates. Through the shrewd selection of influential figures, a scientist can make important connections known to the public, asserting his or her membership in a particular social network. Financial backers, sponsors, and patrons are usually happy to see species named after them, which may leave them disposed to show further generosity.

Personal reasons can also provide the motivation behind new names. Family members, personal supporters, favorite characters from mythology, fairy tales, books, or films, admired artists, historical figures—the number of possible sources of names is nearly limitless.

The reason for a certain name choice is elucidated in the section of the species description known as the "etymology" or "derivatio nominis." As such, this section of the publication is intended for the actual etymology, or linguistic derivation, of a name. Although the nomenclature rules only recommend—but don't require—these explanations, they're common today, and many scientific journals have a policy of requiring them. In addition to providing a linguistic explanation of the name components, their linguistic origins, and the gender and grammatical form of the name, this is also where authors can present the scientific or personal reasons for choosing a name at their own discretion. It's one thing to establish ties to prominent figures through taxonomic names and quite another to provide the reasons for doing so. With descriptive or geographical names, the reason is often obvious, but it's at least assumed that the information contained within the name applies to the species named. This usually isn't immediately evident with personal names, and their actual origins often remain opaque until the original description has been read. An informal survey of my colleagues in taxonomy revealed that when first scanning a new publication, at the sight of a dedication, most will read the etymology section with great interest. Thus, the etymology section of a species description isn't just a linguistic explanation, it's also a mix of social media and gossip column.

The effectiveness of VIP names dedicated to politicians or popstars relies on their being noticed and read and not just by those in the field. In taxonomy today, it has become evident that in selecting a name, many scientists calculate and plan its public impact to a T. Major taxonomic research institutions, such as natural history museums, promote the names through targeted public relations campaigns online and through other mass media channels with large public followings. Although the actual advertising effect of such anecdotal name selections can hardly be measured, taxonomists agree that this is one of the ways to direct public attention to the multitude of undescribed species and the field of taxonomic research.

A nice example for the interwoven reasons behind the creation of patronyms can be found in the description of a variety of new huntsman spiders from Southeast Asia, published by Peter Jäger over the course of many years. Jäger is an internationally known spider expert who works at the Senckenberg Museum in Frankfurt. He has named around 260 spider species, most of which he discovered in Asia. By the end of 2013, fourteen of these names were "VIP names"—as Jäger refers to them in his *Arachno-Blog*—which are good publicity. Twelve others allude to overpopulation, and 81 were named after individuals more or less known to the general public. *Heteropoda davidbowie* and *Pseudopoda amelia* are two such VIP names, and several others were coined in honor of German actors and comedians. *Heteropoda davidbowie* is a Southeast Asian species named after the English singer, songwriter, and actor David Bowie, and the Chinese huntsman spider *Pseudopoda amelia* recalls the title character of the 2001 French film *Amélie*. Jäger views the twelve names that refer to global overcrowding as political statements highlighting the ecological problems resulting from overpopulation. For those who know German, the name *Heteropoda zuviele* (*zu viele* = too many) is easy to understand. *Heteropoda duan* means "urgent" in Lao, the national language of Laos, and the name calls for what Jäger sees as the need for quick action against the unchecked destruction of natural habitats. *Heteropoda laai* is also borrowed from Lao and means "lots." *Heteropoda homstu* is an abbreviation of *Homo stultus*, the "stupid human," which Jäger also translates as "madman" or "idiot," referring again to the environmental destruction by which humans are ravaging their own basis of existence. *Heteropoda opo* comes from "OverPOpulation." *Heteropoda duo* is not based on the Latin adjective for "two," as one might think. Rather, it comes from a Chinese word that means "too much." Finally, there's *Heteropoda hippie*, a general nod to the hippie movement and the long hairs on the male spiders' legs.

In addition to thoroughly unusual name derivations, Jäger's linguistic constructions are also worth mentioning. Most of the artists' names are appended as appositions, meaning they're added to the genus name unaltered. Jäger brushed off the Code's recommendation not to use personal names as appositions. The examples given here are pretty unproblematic because there is little risk that someone would take David Bowie to be the author of the spider genus *Heteropoda*, at least for now, while the artist is

Figure 6.6
Portrait of the huntsman spider *Heteropoda davidbowie*, Jäger, 2008. Courtesy of Mattes Linde.

still sufficiently well known. With the names *Heteropoda zuviele, H. duan, H. laai,* and *H. homstu,* Jäger ignores another recommendation of the Code, namely, that for scientific names, one should avoid using vernacular terms in the original and instead Latinize them. This is also just a recommendation, though, meaning that Jäger's names are formally unproblematic.

But what drives Jäger toward these catchy, unusual names? Certainly these creative christenings are fun, but there's more to it than that. The political statements inherent to *Heteropoda zuviele, H. duan, H. laai,* and *H. homstu* are self-evident. As a biologist whose work is focused in Southeast Asia, Jäger witnesses firsthand the rapid disappearance of the huntsman spiders' tropical habitat. Communicating a political message by means of a species name is certainly an unconventional move, bearing the risk that the meaning will not be understood or even noticed by anyone beyond other specialists, who tend to already share the aforementioned environmental concerns. The meaning inherent to a species name is linguistically encrypted as it is, and the use of German, Chinese, and Lao names presents a further level of encryption that requires no small amount of effort for the user to crack. *Heteropoda homstu* is certainly an extreme example: a name whose political content is beyond recognition, hidden under several layers (environmental destruction—idiocy—translation into Latin—abbreviation—merging of isolated syllables). Because most readers are only able to understand the political statements contained within Jäger's names in combination with the supplemental explanations in the original description, their immediate political impact is limited at best.

And why does Jäger name his spider species after musicians and artists one can assume he doesn't know personally? The explanations in the etymology are definitely worth a read. For instance, in the etymology of *Heteropoda davidbowie,* he writes, "The species name is honouring the rock-singer David Bowie—composer of the music album *The Rise and Fall of Ziggy Stardust and the Spiders from Mars* and interpreter of songs such as 'Glass Spider'—who has been in early years of his career sometimes as painted as the frontal view of the head of this new species, furthermore inspiring the author by his songs full of energy, creativity and open-mindedness." With regard to *Heteropoda ninahagen,* named for the "godmother of [German] punk" Nina Hagen, he writes, "This species is named after German rock and punk singer Nina Hagen, who has inspired the author for many years with her one-of-a-kind songs and lyrics, which are as unusual as the form of the new species' RTA; a substantive in apposition." Not only does the reader learn that Jäger is a longtime Nina Hagen fan, they also discover that her songs and lyrics readily withstand comparison to the form of the new species' RTA. RTA stands for "retrolateral tibial apophysis," which denotes a certain structure in the male spiders' copulatory organs. The RTA and other male genital structures are complex and often provide reference points for species differentiation. Hence, Jäger is saying that Nina Hagen's songs and lyrics are as unusual in the music scene as the male genitalia of the new species are within the genus *Heteropoda*. A truly striking comparison!

Jäger, with his selection of species names, falls within the current trend. Given the freedom of name choice, it's currently in style to use eye-catching monikers. Taxonomic species descriptions are mostly done for specialists. Close colleagues in the field—who are interested in either the animal group at hand or the geographic region the species comes from—are the only people who will read these articles with interest, if not enjoyment. It's more difficult—if not hopeless, and in some instances, perhaps pointless—to garner attention for the approximately 18,000 new species discovered worldwide and described every year. The careful selection of PR-friendly names, however, can bump discoveries like these into the limelight. An online search for Peter Jäger's star names illustrates this point: hundreds of news tickers, blogs, and print media have reported on the new spider names, which is a level of attention the spiders never would have reached had they been given dry, descriptive names. *Heteropoda davidbowie* seems to have had particular appeal to the international press because directly following its publication, there were more than 230,000 Google hits for the name. Music magazines, including the German edition of *Rolling Stone*, reported on it, and Jäger took the stage at the World Science Festival 2012 in New York to present *Heteropoda davidbowie* to the crowd.[1] The species named after German singers haven't made it quite as far, even if Udo Lindenberg does mention "his" spider on his homepage.

It's obvious that this kind of media coverage attracts attention for the spiders as well as for Jäger, which is naturally in his interest and in that of the Senckenberg Natural History Museum in Frankfurt. Such attention needn't be entirely self-serving, and to his credit, Jäger has parlayed his interview time into a platform for raising awareness of the large percentage of undiscovered species worldwide, the plight of biodiversity, and the threat of habitat loss, especially in tropical regions.

In terms of political effectiveness, the art of naming entails more than the quality of the name then—if it is to be heard, the message needs an adept messenger and not only a quirky medium. A colorful name such as *Heteropoda davidbowie* certainly catches the eye, but deeper public impact depends on Jäger's continued efforts and ability to inspire the press to report further research.

Realistically, the burning environmental questions will not be solved by the description of 18,000 new *davidbowie* spiders or *freddiemercuryi* damselflies a year. However, there's also little danger of a glut of celebrity-inspired names; most taxonomists prefer to avoid the limelight, and many are dismissive of such media-friendly names as flashy and flip. Thus, we can expect that most newly described organisms will continue to be named in classic fashion, according to features, geographical origins, and sponsors.

Still, Jäger isn't alone in adopting musicians and other public figures as namesakes for new species and other taxa. A complete list would fill pages.

Figure 6.7
A wandering albatross (*Diomedea exulans* Linnaeus, 1758) egg, labeled in pencil. Museum für Naturkunde Berlin, M. Ohl photo.

Although most musician-based species names simply express the scientists' enthusiasm for their favorite artists, some are chosen because of certain features shared by the species and the human namesake. The Antarctic predatory dinosaur *Elvisaurus*, for instance, has a crested forehead reminiscent of Elvis Presley's pompadour hairstyle. *Elvisaurus* was only informally introduced by its author, Holmes, and under the nomenclature rules, it is considered "nomen nudum," or a "naked name" that doesn't fulfill the Code's requirements. The correct name of this dinosaur genus is *Cryolophosaurus*.

In 2013, the team around paleontologist Jason Head—then of the University of Nebraska–Lincoln—dubbed a giant herbivorous lizard from the Eocene of Myanmar *Barbaturex morrisoni* in honor of Jim Morrison. The reason behind it wasn't just a passion for The Doors' music but because of a lizard that appears in one of their songs: "I am the Lizard King, I can do anything."

More critical attention was raised by a new Australian species in the horsefly family, named *Scaptia* (*Plinthina*) *beyonceae* Lessard & Yeates, 2011. In the etymology, the Australian authors simply state that they named the species in honor of singer Beyoncé Knowles, but they provided further details in several interviews. This horsefly is distinguished by the striking golden tip of its abdomen, which reminded Lessard and Yeates of the singer's curvaceous backside in one of her golden evening gowns. Lessard referred to *Scaptia* (*Plinthina*) *beyonceae* as the "all-time diva of flies." Beyoncé's horsefly received mixed reviews, and some saw sexism (or at least poor taste) at play, another example that species names with even the slightest suggestion of sexual connotation can be a real balancing act.

An alternative possibility, although not widely practiced, is to translate a modern musician's name into a classical equivalent. The result has all the appearances of a scientific and serious name but one whose etymology is often encrypted beyond the point of recognition. The genus name of the ichneumon wasp *Xanthosomnium froesei* Sime & Wahl, 2002 is a translation of the progressive rock band Tangerine Dream. The species name is in reference to Edgar Froese, who founded the band in 1967. Similarly, the specific epithet of the mite species *Funkotriplogynium iagobadius* Seeman & Walter, 1997 combines Iago (James) and badius (brown) in a hidden homage to funk legend James Brown.

The individual members of a band can also be immortalized with species names, grouped together under the same genus. For instance, Jonathan

Adrain and Gregory Edgecombe named new trilobite species after the members of the Ramones (*Mackenziurus johnnyi*, *M. joeyi*, *M. deedeei*, and *M. ceejayi*), the Sex Pistols (*Articalymene viciousi*, *A. rotteni*, *A. jonesi*, *A. cooki*, and *A. matlocki*), and Simon & Garfunkel (*Avalanchurus simoni* and *A. garfunkeli*).

In addition to the well-represented world of musicians, countless species names are based on other famous figures. In 1996, for instance, a conch was named *Bufonaria borisbeckeri* after the tennis champion Boris Becker, notwithstanding the snail's slowness in juxtaposition with Becker's swiftness. The author, Parth, evidently intended it as a tribute, writing in the etymology that the new species was dedicated to the "single greatest German athlete of all time, in my opinion." Comedians have done well; Jäger, among others, has immortalized some with spider names, and there are many examples from other animal groups. The long-legged fly *Campsicnemus charliechaplini* was named after Charlie Chaplin in 1996 by Neal Evenhuis because of its unusual tendency to die with bowed middle legs. A pair of cicada species—*Baeturia laureli* and *Baeturia hardyi* de Boer, 1996—were named after the classic comedy duo.

The world of writers and publishing has also received its due. The eccentric wasp researcher Alexandre Arsène Girault—who will be introduced in greater detail in the chapter 9—appears to have been in a literary frame of mind while searching for genus names for Australian wasps: *Aligheria* (for Dante Aligheri), *Carlyleia* (for Thomas Carlyle), *Emersonella* (for Waldo Emerson), *Goethana* (for Johann Wolfgang von Goethe), *Keatsia* (for John Keats), *Plutarchia* (for Plutarch), *Richteria* (for Jean Richter), and *Shakespearia* (for William Shakespeare). *Arthurdactylus conandoylensis* Frey & Martill, 1994 is a Brazilian pterosaur named in honor of Arthur Conan Doyle in reference to his 1912 novel *The Lost World*, in which an expedition finds its way to the top of an isolated plateau in the South American jungle, only to discover pterosaurs and other extinct animal species still living there. The Cretaceous-era herbivorous dinosaur *Serendipaceratops arthurclarkei* Rich & Vickers-Rich, 2003 was named after science fiction author Arthur C. Clarke, who predicted a future in which all humans would be vegetarian. A now-endangered subspecies of the North American cottontail rabbit, *Sylvilagus palustris hefneri* Lazell, was named after *Playboy* founder Hugh Hefner in 1984. The author is said to have received financial backing from *Playboy*.

Film is another popular source for scientific animal names. In 2002, the entomologist Terry Erwin named several newly discovered Costa Rican ground beetles after actors. *Agra katewinsletae* (for Kate Winslet in her role in *Titanic*) and *Agra liv* (for Liv Tyler in her role in *Armageddon*) are meant to represent catastrophe and raise awareness that these species' habitats are threatened by manmade or natural disaster. On the other hand, *Agra schwarzeneggeri*—described in the same publication as a ground beetle with "markedly developed (biceps-like) middle femora"—is a nod to Arnold's distinct physiognomy. And what could be more appropriate than *Coloborhynchus spielbergi* Veldmeijer, 2003, a pterosaur named after *Jurassic Park* director Steven Spielberg?

Figure 6.8
A specimen of the carabid beetle *Agra schwarzeneggeri* Erwin, 2002, with its biceps-like middle femora. Courtesy of Karolyn Darrow, Smithsonian Institution, Washington, DC.

It's no secret that American arachnid taxonomist Gustavo Hormiga is a big Orson Welles fan and knows his filmography inside and out. In addition to naming a new genus of Hawaiian spiders in the Linyphiidae family *Orsonwelles*, he also commemorated many of Welles's best-known film roles as the species names: *Orsonwelles othello, O. macbeth, O. falstaffius,* and *O. calx*. The Shakespearean characters are easily recognized; "calx," the Latin for "limestone," is a reference to Harry Lime, Welles's role in *The Third Man*. For other species in the genus, Hormiga uses the titles of Welles films, adapting them according to classical rules: *Orsonwelles bellum* (Latin for "war"—*War of the Worlds*), *O. malus* (Latin for "evil"—*Touch of Evil*), and *O. polites* (Greek for "citizen"—*Citizen Kane*).

In the river systems stretching across the American southeast, Steve Layman and Rick Mayden studied the speckled darter *Etheostoma stigmaeum*, a widespread and colorful species of darter. Their genetic data suggest that some in the subpopulation differ significantly enough to be recognized as separate species. They described five of these newly discovered darter species in 2012 and named them after four American presidents and one vice

Figure 6.9
An adult male of *Orsonwelles malus* Hormiga, 2002, from Kauai. Gustavo Hormiga photo.

Figure 6.10
The darter *Etheostoma obama* Mayden and Layman, 2012. Drawing by Joseph R. Tomelleri (www.americanfishes.com). Copyright by Joseph R. Tomelleri.

president: *Etheostoma obama*, *E. gore*, *E. jimmycarter*, *E. teddyroosevelt*, and *E. clinton*. This naming strategy proved effective in capturing the attention of the American media, and in the many interviews Layman and Mayden have given since their publication appeared, they have detailed the reasons for their name selections, pointing to the achievements each of the name-sakes have made in American environmental politics.

Hobbits and Haters

A source of species names as popular now as it was in Linnaeus's day is ancient mythology. There can be many reasons for choosing a certain Roman or Greek figure as a namesake, and the publications of the eighteenth and nineteenth centuries don't usually provide any background information. Here's a small sample of the loveliest patronyms drawn from Greek and Roman mythology.

The death's head hawk moth genus *Acherontia* Laspeyres, 1809, which includes the species *A. atropos* (Linnaeus, 1758), *A. lachesis* (Fabricius, 1798), and *A. styx* Westwood, 1847. Acheron and Styx are two of the five rivers of the underworld in Greek mythology, and Atropos and Lachesis are Greek goddesses of fate. *Aphrodita* Linnaeus, 1758 is a sea mouse that can also be found on German shores, a segmented worm with dense, shimmering bristles. It's said that the hairless, naked underbelly of this seven-to-ten-centimeter-long, two-to-three-centimeter-wide worm reminded Scandinavian seamen of women's genitalia. Linnaeus, who liked using names with sexual connotations, took this image and gave the sea mouse the name of the Greek goddess of love, beauty, and carnal desire. The male members of the Cretaceous shark genus *Damocles* Lund, 1986 have a prominent structure that reaches over the head from the back. Its namesake, Damocles, is a figure from Greek mythology who had a sword suspended over his head by a single horse hair. The impressive Central and South American eagle species *Harpia harpyja* (Linnaeus, 1758) may count as the inspiration for some sagas and legends of mythical creatures. Linnaeus named it after the harpies, the winged hybrid monsters in Greek mythology. *Pegasus* Linnaeus, 1758 is one of two genera of so-called seamoths or dragonfish. The enlarged, wing-like pectoral fins of these demersal fish are reminiscent of the winged horse Pegasus in Greek mythology. In 1758, Linnaeus named the oceanic tropicbird genus *Phaethon* for the sun god Helios's son, who brazenly drove his father's sun chariot into the heavens. *Titanus giganteus* (Linnaeus, 1758), the Titan beetle, and *Dynastes hercules* (Linnaeus, 1758), the Hercules beetle, are the world's largest beetles. The names refer to these figures from Greek mythology, known for their size and strength.

Figure 6.11
A male specimen of *Damocles serratus* Lund, 1986. Carnegie Museum (Natural History), Pittsburgh PA, #CM 35473. Courtesy of Richard Lund and Eileen D. Grogan.

Figure 6.12
The Hercules beetle, *Dynastes hercules* (Linnaeus, 1758), here a specimen of the sub-species *Dynastes hercules ecuatorianus* Ohaus, 1913, from Peru. Muséum d'Histoire Naturelle de la ville de Toulouse, Didier Descouens photo.

Gods and other mythical beings *not* of classical origin are also popular choices for scientific animal names. For instance, *Lucifer* Döderlein, 1882, a deep-sea fish, was initially given the biblical name for the devil that literally means the "bringer of light" but has since been renamed *Photonectes*. *Beelzebufo* Evans, Jones & Krause, 2008, is an amphibian genus from the Cretaceous period that the authors refer to as the "frog from hell." The name is a portmanteau of Beelzebub, another name for the devil, and bufo, Latin for toad. *Murina beelzebub* was the name given to a bat species discovered in Southeast Asia in 2011. *Mephisto* Tyler, 1966 is a genus of spikefish related to pufferfish. *Moloch horridus* Gray, 1841, is the Australian thorny dragon, a spiny lizard, named after Moloch, one of the devils in John Milton's 1667 epic poem *Paradise Lost*. *Anubis* Thomson, 1864, is a longhorn beetle named after the Egyptian god of death. An especially popular namesake is Osiris, the Egyptian god of the afterlife, rebirth, and the Nile. A search of the *Encyclopedia of Life* turns up more than 200 names that contain Osiris, either as a genus or species name. The New World bee genus *Osiris* boasts a couple dozen species alone, but stick insects, moths, and several other animal and plant groups have Osiris as the specific epithet in their name.

New World gods also find their way into scientific names. The enormous pterosaur *Quetzalcoatlus northropi* Lawson, 1975 was named after Quetzalcoatl, a Central American god of the Aztec and Maya, among others. The specific epithet is in honor of aircraft engineer John Knudsen Northrop, whose designs of flying wings still serve as the basis for the stealth bomber B-2 Spirit.

Among taxonomists, *The Lord of the Rings* has its share of fans, and perhaps unsurprisingly J.R.R. Tolkien's fantasy worlds and invented languages have provided a source for many scientific names. Director Peter Jackson's hugely successful film trilogy, released in 2001 to 2003, provided the books with new fans and widespread popularity. In 2013, for instance, an international group of wasp researchers led by Fernández-Triana and Ward described a new genus and six new species of braconid wasps (Braconidae) from New Zealand, where the *Lord of the Rings* movies were filmed. The genus name *Shireplitis* refers to the Shire, the fictional homeland of the hobbits for which New Zealand served as the cinematic stand-in, thus alluding to the wasps' real-world geographical origin. (The suffix –plitis comes from the morphologically similar genus *Paroplitis*.) Five of the new species were named after hobbits: *Shireplitis bilboi*, after Bilbo Baggins, finder of the ring in question; *Shireplitis frodoi*, after his nephew, Frodo Baggins, who bore the ring on the quest for its destruction; *Shireplitis samwisei*, after Frodo's best friend and faithful companion, Samwise "Sam" Gamgee; and *Shireplitis peregrini* and *Shireplitis meriadoci* after his companions Peregrin "Pippin" Took and Meriadoc "Merry" Brandybuck. With the sixth wasp, *Shireplitis tolkieni*, the authors pay "humble homage" to the creator of the epic.[2]

Others have delved deeper into the intricacies of Tolkienian lore. In a 1978 article in *Evolutionary Theory*, the American paleozoologist Leigh Van Valen described a number of prehistoric mammal fossils, assigning names that evince a detailed knowledge of the pseudo-historical Elvish languages invented by Tolkien, including references to *The Silmarillion*, a posthumously published mythological prehistory to *The Lord of the Rings*. Choice examples include *Oxyprimus galadrielae*, after Galadriel, the highest-ranking Elf in Middle-earth from the Elvish language Sindarin. Van Valen does not provide the motivation behind this name choice. *Deltatherium durini*, after Durin I, the King of Dwarves who initiated construction of

Figure 6.13
A male of *Shireplitis frodoi* Fernández-Triana and Ward, 2013. Courtesy of José L.
Fernández-Triana.

the vast subterranean fortress of Khazad-dûm, was chosen for the species'
diminutive size. *Chriacus calenancus*, from the Sindarin "calen," for green,
and "anca," for jaw. The fossil was potentially that of an herbivore. *Than-gorodrim thalion*, in which Thangorodrim refers to a mountain fortress in
The Silmarillion, and refers to the animal's mountainous discovery site.
The species name means "strong" in Sindarin. *Platymastus palantir*, after
Palantír, one of the seven "Seeing Stones" created by Fëanor that can see
through time and space, from the Elvish language Quenya. The name refers
to the species' long record of existence. *Platymastus mellon*, from the Que-nya word for "friend." "Mellon" is also the password to enter the western
gate to Khazad-dûm. In the species, the name refers as well to "melon"
and to the Greek term "mellesis" (hesitation, delay). Mixed in are names
from American Indian languages, for example, *Ellipsodon yotankae*, derived
from Sitting Bull's name in the Lakota language, Tatanka Yotanka, and from
the holy texts of Hinduism, for example, *Haplaletes andakupensis*, based on

Andhakupa, described in the fifth book of the Bhagavatapurana as the hell for those who have killed mosquitos or other blood-sucking insects. The species name refers in equal measure to the fossil's origins in the Purgatory Hills and its proximity to Bug Creek.

Van Valen is best known for his 1973 contribution of a "new evolutionary law," which has since become an inextricable part of modern evolutionary theory.[3] The hypothesis holds that the risk of extinction for every organism group is about the same, independently of how long the organism group has been in existence. All that matters is that the group constantly adapts to ever-changing environmental conditions to assert its earned position and not die out. To illustrate, Van Valen again found inspiration in fantasy literature, naming the hypothesis after the Red Queen from Lewis Carroll's *Through the Looking-Glass*, who explained the natural laws of her realm: "Now here, you see, it takes all the running you can do, to keep in the same place." The Red Queen's Hypothesis has been applied to many other areas of evolutionary biology, in particular the phenomena of evolutionary arms races between predators and prey, hosts and parasites, and to explain the advantages of sexual selection.

The examples in this chapter reflect an imaginative approach to the search for scientific names, a cherry on top of the naming and describing process. For the most part, names dedicated to people—whether in honor of a generous patron or a fictional character—are usually intended as an expression of positive feelings toward the creature named and its namesake alike. However, here, too, are exceptions. At times the temptation to use a name dedication as a platform to express a negative feeling toward a specific person may be irresistible. Because this is rather unusual and generally frowned upon by scientists, one can assume that the authors' conflicts with the targeted colleagues, friends, or relatives must have been serious. Admittedly, however, the entertainment value of spiteful names is usually pretty high, and the scientific community reads them with great interest. A name's negative charge can be emitted from the denigrating meaning of the name itself, or it can come through the dedication of a species with unpleasant features.

No surprise that the Bone Wars should constitute a master class in the art of the insulting name. In 1869, Othniel Charles Marsh described a fossil marine reptile that he named *Mosasaurus copeanus*. The first element of the species name *copeanus* unquestionably refers to his bitter rival, Edward

Drinker Cope. The second element, however, is somewhat ambiguous. The Latinate suffix –anus can be used to make the species name into an adjectival form to modify the genus name, for instance, describing an affiliation or a connection. Common examples include *montanus*, meaning "of the mountains," as in *Suncus montanus*, the Asian highland shrew; or *africanus*, "of Africa," as in *Agapanthus africanus*, the African lily. The suffix is analogous to –an in English, as used in "African." In a few cases, the suffix –anus has been used to express affiliation with an individual person. The braconid wasp *Xiphozele linneanus*, for example, was described and named by the Dutch entomologist Kees van Achterberg in 2008 in honor of Linnaeus on the 250th anniversary of the establishment of binomial nomenclature. With *Mosasaurus copeanus*, Marsh was thus clearly dedicating the name to his colleague Cope. But in this case, one would expect a simple genitive construction based on Cope's name—*copei*—as Marsh had done for so many other fossil names. The choice of the far less common suffix –anus was surely no accident—the scatological associations of *copeanus* are impossible to ignore. This particularly juicy insult would have been keenly felt by Cope, and likely an object of mirth for others in the field.

The ridicule can't have been lost on Cope. Never one to allow his detractors the last laugh, in 1884, he described *Anisonchus cophater*, an herbivorous mammal from the Miocene. On first glance, *cophater* has the appearance of a Greek etymology, but in a letter to paleontologist Henry F. Osborn, Cope revealed that he had named the species in honor of his many enemies: "Cope Haters." The absence of the "e" at the end of Cope's name in *cophater* might have been intended to make the word look Greek by means of the resulting "ph," somewhat disguising the message from those not in the know. Thus, rather than meeting insult with insult, Cope chose the route of self-deprecation.

Then there is the more ambiguous case of the "Hitler beetle." In 1933, German coleopterist and civil engineer Oscar Scheibel, residing in Ljubljana, Slovenia, then part of the Kingdom of Yugoslavia, purchased from a Slovenian biologist several specimens of an unknown beetle that had been found in the caves near the city of Celje. In 1937, Scheibel published in *Entomologische Blätter* a description of a light-brown ground beetle a mere five millimeters long under the name *Anophthalmus hitleri*. After the war, Scheibel is supposed to have claimed that naming the beetle in honor of

Figure 6.14
The holotype specimen for *Mosasaurus copeanus* Marsh, 1869 (YPM VP 000312).
Courtesy of the Peabody Museum of Natural History, Division of Vertebrate Paleon-
tology, Yale University (http://peabody.yale.edu).

Hitler had been a subversive act: after all, this was an unlovely species of
brown, blind cave beetle that lived hidden from view. This defense must
be squared with the original description, the final sentence of which reads,
"Dedicated to Reich Chancellor Adolf Hitler, as an expression of my rever-
ence." No official response from the Reich Chancellery was documented in
this case.

To date, *Anophthalmus hitleri* has been found in but a handful of caves in
Slovenia. Particularly after the media discovered and circulated the Hitler

beetle story in 2000, interest in this species has been rekindled. A well-preserved specimen of *Anophthalmus hitleri* can fetch upward of 2,000 euros on the collectors' market; among the bidders, certainly some wish to add the Hitler beetle to their collection of Nazi memorabilia. Increased demand for the specimens has raised concern in Slovenia, where the beetle has been granted protected status. Despite a required government permit to collect the beetles, poachers continue to scour the caves in search of a lucrative source of extra income. Its name has turned out to be something of a curse: the Hitler beetle is now an endangered species.

At least one other species has been named after Adolf Hitler: the fossil *Roechlingia hitleri*, which belongs to the Palaeodictyoptera, a group of primitive fossil insects. *Roechlingia hitleri* was described in 1934 by German geologist and paleontologist Paul Guthörl. In 1949, entomologist Hermann Haupt attempted to synonymize the genus with an older one and rename the species *Scepasma europea*, as he took *Roechlingia hitleri* to be a nomen nudum, or "naked name," not considered valid without additional information. According to other specialists, however, Haupt's interpretation is incorrect, and consequently *Roechlingia hitleri* remains available (and possibly valid) to this day.

Extensive research has failed to turn up any other species named in honor of Hitler. This seems surprising, as this form of salute could have proven quite expedient to aspiring German scientists from about 1933 until 1945, at the latest. There is no evidence to show that German taxonomists sought to avoid the political implications of such name choices by remaining neutral. The likeliest explanation is that when Hitler patronyms were planned, approval was sought in advance from the Führer (by way of the Reich Chancellery), whether out of respect or perhaps fear of potential consequences. In 1933, for instance, a rose breeder submitted a written request to the Reich Chancellery for permission to introduce to the international market one of his best rose varieties, bearing Hitler's name. Similarly, a nursery owner from Schleswig-Holstein hoped to name a "prized strawberry variety" the "Hitler strawberry," in honor of the Reich Chancellor. They already had a "Hindenburg" strawberry variety in their catalog, he added. In reply to both cases, Hans Heinrich Lammers, Chief of the Reich Chancellery, sent almost identical letters, in which the inquiring parties were informed that, "upon careful consideration, [the Reich Chancellor] requests that a name in his honor most kindly not be used." Although no such letters are known within scientific taxonomy, it can be assumed that any requests for patronyms were declined in a similar fashion. Perhaps this fundamental rejection of honorary names is the reason that so few *hitleris* exist.

In the broader context of naming, it's worth noting that from 1933 onward, German registry offices saw an influx of requests by parents to use the name Hitler as a given name for their children, whether in its original form or in such feminized forms as Hitlerine or Hitlerike. The Reich Ministry of the Interior issued a directive to registrars and their agents, instructing them to advise any potential applicants to choose a different name.

Today, regular public discussions take place as to whether animal species named after dictators, murderers, and their ilk shouldn't be renamed. The International Code of Zoological Nomenclature states that no name should be proposed that "would be likely to give offence on any grounds."[4] Technically speaking, although the rules recommend this, they don't *require* it. The nuance here is significant: because these names have already been successfully published, it is impossible for a later author to simply change the name. The only practical way would be to submit an official appeal to the nomenclature commission, which no one has done yet. It's unlikely that anyone will: when push comes to shove, taxonomists, conservation organizations, and Slovenian coleopterists profit more from this stigma than they are harmed by it, even to the detriment of a beetle species. On the one hand, *Anophthalmus hitleri* is a historical document of the entanglement of politics and taxonomy. On the other hand, by means of its discomfiting implications, the beetle raises public awareness of the background of biodiversity discovery and scientific naming. Thus, the name *hitleri* will probably keep its place in the catalog of life, its significance as a historical anecdote assured by the political implications greatly different today from what Oscar Scheibel originally intended.

Let's return now to *Bathybius haeckelii*, the monera about which Haeckel had theorized, which he and Huxley believed covered the entire floor of the ocean in a primordial slime. Its fame was only fleeting, and by the 1870s, even Haeckel's reputation no longer benefited from association with *Bathybius*. Directly after Huxley's original description was published, British zoologist Sir Charles Wyville Thomson examined several samples from the depths of the Atlantic and reported exultantly that the sediment really was alive. Starting in 1872, Thomson led the *Challenger* expedition, a three-and-a-half-year-long deep-sea exploration aboard the corvette H.M.S. *Challenger*, a voyage considered a watershed in the establishment of scientific marine research. Thomson and the other scientists aboard labored in vain to find fresh primordial slime in their samples of the North Atlantic seabed. The deep-sea slime was indeed teeming with life, but there was no sign of *Bathybius*. Realization gradually dawned: *Bathybius* tended to appear in the sediment samples when alcohol was added to a fresh sample. Highly concentrated alcohol (ethanol, to be specific) has long been used to preserve natural specimens and is still the substance of choice when preserving plants and animals. When alcohol was added as a matter of course to the deep-sea sediment, *Bathybius* was evident, whereas when the fresh samples were examined, it was completely absent. The chemist on board the *Challenger* ultimately determined that the alcohol added to the deep-sea samples resulted in a precipitate of calcium sulfate, which explained the slimy substance. *Bathybius*, whose existence had already been questioned by Berlin zoologist Christian Gottfried Ehrenberg, had finally proven to be a falsity, an inorganic delusion from the depths of the sea. For a brief moment, Haeckel, Huxley, and the entire world, it seemed, had imagined the ocean floor covered in primordial soup: a slimy net of pulsing material that spanned the globe, the glorious manifestation of the theory of life's emergence from inanimate matter, only to be revealed as the result of a simple chemical reaction inside a test tube. *Quel dommage!*

Thomson, who over the years had provided Huxley with the most outlandish deep-sea fish and other zoological samples from the *Challenger*'s nets, sensed that this discovery would spread quickly around the world and discredit Huxley. While still in Queensland, he wrote a personal letter to Huxley, in which he reported that the true nature of the Huxley-Haeckel primordial soup had been discovered, and that he—Huxley—would do well to take an appropriate stance on the matter. Huxley reacted promptly. He had earlier played a decisive role in founding the scientific journal *Nature*, a prestigious publication to this day, and he was in close contact with the publisher at the time, Norman Lockyer. In a letter to Lockyer, Huxley lamented, "My poor dear *Bathybius* appears likely to turn into a *Blunderibus*."[5] Huxley assented to the publication of Thomson's letter in the August 1875 issue of *Nature* and explicitly accepted responsibility for "introducing this singular substance into the list of living things."[6] The wind was thus taken from his critics' sails, should they have accused him of malicious intent or—even worse for a scientist—naïve self-deception. Although Huxley openly admitted to his error in 1875, he continued to mention *Bathybius* in lectures and publications until at least 1879; some residual doubt must have remained as to whether there might still be something to the idea of an oceanic primordial slime. In 1886, German zoologist Hubert Ludwig included *Bathybius haeckelii* in the third edition of *Dr. Johannes Leunis Synopsis der Thierkunde.* Although Ludwig cites the *Challenger's* findings, which state that *Bathybius* is a sulfate precipitate, he goes on to report that "bathybius-like protoplasmic mass" had recently been found at 92 fathoms in the North Pole region, and that this mass contained a network of pseudopods—mutable projections of unicellular organisms—and made amoeboid movements. But this discovery, too, turned out to be a dead end in the search for the primordial slime.

Its fate sealed, Haeckel acknowledged that *Bathybius* had turned out to be a flop. However, he maintained that his monera theory was still true, and that sooner or later the monera-slime would be found. His monera phylum was later elevated to a kingdom, but by 1977, this term was deemed obsolete, and currently no taxon exists with the name monera. *Bathybius haeckelii* also has faded into obscurity, although its namesake is unlikely to lose his place in the history of science, not least for the aesthetic value of his engravings.

As 31-year-old Alfred Russel Wallace disembarked on the Southeast Asian island of Borneo on November 1, 1854, he didn't realize he would be spending more than a year in Sarawak in the island's remote northwest. He was far less able to predict that this was where he would finally commit to paper the ideas he'd been developing with regard to how new species emerge from existing ones. His travel assignment, however, was of a different nature. Wallace had traveled to Southeast Asia on his own initiative with the aim of collecting as many exotic animals as possible, which he sent whenever he could to Samuel Stevens, a London-based natural history agent. Many of the animals were unknown to science, whereas others were familiar but represented in local collections by single specimens in miserable condition and lacking background information. In Europe, the hunger for exotic specimens in science was insatiable, and Stevens ran a lucrative business selling Wallace's extensive materials. With each of the approximately twenty shipments sent intermittently to London, Stevens was able to finance each stage of Wallace's travels around the Malay Archipelago.

Before accepting the invitation to Borneo, extended by the "White Raja" Sir James Brooke—ruler of Sarawak, as appointed by the British Crown—Wallace was in Singapore, where he first encountered the huge species diversity of Southeast Asia. He had already discovered hundreds of new species there, expanding his collection exponentially. In Sarawak, however, the diluvian rains of the monsoon forced him into a months-long recess. Sir Brooke, who found great enjoyment in the spirited conversations with his guest, provided Wallace with a small house located directly on the Sarawak River in the foothills of Mount Santubong. Along with a Malayan cook, Wallace spent a large part of the rainy season from late 1854 to early 1855 in this house. During this forced hiatus, Wallace focused on the observations

Figure 7.1
Alfred Russell Wallace. Senckenberg Deutsches Entomologisches Institut, Müncheberg, Historisches Archiv, Porträtsammlung, image #4358.

he'd made in the Amazon and composed the seminal essay that would provide the underpinning for the "Sarawak Law." He had traveled through the Amazon from 1848 to 1852 with Henry Walter Bates and discovered that many species along the river occupied a distribution area typical of and often limited to themselves, and not only in the Amazon. Other explorers, such as Charles Darwin or Alexander von Humboldt, had also reported on the specific distribution patterns of various animals and plants. Why then,

Wallace wondered, did some species appear only in certain parts of the world and not in others? Then there was the fact that similar species evidently emerged over time in fairly close succession, which geologist Charles Lyell had shown through studies of the earth's geology and fossils in his three-volume work, *Principles of Geology*. Wallace combined the chronology of related species' emergence with their geographical distribution and summarized this as a "law" and the central argument of his Sarawak essay: "Every species has come into existence coincident both in space and time with a pre-existing closely allied species."[1] Although Wallace could not yet explain why species emerged, he was already implying that species had close geographical and temporal ties because they originated from the same ancestors. Wallace sent the Sarawak essay to London for publication, where it soon appeared in a respected British journal in September 1855.

The Sarawak essay represents a significant milestone in the history of evolutionary theory but is often underrated given the impact of subsequent events. To this day, Wallace plays second fiddle to Darwin. Despite having more or less answered the species question at the same time, Wallace ultimately had to cede precedence to Darwin as the father of evolutionary theory in the public eye. In 2013, in commemoration of the hundredth anniversary of Wallace's death, Matthias Glaubrecht published a comprehensive biography of Wallace, which reconstructed the events faithfully and reads like a real-life science thriller.

Namers and Gatherers

In addition to his unclear (as mentioned earlier) role as one of the founders of a substantiated theory of organismic evolution, Wallace is primarily known today for his work in biogeography—that is, the science dedicated to the geographical distribution of organisms. His critical contributions to the study of biodiversity in Southeast Asia, however, are easily overlooked these days. As a collector of natural artifacts, his odyssey led him straight through the Indo-Malayan island world to all of the major islands and most island groups. By the end, he had put away more than 22,000 kilometers, despite sometimes spending months in areas that proved particularly bountiful for his gathering endeavors. At the conclusion of his trip through the archipelago, he had captured more than 125,000 animals, appropriately preparing and preserving, labeling and sorting them, and by no means only insects, although at 110,000 specimens, they did constitute the largest portion of the catch. Wallace also collected great numbers of large animals such as orangutans, crocodiles, and especially birds, all of which were shipped to England.

After his return to England in 1862, Wallace could look back on this unusually successful one-man gathering expedition with satisfaction. Even before the start of the expedition, he had been determined to travel to a region that promised new, spectacular finds and would also provide him with the information he needed to answer the species question that so preoccupied him. It was to be expected that many of the animals caught in the tropics would be new and undiscovered, but even specialists were amazed by the percentage of undescribed species in Wallace's material. Glaubrecht, his biographer, estimates that around 1,500 insect and bird species were described on the basis of his material.

British entomologist Andrew Polaszek combed through the publications released in the decades directly following Wallace's return, counting all of the newly named species that had been described based on specimens Wallace had brought back from Sarawak. Polaszek arrived at impressive figures: Wallace had collected around 80,000 insects, representing 7,000 species, about 2,000 of which had been found on Borneo alone. For example, as far as we know, the species-rich longhorn beetle group comprises more than 1,200 species in the Indo-Malayan archipelago. In Sarawak alone, Wallace had collected 280 of these, 250 of which were unknown and later described by British insect specialist Francis Polkinghorne Pascoe in the 1860s. Wallace estimated he had gathered around 800 new insect species in total in Sarawak, whereas Polaszek suspects that over time, upward of 1,000 new species were described. Similarly for the butterflies, the renowned entomologist Francis Walker alone described 400 new species and 100 new genera based on Wallace's Sarawak material. It goes on. Frederick Smith, another entomologist at the London Natural History Museum, described 150 new bee and wasp species, and Walker—the butterfly guy—took on other insect groups as well. Hundreds of new fly species and 140 cicada species from Sarawak can be traced back to him.

Matthias Glaubrecht's estimate that Wallace provided material for no fewer than 1,500 newly described species is probably too low given the Sarawak figures. More accurate numbers aren't available because in large part Wallace's material was often sold to private collections and not infrequently resold from there. For most of his insects, Wallace used typical but unobtrusive labels. They were small and round and bore only a three-letter-long abbreviation of the respective discovery location, handwritten by Wallace or his assistant, Charles Allen. Several of these labels were unwittingly removed by later owners and replaced by new ones, meaning that not only are the Wallace specimens scattered among many collections, they're also not necessarily recognizable as such. As a result, the material was then processed by many different scientists, who published in many different journals. The largest portion remained in the London Natural History Museum, where it was also put to scientific use. Many other specimens are found in other collections, however, and even the fly collection in Berlin's natural history museum includes original Wallace specimens. Even the specialists—those who'd thrown themselves so fervently into Wallace's material in the mid-nineteenth century—weren't up to the task of processing this enormous number of species. Many remained long untouched and have only been described in recent years. To this day, researchers are discovering and describing new species in unprocessed material that still remains from Wallace's Southeast Asia expedition.

Wallace is undoubtedly one of those collectors whose tremendous activity yielded outsize contributions to the discovery of new animal species. In the field of botany, British botanist Daniel P. Bebber and his team have dubbed such collectors "big hitters." Compared with the majority of plant gatherers, these individuals have gathered far above the average amount of type material, which is later used as the basis for species descriptions. To suss out the significance of big hitters for the discovery of new species, Bebber pulled together the collection and collector data for approximately 100,000 type specimens from four of the world's most important botanical collections. The result was surprising: a mere two percent of all collectors were responsible for more than half of all type specimens (and thus, for the discovery of these new species), whereas the majority of collectors managed only a few specimens—if not just one—of a new species.

Many of the top-ten collectors Bebber researched had been active in the eighteenth or nineteenth centuries. For instance, Scottish botanist Robert Brown collected untold numbers of plants in Australia from 1801 onward, and about 1,700 of Brown's type specimens are still housed in the Natural History Museum in London. He personally described around 1,200 of the species based on these specimens. Like Brown, many big hitters were collecting at a time when the botany of many regions had scarcely been tapped. It was unquestionably easier in those early days to become a big hitter but not exclusively so. Bebber was able to demonstrate that big hitters have existed over the years and into present day, and that they don't necessarily need to be gathering in the world's most species-rich areas. They are, however, defined by five special characteristics: they collect over a long span of their life; they have a good eye for new and unknown forms; they collect in many different areas on Earth but specialize in one, usually within a single country; they collect various plant families, although they typically specialize here, too; and they collect significantly higher numbers of examples of unknown species toward the end of their careers.

Although these characteristics don't apply to every big hitter, Bebber's numbers suggest an interesting conclusion. In theory, the most effective strategy for rapidly growing the catalog of life with unknown species could be as simple as sending a few experienced and competent collectors to the right geographical regions.

The influence of big hitters in zoology hasn't yet been studied as systematically as in botany, but it's probably safe to assume that the situation is similar. In any case, there's no doubt that this strategy began with Wallace, one of zoology's biggest of big hitters. After his experiences in the Amazon, he deliberately sought out his next destination—the Indo-Malayan archipelago—with the expectation of finding mostly unknown fauna there, and in this way, finding many new species. In the nineteenth and early twentieth centuries, a host of other significant expeditions à la Wallace were undertaken—that is, trips characterized by the tremendous personal efforts exerted by the individuals in charge—leading to the discovery of enormous numbers of animals, many of which later turned out to be new species.

In zoology, the best documented are not the people who have performed the gathering but those involved in the scientific evaluation of the gathered materials. Following the explorers' successful return home and after the valuable objects have survived the often months-long passage from distant lands unscathed, a technical—but no less important—step must be taken. The objects must be well packed for shipping to prevent damage. Fish are packed tightly in vats of alcohol, vertebrate skulls wrapped individually in cloth, stacked in boxes. Fragile insects are particularly at risk on long journeys. In collections, they're typically pinned—that is, impaled by

Figure 7.2
A stamped label attached to a dried specimen of *Crocodylus moreletii*, known as More-let's crocodile. Museum für Naturkunde Berlin, M. Ohl photo.

special pins and dried. Pinning the collected insects during the expedition, however, can be problematic. Many collectors, for whatever reason, end up pinning their specimens on location at the end of a long day of fieldwork, preparing insects at night, for hours on end, by the glow of the kerosene lamp. Because insects are often caught in large numbers, the catch from a single day might be in the hundreds if not thousands. Treating every animal one by one, whether it's a big and sturdy beetle or a transparent and delicate mayfly, requires a degree of focus and is certainly time intensive. It must first be taken out of the killing jar, its legs, wings, and antennae manipulated to hold the desired form and direction, before inserting the pin through a specific spot that doesn't damage the animal too much, and finally sticking the freshly pinned insect to a base in such a way (maybe even with other pins to support it) that it holds the painstakingly attained position. On top of that, scientific guidelines call for pinned insects to be arranged in such a way as to allow for various features required for examination to be displayed—for instance, the wings must spread to a precise angle and the legs positioned in a prescribed direction. In the shipping crates, they must be placed a safe distance apart, should they start to loosen from the tight bond with the pin and start turning. Thus, not only are pinned insects fragile, they also take up a lot of space, unfavorably for large-scale collecting expeditions, where the volume of shipped items is bound to be of concern. The alternative is shipping in paper bags, where the insects are placed immediately after their death and dried. Layers of these bags, which can easily be created out of folded newspaper while in the field, are well suited for packing in shipping crates. A further advantage is that, should a leg or head break off, it will stay with the rest of the body in the bag and can later be glued back into place on the correct animal during pinning. Once the specimens make it back to the home museum, professionals must then be enlisted to take on the time-consuming task of pinning the insects, which in this case must be softened beforehand. Insect bags of folded newspaper, which are usually triangular, in this setting inadvertently become artful mementos of faraway lands, fragmented archives of the current events of the day of their packing, even if this can't have been the collector's intention at the time.

Labeling is possibly the most essential step to be taken when doing any kind of preservation back home. After all, labels—or, rather, the information they contain—are what actually turn a collected object into what it's meant to be, namely, a scientific unit. In the field, objects will often have been given a temporary label that provides the most important shorthand details about the location and circumstances of the discovery, along with references to field notes and travel journals. For mammals, in cases where only a handful of individual specimens have been collected, it may be possible to write more detailed labels in the field or during transport, but for the thousands upon thousands of insects, crustaceans, and other animals, these initial bare-bones labels must suffice. A clear specification of the discovery location is the minimum requirement, and the collection date is usually also included. Specimens missing these metadata—save those from a handful of historically significant expeditions—are considered scientifically worthless. Proper labeling, which must promise to fulfill its purpose in the future, is therefore the linchpin of the processing that follows a collecting expedition. This also often includes an analysis of notes on the collection, field books, and journal accounts.

Quite some time before the voyage concludes, the collected material is thus accurately prepared and labeled. Further scientific processing is manifested as a shared group project, at least for the large-scale collecting expeditions, which have yielded new species across nearly all groups, from turtles to blow flies. The material, presorted according to animal group, is sent around the world to the appropriate specialists, who will have agreed to help, usually happily, provided it's coming from remote regions of particular interest to their respective specialty areas. And thus begins the painstaking phase of taxonomic processing and description.

Amassing the Data and Sifting for Species

The species discoverers often encounter utterly unknown diversity. Many of the collected animals represent new species, and especially in "super-diverse" groups such as insects, huge numbers of species can require description. Describing dozens or sometimes hundreds of new species isn't uncommon for full-time entomological taxonomists. For researchers working on a particularly diverse and poorly researched animal group, the number of newly discovered, described, and named species can reach into the thousands or even tens of thousands—a life's work. The number of these "mass authors" is small, a clear indication of the level of exertion required to achieve this feat. Nevertheless, there are a few natural scientists approaching or even exceeding the 10,000 mark—a remarkable achievement over the course of decades of active effort. But what impels a person to dedicate his or her life entirely to the taxonomic pursuit of the tiniest insect species? Can we put this down to the admirable dedication of intellectual heavyweights? Or is it an expression of manic obsession, a sick compulsion that won't let up, until every last specimen has been gathered and organized? What follows is an introduction of every known taxonomist documented as having described more than 10,000 species in an attempt to shed some light on these questions.

Prominent among these characters is Charles P. Alexander, the veritable "lord of the crane flies." Crane fly is a common name for members of the superfamily Tipuloidea. The long-legged, large crane flies, which don't infrequently invade our homes, have a striking appearance and different names throughout the English-speaking world, including gallinipper, gollywhopper, jimmy spinner, mosquito hawk, mosquito lion, and daddy long-legs. According to the most recent count, Tipuloidea includes 16,850 species-group taxa—that is, species and subspecies—11,278 of which were described by Alexander. In other words, a single entomologist discovered and named two-thirds of the world's crane fly species. Not to mention approximately 200 further species descriptions of gnats and flies, along with a species of stonefly. All told, the number of insect species Alexander described totals up to 11,755. An immense number! Its enormity becomes especially obvious considering the following: Alexander was born in 1889 in New York State and published his first work on crane flies in 1910—that is, at age 21. His last publication appeared in 1981. Over those seventy years, he published 1,024 articles, or an average of 1.3 publications per month. Each of these publications contained an average of eleven newly described species, meaning he was managing an output of some three species descriptions per week. Alexander was a constant species author over long intervals of time, even if sporadic years broke the pattern. In 1929 alone, he described 394 species. The year before his death, 50 new names were published, and even in the year he died, a further 18. How on earth could Alexander find the time for all of this? And wherever did he find all that material?

In Alexander, there is no mistaking his tremendous diligence and an almost manic power of concentration. For most of his career, beginning in 1922, he was a full-time faculty member and administrator at the Massachusetts Agricultural College at Amherst (today the University

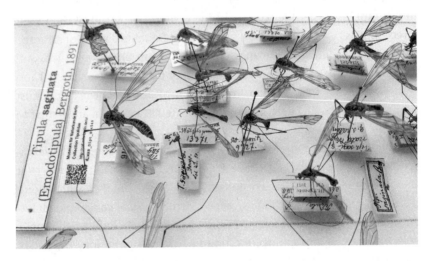

Figure 7.3
A small part of the crane fly collection with labels created at different times. Museum für Naturkunde Berlin, M. Ohl photo.

of Massachusetts). In addition to what was surely a busy workday, he was also president of the Entomological Society of America and repeatedly embarked on extended collecting trips with his wife Mabel. Ah yes, his dear Mabel. Congruent with the times, as is so often the case in life stories like these, Alexander's wife stood behind him as a strong force and beside him as an active assistant. She organized and managed his enormous comparison collection, which was stored in an addition to their home in Amherst, built for this express purpose and known as "Crane Fly Heaven." Thanks to Mabel's work, the collection was superbly organized, such that all of the comparison specimens, microscopic preparations, and literature her husband needed were close at hand. Diligence, an extraordinary overview of the world's crane fly fauna, a continuously growing comparison collection unmatched around the world, and especially the support of his wife Mabel, appear to have been Alexander's recipe for success.

But where did the material that one needs to describe so many species come from? To describe 11,755 species, an absolute minimum of 11,755 individual specimens is required; in practical terms, this will have meant sifting through many times that number of specimens. Many species are common and collected in large numbers, but far more are rare or very rare. Alexander worked on crane fly fauna from every continent with the exception of Europe, and for the majority of his active career, he was the only specialist for crane flies in most of the world's geographical regions. At the same time, crane flies are often caught as by-catch in the nets of specialists looking for other winged insects, and thus a steady stream of unidentified crane flies flowed from other collectors and museum collections toward the East Coast, where it emptied into Crane Fly Heaven. Alexander's collection grew and grew, and his own expeditions only added to it. These factors together were enough to ensure that he never lacked for research material, and should the mood strike to work on crane flies from a certain region, unopened parcels were always ready and waiting for him.

Understandably, Alexander sought to expand his comparison collection with ever more species, necessary to distinguish undescribed species from those already described. In his efforts, however, he overshot the mark. After a specialist has processed material that has been sent to him, it's common practice to keep a handful of individuals for his own collection, even if it's type material and of course only by permission of the specimens' owners. Alexander, however, who usually had to dissect his research material to reveal important features, would keep parts (even of holotypes) for his collection without asking—a wing, a few legs, the male genitalia. He sent back the rest.

On the surface, crane flies don't appear to differ much from each other, at least not to the layperson. Microscopic examinations of the male genitalia and bristles on the body reveal a somewhat unexpected structural diversity. Differentiation between species is thus based on small, inconspicuous features; in addition to a good microscope, a researcher needs a comprehensive comparison collection, a good library, and lots of experience. Alexander possessed all of these in ample measure. The sheer mass of data before him presented its own huge challenge. Even today, when speedy computers with user-friendly databases are essentially part of the natural landscape, this task is no walk in the park. Alexander's work process, by contrast, was entirely object- and paper-based, with introduced errors always a possibility.

A further question comes into play. Whether a certain morphological peculiarity of a certain crane fly individual should be considered an indication of its being a newly discovered species will always depend on the personal assessment of intraspecific variability and speculation as to whether the observable peculiarities represent constant and genetically inheritable characteristics. Two taxonomists can easily differ in opinion here, and what one considers to be two well-defined, distinct species can be interpreted by the other as synonyms of a single species.

Believe it or not, by 2009, only 355 synonyms had been found among Alexander's 11,000-plus species. Twenty-seven of these were the result of objective mistakes, by which Alexander formally described the same species twice—the name, description, and image of the species were accidentally published a second time in the years following the original publication. Most of the remaining synonyms, however, are subjective synonyms—that is, the result of other scientists' conflicting views on the species' status. It's estimated that around five percent of the species Alexander described had already been described, and that approximately one percent of those (about 115 species) he'd done himself.

Considering the high total number of species he described, his number of synonyms at five percent turns out to be low, both proportionately and as an absolute number, in comparison with other taxonomists, as we will see. A low rate of synonymy might be attributed in part to the quality of his taxonomic interpretations, but the poor state of scientific research in several of the regions Alexander studied can't be discounted as a factor either. For instance, from a geographic area rich in crane flies, 3,574 species of South American crane flies are known today, 3,286 of which are on Alexander's account. To date, only 15 of these have been interpreted as synonyms, meaning that Alexander described 3,271 of the South American Tipulidae species considered valid today. In other words, about 92 percent of the total known population of South American crane fly fauna can be traced back to Alexander. There hasn't been any broad reassessment of South American crane flies that could be used as the basis for a new evaluation of the species described by Alexander. Simply put, no one has looked since. Whether his species ultimately prove good and sensible, no one can say, and to this day, Alexander holds the monopoly on the crane flies of South America.

Ultimately, synonyms are mistakes regardless of qualifications. In any case, it's an unpleasant experience for a taxonomist when one's own names, published with the best of intentions, vanish into synonymy. Thus, in a quantitative assessment of the life's work of prolific authors, individual synonymy rates are the measure of quality for their activity. Charles P. Alexander's estimated five percent is the stuff of dreams for other high-volume taxonomists.

Like Francis Walker. It's hard to find another figure in taxonomy who enjoys a reputation as conflicted as his. In 1874, the year of his death, an obituary appeared in *Entomologist's Monthly Magazine*, one of the best-known British entomology journals, that likely spoke from the heart of most of Walker's colleagues. The opening sentence got right down to it: "More than twenty years too late for his scientific reputation, and after having done an amount of injury to entomology almost inconceivable in its immensity, Francis Walker has passed from among us."[2] The author of the obituary, an entomologist named J. T. Carrington, was undoubtedly aware that it wasn't in good taste to speak ill of the deceased in an obituary, and toward the end of the text, he preempts potential criticism of the style he chose: "We earnestly hope that never again will it fall to us, nor to our successors in entomological journalism, to have to write such an obituary notice as this. That the motto, '*De mortuis nil nisi bonum,*' ['Of the dead, nothing unless good'] will be directed against us we fully expect; and we answer before-hand that we have only judged Walker as an *entomologist.*"[3] Other contemporary colleagues, however, saw Walker first and foremost as the "most voluminous and most industrious writer on Entomology [England] has ever produced" and emphasized that they'd never met another person "who possessed more correct, more diversified, or more general information, or who imparted that information to others with greater readiness and kindness."[4]

To this day, Walker tops the list of most productive mass species authors of all time. According to the latest count, prepared by entomologist and fly specialist Neal Evenhuis of Bishop Museum in Honolulu, Walker christened a dizzying 23,506 species. Compared with Charles Alexander, however, Walker did not concentrate on a single insect order—not by a long shot. Butterflies were his obvious favorite, and with 10,628 names, they comprised almost half of all the species he named. After that came Diptera (flies and gnats), with more than 4,000 species; Hemiptera (true bugs and cicadas), of which there were hardly fewer; Hymenoptera (wasps, bees, ants), with 2,500 species; Orthoptera (grasshoppers), with about 1,000; and Coleoptera (beetles) and Blattodea (cockroaches), each with about 400 species. As if that weren't enough, he was also interested in ten other insect orders, and he described smaller numbers of species for each of them: more than 200 Neuroptera (lacewings), more than 100 Trichoptera (caddisflies), nearly 40 Ephemeroptera (mayflies), 14 Isoptera (termites), 7 Psocoptera (booklice), and 3 Mecoptera (scorpionflies). Finally, Walker also contributed a species each to the Odonata (dragonflies), Embiidina (webspinners), Mantodea (praying mantises), and Thysanoptera (thrips) orders.

This number appears to stand in glaring contrast to the total number of Walker's publications. As a reminder, by the end of his life, Charles Alexander had more than one thousand publications to his name, his average number of new species per publication was just over 11, and his number of publications per year about 15 over a span of 70 years. Walker's record is a different story altogether. Although he may have published more than 300 pieces, most were barely more than notes a few lines long. The majority of his species descriptions can be found in about 90 publications, which amounts to an average 261 species per publication. If we take the total number of his publications as the basis, it would still require an average of almost 80 new species per publication. If one then also considers his significantly shorter career span, then the whole business becomes even more striking. While Alexander was active in science for more than seven decades, Walker worked only 42 years. Alexander averaged 168 species per year, Walker 560; that is, Walker described 47 species per month, or considerably more than a species a day.

In view of the standard course of taxonomic work, which involves carefully studying comparison materials, compiling all relevant literature related to the target group, and producing detailed descriptions, possibly even illustrations, Walker's level of productivity is almost inconceivable. It's tedious and protracted work, and to produce an overview of real depth—even after years of experience—is usually only possible for several hundred or maybe a couple thousand species at most. It's with good reason, then, that taxonomists will usually focus on just one animal group. Walker, by contrast, described animals in widely different insect orders, and in huge numbers at that. How could he have achieved this almost industrial productivity? From the first, he published in a format that was conceived for the mass organization and administration of large numbers of species names: the catalog, voluminous tomes that he filled with names, page by page. In this regard, he held a privileged position: his 9-to-5 had him creating a complete inventory of collections at the Natural History Museum in London. Its collections were and are some of the most extensive and diverse in the world. The simple act of cataloging them would be a gargantuan task. In the process of working on his insect catalogs, Walker would frequently come across undescribed species that needed to be included in the collection inventory. What's more, it's new species such as these that enhance a catalog with the new and the innovative, turning it into something more than a mere list. So Walker accepted the challenge and added the as-yet-undefined species to his list, each with a brief description and new name. The majority of Walker's catalogs containing species names always have the same title structure: "List of specimens of xyz insects in the collection of the British Museum. Part abc," in which "xyz" stands for the respective insect order and "abc" for the subgroup. For instance, the "lepidopterous insects," or butterflies, appeared in four "parts," together totaling more than one thousand pages alone. This form of cataloging its own holdings was a long-held tradition at the Natural History Museum, and experts were often contracted to take on their own specialty area, whether mammals or leaf beetles. Most of these contracts were terminated in the 1860s, leaving Walker the sole remaining contract entomologist, most likely because of the productivity promised by his steady stream of catalog publications. Pay was on a fee basis for every publication completed within an established timeframe. Some sources claim that Walker was paid for every processed individual or species, to which they attribute his tremendous productivity, but those are probably just rumors.

Thanks to Evenhuis, an entire host of other numbers, no less impressive, is known from Walker's life's work. He published his catalogs over a period of 27 years, beginning in 1846 with a 238-page catalog on parasitic wasps, through 1873, with the final volume of the eight-part, 1,655-page catalog on true bugs. The number of catalog pages he produced thus totals 16,960; even if they aren't filled with freely written prose, it's still an impressive number. In doing so, Walker listed 46,066 species present in the British Museum. As part of the catalog, he described 15,959 (about one-third) of these species as new. These newly described species are unevenly distributed between the individual insect taxa. Only 9.8 percent of the wasps Walker cataloged are new species, compared with 46.6 percent of butterflies. In other words, nearly half of the butterflies held by the British Museum in the mid-nineteenth century hadn't yet been described, at least in Walker's utterly professional estimation.

The publication of extensive catalogs for the British Museum— particularly those covering little-researched insect groups—was Walker's preferred method of describing batches of new species at once. He became notorious in the scene overnight; owners of large private collections or well-endowed travel collectors who wanted their pieces named turned to him to process and define their specimens. As mentioned in Carrington's critical obituary, it's unknown whether Walker ever turned down this sort of request. In several publications, he thus also processed flies and gnats Alfred Russel Wallace had sent from Southeast Asia.

But what makes Walker so suspect that his death should be so heartily welcomed by some of his colleagues? Upon closer examination, a certain superficiality appears to have afflicted his methodology in direct conse- quence of his breakneck pace. In his 1858 catalog on cockroaches at the British Museum, for instance, he described one and the same species three times, variously as *Ischnoptera ruficeps*, *Nauphoeta ruficeps*, and *Nauphoeta sig- nifrons*. If this treble synonymy weren't enough, all three also happen to be synonyms of an older name, *Oxyhaloa deusta* (Thunberg, 1784). To be fair, synonyms regularly emerge from varying interpretations of intraspecific variability, and if this were so, Walker could be excused for simply emphasiz- ing minimal differences that would come to be considered inconsequential by later roach experts. In Walker's case, the error is more than a problem of subjectivity: the individuals used for the three species descriptions are as alike as peas in a pod, both sexes of the *ruficeps* species were available to him, and they all came from South Africa. At the very least, he should have noticed that both specimens to which he assigned the same species name *ruficeps* had a red head. To crown it all, Walker placed *Ischnoptera ruficeps* and *Nauphoeta ruficeps* in two different cockroach families—that is, in near opposition to one another within his own cockroach system. Cockroach specialists are in agreement that this serial production of cockroach names took a real toll, with plain negligence to blame.

It's worth noting that the "star" of synonymy with one's own names is unquestionably the French entomologist Jean-Baptiste Robineau-Desvoidy, one of the most important early fly taxonomists of the nineteenth century. His 248 newly described tachinid fly species bear particular mention: in a reassessment carried out a century later, every last one of them turned out to be synonymous with a single species, *Phryxe vulgaris*. Typically for Robineau-Desvoidy's work, all 248 species he published are, in fact, based on the slightest nuances of color, and what's more, all originate from around Paris, geographically a pretty manageable area.

As for Walker, instances like the thrice-described cockroach species are common to several groups he worked on. Take the numbers for dipterans, or flies and gnats. Of Walker's 3,917 new species names, 2,691 are still considered valid today, making for a 31 percent rate of synonymy. In other words, about one-third of his fly names refer to species that had already been described. This certainly seems high, but compared with the general rate of 20 to 30 percent synonymy, depending on the animal group, Walker's mistakes here were on the order of many other prolific taxonomists'.

Walker bequeathed to later scientists another problem. Given the huge number of his species descriptions, it's hardly surprising that each individual description succinctly outlines what Walker felt distinguished the species. Walker's descriptions typically consist of three or sometimes five lines of brief description in Latin, followed by ten, rarely more lines of somewhat more detailed description in English. At the end come country of origin and collector. The following catalog entry's relationship to the preceding is unclear: it could be the next new species or alternatively the next known name from the British Museum's stores. Even if Walker's descriptions are certainly more extensive than those of Linnaeus, they are nonetheless too short for many later taxonomists, too sparsely detailed to use to recognize a species. Should the original description be insufficient, the only recourse is a look at the type material, which is cumbersome and time consuming, especially when hundreds of species are in question.

In the league of taxonomists with more than 10,000 new species names, only four other entomologists share the title with Charles Alexander and Francis Walker.

The world of beetles has Frenchman Maurice Pic to thank for around 20,000 species names—some sources say up to 38,000—but no one knows for sure because neither a complete list of publications nor a register of his names exists. In the beetle scene, Pic is probably more contentious a figure than any other taxonomist. His species descriptions were always short, forgoing any use of explanatory illustrations, and he worked without a microscope. What's more, he attempted—quite successfully—to prevent his colleagues from reviewing the type specimens of the species he'd described. Pic published over a period of 67 years, and although the biological sciences—and with them taxonomy—developed and modernized continuously during that time, Pic's species descriptions barely deviated in form, from his first in 1889 to his final publication in 1956.

Thomas Lincoln Casey Jr. just barely clears the 10,000 mark. Casey was the son of Thomas Lincoln Casey Sr., a highly decorated officer in the U.S. Army Corps of Engineers. The United States has Casey Sr. to thank for the Washington Monument, whose completion he oversaw in 1884. Like his father, Casey Jr. became an officer in the U.S. Army Corps of Engineers. From his early days as a young lieutenant, he tried his hand at theoretical and applied astronomy with success; on the side, he collected beetles wherever he was stationed as a soldier. He developed into one of the most productive North American beetle collectors and authors of his time. His collection ultimately included 117,000 beetles representing more than 19,000 species and subspecies. His collection boasts more than 9,200 holotypes, but the number of species he described was far greater. In the end, Casey Jr. was buried with his microscope in the cemetery at the family estate.

Another 10,000 beetle species were described by Austrian Edmund Reitter. The son of a forester and trained agronomist, Reitter was an autodidact when it came to insect taxonomy, which he pursued with élan. From 1867 onward, he undertook extended collecting trips, especially in eastern and southeastern Europe, building an enormous beetle collection through his own finds and habitual trading activities. In 1879, he opened a bookstore in Vienna specializing in insects and entomology, which he initially called the "Natural History Institute." The revenue enabled him to undertake further collecting expeditions and also to send hired collectors as far as Mongolia. To this day, one of the key innovations behind his huge success in collecting was the systematic implementation of an instrument called the "beetle sieve," used to sift through leaf litter in search of beetles. In 1886, Reitter wrote about his experiences with this known but at that point only sporadically implemented method in a publication with the delightful title *The Insect Sieve, Its Significance in Capturing Insects, Particularly Coleopterans, and Its Application.*[5] His five-volume work *Fauna Germanica: The Insects of the German Reich* enabled the identification of German beetles through its detailed images and is still known today.[6] In 1917, only a year after the final volume appeared, a little supplementary pamphlet of about 80 pages was published under the title *Explanation of the Scientific Beetle Names in Reitter's Fauna Germanica* edited by Sigmund Schenkling, curator at the German Entomological Institute, then in Berlin-Dahlem, today located outside Berlin in Müncheberg.[7] The three works are yet to be translated into English. As a young man, Reitter also wrote romantic nature poetry with titles such as "Forest Shadows," "Evening Hush," and "Night of Wild Flowers," and he published a book of verse nearly two hundred pages long at age 20. In his final years, Reitter was also interested in the occult. He told his biographer Franz Heikertinger that during a séance, the death of his close friend Ludwig Ganglbauer had been communicated to him from beyond and was set to occur the following June of 1911. Ganglbauer didn't die at the appointed time, but he did fall very ill and undergo surgery in June 1911. He died of his illness in June 1912, exactly one year later than had been foretold.

Last, there is the Englishman Edward Meyrick, like Reitter an amateur entomologist. His specialty was "micros," as micromoths or microlepidoptera are lovingly known to butterfly experts. Micros encompass everything known in colloquial speech as moths. They are a species-rich, taxonomically challenging group. Especially deserving of respect are those like Meyrick, who have described thousands upon thousands of micros. In a 1955 catalog of the types of micromoths described by Meyrick in the British Museum of Natural History in London, where his collection has been housed since his death, 14,199 names are listed. Adding to that his work on the species-rich group of snout moths (Pyraloidae), omitted from the list, makes about 15,000 species, all told.

Meyrick grew up in England and published his first piece on microlepidopterans at age 21. From 1877, he spent almost ten years as a classics teacher in New Zealand and Australia, where he found an almost untapped world of new micromoths waiting to be discovered. An El Dorado for a micro taxonomist! He collected like there was no tomorrow, publishing scads of new species and genera and sometimes even higher groups. His work with Australian and New Zealand micromoths established his fame in the scene; as one of the only people active in the area of exotic microlepidopterans, from that point onward he was sent material from all over the world. Whether from Sri Lanka or India, China or Japan, South Africa or Zaire, huge numbers of micromoths reached him from every last corner, along with requests to identify or, if new, describe them. Meyrick processed them all. His works appeared in the standard scientific journals, often corresponding to the animals' geographic origins. Thus, he published most of the Australian species descriptions in *Proceedings of the Linnean Society of New South Wales*, those from India and Sri Lanka in the *Journal of the Bombay Natural History Society*, and African species in the *Annals of the Transvaal Museum* and the *Annals of the South African Museum*. Because the publication process was complicated and inconvenient—the author and publisher were separated by oceans, and communication between them was limited to handwritten missives delivered by ship—Meyrick established his own publication organ, *Exotic Microlepidoptera*. Published at his own expense, five thick volumes totaling more than 3,000 pages were ultimately released, in which Meyrick—as the sole author—described approximately 8,000 species. Beyond *Exotic Microlepidoptera*, he produced 428 further publications. Over the course of 64 working years, Meyrick produced an average of almost seven publications per year, describing an average of 234 species annually. For comparison, Charles Alexander tallied 168 species per year, Francis Walker, 560. A happy medium for Meyrick.

In terms of the scope of their texts, Meyrick and Walker's species descriptions are not dissimilar, usually only a few short lines, occasionally maybe a third of a page, almost always without images. Meyrick is credited with being the first to methodically study the venous systems of micros' wings. Insect wings consist of an ultra-thin membrane stabilized by stiff wing veins. The wings' venous network, common to virtually all insect species, is genetically fixed and often species-specific. Particularly the longitudinal veins, which are closely linked to the rather complicated wing joint, are comparable throughout most insect groups. Together with the many crisscrossing veins, the longitudinal veins form the typical, net-like venous pattern. Thus, for many winged insects, wing veins play a large role in the analysis of systematic position. On butterflies, the wing veins are concealed under a thick layer of scales and the optically dominating color patterns. Only after the scales have been rubbed off, the wings moistened or sometimes backlit, do the veins reveal themselves. With the exotic micromoths, Meyrick had recognized the systematic value of the wing veins, described each of them, and built many of his genera and families on the differences and similarities between them. So far, so good. What he wantonly neglected, however, and what has led present-day micro researchers to view his descriptions as minor catastrophes, are the genitalia so important to species recognition. Barring a reevaluation of his type material, the majority of his species descriptions are incomprehensible—in other words, they can't be applied to today's various species without further effort. Simply put, it's impossible to know which species he was actually specifying.

Besides his general disregard for micromoth genitalia, there was another much simpler reason for his excluding them: Meyrick didn't own a microscope. Instead, he performed all of his taxonomic comparison work with the help of a magnifying glass, securing the pinned animals in a small watchmaker's tripod for examination under lighting. A magnifying glass, good eyesight, and his tremendous knowledge replaced the microscope for him, as one of his colleagues wrote after his death. Nevertheless, these strengths were his undoing: the notion of preparing the minute butterfly genitalia as embedded micropreparations didn't even cross his mind. Meyrick simply didn't possess the equipment needed for this method so crucial to proper identification.

It's for good reason that all of the 10,000-species taxonomists are entomologists. Not only are insects the most species-rich animal group, but, depending on the particular insect group, they're also relatively easy to catch and to handle, technically speaking. It's not by chance that insects have been skewered and dried on pins for more than 250 years, a simple, effective method of preservation that ensures the insects will retain the chitinous exoskeletal form and often even the color they had in life. For one person to keep an eye on all insects—with a diversity in the hundreds of thousands, bordering on millions—is impossible. Thus, for the sake of efficacy, most entomologists specialize in a more or less narrow field. For Walker to publish huge numbers of new species in nearly twenty insect orders was highly unusual even if he did stick to insects.

Narrow specialization had not always been the norm. In the eighteenth-century tradition of natural history collections, Carl Linnaeus hoped to produce a comprehensive representation of all three natural kingdoms of animals, plants, and minerals: a feasible goal in an era when the known species to take into account numbered at the most a few ten thousand. In that context, Linnaeus managed to emerge as the author of species in nearly every animal group, from the common house mosquito, *Culex pipiens*, to the blue whale, *Balaenoptera musculus*, all the way to humans, *Homo sapiens*. In total, by the tenth edition of his *Systema Naturae*, he had reached 4,376 species, about half of which were new and discovered by him. Still no mean feat.

With the birth of modern taxonomy, of which Linnaeus can be considered the father, naturalists found themselves increasingly confronted by what medical and biological historian Staffan Müller-Wille has described as "information overload." The burgeoning wealth of knowledge about the earth's living diversity ultimately required new approaches to managing large amounts of information. Initially, researchers into the early nineteenth century pursued a universalist project aimed at the complete compilation of every known thing. Encyclopedic books, tabular compilations, and tree-like visualizations of heredity—often in combination with individual methods of annotation and filing—represent attempts to control the flood of new data. Such innovations in the techniques of information management, in keeping with the times, were both enabled and constrained by the possibilities provided by paper and writing utensils. With classic "paper technology," it was certainly possible to effectively organize and memorize thousands—perhaps even tens of thousands—of objects in tables and encyclopedias. In Linnaeus's time, completeness was thus a thoroughly tangible goal for individual encyclopedists. By the second half of the nineteenth century, the corpus of knowledge had exploded such that described insects alone now numbered approximately 250,000 species. In the face of such volume, entomologists began to limit themselves to just one group within the array of described insect diversity. By now, this is standard practice for most taxonomists; in many cases, a taxonomist will specialize further, dedicating his or her entire career to a single genus of beetles, wasps, or butterflies.

Clearly, taxonomists who describe more than 10,000 species in their lifetime represent an extreme exception. In today's context, a changing understanding of science toward increasing pressure to roll out high-level, synthesized publications instead of species descriptions makes it more unlikely than ever for a taxonomist to aspire to join this league. In addition to diligence, time, and access to the appropriate material, a certain mental disposition—to be less kind, an obsession—is a requirement if one is to dedicate one's life to the description and naming of species. In a frank assessment, at nearly three species descriptions per week, including the time consumed by the necessary "side work," such as collecting animals, correspondence, and the actual examination, not to mention the demands of his job at the university as well as the purely physical necessities, such as eating and sleeping—Charles Alexander can't have had much spare time. In his married life, he was fortunate enough to find in Mabel a spouse willing to facilitate such a rigorous work regime.

Particular to all 10,000-plus taxonomists is the high percentage of publications for which they are the sole author. Granted, publications with multiple authors weren't nearly as widespread in the nineteenth century as they are today. Even so, this can be taken as further evidence of the obsessive nature of the lone scientist, who can attain his high yield in a seemingly endless task only if he focuses on the next species, the next publication, without becoming mired in the tedious exchange with colleagues of potentially differing opinions. It's not uncommon for these mass authors to attract attention through their eccentric behavior. To their mind, social interactions, in particular, are more a nuisance than a welcome distraction. Dedicating oneself in monomaniacal fashion to a certain insect group invariably turns these insects into the lodestar of one's personal universe. When Wojciech J. Pulawski, the world expert on the digger wasp genus *Tachysphex*, relocated to the United States several decades ago, his friend and fellow wasp researcher Arnold S. Menke had *"Tachysphex* Forever" printed on a custom t-shirt for him. And it's true that all his life, Pulawski has worked primarily on this genus.

Let's come back once more to Francis Walker, the leader of the pack among mass authors. As previously mentioned, his reputation in the guild is understandably poor, and his colleagues seldom shy from scathing ridicule. In 1863, the Austrian butterfly expert Julius Lederer, for instance, circulated the derisive commentary that it must have been so dark in the basement of the British Museum where Walker worked that one couldn't have recognized if one had described the same species "five, six, or even eleven times, and in different genera, no less."[8] Lederer mused further that it wasn't actually a basement but an entresol, a mezzanine, and wondered moreover that, despite the terrible lighting, other colleagues were producing "sound" work. Besides, on foggy days, the museum was dark everywhere, basement or not.

Even today, when speaking about Walker with colleagues in taxonomy who are active in his specialty area, the response is largely deprecating, although the impression arises that the complaints about Walker are at least partly the result of a tradition we've grown fond of. I've had to recognize this in myself as well. Although I never had an unpleasant experience with Walkerian species among the wasps I was researching as an undergraduate and later a doctoral candidate, the consistently negative opinions of my older colleagues were enough to tarnish my views on Walker for a long time. I almost reflexively anticipated trouble with every wasp species Walker had described. Against this background, I prepared myself for the worst when researching Walker and his species, seeking out hard figures for the synonyms since discovered for the species he'd described. The synonymy rate is a common touchstone of taxonomic quality, provided enough time has passed to allow later scientists a critical perspective on these species. Not many figures exist for Walker's synonymy rate, but the few that do were surprising and in no way met my expectations. As mentioned, Walker's synonymy rate of 31 percent for flies and gnats isn't even so bad, compared with those of other fly experts. Among the thirteen most productive dipterologists of all time, there are three whose synonymy rates are higher than Walker's: Jean Baptiste Robineau-Desvoidy, who will eternally bring up the rear with 49 percent; Pierre Justin Marie Macquart, with 37 percent; and even one of the founding fathers of dipterology, Johann Wilhelm Meigen, with 36 percent. All of the top-13 dipterologists active in the nineteenth century are hardly better, with double-description rates between 25 and 50 percent. The picture is more varied in other insect groups described by Walker: 74 percent of his aphid species are synonyms, 55 percent of his cockroaches, 23 percent of his caddisflies, and only 6.9 percent of his North

American chalcid wasps. Overall, the synonymy rates confirm that Walker's taxonomy was of average quality.

Apart from Crane Fly Alexander, whose active period is still too recent to allow for a critical synonymy assessment, the synonymy rates of the other mass authors are scarcely better, many even significantly worse. However, they're frequently praised in the literature for their tremendous productivity, whereas Walker is regularly denigrated. This raises the question as to why the entomologist guild's distrust should be so targeted at Walker.

An answer may be found in a further criticism leveled against Walker's work by his contemporaries: the linguistic quality of the names. In 1863, for instance, Julius Lederer wrote that Walker's name creations were "largely horrific." True, many of his names are unusual, classically upvalued word combinations that many taxonomists at the time—who preferred names based on morphological features—found objectionable. Of course, it is challenging to come up with more than 20,000 new names, and although understandable from a historical perspective, no one today focuses their umbrage on Walker's nomenclature decisions.

Nevertheless, quality of description, synonymy rates, and perceived linguistic deficiencies are all criticisms that Walker's contemporaries also faced to varying degrees. The quality of his scientific work thus doesn't seem to be the reason for his poor reputation, nor was it his social behavior if the few extant accounts of Walker's personality are to be believed. Even Carrington, who caustically rued Walker's death as having come 20 years too late, acknowledged that Walker was "amiability itself, and probably there are few men who have lived to the age of 65 (his age at the time of his death), and made so few enemies."[9] A description from the minutes at a meeting of the Entomological Society in London records the following introduction: "This is Mr. Francis Walker, a perfect ambulatory encyclopaedia of entomological knowledge; you will find him very agreeable, and always ready to impart information."[10]

In the final years of his life, Walker suffered from deteriorating eyesight. It's unclear at which point this became a serious problem for him, but by 1873, his handwriting had been significantly impacted. Visual impairment didn't stop him from his taxonomic study of tiny chalcid wasps, whose features were scarcely visible, even with the magnifying glasses common in those days. Chalcid wasps were the focus of his final publication, published posthumously in 1875.

Francis Walker didn't leave behind an autobiography. The archive of his correspondence and, ultimately, his tremendous productivity bespeak an obsession with catalogs and the description and naming of insects. Whether driven by vanity and ambition, scientific curiosity or even a manic relationship with cataloging, his motivations remain obscured in the shadows of the past. Equally so the explanation for why he is admired by some, while others consider him a butcher.

Many of the animals Walker processed in the entomological collections of the British Museum had been gathered as material by Alfred Russell Wallace. Besides Walker, many other specialists occupied themselves with Wallace's spoils, and consequently there are hundreds of plant and animal species with the name *wallacei*. To this day, undescribed species are still being discovered among the Wallace insects and named after him.

Wallace did not see himself exclusively as a taxonomist, even if he did describe and name around 300 new species. This included a dozen palm, 120 butterfly, 70 rose chafer, and more than 100 bird species. One of the best-known and most beautiful species he caught, discovered, and ultimately named himself, is the butterfly *Ornithoptera croesus*, also known as Wallace's golden birdwing butterfly. In his 1869 travel report, *The Malay Archipelago*, Wallace describes his discovery:

During my very first walk into the forest at Batchian, I had seen sitting on a leaf out of reach, an immense butterfly of a dark colour marked with white and yellow spots. I could not capture it as it flew away high up into the forest, but I at once saw that it was a female of a new species of *Ornithoptera* or "bird-winged butterfly," the pride of the Eastern tropics. I was very anxious to get it and to find the male, which in this genus is always of extreme beauty. During the two succeeding months I only saw it once again, and shortly afterwards I saw the male flying high in the air at the mining village. I had begun to despair of ever getting a specimen, as it seemed so rare and wild; till one day, about the beginning of January, I found a beautiful shrub with large white leafy bracts and yellow flowers, a species of *Mussaenda*, and saw one of these noble insects hovering over it, but it was too quick for me, and flew away. The next day I went again to the same shrub and succeeded in catching a female, and the day after a fine male. I found it to be as I had expected, a perfectly new and most magnificent species, and one of the most gorgeously coloured butterflies in the world. Fine specimens of the male are more than seven inches across the wings, which are velvety black and fiery orange, the latter colour replacing the green of the allied species. The beauty and brilliancy of this insect are indescribable, and none but a naturalist can understand the intense excitement I experienced when I at length captured it. On taking it out of my net and opening the glorious wings, my heart began to beat violently, the blood rushed to my head, and I felt much more like fainting than I have done when in apprehension of immediate death. I had a headache the rest of the day, so great was the excitement produced by what will appear to most people a very inadequate cause.

I had decided to return to Ternate in a week or two more, but this grand capture determined me to stay on till I obtained a good series of the new butterfly, which I have since named *Ornithoptera croesus*.[11]

Over the course of several weeks, Wallace returned daily to the *Mussaenda* bush, where he was able to capture one to two specimens almost every day. His assistant Lahi contributed additional butterflies netted alongside a nearby river. By the end, Wallace possessed more than one hundred specimens of *Ornithoptera croesus*.

In a January 28, 1859, correspondence addressed to Samuel Stevens, Wallace reports on his newest finds, then en route to the natural history agent in London. Regarding his new butterfly, Wallace writes, "For the *Ornithoptera* I propose *croesus* as a good name."[12] Excerpts of the letter to Stevens were read at a meeting of the Royal Entomological Society on June 6, 1859, and published in the Society's proceedings. Some of Wallace's contemporaries were not satisfied with this brief sentence as a serious species description, and as a result, George Robert Gray, then president of the society, took it upon himself to examine this gorgeous new species. In November of the same year, he published the description—based on Wallace's gathered materials, which had since arrived in England—in the proceedings of the Zoological Society of London. It really should have been named in Wallace's honor, Gray argued, but because the butterflies on hand already bore Wallace's *croesus* labels, and because Wallace had already announced the name to the Royal Entomological Society in June, Gray adopted the name proposed by the discoverer. Without question, only Gray's publication can be counted as the proper detailed description in the truest sense. In fact, many lepidopterists have taken the stance that the name *croesus*, which appeared in the letter excerpts published in June 1859, only held the status of an unpublished manuscript name, rendering it unavailable with Wallace as author, although ultimately this view didn't gain much traction. Perhaps because the availability clauses are fulfilled (albeit with a looser interpretation of the nomenclature rules), or simply out of respect for Wallace's names and his poetic description of the capture of this extraordinary butterfly, Wallace remains recognized as the author of Wallace's golden birdwing butterfly to this day.

8 Who Counts the Species, Names the Names?

Upon climbing the simple, Prussian-style steps to the entrance of the Museum of Natural History in Berlin, one glimpses through the glass doors that holiest of exhibit halls—the dinosaur room, a light-flooded hall dominated by the iconic *Brachiosaurus brancai*. To pause before heading into that beckoning light, one might notice two weathered figures standing guard above the entranceway: flanking the main entrance, several meters tall, two corner *risalits*—architectural embellishments that jut out from the facade—present the stony likenesses of two men. To the right stands Johannes Müller, whom Ernst Haeckel called the "most significant German biologist of the nineteenth century" and who helped lay the foundation for modern marine biology through the systematic study of plankton and other microscopic organisms. He also published seminal works in the area of comparative human anatomy and physiology. On the left is geologist Leopold von Buch, who was responsible for coining key terms in geology and paleontology, such as "caldera," the term for volcanic craters, and "index fossil."

Affixed to the left of the main doors, just outside the foyer, is a small bronze plaque of more recent origin, dedicated to a scientist of rather humble stature by comparison with the historic luminaries overhead: zoologist Walther Arndt, an expert on sponges and a former curator at the museum. The plaque's inscription eulogizes Arndt's horrible fate.

Arndt was born in 1891 in Landeshut, Lower Silesia, known today as Kamienna Góra, Poland. He trained in medicine and served in World War I, and in 1921, he followed his teacher, Willy Kükenthal, to the Museum für Naturkunde in Berlin, at the time called the Zoological Museum. First as an assistant and from 1925 as primary curator, he oversaw the sponge, worm, moss animal, cnidarian, and echinoderm collections. His tenure passed without incident through the Nazi period and the first years of World War

Figure 8.1
Boxes containing brachiopod (Brachiopoda) shells. Museum für Naturkunde Berlin,
M. Ohl photo.

II. By 1943, however, the tide of the war had begun to turn: Allied bombardment of Berlin was mounting, Mussolini was toppled on June 25, 1943, and Arndt was becoming increasingly pessimistic about developments in Germany. By July 1943, Arndt was convinced that the Nazi regime would fall next, and that the guilty would soon face judgment. He said as much to his colleague Günter Tembrock, who would later become a prominent behavioral researcher and zoologist in Berlin. Tembrock and others warned him to be careful in his choice of conversation partners.

In September 1943, while visiting his hometown, Arndt bumped into an old school friend, Hanneliese Mehlhausen. As she later reported, Arndt said the following: "What's bad is that we all suffer from what's been foisted upon us by others. But now they'll face judgment. Just like Mussolini was vanquished in Italy—the same will happen here. You'll see. In four weeks' time, the Party will be vanquished here, too." Mehlhausen, a Nazi Party member since 1930, informed the local Party chief, who alerted the Gestapo in Berlin. Later that year, Arndt ran into Wolfgang Stichel—an expert on bugs—in front of the state library in Berlin. Following a similar conversation, in which Arndt allegedly described the 1933 Reichstag fire as part of a Nazi conspiracy, Stichel—who happened to be a member of the SS—denounced Arndt to his superiors. Aside from political proclivities,

Figure 8.2
Walther Arndt in 1940. Museum für Naturkunde Berlin, Historische Bild- u. Schriftgutsammlungen (MfN, HBSB) Bestand: GNF, Signatur: FM X,1.

it's likely that personal motives also played a part in denouncing Arndt.
Mehlhausen described herself as having once been Dr. Arndt's fiancée, but
he had rejected her. Stichel had been trying to get hired at the Zoological
Museum for years and is said to have complained repeatedly that Arndt was
standing in the way. Whatever the case, Arndt was arrested by the Gestapo
in his office at the Zoological Museum on January 14, 1944.

On May 11, 1944, the case against him was opened and closed in the
People's Court, Judge Roland Freisler presiding. Freisler was undoubtedly
the most notorious judge in Nazi Germany; he issued thousands of death
sentences, including those in the show trials of members of the White
Rose resistance group and the conspirators in the failed Hitler assassination

attempt of July 20, 1944. According to Günter Tembrock's eye-witness account, Arndt's hearing was also defined by Freisler's irascibility. After just two hours, based wholly on the testimonies of Mehlhausen and Stichel, the sentence fell—Arndt was found guilty of "eternal dishonor [in] disparaging the military prowess" of the German state and sentenced to death. Several prominent scientists issued appeals for clemency, including Hanns von Lengerken, Director of the Zoological Museum; Oskar Heinroth, Director of the Berlin Aquarium; his wife Katharina Heinroth, who would later become Director of the Berlin Zoo; as well as the famous surgeon Ferdinand Sauerbruch. Tembrock even solicited Hans Hass—a well-known diver and marine biologist with close ties to high-ranking Party officials—to request a pardon. All in vain. On June 26, 1944, Arndt was beheaded by guillotine in Brandenburg-Görden penitentiary. His sister was then sent a bill for 300 reichsmark for the execution, plus 20 cents postage and sundry other charges.

Neither Organs Nor Muscles, Nor Nerves, Nor Sensory Cells

Arndt's murder signified the violent end of a scientific career spanning two decades. From his first publication in 1907 regarding the "Yearly Food Consumption of an Aquarium-Held Pike"—which he wrote at age 16—to his final article, which appeared shortly before his death, Arndt published around 260 pieces, over 220 of which he wrote while employed by the Zoological Museum. Approximately 15 manuscripts remained unfinished or were published posthumously. His scientific activities ranged broadly, but they were linked nearly throughout to certain topics that he clearly held dear—for instance, the work done at natural history museums, generally ("Occupational Diseases at Natural History Museums," 1931), technical matters concerning preservation techniques ("Questions Regarding Alcohol at Natural History Museums," 1937), and preservation issues specific to certain animal groups ("Dermoplasty, Then and Now," 1934).

In the zoological scene, however, Arndt became known internationally for his research on sponges. Sponges—known scientifically as Porifera—are an ancient group of multicellular animals, about 8,000 species of which are known. Typically sea dwellers, some species of sponge may also be found in freshwater. As animals, sponges have a strange physique, exhibiting neither organs nor muscles, nor nerves, nor sensory cells. Their physical structure—by means of which they filter particles floating in the water—is generally porous, and their unusually varied forms depend largely on their food situation and habitat. In possession of only three different cell types, sponges tend to have needle-like skeletal elements called spicules, whose chemical composition, form, and arrangement serve as important properties for taxonomic and systematic classification. One exception is the demosponges or "horny" sponges, which lack hard spicules but instead possess flexible, horn-like spongin fibers. The cellular matter can be removed through the process of maceration, and the flexible, soft, and absorbent spongin skeleton that remains has long held commercial appeal. Many varieties of sponges are now farmed in aquaculture and harvested for medical and pharmaceutical purposes.

Arndt was particularly interested in "practical sponges" such as these. Over the course of several years, he built up one of the largest—if not *the* largest—collections of practical sponges and related literature in the Zoological Museum. He studied sponges from almost every angle imaginable. For instance, not only did he examine "The Oldest Pictorial Representations of Sponges" (1931), but after extensive research, he revealed with regret in "Goethe and Sponges" (1939) that the sponge believed to have been left behind in Goethe's Weimar residence by the prince of poets himself could not possibly have belonged to him. Instead, the bath accoutrement in question was an unbleached velvet sponge from the West Indies; these sponges were not regularly imported to Europe until the 1840s, about a decade after Goethe's death in 1832.

In a 1943 publication, Arndt examined 119 dried sponge skeletons from the Zoological Museum collection for their acoustic properties. To do so, he percussed the sponges "in the manner typical of 'knocking,' with the middle knuckle of the right pointer finger," or with the pointer or middle finger nail if the tones were too quiet. He recorded volume and pitch using various physical methods of measurement, compiling the results in a nine-page table in the article's appendix.

Beyond sponges and the central role they play for reefs and other marine habitats, Arndt published pieces on the diverse underwater communities living in caves; the cohabitation of sponges and polyps; Bulgaria's hydrobiology; and the sponges of the North and Baltic seas, as well as various freshwater lakes. His contribution to the series "The Raw Materials of the Animal Kingdom"—a collaboration between Arndt and his colleague Ferdinand

Pax—was a comprehensive manuscript on sponges that filled nearly 500 pages.

Finally—and perhaps most characteristically—Arndt published numerous indexical works that could easily be categorized as catalogs or lists, drawing heavily on his meticulous analysis of the available literature. These included *Museologische Literatur*, the *Tabulae Biologicae*, a multivolume work filled with tables and data on various biological topics and a whole series of publications on species numbers in Germany and other habitats: "The Percentage of Parasites on and in Animals Within the Known Animal Population of Germany" (1940); "The Number of Animal Species Found Living in Caves and Groundwater in Germany (Old Reich)" (1940); "How Many 'Microscopic' Animal Species Do We Know in Today's Animal Kingdom in Germany?" (1940); "How Many Living Animal Species Do We Know from Germany?" (1941); and "The Number of Proven Extant Animal Species in Germany (Old Reich)" (1941).

This final list is remarkable, even from today's perspective. In extensive tables, systematically subdivided by animal groups, Arndt broke down how many species existed on land, in fresh and saltwater, and in all of Germany. He included remarkably precise calculations for the respective percentages of all German fauna. Thus, he could demonstrate that marine wildlife represented 9.7 percent of total German animal life, and that omitting the 300 species of beach and parasitic insects would reduce that percentage to 8.9.

In part, Arndt's goal was to determine the proportion of German animal species in each animal group as a percentage of species known worldwide in each. Previously he had attempted to derive a realistic estimate of known biodiversity from existing appraisals, coming up with 1,025,000 described species worldwide, 3.8 percent of which were German fauna. Although many species-rich groups such as insects—particularly abundant in the tropics—were found in much smaller numbers in Germany, groups such as worms and microscopic vermiform organisms—such as hairybacks (Gastrotricha), wheel animals (Rotifera), and water bears (Tardigrada)—represented much higher percentages. These organism groups were first discovered in the nineteenth and early twentieth centuries, in part by German zoologists. As such, their high numbers are more likely due to the special attention and research focus prompted by new discoveries rather than to uniquely large populations in German waters.

Counting and Cataloging

Our picture of the extent of species diversity is essentially determined by two equally uncertain numbers, although their uncertainty results for different reasons and in different ways. The first is the number of known species, and the second is the number of all biological species existing on earth, both known and yet to be discovered. In the early days of animal research, zoologists unfortunately failed to establish a central, required registry of all valid published scientific names, although several attempts were made in the nineteenth century to rein in the continuously growing multitude of names in catalogs and rosters. British researcher Sheffield Airey Neave, for instance, published the multivolume *Nomenclator Zoologicus*, a catalog aimed at the comprehensive presentation of all genera and subgenera published since the tenth edition of Linnaeus's *Systema Naturae*. The catalog was continued after Neave's death and survives online in digital form, its entries updated through 2004. Another epochal catalog available today is the *Zoological Record*, which first appeared in print in 1864. Now in electronic form, the continuously updated database aims to record every new publication in every branch of zoology.

These are just two of many cataloging initiatives that have—and have had—great significance in systematic zoology and beyond, and yet they've ultimately failed to determine the number of known species for a variety of reasons. One major reason is the way in which scientific names come into being, both in times past and today. The "baptism" of a species occurs through the publication of its name, and only then can it be considered available—that is, valid in nomenclatural terms. The criteria for what counts as a publication are outlined in the zoological nomenclature rules, which serve as the yardstick for all things taxonomical. In reciprocal terms, scientific journals, the primary platform for the publication of taxonomic decisions and the discovery of new species, commonly require authors to observe the Code. The list of criteria is short: a work considered valid by the nomenclature rules must be accessible to the public, available for free or purchase, and "[be] produced in an edition containing ... numerous identical and durable copies."[1] As one can easily see, this is a slightly roundabout way of stipulating that the publication must be in a book or journal format, and that's about all there is to it. According to the nomenclature rules, every book or journal that fulfills these minimal criteria counts as a publication;

every scientific name printed there—provided it otherwise complies with the rules of name creation and a few other requirements—counts as available. This, in turn, means that all species names printed in any such qualified publications, even the most obscure, must therefore be recognized as available. For instance, species have been described in appendices to travel reports, footnotes of longer scientific works that have nothing to do with taxonomy, eighteenth-century natural philosophy magazines that only appeared in a handful of copies, and many other often surprising places. Any attempt at compiling a comprehensive record of all names ever published must reckon with this situation.

To find their way into one of the major catalogs, scientific names must have either appeared in a publication regularly combed by the catalog's editor or been submitted to the catalog by the authors of the article. To this day, there is still no requirement to register newly published names. Whether the majority of new names ends up in the *Zoological Record* depends largely on its editors' research strategies, the authors' readiness to cooperate, and a good dose of luck. There's hope for future species descriptions at least: a registration requirement for new zoological names in ZooBank—an online database launched by the Commission—is currently in the works.

Lurking in the background is a much more fundamental problem for zoological taxonomy and nomenclature: the critical difference between availability and validity. As discussed, a name must first clear the hurdle of availability. Should it fail, it's out the window: once it has been deemed unavailable, there's no way a name will ever become a species name. Passing the availability test doesn't necessarily make it the valid name—that is, the one actually used for the species. As we have seen in chapter 7, species may be described multiple times for a variety of reasons, resulting in several synonymous names referring to the same species. Of all the available names, the oldest is given priority, and this then counts as the valid name.

What's more, as many biologists will point out, the question as to what actually defines a species has never been decided conclusively. Still, there is a generally accepted standard, and to this day species concepts that deviate from it have carried little weight.

The increasing significance of molecular systematics and use of genetic methods to differentiate species is seen as a Copernican revolution within the centuries-long organic development of taxonomy by many scientists. In

2011, for instance, zoologists Colin P. Groves and Peter Grubb published an extensive, revised taxonomy of the world's diversity of hoofed mammals. Beside the familiar members of this lineup, it also included hippos and several other lesser-known groups barely recognizable as hoofed animals. One of the most species-rich groups of hoofed mammals is the Bovidae family, which includes cattle, sheep, goats, and various species of antelope. Until 2011, 143 species of bovids were known worldwide. Few newly described species had been added to the group in recent decades, and researchers were quite certain that there wouldn't be a spike in discoveries in the future either. Groves and Grubb disabused them of this belief. With the publication of their work, the scope of worldwide Bovidae diversity mushroomed from 143 to 279 species. Nearly doubled! The scientific world was outraged and unleashed a storm against Groves and Grubb. How could the number of bovids on earth suddenly be doubled after science had long agreed there were fewer than 150 species? Where did all these new species come from?

True, Groves and Grubb hadn't discovered a single one of the 136 "new" species, in the physical sense, nor had they examined any previously unknown materials that revealed new features. Instead, they had looked at known and named species from an utterly different perspective, known as the "Phylogenetic Species Concept," according to which "a species is the smallest population or aggregation of populations which has fixed heritable differences from other such populations or aggregations."[2] Fixed heritable differences, as described by Groves and Grubb, can exist within geographically separated populations of the same species. Applied to the taxonomy of bovids, many populations that had long been considered the same species now counted as their own. For instance, whereas the scientific world had long recognized the African klipspringer, one of the smallest species of antelope, as the single species *Oreotragus oreotragus*, Groves and Grubb saw eleven separate, clearly defined species of klipspringer. Intense debate about this is ongoing, and it remains to be seen which concept ultimately prevails.

In practical terms, this question is of great significance to the klipspringer and its kin. All klipspringers, whether they are counted as eleven species or just the one, are on the International Union for Conservation of Nature and Natural Resources (IUCN) Red List of Threatened Species. Conservation measures, however, are typically species-specific. It's easy to see that there's a huge difference—politically and financially, as well as in practical terms—between designing a conservation roadmap for eleven species and just one. For many large animals in Africa, conservation initiatives often include resettlement, and the practical challenges of introducing new animals to existing populations are obvious. These are just some of the implications of Groves' and Grubb's "biodiversity doubling," which accounts for the vehemence with which so many other scientists and conservationists have rejected their work.

These high-resolution genetic methods will unquestionably help in cracking the "cryptic" species, whose numbers remain obscure to this day. Cryptic species are those that have remained unidentifiable using all existing methods but genetic testing shows to be distinct. Many of these species truly seem to be morphologically indistinguishable. In some cases, genetic data have prompted new examinations of the morphology, which have at times resulted in the discovery of external distinguishing characteristics that had previously gone unnoticed. Estimates regarding the extent of cryptic diversity vary drastically, and in some cases, one morphologically established species has proven to be ten. These cases appear to be exceptions; many scientists believe that among the truly existing total number of species, the percentage of cryptic species hovers between five and ten percent, whereas others contend it's as high as thirty.

Because there has never been a central registry of names, and because names can be published wherever the author chooses, an exact census of what we already know is essentially impossible. Past attempts at determining this sum have always focused on known—that is, named—species. It's much more difficult to estimate the number of all species existing on earth—in other words, the sum of both described species and those yet undiscovered. For many scientists, this global species number is the Holy Grail of biodiversity research: for taxonomists, who wish to anticipate the task that lies ahead; for ecologists, who wish to better understand ecosystems; but especially for environmental policymakers, conservation organizations, and others who would stand to benefit from the ability to quantify the diversity and value of nature. In pursuit of relatively reliable calculations, the spectrum of methods employed ranges from simple estimates—the product of gut feeling, more than objective evaluation—to extrapolations based on the increase of species descriptions within certain animal groups, and on to algorithmic processes and statistical analysis.

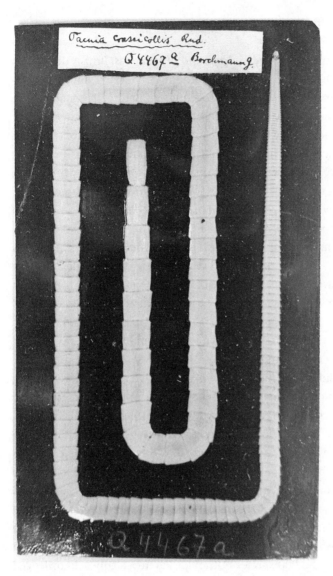

Figure 8.3

A glass slide preparation of the feline tapeworm, known today as *Hydatigera taeniae-formis*. Museum für Naturkunde Berlin, M. Ohl photo.

Quantifying Creation

By the seventeenth century, decades ahead of Linnaeus, British theologian and botanist John Ray was already attempting to develop numerical estimates for the extent of earthly life. The study of nature, Ray maintained, "may be justly accounted a proper Preparative to Divinity." As an adherent of "natural theology," Ray believed he saw proof of the existence of God in the manifest perfection and beauty of the environment and its systems of interdependence. What better way to serve God than to study nature as an expression of godly omnipotence, wisdom, and grace? Ray's famous 1691 book, *The Wisdom of God Manifested in the Works of the Creation*, opens with Psalm 104:24 from the Old Testament: "How many are your works, Lord! In wisdom you made them all; the earth is full of your creatures." Although most of the work focuses on the essence of a godly natural order, Ray first attempts to answer the question drawn from the psalm's opening line. Can the extent of godly creation and creativity be counted? Ray was convinced that the absolute, true number of natural objects—created by God in all His wisdom—was fundamentally incalculable for us, and that this was proof of the limitlessness of God and of the "fecundity of His Wisdom and Power." However, that didn't stop him from trying. Ray was a great authority on the natural research of the time, and based on a burgeoning understanding of compartmentalized animal groups (e.g., the butterflies of the British Isles), he estimated that about two thousand British insect species exist. Extrapolating from this estimate, he figured the total worldwide insect diversity was probably somewhere around 20,000. He applied the same logic to produce an overall tally of animals in all categories: besides insects, Ray recognized quadrupeds (which he called "beasts"), birds, and fish. By his estimate, 150 quadruped species (including snakes) and 500 species each of birds and fish had been discovered and described. With "shell-fishes" included in the fish category, it totaled 3,000 species. Although Ray repeatedly acknowledged that one could not come close to knowing the true number of species in these groups, he kept trying. He added another third to the "beasts" and birds, another half to the fishes. That's 5,350 species for the noninsects, and the total for all animals—including insects, a category Ray extended to other arthropods such as spiders and crabs—comes to just over 25,000 species.

While he played with numbers, Ray recorded an observation that would puzzle systematic biologists for many years to come. He described a connection between species diversity and morphological complexity, in which a group's greater or lesser ability to adapt to its environment would express itself in tiers of higher development. In other words, the "less perfect" an animal group, the more species it would have, whereas the "more perfect" an animal group, the more economical would Nature—or rather the Creator—be in its distribution. It was no surprise, then, that there were more birds than fish and quadrupeds and more insects than all the others together. What do these numbers tell us? First, they demonstrate "how great, nay immense, must needs be the Power and Wisdom of Him who formed them all." Second, they show that all this was exceedingly joyous, an argument popular in the seventeenth century. Because the greater the diversity of Creation, the greater the glory of Man, for in all His wisdom, it was for human enjoyment that God had created plants and animals.

As a child, Pieter (Latinized as Petrus) van Musschenbroek came into direct contact with the technical and natural scientific developments of the seventeenth century, thanks to his father, the renowned Dutch scientific instrument maker Johann Joosten van Musschenbroek, best known for his microscopes and telescopes. Strongly influenced by Sir Isaac Newton, whose lectures he attended in England, Pieter experimented with the physics of electricity and invented an array of instruments for the natural sciences, publishing a number of books on physics and geometry. Like John Ray's *The Wisdom of God*, van Musschenbroek's 1744 *Oratio de Sapientia Divina* was rooted in the tradition of natural theology and honored God's wisdom and power through the study of "well-conceived natural things" and the connections between them. This included an estimate of the number of animal and plant species, which van Musschenbroek determined as follows: of known animals, there were 500 bird, 450 terrestrial vertebrate, 600 fish, 1,000 mollusk, 50 amphibian, and 5,000 insect and aquatic vertebrate species, for a total of 7,750. There were also 13,000 known species of plants. At this point, he made a remarkable calculation. He assumed that every plant species must have five insect species directly dependent on it. (Two and a half centuries after van Musschenbroek, in the 1980s, this kind of ecological symbiosis and its implications for species numbers would provide the basis for Terry Erwin's famous calculation of global diversity, which would forever change our sense of real diversity; more on that later.) Five insect species per plant species entailed 65,000 further insect species.

The 7,750 known animal species were added to equal 72,750 species. If one further assumed that every animal had at least one specific predator, then the number doubled to 145,500. Finally, van Musschenbroek accounted for his suspicion that, because so little of the earth's surface had been explored, even this number represented only half of all the species really out there. So, another doubling, allowing van Musschenbroek's estimate of the world's total species number to reach 291,000. Given advancements in knowledge—particularly regarding ecological interdependence—the assumed possible number of species had grown more than tenfold a mere half century after Ray's first calculations.

Carl Linnaeus—the "father of taxonomy"—had little to say about the actual number of the world's species. The number of plant and animal species known in his day corresponds closely to the species named in his books. In the tenth edition of *Systema Naturae* from 1758—that seminal volume for zoology—he names 4,376 animal species. Although Linnaeus strove for a complete account, and despite claiming in his autobiography that "none have written more works, nor better, more ordered, or from personal experience" than he, he was fully aware of the holes in his catalog. How could it be otherwise? On trips to far-off places, he had seen with his own eyes the plants and animals just waiting to be discovered. The students he sent on collecting trips around the world (whom he called "apostles") sent back previously unknown species with every communication. This expanded Linnaeus's perception of the extent of godly creation over time, which was reflected from edition to edition of his systematic works.

The first edition of *Systema Naturae* appeared in 1735. It comprised fourteen large-format folio pages, and each of the three natural kingdoms—minerals, animals, and plants—was presented in a two-page table. Linnaeus cataloged 561 species here. Given this background and the treasures slumbering in the natural history collections of the time, it seems unlikely that Linnaeus really thought he was approaching totality in his record. In 1758, in the tenth edition of *Systema Naturae*, Linnaeus named 4,376 animal species, and five years earlier he had compiled around 6,000 plant species in his *Species Plantarum*. In the preface to this book, he estimates that the actual count was somewhere around 10,000, and he assumed a similar number for the animal kingdom. It's easy to see that Linnaeus probably placed more value on botany than zoology. Scarcely anyone at the time doubted that the number of animal species considerably surpassed that of plants. But

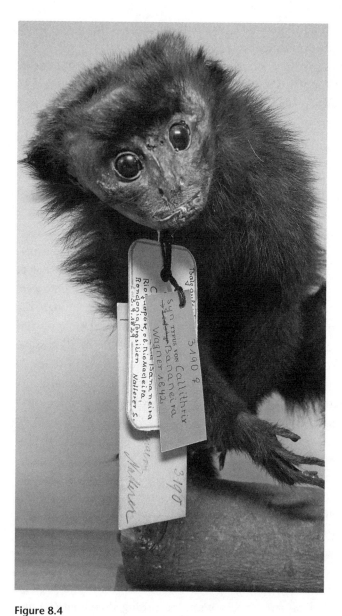

Figure 8.4

One of the type specimens of the brown titi monkey, *Callicebus brunneus* (Wagner, 1842), originally described in the genus *Callithrix*. Museum für Naturkunde Berlin, M. Ohl photo.

Linnaeus was first and foremost a botanist, and as such he collected and studied plants with far greater care.

Linnaeus, however, had indirectly established upper limits of possible diversity, if only for plants. In the fifth edition of *Genera Plantarum* (1754), he introduced an alphabetical system—the language or alphabet of botany. The 26 letters of the alphabet stood for the 26 features with which any plant could be comprehensively described. The combination of any two of these features, along with additional consideration of four "specific and mechanical principles"—namely, number, position, form, and relative position—sufficed to clearly define any plant's genus. The total number of combinations was thus 26 times 26 times 4, equaling 2,684 combinations—and thus the maximum number of possible genera.

A decade later, in the sixth edition of *Genera Plantarum*, Linnaeus performed another calculation yielding similar results. He assumed that at the beginning, God had first created "natural orders," of which there were 58, according to Linnaeus's calculations. Genera emerged through the "mixture" of orders, or 58 times 58, equaling 3,364 genera. Through a further "mixture" of the God-given structure, the total radius of all possible species expanded according to combinations of features, so 58 times 58 times 58, totaling 195,112 species. Linnaeus believed the random mixture of species gave rise to another layer, known as the "varieties." He argued, however, that this random process occurred constantly and to such an extent that botanists needn't necessarily concern themselves with all of its results.

Likely the most ambitious attempted estimate of the eighteenth century, based on a combination of mathematical processes and intuition, was made by German biologist and geographer Eberhard Zimmermann. Zimmermann's *Geographical History of Humans and Common Quadrupeds*, published in three volumes between 1778 and 1783, established his fame and reputation as a founder of animal biogeography. Mathematics was tremendously important to Zimmermann, especially in connection to biology, medicine, and other natural sciences. It's not surprising, then, that Zimmermann prepared extensive calculations of the "Size of the Animal Kingdom" and the "Size of the Earth." But there was something else at work here. One of Zimmermann's basic natural philosophical assumptions was that the three natural kingdoms existed in proportion to one another, as if by law. The higher the degree of organization, the greater the natural diversity.

To wit, Zimmermann assumed that, as the "highest level of life," the animal kingdom should possess the greatest diversity of species, compared with the plant and mineral kingdoms. After a thorough review of the relevant literature, Zimmermann was certain that a significant part of the world's diversity remained undiscovered, and he was convinced that mathematical methods were critical to determining an even remotely reliable estimate of the world's diversity.

For the total number of animals, Zimmermann started with the plant kingdom: as a source of food and medicines, it had been more extensively studied and was more physically accessible. Through empirical observations, earlier naturalists such as Charles Bonnet, August Johann Rösel von Rosenhof, and others had concluded that every plant must be seen, Zimmermann wrote, as a "small republic" populated by many citizens—in other words, as home to countless animal species. From this, Zimmermann concluded that every species of plant must have at least five insect species particular to it. By including information from Linnaeus's *Systema Naturae* and knowledge of the range of marine diversity, Zimmermann projected that the sum of animals would "easily climb to greater than seven million," meaning an optimistic estimate of the plant kingdom's reach would "exceed [it] by more than tenfold." Zimmermann must have known how outrageous his estimate seemed. His 7,000,000 animal species exceeded all earlier published calculations by several orders of magnitude. Even Zimmermann was awestruck by the extent of possible diversity in all its glory and functionality: "And these species, what an immeasurable sum of individuals must they hold! Each of the same just as artful, just as useful, just as balanced in structure as a solar system! All of it on this tiny speck, on this inconsequent planet unknown to the denizens of Jupiter, whose own sun is naught but a peripheral star to the observer residing in Orion's celestial bodies! A dumb amazement were the single true appreciation, were one not harassed by the thought of being so insignificant, and yet to think even this would leave in the eye a tear of gratitude."

From today's perspective, Zimmermann's estimate in the millions seems to have hit the mark in its general scale. Almost 150 years would pass, however, before another zoologist's estimate would exceed the seven-digit threshold. Zimmermann's numbers went unmentioned over all those years, and nineteenth- and twentieth-century authors trailed him substantially. Through the steady increase in species discoveries, which ran in tandem with the geographic exploration of the globe, the general perception of the scope of species diversity continuously expanded.

American evolutionary and systematic biologist Louis Agassiz—who prepared the first New World calculation of global species in 1848—has the questionable reputation of having been one of the last paleontologists to tie diversity of species back to a godly act of creation. He also rejected Darwinian evolutionary theory up to a point—namely, he believed it unlikely that new species could truly emerge from the interplay of intraspecific variability, known principles of inheritance, and environmental changes. Agassiz also tried his hand at estimating the total number of animal species on earth. He started with the 150,000 species already described and proposed a total of 250,000; as a paleontologist, he suggested the same number for fossils. Although this tally was a good deal smaller than van Musschenbroek's or Zimmerman's, which by then were largely ignored as relics from an era of less advanced scientific knowledge, Agassiz's was all the more shocking because it came from one of the foremost zoologists of the nineteenth century, when mass production of books also allowed for a much wider distribution than his precursors had enjoyed. Agassiz and his co-author, Augustus Addison Gould, were aware of the size of their estimate, and they tried to emphasize that this monstrous number should encourage naturalists—rather than scare them off—because each newly described species represented a "radiating point" that shed light on everything surrounding it. Thus, they argued, taxonomists' painstaking work would serve to expand and illuminate the overall picture.

Agassiz and Gould published their findings in a textbook, and only a few years later, a similar book containing animal species numbers appeared in German schools. Johannes Leunis was a clergyman in the northern German city of Hildesheim, but his primary focus was on teaching and natural history. In the introduction to his 1851 text, *Natural History for School*, Leunis took a stab at estimating the number of species worldwide. He established that since the sixth edition of *Systema Naturae* in 1748, the number of known species had increased by three-quarters every 10 years. Leunis predicted that the extent of registered worldwide diversity would "assuredly increase significantly," should non-European parts of the world be studied more closely. He then introduced a new aspect to the conversation: Leunis believed that the actual number of known animal species should be reduced by one-fifth "as the same species is often included in publications under two different names and the species-smithing authors will employ may result in certain 'play-species.'" Whether stemming from "species-smithing" or simply changing notions of species definitions, the double description of species was and remains a factor to be reckoned with. To this day, a 20 percent rate of synonymy is assumed, which corresponds directly to Leunis's prescient estimate.

In 1898, Karl August Möbius set about determining a reliable estimate of species diversity but for a different reason than the scientists before him. In 1888, after two decades of research as the first professor of zoology in Kiel, Möbius was called to Berlin to serve as professor of systematics and zoo-geography at Friedrich Wilhelm University, as well as director of the Zoo-logical Museum. In his first months of service, Möbius oversaw the transfer of the museum's extensive collections from their university location on Unter den Linden to the new museum building on Invalidenstrasse, both in the city center. The opening of the new museum had been celebrated in December 1889 in the presence of Emperor Wilhelm II. From 1896, Möbius served as administrative director of the entire museum, which included zoological collections as well as mineralogical and paleontological stores. In the 1898 volume of the *Proceedings of the Royal Prussian Academy of Sciences in Berlin*, Möbius published an account of the museum's status quo, which served a variety of purposes. The article was titled, "Regarding the Capaci-ties and Facilities of the Zoological Museum of Berlin." In just a few pages, Möbius outlined how quickly knowledge of animal species diversity had grown since Linnaeus, how past representations compared with current understanding, the role and function that large zoological museums served as educational and research institutes, how the collections were organized in an effort to manage the overwhelming diversity, and how many people the museum employed. In the single table included in the publication, Möbius compared the known animal groups with Linnaeus's species count from 1758, his own estimate of species known at the end of the nineteenth century, the approximate number of species in the Zoological Museum, and the approximate number of specimens in the museum. According to his estimates, 418,600 animal species had been described, 270,370 of which were represented in the 1,776,253 specimens housed at the Zoological Museum. These unquestionably impressive numbers revealed the scale of such museums' ambitions, as a home to "good specimens of all attainable species,"[3] and the measure of support they would require to achieve this end. Möbius did not explicitly address the actual extent of animal diversity, although he did acknowledge that a "presumably protracted stream of new animal species" was to be expected.

The Magical Million Mark

Möbius's numbers were the last significant calculation of the nineteenth century and one of the last that remained under the magical threshold of one million. Just three decades later, German zoologist Richard Hesse braved the leap into the millions in his 1929 "Report on the 'Animal Kingdom,'" published in the proceedings of the Prussian Academy of Sciences. However, Hesse's "animal kingdom" didn't denote the actual animal world. Instead, it represented an ambitious catalogic book project to "compile and identify all extant animal species." After the German Zoological Society was established on May 28, 1890, its member scientists felt empowered to push the implementation of such projects that had been discussed in the run-up to the society's founding. By now, most taxonomists were aware that the need to document what had been learned since Linnaeus's time regarding the extent of the animal world had led to two closely related problems. On the one hand, the majority agreed that Linnaeus's binomial nomenclature represented the best method for the naming of species. On the other hand, Linnaeus's version provided little more than a basic framework that urgently needed to be formalized through binding guidelines. There were too many exceptions and conflicts amid the hundreds of thousands of known names, and opinions regarding how best to handle them were both a common topic of debate and cause for deep enmity between colleagues.

The need for binding conventions—in the form of nomenclature rules—was glaring. The international community of zoologists also bemoaned the fact that since Linnaeus's time, the continuous stream of new descriptions and species names had not been registered and cataloged in step. No reliable overview showed what had been published to date. All emerging scientists who started working with long-neglected animal groups were faced with the same problem. If they weren't lucky enough to have chosen a group that an earlier scientist had cataloged, then they had to force their way through the thicket of historic literature, all the way back to Linnaeus, if not further—a ludicrous proposition for the quick, effective advancement of the ambitious zoology of the late nineteenth century. The newly founded German Zoological Society provided an opportune platform for addressing both concerns. At the inaugural congress in Leipzig in 1891, two motions were brought forward by zoologists Otto Bütschli, Alexander Goette, Ludwig von Graff, Hubert Ludwig, and Johann Wilhelm Spengel. The first motion called for the society to establish a commission "with the purpose of [creating] standardized regulations for systematic nomenclature." The second motion expressed the hope "that the German Zoological Society might set itself the task of revising the 'Species animalium recentium.'" The same commission should thus be charged with developing a plan for creating such a catalog of all extant animal species and presenting it at the following year's congress.

Considering the aim of standardizing the nomenclature, the unilateral German approach didn't make much sense. The motion to establish a commission for setting the rules was expanded in 1895 by a further motion to create an international commission to "unify in a single, trilingual codex the rules for the designation of animals, as they have been formed and recommended in various countries and languages." As proposed, the Code was prepared in French, English, and German. The currently valid fourth edition of the international nomenclature rules—first introduced in 1905— now contains thoroughly revised French and English text. A German translation appeared in 2000.

The other proposed project—"Species animalium recentium"—proved significantly more challenging, which can be seen in the fact that the initiative launched in 1891 wasn't finished until 1999, and even then it wasn't fully complete. Initially, the undertaking remained in the hands of the German Zoological Society and was christened in 1894 with the monumental title, *Das Tierreich: A Compilation and Guide to Extant Animal Lifeforms* (the German main title, which translates to "the Animal Kingdom," was retained even by the authors writing in English, and it was under the German *"Das Tierreich"* that the project became internationally known). Franz Eilhard Schulze was appointed editor, and he subsequently approached potential authors for the various animal groups, with mixed results. By 1896, however, Schulze did manage to finalize a sample entry for one of the smaller animal groups—namely, the unicellular sun-animalcules (Heliozoa), which had been prepared by German protozoologist Eduard Reichenow. In his progress report on *Das Tierreich*, delivered to the Royal Prussian Academy of Sciences in Berlin—which assumed responsibility for the project from 1901 onward—Schulze complained about the immense difficulties "inherent to publishing a work this gargantuan in scale." Still, in the two decades following the sun-animalcule entry, 42 further articles were completed, ranging in length from a few pages to several hundred. Although Schulze maintained that the end was nowhere in sight, he left no doubt that the *Tierreich* project was well on its way.

In 1927, Richard Hesse took over editing the series. Two years later, he reported to the Prussian Academy of Sciences, but his view of the future was far less optimistic than Schulze's had been in 1919. Hesse wanted to demonstrate how far *Das Tierreich* had come in more than three decades, and he was especially keen to estimate how much work remained. In 1915, for example, 9,712 pages of material had been submitted; by 1929, this figure had increased to 14,624 pages.

The question emerges as to just how long it might take to realize the intended vision for *Animal Kingdom*—namely, to catalog—if not describe— all known animal species. Hesse explained, "with the help of specialists and consulting the latest literature," he had calculated between 700,000 and 1,000,000 known species depending on how large a count was used for insects, which proved to be the group most difficult to gauge. He was more precise in a table arranged by animal group: he arrived at 1,013,773 animal species already known to science. Hesse calculated further: if one were to process all of these species at the same rate that *Das Tierreich* had been compiled to date—allowing for minor setbacks, such as another world war—it would take 750 years to complete the work. This calculation was based on the conservative estimate of about one million species, not taking into consideration the constantly growing number of newly discovered animals. Measured in "literary [time]," and even if production speed were doubled, he continued, the project would become an endless catalog—totally unrealistic. So what needed doing to further develop the "animal kingdom" in a sensible way? According to Hesse, the only workable way forward was to set priorities and not even try for global completeness. It started with bugs, which a friend and leading entomologist had described to him as a "Danaidean task," evoking the mythological image of filling a bottomless vessel with water. Besides, Hesse argued, the systematic work being done with insects generally demanded better organization and support before one could even consider including them in the *Animal Kingdom*. No, for the work to be successful—that is, to achieve something "conclusive and complete"—smaller classes had to be singled out and developed as thoroughly as possible. Only then, Hesse concluded, could the *Animal Kingdom* "represent a solid foundation, saving future scientists endless toil, and providing a reliable overview of a defined area." And so it came to pass, extending into the present day. After the appearance of volume 113 in 1999, publishing house De Gruyter declared the "gargantuan work" finished. It was still not complete, but the prospect of continuing was untenable.

One of the most effective calculations of species diversity—notable in its level of detail and support—was prepared by Walther Arndt, whom we met at the opening to this chapter. Arndt was clearly fond of numbers and counting. Had he been interested only in reporting the number of species in Germany as compared with other regions and the world at large, any of the tables outlining animal groups published before his time would have sufficed. The major animal groups, the current number for the desired region, the respective source—done. But Arndt proceeded far more meticulously. First, the classifications underpinning his calculations were as finely detailed as the literature would allow. He managed to divide unicellular organisms into more than 25 subgroups, and his table for multicellular animals spanned six pages. Then came more tables. Naturally most important was how many species were known in Germany by 1939 and where they stood in relation to global figures. Ultimately, Arndt compared the German numbers to those published on local fauna in Greenland, Hungary, and India.

Most interesting for us is the chapter, "German Animal Species Recognized to Date and the Number of Known Animal Species Overall." By placing the German animal world at the center of the study, Arndt was most likely abiding by conventions of the day. Regarding the total number of known species, he heavily referenced Richard Hesse, and after minor revisions to account for discoveries made since 1929, he landed on 1,025,000. Regarding the actual number of all animal species, Arndt remained vague, stating generally that, "provided the continued study of fauna in other countries, the final figure will grow considerably, the proportion of German animal species diminishing at a relative rate." At that time, according to Arndt, German species (including unicellular organisms) represented 3.8 percent of fauna worldwide. By comparison, Greenland was species-poor— at least on land, while a far greater wealth of species was to be found in its seas. Even when considering the grave effects of the First World War on

Hungary's borders, the country's representation of species was still "quite high." Not to mention India. While British zoologists were working feverishly to compile the *Fauna of British-India* monograph series, it remained unfinished at the time Arndt referenced it, although it provided "a few, in some cases significant insights."

Leading up to Arndt's time, whenever species were counted, the main conclusions followed the same trend. The exact number of species that had already been described couldn't reliably be determined. However, since Linnaeus, discoveries had continued in a pattern that was more exponential than linear. Besides, an end to this growth wasn't anywhere in sight. Every calculation of the world's diversity had thus proven so riddled with error that scientists did well to avoid the attempt. So it seems, at least, because after Agassiz and Gould's efforts, it wasn't until the 1980s that someone would explicitly approach the calculation of potential species again.

Gotta Count 'Em All

From that point onward, nothing would remain as it had been. Human-made changes to the environment and destruction of habitat worldwide had reached a magnitude that could no longer be ignored. At first, only scientists were interested in questions of biological diversity and the challenges to international conservation efforts, but public and political interest soon started growing. A host of critical questions were discussed: Is the environmental impact of human society's growth and development simply a "natural," evolutionary result of the spread of *Homo sapiens*? What degree of encroachment and change can the Earth system tolerate before collapsing and endangering human survival? Then questions regarding biodiversity arose: What role does it play within the Earth system? Do we need this ineffable diversity, particularly with regard to the extremely species-rich habitats of the tropics? What about the fact that we can't even approximate how many species live on Earth, that the vast majority of species are distributed locally, and that they must therefore play a marginal role in the world's overall diversity? Doesn't that mean that most species diversity is unimportant, and that losing it wouldn't be such a big deal? Thus, how are governments justified in earmarking tremendous resources to research things such as tiny slime fungi in the hidden corners of the Amazon or unfamiliar worms in the endless darkness of the deep sea?

As the twentieth century advanced, a consensus emerged: a well-founded estimate of species diversity was important for understanding the complexity of Earth's habitats as well as shaping public opinion and influencing political support for conservation initiatives by demonstrating the sheer magnitude of living creatures with whom we share our planet. Ample quantitative data already existed, but both scientists and politicians required more information to justify big decisions and costly expenditures.

It was within this context that the first large-scale projects were launched in the 1970s to document species diversity in specific habitats, especially in the tropics. One of these expeditions took place in Panama, and an ambitious beetle guy was in on it. Terry Erwin, born in California in 1940, had emerged early as an enthusiastic and talented coleopterist, or beetle specialist. After defending his dissertation (which addressed concerns germane to beetle studies) in Alberta, Canada, he wound up at the Smithsonian. After spending time in Sweden under the tutelage of Carl Lindroth, one of the most important beetle specialists of the day, Erwin decided to return to his North American beetles. He wanted to work with Californian fauna, but Paul Hurd—chairman of the Department of Entomology at the Smithsonian and thus Erwin's supervisor—spotted a problem. Funding for research in California was hard to come by, but Central America, with its tropical habitats and proximity to the United States, was the current focus of research institutes. He unceremoniously struck through "California" on Erwin's application form, replacing it with "Panama." Erwin, who had just returned from Sweden, was at a faculty meeting when he learned that his application for research funding had been approved but not for California. Instead, he would be sent a good 4,000 miles southeast. Erwin was beyond surprised and initially baffled. He had never worked in the tropics, and the $8,000 he'd received would have to be carefully disbursed. In December 1971, he flew to Panama; bought a machete, hat, and notebook; and set about studying beetles of the tropical rainforest. From the first, Erwin trained his attention on the canopy layer, where a largely unknown diversity was just waiting to be discovered, but he wasn't even on the hunt for diversity. Erwin just wanted to find rare beetles and describe new species—in other words, pursue the classic craft of a taxonomical entomologist.

He soon realized which technical issues had to be addressed to allow him to work and collect reasonably well in the canopy. He learned to use professional equipment to scale trees, but it quickly became clear how tedious and time-consuming this method was. In 1979, he made a radical decision. He started fogging the trees: using a technical contraption, he sprayed insecticide into the treetops and waited for the insects to come to him rather than making the tricky climb up to them.

Within no time, Erwin was able to collect masses of insects—which the poisonous fog had killed or nearly killed—that had fallen out of the trees and into sheets laid on the ground under them. As he'd hoped, Erwin saw scads of carabids but also thousands upon thousands of exotic representatives of other insect groups. He was faced with the question of what to do with this enormous diversity of forms, colors, and species. One possibility would have been to pick the carabids out of the samples, return to the Smithsonian after months of intensive field work, and spend the better part of the next decade analyzing the unbelievably varied material and describing all the new species. But Erwin decided differently. He was fascinated by the biodiversity but also knew that it represented only a tiny sliver of what was out there. Wouldn't Papua New Guinea or Central Africa have species groups as manifold and varied in detail as these? And if the canopy of a single tree somewhere in Panama was home to this many beetles, what might that mean for the whole tree, from canopy to forest floor? And for all of the trees in Panama's rainforest? Or for that matter, all of the trees on Earth?

Erwin prepared a bold calculation. While studying the canopy of nineteen individual *Leuhea seemanni* trees—a relative of the linden tree—he had collected 8,000 beetles representing at least 950 species. Some of the species were known, but many weren't. These 950 species did not, however, include weevils. As the most species-rich beetle group, weevils are a taxonomical nightmare, and Erwin simply couldn't identify them reliably, but he knew a few tricks. Studies in Brazil had shown that the number of weevil species was about equal to the number of leaf beetle species there. Thus, Erwin simply doubled the number of Panamanian leaf beetles he'd found and came up with 1,200 species of beetle—on *Leuhea seemanni* alone.

Next, he assumed that per *Leuhea* tree, there were 163 species of beetles endemic to that specific plant species. If this number applied to every species of tree, and about seventy different species grew per hectare of rainforest, then 70 times 163 would result in 11,400 beetle species living in the canopy of a single hectare. Include about a thousand itinerant species that didn't stick to certain tree species, and you've got 12,400 species, and that's just the canopy.

Erwin further assumed that beetles comprised about 40 percent of all arthropods, which would suggest that 31,120 arthropod species (including beetles) per hectare lived in the canopy. It was believed that two-thirds of rainforest arthropod species lived in the canopy, while the other third resided in the understory and forest floor layers, which would increase the total count in one hectare of Panamanian rainforest to 41,389 species.

As if this list of minimally substantiated assumptions weren't long enough, here comes the most controversial point: rather than contenting himself with the 70 Panamanian tree species, Erwin expanded his calculation to include the 50,000 species botanists had concluded existed on Earth. If one performs the calculation using 50,000 instead of 70 tree species, the result is 30 million arthropod species living in the Earth's forests, "not 1.5 million," as Erwin once reiterated. Although some taxonomists may have been offended that he counted only arthropods, ignoring all other groups, on this scale, thousands or even tens of thousands of roundworm or other invertebrate species would be a drop in the bucket of all the world's species. Never mind such "tiny" groups as mammals, with their six thousand, or birds, with barely 10,000 species. Small potatoes compared with the overwhelming diversity of 30 million bugs. Surely Erwin would admit that the margin of error for an estimate such as 30 million would be in the millions.

Nevertheless, Erwin opened the field for anyone who wanted to prepare similar calculations for any non-insect groups. As far as arthropods went, Erwin had set a pretty clear lower limit, which he would argue should not be undercut. However, he would be more than happy if someone used his samples as a starting point and surpassed his count.

Erwin's number was political dynamite, although several years would pass before the explosion. He first published his results in 1981 in a pretty obscure journal, unknown outside his immediate field, called *Coleopterist's Bulletin*—one could almost say he hid it there. It was met with a fitting response: silence. Nothing happened because beyond a handful of coleopterists, no one took note of it. That would soon change, though, as Erwin began speaking out about his calculations. He would talk about his 30 million at conferences, at workshops, and in interviews, and the number started getting out—fast. In his book, *Every Living Thing*, author Rob Dunn describes the reactions: amazement, shock, and open aggression.

The criticism of Erwin's calculation had less to do with the equations and conditions he assumed and more with the numbers he introduced to it himself. Save those he had drawn from his own studies, his figures were based on reckless, faulty estimates; once introduced to his calculations, they soared to truly unbelievable places. Maybe Erwin was right, and global biodiversity really was that high or even higher, but he was missing the empirical evidence. He was missing data to underpin his thinking—to show that his bold calculations were more than just an attempt to chase a dream.

Through his simple calculation, however, Erwin had directed the attention of both scientists and the public to a new aspect of the biodiversity debate. Everyone knew that the world's species diversity was large, if not enormous. But maybe the estimates to date still lay far below the actual size. Maybe life on Earth was much bigger, more diverse, and more complex than we had ever imagined. Within a few years of its publication, Erwin's 30 million had become a metaphor for global diversity. Even today—four decades later—there is scarcely a publication or review regarding worldwide species numbers that doesn't include a reference to him. Shortly after the discussion began, many new research projects—in particular those in the tropics—received funding to close the painful data gaps exposed by Erwin's admittedly poorly substantiated empirical forecasts. The objections he encountered proved sufficient to unleash this wave of localized biodiversity studies. In retrospect, regardless of whether Erwin was in the right, his inconspicuous work from the early 1980s seems to have been a well-timed provocation that stimulated the biodiversity debate tremendously.

The magical 30 million keeps coming up. Edward O. Wilson—the famous American ant specialist and biodiversity researcher—has used Erwin's number in many publications regarding the issue of extinction and possible solutions, sometimes even increasing it to 40 million. He isn't opposed to considering much higher figures—why *not* a billion species? Lord Robert M. May, too—another popular physicist and biologist who has been active in the biodiversity debate for years—refers almost exclusively to Erwin's numbers. At the end of the 1980s, however, both Wilson and May began to map the functional connections between the sterile species numbers and the species themselves. Their analysis shows a more or less linear relationship between the absolute body size of various taxonomic groups and these groups' manifest species diversity. The larger the animal, the fewer species it will have, whereas the smaller the body size of a certain group, the more species will have emerged through evolution.

This reverse proportional relationship falls flat in the smallest size category, though. There appear to be far fewer species in the group of animals less than a centimeter in size than this relationship would predict. Although many scientists went so far as to assume that the biodiversity among creatures smaller than a millimeter would have exploded over the course of world history, the data told a different story. The smallest within a mid-size range proved the most species-rich—that is, those species that managed to grow between a few millimeters and a centimeter in size. Critics argued that the smallest size categories had been studied insufficiently perhaps for methodological reasons. In any case, with the discovery that the microscopic world wasn't some El Dorado of biodiversity, greater doubts emerged: under such circumstances, how could a number such as 30 million ever be attained? These doubts would prove to have good cause.

In 1997, Australian biologist Nigel E. Stork published a comprehensive literature review and concluded that approximately 1.8 to 2 million species were already described; with a synonymy rate of 20 percent, the true number of known species would shrink to between 1.4 and 1.8 million. As for the scope of undiscovered diversity, Stork calculated 4.9 to 6.6 million insect species and more than 1.5 million species of fungus.

In 2009, just over ten years later, Arthur C. Chapman—another Australian biologist—assessed the available literature and various compilations of Australian fauna to develop an overview of Australian and global biodiversity. His results indicated 1,424,153 known species, with a projected total of 8 to 9 million species in existence worldwide.

Several articles have recently appeared by the New Zealand team around Mark J. Costello, which set the global species numbers significantly lower than most authors since Erwin. They state that approximately 1.5 million known species exist, and that the total number of species hovers around 5 million—give or take a margin of 3 million, that is. So, we're possibly near the lower limit of 2 million, but maybe the real count is closer to 8 million, which would mean a fair amount of work remains. Costello appears inspired to use his numbers to show that there's reason to believe we could describe every species before they died out. His work bears the fitting title, "Can we name Earth's species before they go extinct?" His response is clearly, "Yes, we can."

In the last twenty years, several calculations of species counts have been published, for which scientists had digital databases at their disposal. These databases simplify the calculations and make them much more precise. Over time, more and more databases for individual organism groups have appeared. Global, Internet-based portals such as the *Encyclopedia of Life* or initiatives such as the *Census of Marine Life* are scientifically and politically welcomed registers of earthly life that have developed as quickly as their financial backing will allow. Today, at the start of the twenty-first century, the data are better than ever before. Yet the complete retroactive cataloging of all available species names remains a distant reality.

Again, to be clear, we are referring to species names, not species. What's being cataloged are exclusively linguistic elements—names, which are labels or linguistic placeholders for biological concepts. Within the framework of such extensive calculations, however, the scientific quality of the concept behind each of these names cannot be verified. As a basis for counting the names, it's naturally a good idea to reference the most recently updated literature, in which experts have already distinguished between these substantiated and unsubstantiated concepts—that is, between valid and invalid names. Although the issue of synonymy—which in all likelihood is actually more than 20 percent—is enormous, when it comes to name cataloging, the real devil is buried in the details. Homonyms—or different species bearing the same name—are just as problematic as the same species bearing different Latinate name suffixes in different genera. According to the nomenclature rules, an adjectival-specific epithet must have the same grammatical gender as its genus. Should the genus change, it's possible that the species name will have to be adjusted. For instance, *niger* in a grammatically male genus would become *nigra* in a grammatically female genus. There are thus two versions of the same specific epithet. This is easy enough for the human mind to comprehend and compute but not so much for an actual computer.

An interesting aspect is revealed here regarding the increasing reliance on computers in the organization and management of scientific names. Because taxon names are subject to declension and other variables in notation, it can be difficult for machines to read them. To a computer, the difference between *niger* and *nigra* is fundamental because it's looking at different character strings. Too many exceptions make it difficult to interpret names as computer-readable alphabetic strings while maintaining their function as dynamic linguistic elements of communication between scientists. To solve this problem, so-called Life Science Identifiers (LSIDs) were introduced a few years ago: these permanent references for specific online information were generated and published for every electronic species description in ZooBank. The use of LSIDs is controversial, and several platforms assign their own LSIDs without aligning them with the others, which undermines efforts toward uniformity. The understandable desire to replace slippery human speech with machine-readable codes appears to come at a significant cost. One of the greatest drawbacks to these codes is that, although computers can process them easily, the human mind is totally unsuited to reading and memorizing the almost random chains of around sixty letters, numbers, and special characters. To illustrate, imagine how confusing it would be if product brand names and labels at the supermarket were suddenly replaced with bar codes. It wouldn't be so easy to find your favorite chocolate bar in the candy aisle anymore.

This isn't the case with scientific names. Although some may contain complex, tongue-twisting Latin or Greek constructions, they can basically be treated like any other foreign term and absorbed into one's own spoken language. The naming of species—by linguistic means and with the support of a customized nomenclature code—has always been an integral part of the discovery and description of existent biodiversity. This also applies when literally millions of species are waiting to be identified. We need lots of names for these species, although far fewer are needed than the actual number of species. A specific epithet must be unique only within its genus—it is thus irrelevant whether both a jellyfish and a rodent species share the name *niger*. Some common names, such as *bicolor*, are used in major registers like the *Encyclopedia of Life* for more than 3,000 species and subspecies. Yet for millions of species, we'll need names, lots and lots of names. Now more than ever before, to keep the current stock of knowledge usable and organized, a standardized process with uniform guidelines is needed. Naming—even with so many species left to discover—will thus remain the crowning moment of the scientific process of species discovery.

We don't know where Walther Arndt stood when it came to name creation. In many ways, he fulfilled the traditional image of a museum curator with the proclivities of an accountant. He was fussy and strict, and he put his work first. After his father retired in 1928, father and son moved into a shared apartment in Berlin. Until he died in 1943, Arndt's father assisted his son, particularly with his cataloging. Walther Arndt structured his day precisely to optimize his use of time. The day was broken into two working blocks and two short sleeping blocks. Every day, he left the museum at the same time in the late afternoon, had tea with his father, slept for a few hours, worked uninterrupted through most of the night, slept another few hours in the early morning, and arrived punctually at his desk in the museum for the start of the new workday. He neither smoked nor drank, as he believed it would harm his work. He swore off other forms of distraction, such as films or theater, because his time was too precious. It's possible that he never married because of his need for total concentration and because of the unabating feeling that he never had enough time. His life seems to have been defined by austerity and modesty, and one of his biographers was probably right in describing him as a "monk of his science." Arndt's modus operandi and publications are thus characterized by thoroughness and an encyclopedic sensibility, which—as for so many of the systematic scientists and taxonomists introduced in this book—have an undeniably eccentric quality. This manifested itself clearly in his pronounced passion for collecting. Arndt was a collector par excellence. He would collect anything that had to do with either museums or sponges. On the one hand, his obsession with collecting focused on sponges and literature on sponges; on the other hand, he sought numbers. With unparalleled thoroughness, Arndt numerically evaluated whatever crossed his desk. These figures, along with various simple statistical preparations, form the backbone of many of his publications. Theoretical, abstract interpretations didn't suit him; he was, as another biographer put it, "more descriptive empiricist with a bent for the extensive, the broad—in other words, the comprehensive." For odd birds such as Arndt and others we're about to meet, the museum—at least in its classic form—is the one place they can tap on their sponges and make their lists, undisturbed by the commotion of the outside world. Professor Arndt cuts a clear picture, striding through the hallowed galleries of the Zoological Museum every morning—rather thin-lipped, with a crew cut and little mustache, in a snow-white shirt with old-fashioned high-starched collar and tie, a stiff hat atop his head, which he would lift in friendly—if distant—greeting, and driven at every step by an almost enviable inner force. Like so many dedicated collectors with a tendency toward eccentricity and a love of details difficult for others to fathom, Arndt attained what can be described as nothing other than joy—the joy of immersing and abandoning oneself to numbers, catalogs, and lists that had the power—in the comforting indifference of columns and tables—to quiet the unease born of an unquantifiable diversity.

9 Naming Nothing

Innumerable stories remain to be told about the people who have dedicated their lives to the study of the world's natural diversity—stories of self-sacrifice and deprivation but also of enthusiasm and joy. Few have managed to capture this as well as Swedish author and hoverfly taxonomist Frederik Sjöberg does in his 2004 book *The Fly Trap*. Part personal memoir, part literary reflection on the meaning of entomology, Sjöberg describes with gentle self-deprecation the passion for collecting, classification, and naming. What's special about Sjöberg's account is that he knows what he's talking about, writing as he is from inside the world of taxonomy. This authenticity, in combination with the author's sense of irony, makes for a charming illustration of how the eccentricity so closely tied to taxonomists' love of organization is at once a burden and a boon to this form of scientific research.

While it isn't hard to find eccentric characters in the sciences, there's a veritable line out the door when it comes to taxonomists (and perhaps especially entomologists). Working with entomologists means getting mixed up with a bunch of eccentrics, and as an entomologist, I can attest to that. In their attempt to rein in the seeming endlessness of global lifeforms, insect researchers are especially prone to losing themselves in illusory or parallel universes that are difficult for the uninitiated to access, should they even care to try. The often solipsistic world of entomological taxonomy can be staunch in its refusal to offer a plausible justification of its purpose. Why bother discovering and describing hundreds of thousands, if not millions, of insect species according to the ritualized standards of the field? Well, because they're there and just waiting to be discovered, those countless diverse species! On the strenuous, months-long marches through the jungle, in the endless and often fruitless battle to protect the collected insects from mold, decay, and ants, and through the subsequent years of laborious microscope work between library and museum—it's here that taxonomists will find what Sjöberg would call happiness.

Taxonomania

It's not necessarily considered socially unacceptable to be an eccentric, to find oneself "ex centro"—that is, outside the center of social convention. Eccentrics think outside established norms, often happy to forgo social recognition in unapologetic pursuit of their convictions and ideals. But they choose to do this all voluntarily, and this choice is what distinguishes socially accepted forms of such behavior from unhealthily compulsive conduct. In many of the stories told in this book, the amusement elicited by the weird behavior and strange passions depicted is commingled with a sense of unease. When considering the taxonomists who've become famous through unusual feats or initiatives, who have dedicated their lives to the classification of natural objects and thus broken from societal convention, who've decided against what most would consider a fulfilling social and family life and risk their necks on dangerous journeys—can one really be certain that they're doing this by choice? Or might some be driven by an urge outside their control, an urge to record, organize, sort; an urge that follows rules other than actual free will? It's safe to assume that every taxonomist could name colleagues whose interpersonal skills are noticeably unorthodox. The borders are fluid between a manageably eccentric state and a pathological one, and many an obsessive-compulsive individual has felt comfortably at home in these surroundings defined by order and classification.

Alexandre Arsène Girault was one of those eccentrics unable to keep his own insanity at bay. Like so many entomologists, he started as a fifteen-year-old interested in bugs and—many detours and mishaps later—ended up becoming one of the most unusual figures in the history of insect taxonomy. Born in 1884 in Maryland, Girault—who was of French extraction—worked sporadically as a math teacher, but his passion in life was the superfamily Chalcidoidea (chalcid wasps), an enormously species-rich family thought to comprise tens of thousands of species, many of which are parasites of garden pests, making them critically important to agriculture. Most chalcid wasps are small, even tiny, and their taxonomy is challenging.

Figure 9.1
Alexandre Arsène Girault. Courtesy of the National Archives, image #7-H-15-H79.

After Girault had worked for a number of years in the United States, he lived in Queensland, Australia, from 1911 to 1914. During this time, Girault was engaged as an entomologist on a sugar cane plantation, where he studied crop pests and their natural enemies, which included chalcid wasps. He encountered an unbelievably rich and widely unstudied population of chalcid wasps. After only a few years, Girault quit his post in applied agronomics, dedicating the rest of his life to what he called the "pure taxonomy" of chalcid wasps. It was already clear by this point that Girault was a man of strong principles, with an unwavering view of what was good science—and good taxonomy, in particular. For him, taxonomy represented the most important basis of biology, and in his opinion, taxonomists should be highly educated individuals for whom the work took precedence over everything else. Girault's objective was to discover the truth, and in his estimation, he was one of the greatest authorities on recognizing it. When it came to his convictions, he was uncompromising and intolerant.

People can be like that, but Girault's intractability in pushing his views unfortunately didn't stop at his colleagues and superiors. Within three years of his returning to the National Museum of Natural History in Washington, DC—where he was also officially employed during his time in Australia— he had fallen out with the entire staff, and in 1917, he was terminated. He returned to Australia the same year and again found work on a sugar cane plantation. By 1919, after sustained conflict with his boss, James Franklin Illingworth, he was fired there, too. The next twenty years were defined by a constant cycle of unemployment, short periods of work, and, throughout, tremendous productivity in the taxonomic recording of Australian chalcid wasp species. By 1939, Girault's behavior had grown increasingly erratic, and following an incident with the police, his children checked him into a psychiatric hospital. Over the next two years, he was repeatedly released from the hospital—only to be readmitted—until his death in the ward in 1941.

Girault was an exceptional taxonomist. He published 462 titles, many of which were hundreds of pages long. At his death, he also left behind 2,483 handwritten pages of unpublished manuscripts. Over the course of his life, Girault described around three thousand genera and species of chalcid and a few other wasps, most from Australia. Recent reviews of several chalcid wasp species have shown that most of those he described are both recognizable and nomenclaturally valid. For a long time, about sixty works he had published privately between 1917 and 1937—in which he described hundreds of new species—were fervently disputed. Taxonomists usually publish their findings in official scientific journals. Privately printed works—even those with a sizable print run—are frowned upon in taxonomy because of the danger that they won't fulfill the conditions for a nomenclaturally admissible publication. For a long time in the chalcid wasp scene, it was unclear how to treat Girault's privately published works, which were also more than a little unusual. For instance, because they weren't officially published, none of the names was included in the *Zoological Record*, the standard reference work for research on zoological publications and names. Other catalogs, however—such as Sheffield Airey Neave's multivolume *Nomenclator Zoologicus*, published from 1939 onward—included Girault's names, thereby lending them substance. They couldn't be ignored, but they also didn't seem especially usable. One possibility may have been to petition the International Commission on Zoological Nomenclature to declare Girault's privately published names invalid—a common practice with a clear outcome. Ultimately, however, the community of chalcid wasp specialists moved differently: they performed a cost–benefit analysis and found that invalidating Girault's names would have such a devastating impact on chalcid wasp research that it seemed to make more sense to simply recognize the private publications as legitimate in the eyes of the Code. Because they mostly had limited distribution, Girault's privately published works were rereleased in 1979 in an American entomology journal. They were thus made available to the wider public, clearing the path for anyone to use the descriptions and names.

Girault's private publications, which were not subject to the scrutiny of colleagues in the field, provided him a space to let his opinions and feelings flow. He wrote obsessively on many topics, ranging from "economic entomology and entomologists" to trade, the economy, politics, the state of U.S. society, women, and colleagues. Some topics were especially important to him and ran through his publications like a golden thread: truth in science, the changing status of taxonomy, and himself and his own position within his complex worldview. His criticism is formulated as if axiomatic, its tone often scathing, and it was particularly injurious to colleagues and politicians. The style varies, expressing his embittered views in long, epic scenarios, pithy bon mots, and poems, as well as species descriptions.

Of the hundreds of serious species descriptions Girault published on these tiny wasps, two names break the mold. Neither was intended to describe a species that truly existed in nature. Instead, both are Girault's invective masquerading in the formal trappings of a taxonomic publication. Not only are these names constructed as formal species descriptions, they're also published alongside names that really are, which furthers the illusion.

The first is the wasp species *Shillingsworthia shillingsworthi*. It's worth reading the original description—which prefaced the sober description of three new species and a new genus—in its entirety:

Like *Polynema* [another chalcid wasp species], but petiole, head, abdomen, mandibles absent. *S. shillingsworthi*, blank, vacant, inaneness perfect. Nulliebiety remarkable, visible only from certain points of view. Shadowless. An airy species whose flight cannot be followed except by the winged mind. From a naked chasm on Jupiter, August 5th, 1919.

This so thin genus is consecrated to Doctor Johann Francis Illingworth [sic], in these days remarkable for his selfless devotion to entomology, not only sacrificing all of the comforts of life, but as well his health and reputation to the uncompromising search for truth and for love of "those filmy people of the air." Honour him![1]

The title of the 1920 publication in which this description appeared is itself striking: *Some Insects never before seen by Mankind*. It opens with a short tirade on one of Girault's favorite topics, the corruption of scientific pursuits harnessed for commercial ends:

Research is a labour of love. [...] Must love, too, be a matter of cash? [...] By Heaven! it has come to that. [...] Will not [lovers] be scarcer and scarcer, bastardy at that, the mothers prostitutes? What a spectacle! In the meanwhile, all true loves may go to the Devil; incidentally, also all men and all things whatsoever without cash.

But who cannot see that these copper-hunting men are not true lovers, but only poachers, snarers, and cunning trappers (not likely to become good fathers!)? Courage, Huntsmen![2]

At the time of publication, Illingworth—who was namesake to both *S. shillingsworthi* and another, genuine species in the same work—was Girault's superior. During Girault's sojourn in the United States, Illingworth had moved into his vacated position; upon returning to work in Australia in 1917, Girault was thus required to function as Illingworth's assistant and complete tasks only as assigned. Girault agreed to the terms and started his new job at the sugar plantation research station in Meringa (known today as Gordonvale, Queensland). Given his job responsibilities, he was forced to start using his free time for his taxonomic studies. Within a few short months, Girault was already engaged in a serious dispute with his boss. His employer suspended him in early 1919, after he'd repeatedly failed to come to work. Girault claimed he'd been "on strike" after Illingworth had spoken "roughly" to him. Illingworth, Girault, and research station administrators clashed so intensely in the following weeks that, by May 1919, Girault had been terminated. Girault expressed his resentment and frustration in his description of the new species. The species and genus names contain a criticism of the commercialization of science, as Illingworth becomes "shilling's worth."

In another, perhaps even more abstruse species description, Girault had a different objective in mind. In *Homo perniciosus and New Hymenoptera*, a four-page article published privately in 1924, Girault described a new species of human:

Since W. Shakespeare described Woman, I have explored America and elsewhere and on Mars I thought I had found a notable new kind of female Man like her, and which had caused some commotion up there (heard even on Earth as faint squabbling). This form was, however, soon recognized upon earth (in America first) by men in general, and called New or Business Woman. [...]

Homo perniciosus was thus described and this description is confirmed: Abnormal female (loveless, without offspring); heart functionless; mammae aborted; psychology novel (as supposed) but artificial; gay, high-coloured, feral, brass-cheeked, shape lovely like Woman but nature hard (selfish, thoughtless, proud, unsympathetic, irresponsible, aggressive, irritant, insensible, luxurious, pugnacious, over-active, inquisitive, mischievous, voracious and even carnivorous; antagonistic, ungentle, immodest, critical, competitive, poisonous); conduct unstable (even inclined to treachery), the lips compressed, body strong. Everywhere but rare in natural habitat.

From young adults, these commonest, 1923, Australia.

This abnormality of Woman, which at first I mistook for a new morphological variation, is serious and needs attention, as all know by this time. [...] [Some call] them weeds, nuisances, unbalanced, ugly—what the devil are they? [...]

When I discovered what was wrong and that Woman had not discovered but had invented, a New Psychology, by Heavens! I shook with laughter. Humorous enough, but more sad and even becoming grim. [...] God aid us! War would be nothing to this moral scourge and when, in my suffering and shame, I think of the cause, many is the time I have uttered this fearful cry from the heart: —

God curse and smite all free-acting women.

Is Earth free from Sun? How, then, can Woman be free from Man, or Man from Woman?[3]

Following this tirade against the new working woman of the 1920s follow two and a half pages of the driest wasp taxonomy imaginable. By now, it should be abundantly clear why Girault would have opted to publish privately rather than submit his works for peer review.

Homo perniciosus, the pernicious human, seems to have worried Girault because it appeared in two further private publications. *Hymenoptera Minutae Nova Australiensis* (or "new, small hymenoptera from Australia") was published in 1926. It consists of four paragraphs printed on a single page.

In the first, he describes the chalcid wasp *Mozartella beethoveni*, made famous by its name. The second paragraph describes another wasp genus; the fourth, a new species. Between them lies a single sentence: *"Homo perniciosus* Girault. This aberrant cosmopolite is due to Modern Commerce, certainly the cause of more than one perversity."

A further pamphlet appeared in 1928, titled "Some Insecta and a New All Highness: Notes compiled in fear and sorrow." In it, Girault expanded on his vision of a changing female paradigm, concluding that this change represented a concrete threat against society—and in particular, against those men searching for truth. The two opening sentences say it all:

A revolution has occurred in Nature. Woman—*Homo perniciosus*—has usurped the earthly throne and is now our King-despot, the All-highest Majesty to whom all (men) must bow.

Naming the Imaginary

Such spurious, wide-ranging passages litter the pages of Girault's private publications, which, it bears repeating, are taxonomically valid, having been accepted by the community as Code-compliant. Considering his personal background, it isn't always clear why he pursues certain topics with such acrimony and intransigence. Despite his incredible productivity in chalcid wasp studies, Girault's clear professional failings can be attributed to a life-defining attitude of universal defiance. In the years directly following his death, attention to the emotional parts of his publications largely eclipsed recognition of his complete works. His taxonomic work has since been rehabilitated, as mentioned, whereas his other pieces, composed with such ardor, are now regarded as little more than the bizarre excesses of an eccentric.

But what's really going on with *Shillingsworthia shillingsworthi* and *Homo perniciosus*? Many, if not most, species names have a certain linguistic appearance—a certain morphology—that makes them easy to recognize within a text: they're two-part, the genus name is capitalized while the species name is lowercase, both are typically italicized, and both will usually be of classical origin or at the least have a Latinate ending. When a word combination fulfills these requirements, it tends to signal that it's a taxonomic name, which is thus subject to the nomenclature rules. *Shillingsworthia shillingsworthi* and *Homo perniciosus* appear to meet these standards, and it's not hard to see them morphologically as species names. Yet there's obviously a huge difference between them and other names because they don't represent real species. Is this an issue for the nomenclature rules? In other words, does a systematic scientist have to pay them any attention or can they be written off as the amusing issue of a creative mind?

Let us remember: only available names—that is, those that fulfill certain criteria for formation and publication—are subject to the nomenclature rules, and thus endure in the taxonomic literature, even if they're later discovered to be synonyms and lose their validity. The question of validity is addressed at the beginning of the Code; in short, it applies to the scientific names of all animals living or extinct. A later paragraph is decisive in determining the status of Girault's names. It explicitly states that names introduced for hypothetical concepts are not subject to the provisions of the nomenclature rules. The Code thus states that only those names should be accepted that name something whose biological existence is accepted.

When it comes to *Shillingsworthia shillingsworthi*, the case is pretty obvious, and it's unlikely that a chalcid wasp taxonomist would want to touch it. A species characterized by shadowlessness and a lack of material existence clearly can't have been observed in nature as a tangible entity. With regard to the Code, *Shillingsworthia shillingsworthi* is unquestionably the name for a thoroughly hypothetical concept.

Despite the fundamental absurdity of the species description for *Homo perniciosus*, a hairsplitting taxonomist could take the nomenclature rules to the extreme and demand a serious analysis of the description. Because unlike the ethereal, immaterial wasp, the working woman who caused Girault such distress was as real then as she is now. Girault presumably had a few women in mind when he sat down to write the description, although he didn't designate anyone as the type specimen. He didn't assign types in his wasp descriptions with the specificity expected today, however, so the missing type for the working woman isn't grounds for stripping Girault's *Homo perniciosus* of its validity. Further, it doesn't matter that it's all biological nonsense. Species names are labels for scientific hypotheses, which—as with all hypotheses—can be disproved. From the perspective of the nomenclature, there's nothing wrong with describing a new species based on a single, unusual-looking animal, which Girault also did hundreds of times. Only time will tell whether the name will endure—in other words, whether the hypothesis behind the name will withstand further tests, such as comparisons with new discoveries and other species. Is *Homo pernicio-sus* an available name, then, that would have to be included as a younger addition to the synonym list for *Homo sapiens*? That is, do the zoological nomenclature rules apply to *Homo perniciosus*? The answer would probably be yes because, given the understanding that Girault's private publication fulfilled the Code's requirements for regular publications, no fundamental difference exists between the description of *Homo perniciosus* and that of the braconid wasp *Phanerotoma coccinellae*, which follows on the very same page.

The nomenclature rules ultimately require a healthy dose of sound judgment in this case. Girault's description, in light of his bellicose comportment, leaves no doubts as to his intentions: he viewed the task of taxonomical writing as an opportunity to impart a personal, perhaps even political statement about his observations of societal change—no more, no less. Let's say a taxonomist seriously decided to ignore Girault's contextually embedded intentions and apply the Code literally, concluding that *Homo perniciosus* was an available name. What would be the point? The population of enterprising women denoted by this name could hardly be defined by any species concept as a meaningful biological entity, which would leave no option for the name but synonymy with *Homo sapiens*. As a result, the list of invalid names for the sole human species still living on Earth would be one invalid name longer. The discussion will thus remain in the academic realm, and *Shillingsworthia shillingsworthi* and *Homo perniciosus* will maintain their commonly accepted status as the names of hypothetical constructs—and as anecdotes in the history of biology.

It seems to go without saying that scientific animal names are meant to name something that exists in nature. As demonstrated, the concept of existence isn't entirely straightforward, but we don't need to spend any more time on that here. What's certain is that a scientific name should signify something that, in the biological context, has a clear referent in nature. Now, to join the chorus of linguists: naming is the verbalization of an idea. Therefore, the naming as such does not demand an evaluation of the meaningfulness or credibility of the idea verbalized. In other words, when it comes to the act of naming, it doesn't matter whether the object named makes biological sense. Now, as a rule, biologists attempt to name only those entities whose real existence in nature can be proven empirically

Figure 9.2
Mounting stands for preserved birds displaying historical labels with the species name, synonyms, geographical origins, and the collector's name. Museum für Naturkunde Berlin, M. Ohl photo.

for an obvious functional reason: the key purpose of naming in biology is to make substantiated claims about the natural world.

Sound Science and Flights of Fancy

Because ideas find themselves verbalized through the act of naming, however, it's immediately clear that names aren't reserved exclusively for the hypothetically existing. We can have lots of ideas, plenty of which don't exist in nature or, for that matter, beyond the realm of the human mind. *Shillingsworthia shillingsworthi* and *Homo perniciosus* are examples of names for imaginary biological entities. Their naming doesn't differ fundamentally from the act of naming real species. The difference is that these two "species" exist solely in Girault's mind.

An astonishingly great number of names for decidedly fictitious species are found in zoology (i.e., names created according to the nomenclature rules that were published with the clear intention of describing fantastical creatures and made-up species). The motivations for doing something like this vary. Girault wanted to give outlet to his contempt. For others it's a fun taxonomic exercise to unleash the precepts of anatomy, evolution, and naming on a fictitious diversity. Humans have a natural impulse to invent and write fantastical tales, and this urge appears to extend to taxonomists as well.

One of the most wonderful and endearing classics in imaginary species diversity are the rhinogrades or snouters, members of Rhinogradentia, a fictitious order of mammal described in 1961 in an eighty-page book released by the esteemed scientific publishing house Gustav Fischer Verlag, Stuttgart. The author is Dr. Harald Stümpke, a pseudonym for University of Karlsruhe zoology professor Gerolf Steiner. His book, *The Snouters: Form and Life of the Rhinogrades*, has appeared in many editions and languages, including a 1967 translation into English. Snouters were incredibly popular among biologists in the 1960s and found their way into various other textbooks. For instance, they're included as their own order of mammal—just after rodents—in Rolf Siewing's *Zoology Primer*, a systematic volume formatted according to the standards of the field. A short sentence stating that the animal's existence was widely doubted, despite Stümpke's book, is the only explicit reference to the rhinogrades' constructed character.

Steiner (a.k.a. Stümpke) was inspired by a poem by Christian Morgenstern, whom Steiner credited with having made early reference to this unknown group of animals he called nasobames:

Along on its probosces
there goes the nasobame
accompanied by its young one.
It is not found in Brehm,
It is not found in Meyer,
Nor in the Brockhaus anywhere.
'Twas only through my lyre
we knew it had been there.
Thenceforth on its probosces
(above I've said the same)
accompanied by its offspring
there goes the nasobame.[4]

In truly amusing attention to detail and using what is immediately recognizable as a practiced scientific patois, Steiner exhaustively outlines the story of the animals' discovery, their geographic distribution and embryonic development, and their extinction following nuclear weapons testing in the (likewise invented) Hy-yi-yi Archipelago. The snouters' grim atomic obliteration, which came shortly after Stümpke's purported visit to the islands, was fitting for the time. In 1961, a good decade had passed since the end of World War II and the first use of nuclear weapons against Japan. The fear of further atomic conflict was a prime component of the Cold War, which defined the global politics of the time. Given the context, it comes as no surprise that the Liberal Democratic Party of Germany took Steiner's zoological humoresque at face value; in the *Liberal Democratic Newspaper*, distributed primarily in East Germany from 1945 to 1990, the party reported that the wonderfully strange animal world of Hy-yi-yi would have survived, "had we, the peaceable powers, managed in time to implement widespread disarmament and prohibit the production and testing of nuclear weapons."

Most of Stümpke's monograph, however, is dedicated to the systematics and taxonomy of the rhinogrades, and the author shines here. With great precision, he creates an inherently consistent image of a species-rich animal group, complete with internal genealogical order.

The diversity of scientific names that Stümpke coined is truly remarkable. He wrote perfect descriptions for 15 families, 26 genera, and 138 species. However, the names are clearly not from the pen of one versed in classical languages, a point that led renowned evolutionary and systematic biologist George Gaylord Simpson to write a review of the book in *Science*. Although he considered the rhinogrades "the most startling zoological event so far in the 20th century," he also criticized Stümpke's name creations as "criminal violations of the International Code of Zoological Nomenclature." Simpson seized on Stümpke's tone, lamenting the missing "rotated matrix" (a concept in mathematics that plays no part in zoology), along with the fact that Stümpke's taxonomy was "painfully phylogenetic." Simpson also notes that, "it is a custom, if not a duty, for a reviewer to hint that he knows more about the subject than the author and that the book would have been better if he, the reviewer, had taken time out from more important things to write the book himself."

Other reviewers of Stümpke's book oriented their analyses on the seeming seriousness of the book and wrote their own commentaries in the argot of scientific book reviews. To this day, Rhinogradentia comes up occasionally in publications that creatively and humorously expand on the snouter universe. For instance, the Max Planck Institute for Limnology in the northern German city of Plön announced a new species discovered in Lake Plön, while French scientists discovered a cache of amazingly well-preserved snouter fossils. Alleged sightings are posted as photos or videos online every so often, and natural history museums curate whole shows on rhinogrades. In 1988, Gerolf Steiner dropped Stümpke for the new pseudonym Karl D. S. Geeste, but working with the same publishing house—the success of the first edition was such that the editor agreed to continue the joke—released a little hundred-page book cataloging the papers, reviews, and further studies that had taken place since the snouters' discovery.

The central trait unique to all snouters is, "as the name indicates," a snout known as the "nasarium,"[5] which takes on a range of appearances across species and serves as the animals' primary organ for locomotion and a wide range of other actions. As such, Steiner made an effort to indicate the specific nasal forms and functions in his names. He includes each species' vernacular name in the description, allowing those readers less familiar with classical languages to understand each name's derivation (perhaps this was also meant to redress Stümpke's maladroitness in classical languages, criticized by Simpson as well as "Geeste" in the second book). For instance, Georrhinidia are Burrowing Snouters,[6] the genus *Holorrhinus* represents the Wholesnouters,[7] and *Hopsorrhinus aureaus* is known more commonly as the Golden Snout Leaper.[8] Add to that a whole host of inspired name creations such as *Archirrhinos haeckelii*, Haeckel's Primitive Snouter, in honor of our old friend Ernst Haeckel.[9] Not a bad alternative to *Bathybius haeckelii*, that doomed primordial soup. Throughout, Steiner's text is an absolute delight:

Tyrannonasus imperator is especially noteworthy for two reasons: like all polyrrhine species the animal is not particularly swift on nose, and yet it travels at a more rapid pace than the nasobemids. But now, since all polyrrhine species, because of their intranasal pneumatic apparatus, when walking give out a whistling hiss that can be heard from afar, *Tyrannonasus* is unable to creep silently upon his victims; but—since they flee while he is still at a distance—must first lie quietly in wait and then stride after.[10]

And so on, for nearly eighty pages.

Another slightly less celebrated example of an entirely invented monograph by another entirely invented persona is the thirty-four-page description of *Eoörnis petrovelox gobiensis*, written in 1928 by Augustus C. Fotheringham. Fotheringham—an alias for botanist Lester W. Sharp—reports that the long-disputed existence of this rare bird species had finally

Figure 9.3
The snouter, or rhinograde, *Tyrannonasus imperator*. Harald Stümpke, Bau und Leben der Rhinogradentia, Tafel XI (München: Spektrum Akademischer Verlag, 2006). Courtesy of Springer Nature.

been confirmed after a four-year expedition to the Gobi Desert. The local name for the bird was said to be woofen-poof, an onomatopoeic name that captured the sound of the bird taking flight: "a 'woof' or 'whiz' in the air, followed by a 'poof' or 'shush' made by the bird's feet in striking the loose desert sand." The expedition was led by Brigadier-General Sir Cecil Wemyss-Cholmondeley, Fotheringham serving as its scientific director. The average woofen-poof is approximately 17 centimeters in length and has a beak and throat pouch reminiscent of a pelican's. It has markedly short, crescent-shaped wings that produce a tone in flight, "three octaves above middle C," given its rapid wing-beat. The woofen-poof's plumage consists of small, sand-colored feathers with a smooth, glossy, almost metallic appearance.

As the observant reader will have noticed, the genus name doesn't conform to the nomenclature rules because it contains a special character. However, the "ö" doesn't represent an umlaut; instead, it's a dieresis to indicate the separated syllables of the adjacent "o"s. The correct pronunciation is thus "*Eo-ornis*," and the name would have to be rewritten as *Eoornis* to meet nomenclature requirements. Not *Eooernis*, although the Code requires that umlauts be replaced by the stem vowel, plus an appended –e in names published before 1985. Because it's not an umlaut, the dieresis would simply have to be removed, leaving an "o" where once there was an "ö." However, as will be discussed later, the taxonomic status of *Eoörnis petrovelox gobiensis* is beyond questionable, and as long as that's the case, we don't need to think too seriously about correct notation.

The history of the bird's discovery dates back 12,000 to 40,000 years to the Cro-Magnon period, as evidenced in the cave paintings of the Dordogne. According to Fotheringham, amulets bearing the woofen-poof's likeness were found in Tutankhamun's tomb. A number of narrative accounts of *Eoörnis petrovelox gobiensis* were also said to exist, written by figures such as Ancient Roman historian Eutropius, Marco Polo, and Thankgod Pillsbury, the alleged ship's doctor on Captain James Cook's expeditions in the Pacific Ocean.

Beyond its unique skeletal features, which Fotheringham describes in detail, the woofen-poof is characterized by its unusual lifestyle. It is exceedingly social, living in groups of 25 to 250 individuals. In flight, the birds exhibit their distinctive "Sumerian arrow" formation. Woofen-poofs mate for life, and interestingly, each bird pair will produce twins—a male and a female. Upon reaching maturity, these siblings will then mate and remain paired for life.

Curiously enough, in his 1933–1934 article, "Eugenics and Consanguineous Marriage," philosopher and anti-Semite Anthony M. Ludovici cited this latter detail of the woofen-poof's behavior as proof of instinctual incest existing among animals. Sharp's work on *Eoörnis petrovelox gobiensis* has also been cited in many renowned scientific journals, usually seriously in tone but with full awareness of its being a "fabrication." The original booklet has gone through several editions and can still be found in bookstores.

What the snouters and woofen-poofs have in common is that both were created by and primarily for scientists. Both Steiner (a.k.a. Stümpke) and Sharp (a.k.a. Fotheringham) managed to create closed systems of invented information on invented animal groups that emerged in the reader's mind as believable, detailed worlds. The many editions still appearing today are a testament to the popularity—as well as the plausibility—of the snouter and woofen-poof worlds.

In 1982, paleontologist and evolutionary biologist Dougal Dixon published *After Man: A Zoology of the Future*, a hugely successful book that established his reputation as an author. It was meant for a wider readership, and, as such, the inspired and well-studied scientific names he coined played only a marginal role. *After Man* is an extensive, illustrated volume that depicts what the animal world might look like in several million years—fifty, to be exact, at which point humans will have long gone extinct. In the first thirty pages of the book, Dixon gives a quick overview of the salient evolutionary mechanisms at play, as well as the genealogical changes seen in today's animal world. He emphasizes that these theories, mechanisms, and data form the basis for his projections of the future. Indeed, he applies them to imaginatively develop the "tree of life" beyond its current ending point. Dixon also invents a number of species, providing Latin names for all and colloquial names for many. In text and images reminiscent of old high school biology textbooks, we learn that rats have become the planet's chief carnivore group. The falanx (*Amphimorphodes cynomorphus*), for instance, is a dog-sized rat that hunts its prey—the equally fictitious rabbuck—in packs.

Dixon thus allows his imagination to run free but in a scientifically sound way. The antelope—now known as *Megalodorcas borealis*, or the woolly gigantelope—has evolved into a massive, long-haired creature whose horns grow out in front of its face. The penguin has developed into the largest animal in the world, known as the vortex (*Balenornis vivipara*). Penguins had moved into niches made available following the extinction of baleen whales many millions of years prior, ultimately producing their own twelve-meter-long species whose beak had developed into a plankton sieve. Although penguins originally laid their eggs on land, *Balenornis* carries its eggs internally until ready to hatch. These characteristics are reflected in the name: "Balen" refers to whales, especially baleen whales (a small error on Dixon's part: "Balaen" would be the correct formulation); "ornis" to birds; and "vivipara" to viviparity, or giving birth to living young.

And so life merrily continues in Dixon's animal world. The young para-shrew (*Pennatacaudus volitarius*) can spread the hairs of its tail into a para-chute that allows it to glide for up to 24 hours on summer updrafts in the mountains where it lives. The flunkey (*Alesimia lapsus*) possesses a fly-ing membrane between its extremities, much like today's flying squirrels, which will long have died out by then. *Florifacies mirabilis*, the flooer, is a flightless, largely sedentary bat with bright red ears and nasal flaps. By positioning these colored features skyward and sitting amid foliage, the flooer mimics the blossoms of a particular flower. Insects that land on the imitation, rather than the flower, are the bat's welcome prey. From ants to antelopes, opossums to ostriches, all have undergone an evolution into the strangest forms. At least that's how it seems when compared with the fauna currently familiar to us. Beyond the pure joy of zoologically sound inven-tion, Dixon's message to his readers is: Today's animals appear familiar, if not normal, to us. But it's worth taking a step backward and regarding today's animal world through the eyes of extraterrestrials or early humans. Through this lens, suddenly our animals seem no less weird than Dixon's extraordinary and not-so-implausible evolutionary advancements.

Figure 9.4

The "Flooer" (*Florifacies mirabilis*), a ground-living bat, which imitates a flower to attract insects. Dixon, D., *After Man: A Zoology of the Future* (New York: St. Martin's Press, 1981). Courtesy of Dougal Dixon.

Naming the Lie

From time to time, sandwiched between the more comprehensive real articles, brief fictional descriptions will find their way into scientific journals. The motivation for doing so varies, but it's usually with humorous intent. The problem that scientific journals face in publishing such entries is their scientific nature—that is, their responsibility to publish only articles that make verifiable claims about the natural world. Because the journals expect this of their authors, readers expect the same of the journal and rely on the belief that every article will meet general scientific standards. Unless directly obvious, fantastical works not based on scientific methods can quickly and often irreparably damage the reputation of a journal.

Austrian entomologist Hans Malicky used this to his advantage. Malicky is known outside Austria as a prominent expert on caddisflies. In the late 1960s, he chaired the Entomological Society of Austria; in this position, he also published the society newsletter, the *Entomologische Nachrichtenblatt*. The bulletin primarily published anecdotal and not infrequently irrelevant articles on a range of insect-related news items. As its editor, Malicky pushed for raising the scientific standard. The society saw things a bit differently, it has been said, and Malicky was summarily relieved of his post. A short time later, Malicky submitted an article to the society's other publication, the *Zeitschrift der Arbeitsgemeinschaft Österreichischer Entomologen*, using the pseudonym Otto Suteminn. The focus of the piece, which appeared in 1969, was two new flea species from Nepal, *Ctenophthalmus nepalensis* and *Amalareus fossorius*. At first glance, nothing jumped out as peculiar about the article: two new species names, complete with morphological descriptions, location of discovery, and author. At first glance, no one could tell that it was all completely fabricated, and because none of the manuscripts submitted to either of the society's journals went through a process of peer review—something Malicky had wanted to change as editor—the new editor didn't notice anything was amiss either. The article was published. While insiders close to Malicky saw what was happening, it wasn't until 1972 that a short article was printed in the *Entomologische Nachrichtenblatt* by F. G. A. M. Smit, a well-known flea researcher at the Natural History Museum in London. Its title was "Notes on Two Fictitious Fleas from Nepal." Smit went through the original article line by line, showing that most of the information was invented. Not only the fleas, but also their mammal hosts,

Canis fossor (literally, the "canine gravedigger") and *Apodemus roseus* (the "pink wood mouse"), are both fictitious, although some of the flea species used for comparison are real. With a little imagination (and linguistic access), a number of the discovery locations provided reveal themselves to be thinly concealed expressions in Austrian dialect. Thanks to an Austrian colleague, Smit was able to provide an explanation for these names: "'Khanshnid Khaib' probably stands for 'Kann's nit geiba' (cannot exist)" and "'leg. Z. Minař' can sound like a very vulgar (unprintable) expression."[11] Whether this form of humor is actually funny must be left to the reader to decide. Despite their debunking, Malicky's two flea descriptions remain in effect to this day, and *Ctenophthalmus nepalensis*—the fictitious flea hosted by the fictitious "pink wood mouse"—even has its own Wikipedia page. As for Otto Suteminn—supposedly stationed at a regional museum in Košice, Czechoslovakia—he remained a mystery to Smit. The latter had even sent a letter to Suteminn's address, requesting to borrow the fleas, but he received no reply, nor had the letter been returned. "Suteminn" itself was a pseudonym for Otto von Moltke, a fictitious knight from the region of Mecklenburg in a book by Karl May—a nineteenth-century adventure writer treasured by Germans and best known for his tales of the American Wild West. At times, the knight secretly retreats to a magical house, where he performs all manner of scientific experiments under the alias "Suteminn."

In 1978, the *Journal of the Herpetological Association of Africa*, a journal dedicated to the scientific study of reptiles and amphibians, published the description of *Rana magnaocularis*, the "pop-eyed frog." The fictitious author is Rank Fross of the Loyal Ontario Museum, a malapropism of the Royal Ontario Museum in Toronto. It's a short article, little more than a page in length, composed with the structure and style of a legitimate species description. It opens as follows: "Night collecting along roads in Ontario has revealed a new species of frog strikingly characterized by enormous eyes and a flattened body. The species is described below and the adaptive significance of its diagnostic features are discussed." The diagnosis: "Eyes enormous, protruding tongue usually extended, body and limbs highly flattened dorso ventrally. Dorso lateral fold absent. Otherwise resembles *Rana pipiens*." The species could regularly be found in or alongside busy paved roads, especially in the spring. The discussion section is particularly amusing:

Three questions require attention. Of what significance is the peculiar morphology, why is it restricted to a single habitat and how does it move?

Why is the body so flattened and why are the eyes so large? We believe that these are adaptations to the peculiar habitat. Normally frogs are at least partially hidden from potential predators by reeds, grass or bushes. On the road they are completely exposed, however. In evolving a two-dimensional body, the pop-eyed frog is enabled to escape the attention of all predators excepting those immediately overhead. [...]

We were at first puzzled as to how it moved from one place to another, observations on live specimens being lacking. Initially we found the tread-like markings found on the upper surface puzzling. Of what use were the treads in locomotion when they were not in contact with the ground? Analogy with the hoop snake offered a hypothesis; the frogs roll themselves into a ring, insert the extruded tongue in the posterior, and roll themselves neatly along, thereby engaging the treads with the road surface.

The description includes a cartoonish sketch of a frog lying in the street with bulging eyes, its tongue fully extended.

It's clear that this is a description of the many leopard frogs (*Rana pipiens*) that are squashed in the road each spring. What's less clear is whether the name can be considered available, according to the nomenclature rules. There certainly aren't any amphibian taxonomists who would want to include the name in their species lists. If one used the zoological nomenclature rules as the yardstick, surely it would be possible to find an article violated by this species description, thus rendering the name formally unavailable. Many of the basic requirements appear to have been fulfilled: the description is properly published, and it has a scientific name, diagnosis, description, and explicit designation of type material. It's highly likely that this flat frog hasn't really been inventoried as a holotype in the collections of the Royal (or Loyal) Ontario Museum. But it isn't the purpose of the nomenclature rules to assess the credibility of statements made. Even with serious species descriptions, it's only in exceptional cases that the inventory number and existence of type material are reviewed.

All that remains, then, is the disqualifying factor used in Girault's case, namely, that regarding hypothetical concepts. Nowhere does the publication state that *Rana magnaocularis* is a hypothetical concept, and what makes the situation even stickier is the fact that the description is based—at least potentially—on a real, physical animal. Reading between the lines, one must therefore conclude that the author's explicit intent was to publish a name for a hypothetical concept, which would thus preclude him from the responsibility of adhering to the nomenclature rules. It's safe to assume that the scientists affected by this case (i.e., amphibian taxonomists) would welcome this opportunity to banish *Rana magnaocularis* to the group of unavailable frog names, and it's likely the author would agree.

It's no accident that when considering whether *Rana magnaocularis* is nomenclaturally relevant, the intent of the author should be emphasized so strongly. If the consensus were that the author was naming a hypothetical concept, it's unlikely that anyone would argue that the name signified a tangible biological entity and was therefore made available through its publication. The question as to the author's intent becomes tricky in cases where it's not immediately clear. But what's even trickier is when the author's explicit intent is to name a species he or she believes is real but whose existence other scientists doubt or view as totally hypothetical.

These two criteria—the author's intent and the physical existence of a biological basis—could actually be enough to separate the wheat from chaff. When it comes down to it, however, it's anything but easy, and the Loch Ness Monster will show us why.

Since the sixth century, there have been reports of a large animal—or even a group of large animals—in Loch Ness, a deep freshwater lake in the Scottish Highlands. Along with the Yeti and Bigfoot, the monster known as Nessie is one of the best-known zoological mysteries studied by cryptozoologists. The field of cryptozoology examines legends and myths about large animals for their substance, guided by the belief that a significant number of folktales worldwide are based on truly existent but well-hidden animal species. As one of these mysterious mythical creatures, Nessie has grown enormously popular and plays a huge role in the Scottish tourism industry. Alleged sightings are reported to this day, but even systematic searches using sonar and automatic cameras (a necessary strategy, given the unfathomable depth of Loch Ness, which consequently contains by far the most water of all Scottish lakes) have failed to turn up indisputable proof of the existence of an unusually large animal inhabiting the loch.

One of the most widely circulated theories about Nessie is the suggestion that it's a surviving plesiosaur—part of a group of sea reptiles that otherwise went extinct at the end of the Cretaceous Period, itself the final chapter of the Mesozoic, or the planet's Middle Age. Plesiosaurs are characterized by an oblong body, long neck with a small head, and four large, paddle-like swimming extremities. The long neck, in particular, is a regularly recurring motif in popular representations of Nessie. And while there are plenty of scientific reasons that speak against the possible existence of a *Plesiosaurus* or plesiosaur-type creature in Loch Ness (such as the lake's geological history or its having too little water and too few nutritional resources, even for a small population), the image of the aquatic dinosaur seems to have become permanently fixed to Nessie.

Many images allegedly show that the Loch Ness Monster exists. The first was taken in 1934 by R. K. Wilson, a respected surgeon, and laid the foundation for the plesiosaur myth. It depicts a large, long-necked creature gliding through the water. The photo was printed in the *Daily Mail* in 1934 and considered by some to constitute conclusive evidence for the existence of Nessie. However, in 1994, a rigorous study of the image revealed that Wilson had faked the photograph with the help of some accomplices.

The best-known images of Nessie in recent decades were automatic underwater photos taken by patent judge Robert Rines and team. The group produced around 2,000 photos, which were taken in brief, regular intervals during an expedition in 1972 and another in 1975. Six of the photos contained noticeable forms, and of the six, two supposedly showed Nessie. The photos—which are rather grainy, despite their having been extensively retouched using the computer technology of the day—show what the authors were convinced were rhomboidal fins, as well as part of the body of a large animal. Using the camera's magnification, it was calculated that the back right fin was approximately two meters in length.

Based on some of these underwater photos, as well as sonar diagrams created around the same time, Rines and Sir Peter Scott—a photographer and conservationist—decided to formally describe and name the monster of Loch Ness. They published the description in *Nature*, one of the world's most respected scientific journals, which guaranteed them international attention. The scientific name they selected was *Nessiteras rhombopteryx*, which is derived as follows: the first part of *Nessiteras* is obvious, referring to Nessie and thus the name of its home, Loch Ness. The second part ostensibly derives from the Greek *teras*; the authors write that since Homer, this term has been used to mean "a marvel or wonder, and in a concrete sense for a range of monsters which arouse awe, amazement and often fear." The specific epithet is a combination of the Greek *rhombos*, for rhomboidal, and *pteryx*, for fins or wings. Scott and Rines write that, literally translated, *Nessiteras rhombopteryx* means "the Ness wonder with a diamond fin."

The existence of the Loch Ness Monster is anything but obvious, but Scott and Rines substantiate their comprehensive description with information from their photos and other sightings to date. Granted, at first glance there's not much to see in the photos: a few shadowy and light fields bleed into each other, making any discernible forms hard to interpret. A larger photo shows a white structure that seems almost to suggest a horned head, despite the image's flaws. Scott and Rines draw what they can from the photos: they describe the approximately two-meter-long fin (the right rear?), areas of the back and belly displaying rough skin texture, and maybe a few ribs. These two small photos, which the authors believe exhibit these structures, represent the actual basis for the *Nessiteras rhombopteryx* description. All other information provided is guesswork. Based on a fin length of two meters, and with the help of the calibrated photographs, Nessie is said to be 15 to 20 meters in length, with a neck three to four meters long and a small head, which might feature a few horn-like protrusions. The spotty description is completed by two reconstructions that depict a plesiosaurus-type animal, whose body is rather fat and ungainly around the front extremities. The authors pointedly avoid the question as to which animal group Nessie would belong to. The existence of the rhomboidal fins means it would be a vertebrate, no question. According to Scott and Rines, there are no living whale species with even remotely similar fins. *D'accord.* All that leaves us with is a reptile of some sort, but as the authors concede, any more precise definition would be pure speculation.

Scott and Rines could easily foresee that the description of *Nessiteras rhombopteryx* would be met with criticism. They point out that the nomenclature rules allow species descriptions based on photographs, and that they had to rely on this allowance because unfortunately there wasn't any type material for Nessie. This isn't entirely true because technically speaking all that's missing is the physically available holotype. There was, however, most certainly a type specimen from August 8, 1972, onward because they took a picture of it.

At the end of the description, Scott and Rines state that it "had been calculated" that the biomass available in Loch Ness was sufficient to sustain animals of this size, given the ample populations of salmon, sea trout, and large eels at their disposal. They also believe it possible that 12,000 years ago, at which point Loch Ness was an estuary, it was cut off from the

Figure 9.5

Photograph taken with a strobe flash in Loch Ness on June 20, 1975, showing the head and neck, 7 to 12 feet in length, of *Nessiteras rhombopteryx*. According to the authors, adjacent frames, taken 1 minute before and after, show nothing. Reprinted by permission from Macmillan Publishers Ltd: NATURE (vol. 258, Scott, P., Rines, R., Naming the Loch Ness Monster), copyright (1975).

ocean by an encroaching isthmus. A small population of *Nessiteras rhombopteryx* could thus have been isolated and contained within Loch Ness, where they've been living ever since.

It's worth noting that Scott and Rines open their article with an explanation as to why they want to name the Loch Ness Monster in the first place. Schedule 1 of the Conservation of Wild Creatures and Wild Plants Act, passed by the UK Parliament in 1975, extends full protection to any animal whose survival in nature is threatened. To fall into this category, the organisms must have both a scientific and a colloquial name. Although Scott and Rines grant that Nessie's existence remains controversial among specialists, they propose to operate under the principle of "better safe than sorry." Accordingly, if lawmakers are to undertake measures to protect this species of no more than a few individuals (at best)—should its existence ever actually be proven—then it should be acknowledged, they reason, that its inclusion in Schedule 1 has already been cemented through its formal naming.

It's not unprecedented for a possibly fictitious organism to fall under official protection. In 1969, Skamania County in Washington State put Bigfoot on the list of protected species. Bigfoot (also known in Canada as Sasquatch) is the legendary ape-man of the Rockies and Appalachians; alleged sightings continue to this day, but its existence has yet to be proven through indisputable evidence. Various theories regarding Bigfoot's systematic assignment have been discussed. One of the most popular ideas is that Bigfoot is a descendant of *Gigantopithecus*, an extinct genus of giant ape from Southeast Asia known to us only through fossils. The Yeti, or Abominable Snowman, is also thought to be related to *Gigantopithecus* and, thus, to Bigfoot. In his book *Big Footprints*, anthropologist and Bigfoot researcher Grover S. Krantz, who died in 2002, discusses the plausibility of the Bigfoot and Sasquatch legends and suggests a few vague possibilities for scientific names. Should Bigfoot be proven to belong to *Gigantopithecus*, then *Gigantopithecus canadensis* would suggest itself as an appropriate choice. Should Bigfoot ultimately require its own genus, then it should be called *Gigantanthropus*, presumably with the same specific epithet, *canadensis*. Krantz also considers a possible connection between Bigfoot and *Australopithecus*, an extinct genus of early humans found in Africa, which would lead to the name *Australopithecus canadensis*. Gordon Strasenburgh, another Bigfoot expert, had already published in 1971 on potential family ties between

Bigfoot and another genus of hominids, resulting in an altogether different name: *Paranthropus eldurrelli*.

But let's return to the question of whether *Nessiteras rhombopteryx* is nomenclaturally available, which remains unanswered. Is it a valid name, according to the zoological nomenclature rules? Description, diagnosis, name, publication—check, check, check, check. The discussion is therefore focused instead on whether *Nessiteras rhombopteryx* names a hypothetical concept, in which case it wouldn't fall under the purview of zoological nomenclature. Many people would surely assert that Nessie is a creature of myth and legend, lacking a biological manifestation in Loch Ness or anyplace else on Earth, which would therefore indicate a hypothetical concept. However, an important tenet of taxonomy is that, first and foremost, what is published is valid. Based on the publication, there's no doubt that both Scott and Rines are thoroughly convinced that Nessie exists. In other words, the description of *Nessiteras rhombopteryx* was not published explicitly for a hypothetical concept, and it's doubtful that the opinion held by many, if not most, scientists—that is, that Nessie is not real—could be reason enough to strike the name from the list of animal species in Great Britain. So there's a lot to suggest that *Nessiteras rhombopteryx* can be accepted as a real, earnest, and, yes, valid name.

Interestingly, Scott and Rines compare their new species *Nessiteras rhombopteryx* with other mythical sea serpents, but specifically those that have also been formally named. The oldest is the Massachusetts Sea Serpent, named *Megophias monstrosus* in 1817 by naturalist Constantine Samuel Rafinesque-Schmaltz. It wasn't until 1958 that Bernard Heuvelmans—the founder of cryptozoology and one of its most colorful characters—described *Megalotaria longicollis*, another fabled species with the appearance of a plesiosaur said to live in North American waters. After comparing their photos to the other species' descriptions, however, Scott and Rines conclude that the older names aren't applicable to the "owner of the hind flipper in the photographs."

Bernard Heuvelmans did more than just provide an American sea serpent with a name. Following the Second World War, Heuvelmans—who was born in Normandy in 1916 and was torn for many years between his two great passions, jazz and biology—began to systematically study enigmatic, mythical animal species. His two-volume *Sur la Piste des Bêtes Ignorées* (*On the Track of Unknown Animals*) from 1955 was a bestseller and made him famous overnight. The book provided the cornerstone of modern cryptozoology.

In this work and others, Heuvelmans published scientific names for a host of mythical creatures whose existence is disputed. In 1969, for instance, he described *Homo pongoides* based on the so-called Minnesota Iceman, a humanoid body frozen in a block of ice that was exhibited in malls and state fairs throughout the United States and Canada in the 1960s and 1970s. Heuvelmans believed that *Homo pongoides* represented a human species closely related to the Neanderthals that had presumably gone undetected until somehow being shot in the Vietnam War. There's a lot to suggest that the Minnesota Iceman was a hoax.

Like the Minnesota Iceman, the Yeti also has Heuvelmans to thank for its scientific name: *Dinanthropoides nivalis*. Heuvelmans translated the name as the "terrible anthropoid of the snows."[12] If the Yeti, like Bigfoot, potentially represented a survivor of the extinct giant ape genus *Gigantopithecus*, then *Dinanthropoides* would be its younger synonym because the former name was published in 1935 by Gustav von Koenigswald. If this were the case, Heuvelmans concludes, then the Yeti's scientific name would be adjusted accordingly to *Gigantopithecus nivalis*.

In this fashion, Heuvelmans works his way through the world of cryptids—the world of marvelous animals that so determinedly elude human detection. Not all are as popular as the Yeti, but Heuvelmans wants to use proper scientific names as the key to acknowledging their existence: the long-necked sea cow, 18 meters in length and quite possibly a sea lion (*Megalotaria longicollis*); the merhorse, an 18-meter-long, whiskered sea monster (*Halshippus olaimagni*); and the "Super Otter" (*Hyperhydra egedei*), a sea serpent twenty to thirty meters in length resembling an otter.

Whether Heuvelmans's names would pass the test of the zoological nomenclature rules is questionable. But there is as little possibility here to oppose the status of a hypothetical concept as there was for Nessie. Even if Heuvelmans were the only person worldwide to believe the cryptids he named actually exist—which he isn't, by the way—one would have to accept that the names were published for biological entities believed to truly exist. Whether parts of the Code beyond this stipulation were violated would have to be tested for each individual case.

Let us return to a central theme of this book: the Code is a convention developed over many years and by many minds, meant to standardize and thus simplify the management of droves of taxonomic data. How taxonomy—the science of recognition, description, and naming—relates to nomenclature—the rules for creating and managing names—is a regular topic of debate. In most cases of species description, the entities addressed by taxonomy and nomenclature coincide so elegantly that it can be difficult to tell the difference between them in everyday scientific work. The taxonomic process of species recognition and description is so closely intertwined with the naming process that it doesn't seem necessary to differentiate between the two. Both taxonomy and naming are trained on the same object: a species or other biological entity waiting to be both described and named. As for "naming nothing," however, the difference is especially striking. In these cases of cryptozoology, the object range for taxonomy is empty because most systematic scientists would agree that the species being described do not exist. The process of naming, however, continues as it always has and as it always should. It's a linguistic process not an empirical one—it needn't be bound to reality. Empirically oriented taxonomy and linguistic naming finally overlap when it comes to the range of validity determined by the zoological nomenclature rules. The Code applies only to those names intended for tangible biological entities. By excluding names for hypothetical concepts, the verdict has been issued for most of the names mentioned in this chapter. They don't fall under the purview of the nomenclature rules and therefore don't belong in the catalog of life. Were a bureaucratic taxonomist to adopt the view that some or even all of these names were formally relevant to the nomenclature, the question would remain as to what could be gained from this stripe of formalism. Whether the list of all organism names includes a few dozen cryptids—which could turn out to be either fairytale creatures or actual species—is mostly irrelevant to the big questions surrounding the inventory of global species diversity. Considered within this context, names like these are merely the stuff of academic jest, humor notwithstanding.

The publication of *Nessiteras rhombopteryx* in *Nature*, one of the best-known and most highly regarded scientific journals in the world, would ultimately prove to be its Disaster of the Year in 1975. The publication, which came out in early December, was followed by a global media response: the whole world was talking about Nessie and its new name. It was precisely the type of media presence a scientific journal like *Nature* had always dreamed of—and all because of a single scientific article. Before the

Figure 9.6

A jumble of old labels from the mammal collection. Museum für Naturkunde Berlin, M. Ohl photo.

year was out, however, Scottish parliamentarian Nicholas Fairbairn made a surprising discovery. He had played around with the letters of *Nessiteras rhombopteryx* and found it was an anagram of "monster hoax by Sir Peter S." He informed the *New York Times* by letter, and by December 18, the *Times* had printed a brief note on the matter, citing the anagram as proof that *Nessiteras rhombopteryx* was a canard. For *Nature*, although Rines had countered that the letters could also be rearranged to spell "Yes, both pix are monsters. R.," it was reason enough to realize it had been given the runaround. We'll never know whether Robert Rines and Peter Scott had intentionally planted this anagram or it was merely a happy accident. Certainly, that a name formed with such serious scientific intent should contain within itself an admission of deceit constitutes a particularly beautiful example of the art of naming.

Epilogue: On Labeling

There's a special place reserved for taxonomic thought and practice, for the description, designation, and naming of species: the enchanted collections of natural history museums, where the diversity of nature is revealed unlike anyplace else, save nature itself. At the same time, the collections are a universe of names that cannot exist independently of their material counterparts. Scientific names are endowed with significance in that they refer to natural entities we are capable of perceiving.

Nowhere is the connection between names as linguistic elements and the biological entities they designate more clearly manifested than in the label. Through its labeling, the museum object crosses the threshold from individual to species, the species formally emancipating itself from the unique attributes of the individual organism. Not only do these natural specimens lose their individuality through their naming, they also become objects within a system of organisms that represents a general idea rather than the concrete. The label turns a formerly living creature into the object of a hypothesis on the existence of a certain biological species.

But hypotheses can change. Indeed, in the realm of language, this type of change takes place in the connection between an object and its name. New names follow the changes, and new labels follow the names. Still, the physical arrangement of objects in a natural history collection is anything but random; instead, it's dictated by our understanding of the objects' nature. Species within the same genus are placed alongside one another, as are genera within the same family. If our understanding of things changes, then objects lose the right to their familiar neighbors and are moved elsewhere within the room. "If new knowledge comes to light about an object, it will suddenly be whisked from one shelf into the company of other objects," Hanns Zischler writes. The "dynamics of abstract concepts" in museum collections are thus expressed further through this movement within the space of the museum.

Language forms the framework within which scientific knowledge is gained and secured. And even if the assigning of a name to an object manifests itself in spatial terms, these physical expressions of order are ultimately subordinate to the linguistic order. It is naming—fastening a name to an object—that creates order within a natural history collection. The physical placement of objects is thus secondary, provided the unambiguous name assignment is ensured by means of the tangible name bearer and its documented inclusion in catalogs and databases.

Even through the act of naming, however, one isn't entirely uncoupled from the individual in museum collections. It's still an animal, after all—sitting in the collection, waiting for attention—and as a documented collection piece, individual traces of its life and death can often be reconstructed in some detail. Behind all scientific names are the stories of their objects, of the animals collected in faraway lands that then became the properly preserved objects of scientific fascination. Yet again names and their objects are tied inextricably to the collectors and researchers, experts and amateurs who make the study of nature their life's work.

Scientific names represent a multidimensional culmination of knowledge and its many forms. Their structured use creates a linguistic likeness of the Book of Life, whose readability is also determined by how closely the established conventions of name creation and use are followed. But as couched in scientific language as the names may be, scientific name creation will continue to be shaped by myriad not infrequently nonscientific influences. It's to these imperfections that the names owe a great part of their appeal.

Notes

Chapter 1

1. "titmouse, n." OED Online. March 2017. Oxford University Press. http://www.oed.com/view/Entry/202615?redirectedFrom=titmouse& (accessed May 26, 2017).

2. International Commission on Zoological Nomenclature, *International Code of Zoological Nomenclature, 4th edition.* London: The International Trust for Zoological Nomenclature, 1999. The website of the Natural History Museum in London hosts the digital edition of the Code online: http://www.nhm.ac.uk/hosted-sites/iczn/code. Henceforth abbreviated as ICZN.

3. English names: Common shrew, Pygmy Shrew, Alpine shrew, Water shrew, Miller's Water shrew, Bicolored shrew, Lesser White-toothed shrew, Greater White-toothed shrew.

4. English names: Pond bat, Long-fingered bat, Daubenton's bat, Notch-eared bat. Literal translations of their German names: pond bat, long-foot bat, water bat, eyelash bat.

5. Friedrich Kluge, *Etymologisches Wörterbuch der deutschen Sprache*, Strassburg: Karl J. Trübner, 1881: p. 219.

6. Eel, eagle, ant, leech, trout, vulture, hamster, toad, snail, stork, toad, wasp.

7. Robin redbreast ("red throat"), Stentor roeseli ("little trumpet animal"), compass jellyfish, Eurasian water shrew, shrimp ("flea crab"), azure damselfly ("azure virgin"), digger wasp.

8. "crayfish | crawfish, n." OED Online. March 2017. Oxford University Press. http://www.oed.com/view/Entry/43985? (accessed May 26, 2017).

9. In both cases, the words translate to "mouth," "drink," "eat," and "die." In the first instance, these terms are typically reserved for use with animals or used pejoratively in the human context (e.g., "yap," "guzzle," "scarf," and "croak").

10. Mole-like rice tenrec, black forest wallaby, Virginia opossum, striped bandicoot, Chinese pangolin, Goldman's spiny pocket mouse, Mediterranean pine vole.

Chapter 2

1. ICZN, Article 11.3: Derivation.

2. Ramey, Paul, "UF's new owl butterfly species naming rights auctioned for $40,800," *University of Florida News*, November 21, 2007. http://news.ufl.edu/ archive/2007/11/ufs-new-owl-butterfly-species-naming-rights-auctioned-for-40800. html (accessed May 26, 2017).

Chapter 3

1. ICZN, preamble.

Chapter 4

1. William H. Ballou, "Wrong End Foremost," *New York Herald* (January 19, 1890).

2. C. D. Fryar, Q. Gu, and C. L. Ogden, *Anthropometric reference data for children and adults: United States, 2007–2010*, National Center for Health Statistics, *Vital Health Stat 11(252)* 2012, at https://www.cdc.gov/nchs/data/series/sr_11/sr11_252.pdf (accessed May 26, 2017).

3. ICZN, Article 75: Neotypes, 75.2.

4. Sources are Spitzka's 1907 article, Jaffe's *The Gilded Dinosaur*, and Gould's *The Mismeasure of Man*.

5. http://psihoyos.photoshelter.com/image/I0000dzGjaqVa3aA.

6. Louie Psihoyos and John Knoebber, *Hunting Dinosaurs* (New York: Random House, 1994): 27.

7. Ibid., 21.

8. Ibid., 27.

9. Ibid., 29.

10. J. E. Bishop, "Bones of Contention: Should Dr. Cope's be the human model?" *Wall Street Journal* (November 1, 1994): A5–A6.

11. William Thomas Stearn, "The Background of Linnaeus's Contributions to the Nomenclature and Methods of Systematic Biology," *Systematic Zoology* (Vol. 8, 1959): 4.

Chapter 5

1. The work was published in German under the title *Synoptisches Verzeichnis mit kurzer Besprechung der Gattungen und Arten dieser Abteilung der Baikalseeflohkrebse* and has yet to be translated into English.

2. International Commission on Zoological Nomenclature, "Opinion 105. Dybowski's (1926) names of Crustacea suppressed," *Smithsonian miscellaneous collections* 1941 73(6):1–3, at biostor.org/reference/67131 (accessed May 26, 2017).

3. Arthur Maitland Emmet, *The Scientific Names of the British Lepidoptera: Their History and Meaning*, p. 13.

4. ICZN, Article 11.3: Derivation.

Chapter 6

1. Daniela Reichert, "David Bowie: Seltene Spinnenart wird Heteropoda davidbowie genannt," *Rolling Stone Magazin*, September 10, 2009, at https://www.rollingstone.de/david-bowie-seltene-spinnenart-wird-heteropoda-davidbowie-genannt-369801/ (accessed May 26, 2017).

2. J. Fernández-Triana et al., "A review of Paroplitis (Braconidae, Microgastrinae), and description of a new genus from New Zealand, Shireplitis, with convergent morphological traits," *Zootaxa* 3722 (4): 565, at http://biotaxa.org/Zootaxa/article/view/zootaxa.3722.4.6/5186 (accessed May 26, 2017).

3. So revolutionary was the hypothesis at the time that Van Valen could not get his paper accepted by any of the established journals; his only recourse was to found his own journal and publish it there. Leigh Van Valen, "A New Evolutionary Law," *Evolutionary Theory* 1: 1–30.

4. ICZN, Appendix A, Code of Ethics.

5. Charles Blinderman and David Joyce, *The Huxley File*, at http://aleph0.clarku.edu/huxley/guide9.html (accessed May 26, 2017).

6. G. C. Wallach, "On the true nature of the so-called *Bathybius*, and its alleged function in the nutrition of the protozoa," *Annals and Magazine of Natural History*, Series 4, vol. 16, 1875: pp. 325–326.

Chapter 7

1. Alfred Russel Wallace, "On the Law Which Has Regulated the Introduction of New Species," *Annals and Magazine of Natural History*, Series 2, vol. 16, September 1855.

2. J. T. Carrington, "Obituary: Francis Walker," *The Entomologist's Monthly Magazine* 40 (1874–1875): 140, at http://biodiversitylibrary.org/page/9265824 (accessed May 26, 2017).

3. Ibid., 141, at http://biodiversitylibrary.org/page/9265825 (accessed May 26, 2017).

4. Edward Newman, "Death of Mr. Walker," *Entomologist* 7 (1874): 260–264.

5. *Das Insektensieb, dessen Bedeutung beim Fange von Insekten, insbesondere Coleopteren, und dessen Anwendung.*

6. *Fauna Germanica. Die Käfer des Deutschen Reiches.*

7. *Erklärung der wissenschaftlichen Käfernamen aus Reitter's Fauna Germanica.*

8. J. Lederer, "Beitrag zur Kenntnis der Pyralidinen," *Wiener Entomologische Monatsschrift* 7 (1863): 241–504.

9. J. T. Carrington, "Obituary: Francis Walker," 140, at http://biodiversitylibrary.org/page/9265824 (accessed May 26, 2017).

10. H. T. Stainton, "The Entomological Society," *The Entomologist's Weekly Intelligencer* 14 (1856): 105–106.

11. Alfred Russel Wallace, *The Malay Archipelago: The land of the orang-utan, and the bird of paradise. A narrative of travel, with studies of man and nature*, London: Macmillan and Co., 1869, pp. 257–258.

12. Alfred Russel Wallace [Letter from Batchian], *Proceedings of the Entomological Society of London* (1859): 70–71, at http://www.nhm.ac.uk/research-curation/scientific-resources/collections/library-collections/wallace-letters-online/4749/5107/T/details.html (accessed May 26, 2017).

Chapter 8

1. ICZN, Article 8.

2. Colin Groves and Peter Grubb, *Ungulate Taxonomy* (Baltimore: The Johns Hopkins University Press, 2011): 1.

3. Karl Möbius, "Über den Umfang und die Einrichtung des zoologischen Museums zu Berlin," *Sitzungsberichte der Kgl. Preußischen Akademie der Wissenschaften zu Berlin* 29 (1898): 363–374, at http://biodiversitylibrary.org/page/40428098 (accessed May 26, 2017).

Chapter 9

1. A. A. Girault, "Some Insects Never Before Seen by Mankind," privately published pamphlet, Brisbane, Australia, October 30, 1920, at http://www.nhm.ac.uk/

resources/research-curation/projects/chalcidoids/pdf_X/Giraul920f.pdf   (accessed May 26, 2017).

2. Ibid.

3. A. A. Girault, "Homo Perniciosus and New Hymenoptera," privately published pamphlet, Brisbane, Australia, April 10, 1924, at http://www.nhm.ac.uk/resources/research-curation/projects/chalcidoids/pdf_X/Giraul924c.pdf (accessed May 26, 2017).

4. H. Stümpke, *The Snouters: Form and Life of the Rhinogrades*, Leigh Chadwick, trans. (New York: The Natural History Press, 1967): xii.

5. Ibid., xvi.

6. Ibid., 23.

7. Ibid.

8. Ibid., xxiii.

9. Ibid., 1.

10. Ibid., 60.

11. F. G. A. M. Smit, "Notes on Two Fictitious Fleas from Nepal," *Entomologisches Nachrichtenblatt*, 19. Jhg., 3, 1972 (1974), at http://www.zobodat.at/pdf/ZAOE_24_0130.pdf (accessed May 26, 2017).

12. Bernard Heuvelmans, *On the Track of Unknown Animals*, English edition (London: Routledge, 1955): 210.

References

The scope of literature on the meaning and creation of biological names is relatively small, although many books on systematic biology will include more or less detailed cross-references. I have taken up the history of biological naming—especially that done before Linnaeus's time—anecdotally and without the claim of comprehensiveness. Regarding the history of biology, as far as evolution and systematic biology are concerned, Ernst Mayr's *The Growth of Biological Thought: Diversity, Evolution, and Inheritance* (Belknap Press, 1982) is a must-read. Mayr is one of the most important evolutionary biologists in recent history and has been a great force in popularizing evolutionary theory. He has written a number of other books that approach the topic from various angles. Leading the charge is *Principles of Systematic Zoology* (McGraw-Hill, 1969), which builds on the book Mayr coauthored with Gordon Linsley and Robert Usinger, *Methods and Principles of Systematic Zoology* (New York 1953). This first book of Mayr's on systematic biology is rarely referenced today, but it includes a number of fascinating observations on taxonomy and naming that are missing from the later books.

A nicely written, popular account of scientific animal and plant names and their history, if somewhat light on theory, is provided by British mycologist John Wright in *The Naming of the Shrew: A Curious History of Latin Names* (New York: Bloomsbury, 2014).

Chapter 1: Hitler and the *Fledermaus*

The literature relevant to this chapter was referenced in the text and should thus be accessible to readers. The history of Hitler's intervention in the (re)naming of shrews and bats was especially well documented by Rainer Hutterer at the Zoological Research Museum Alexander Koenig in Bonn (Rainer

Hutterer: "Berlin und die Deutsche Gesellschaft für Säugetierkunde," in: *Bongo* 31 2001).

Chapter 2: How Species Get Their Names

For those who'd like to try their hand at describing a new species or learning the intricacies of animal naming, there's no way around diving into the nomenclature rules. The original 1999 version is available in print in French, English, and German (published in 2000). The International Commission on Zoological Nomenclature also has a website (http://iczn.org) where users can access the Code in various languages. The page also includes a link to ZooBank, the official online register for zoological nomenclature.

Surprisingly few books could be considered taxonomy textbooks in a broader sense. Although this title largely neglects theoretical bases, the most comprehensive and current presentation of practical taxonomic methods is Judith E. Winston's *Describing Species: Practical Taxonomic Procedures for Biologists* (New York 1999).

The history of pre-Linnaean nomenclature and the examples given in this chapter are drawn in part from Winston's book and from Mayr, Linsley, and Usinger's *Methods and Principles of Systematic Zoology* (see above). The information on Gessner's bird book and its historical connections to authors of antiquity was borrowed from *Das Vogelbuch von Conrad Gessner (1516–1565). Ein Archiv für avifaunischen Daten* (The Bird Book of Conrad Gessner (1516–1565): An Archive of Avifaunal Data) by Katharina B. Springer and Ragnar K. Kinzelbach (Berlin, Heidelberg 2009).

More has been written on the honeybee than on most other insects, but a formal clarification of its confused nomenclature is hard to come by. American bee researcher Michael Engel composed a summary of all 178 species-group names and synonyms in the genus *Apis* in "The Taxonomy of Recent and Fossil Honey Bees (Hymenoptera: Apidae: Apis)," in the *Journal of Hymenoptera Research* (No. 8, 1999).

Embedded within a cultural history of the London Natural History Museum, Richard Fortey illustrates the art of species description with inimitable élan in *Dry Store Room No. 1: The Secret Life of the Natural History Museum* (London 2008).

General information on the "Chilean Blob" can easily be found online. A year after the find, biologist Sidney Pierce and his colleagues published the findings of their scientific evaluations of the tissue, including determining that it was the remains of a sperm whale, in "Microscopic, Biochemical, and Molecular Characteristics of the Chilean Blob and a Comparison With the Remains of Other Sea Monsters: Nothing but Whales," in *Biological Bulletin* (206 [3], 2004).

I drew the tangled synonymy of *Mellinus crabroneus* from the Internet-based *Catalog of Sphecidae sensu lato* (http://www.calacademy.org/scientists/projects/catalog-of-sphecidae) with the permission of my dear friend and colleague Wojciech J. Pulawski at the California Academy of Sciences in San Francisco. I had some previous experience with this exercise in zoological nomenclature—albeit in different form—working with Ulrich Moritz, Agnieszka Pufelska, and Hanns Zischler's book, *Journey to the Interior: A Tour Through Berlin's Museum für Naturkunde* (Berlin 2010).

Herbert Wendt's *Out of Noah's Ark: The Story of Man's Discovery of the Animal Kingdom* (Houghton Mifflin, 1959) contains a trove of information on the discovery of many extraordinary animal species. For instance, it contains extensive accounts of David's discovery of the giant panda, the Père David's deer, and the golden snub-nosed monkey. Given space constraints, I was able to include only the first two, but it would have been worth including the story of the golden snub-nosed monkey—that beautiful ape with the colorful face.

BIOPAT has an informative website that can be viewed in English (http://biopat.de). Thanks to extensive press coverage, especially in its first years, numerous articles on the organization can also be found. Worth reading is "What's in a Species' Name? More Than $450,000" by Bijal P. Trivedi (in: *Science* 307, 2005).

Chapter 3: Words, Proper Names, Individuals

The source I relied on most heavily for information on Henry Fairfield Osborn was Louie Psihoyos and John Knoebber's *Hunting Dinosaurs* (New York 1994), which also provided the bulk of information on the absurd tale of Edward Drinker Cope. The history of the American Museum of Natural History in New York was presented rather anecdotally in Douglas J. Preston's *Dinosaurs in the Attic* (New York 1986). It's a worthwhile book that contains lots of information on Osborne, Roy Chapman Andrews, and the museum's many expeditions. Much has been written about the Bone Wars, but my primary resource was *The Gilded Dinosaur: The Fossil War Between E.D. Cope and O.C. Marsh and the Rise of American Science* (New York 2000) by Mark Jaffe.

Andreas Sentker's commentary on the *Oviraptor*, "Ausbruch aus der Vitrine" ("Escaping the Display Case"), appeared in the January 19, 1996, edition of the German daily newspaper *Die Zeit*.

One of the sources I used most extensively for the linguistic perspective on proper names was Damaris Nübling, Fabian Fahlbusch, and Rita Heuser's fantastic book, *Namen. Einführung in die Onomastik* (Names: An Introduction to Onomastics) (Tübingen 2012), which thankfully appeared at the moment I needed it. Plenty of other works have been published on the topic, but I drew concrete points from the following works: *Einführung in die Terminologiearbeit* (Introduction to Terminology Practices) by Rainer Arntz, Heribert Picht, and Felix Mayer (Hildesheim, Zurich et al. 2009), *Eine Zeitreise zu den Ursprüngen unserer Sprache. Wie die Indogermanistik unsere Wörter erklärt* (A Trip Back in Time to the Origins of Our Language: How Indo-European Studies Can Explain Our Words) by Harald Wiese (Berlin 2010), and *The Science of Words* by George A. Miller (W.H. Freeman & Co., 1991).

When it comes to questions about the definition or history of biological terms, Georg Töpfer's impressive three-volume *Historisches Wörterbuch der Biologie* (Historical Lexicon of Biology) (Stuttgart, Weimar 2011) is the superlative source. Its entries can also be found online, some including supplementary details, at http://www.biological-concepts.com.

Wilhelm Kamlah and Paul Lorenzen's modern classic, *Logical Propaedeutic: Preschool of Reasonable Discourse* (Rowman & Littlefield, 1984), proved helpful. I also consulted the Wikipedia pages on the following search terms: "Name," "Proper Name," "Appellative," and "Semiotic Triangle."

It's difficult to recommend literature on species concepts in biology, given the sheer number of books and journal articles written on the subject. Many publications will exhaustively argue a certain preferred concept, and it's not uncommon to be left wishing for a more measured approach with regard to other concepts as well.

Ernst Mayr, who was mentioned earlier and whose books are considered classics at this point, provides a good—albeit somewhat dated—overview in his publications, including references to seminal works written on the major species concepts. *Toward a New Philosophy of Biology: Observations of an Evolutionist* (Harvard University Press, 1989) provides a good introduction to the "species-as-class-or-individual" quandary. There are too many other publications on the topic to list here. Zoologist Johann Wolfgang Wägele provides a helpful introduction to the theoretical underpinnings relevant to systematic biology in his textbook, *Foundations of Phylogenetic Systematics* (Friedrich Pfeil, Munich 2005). As far as I know, this book contains the only competent representation of the function of language for systematics and taxonomy.

Chapter 4: Types and the Materiality of Names

The documentation of Louie Psihoyos and John Knoebber's journey with Edward Drinker Cope's skull in the backseat of their van is truly worth seeing, and *Hunting Dinosaurs* (1994)—which has long since gone out of print but can be found from time to time in used bookstores—comes highly recommended. It's worth taking a look at the book if only for Psihoyos's photographs of dinosaurs and dinosaur researchers, not to mention his entertaining prose. It also includes a brief section on Cope's life, as well as a summary of the history of North American dinosaur research.

Otherwise, I used the following literature:

Biographical information on Cope: Davidson, Jane, *The Bone Sharp. The Life of Edward Drinker Cope* (Philadelphia 1997).

Type specimen of *Archaeopteryx siemensii*: Ohl, Michael, "Von Namen und Namensträgern: *Archaeopteryx* und der Typus des Menschen" ("On Names and Name-Bearers: *Archaeopteryx* and the Human Type Specimen"), in: Damaschun, Ferdinand / Hackethal, Sabine / Landsberg, Hannelore / Leinfelder, Reinhold (ed.), *Klasse, Ordnung, Art. 200 Jahre Museum für Naturkunde* (Class, Order, Species: The Museum für Naturkunde Celebrates 200 Years) (Rangsdorf 2010).

Does a species description need a dead holotype? A number of publications on this topic are available in the journal *Zootaxa*, such as "New Species and Subspecies Descriptions Do Not and Should Not Always Require a Dead Type Specimen" by Thomas M. Donegan, in: *Zootaxa* (No. 1761, 2008) or "Nomenclatural Availability of Nomina of New Species Should Always Require the Deposition of Preserved Specimens in Collections: A Rebuttal to Donegan" by André Nemésio, in: *Zootaxa* (No. 2014, 2009). Ramana Athreya's original description of *Liocichla bugunorum* was published as "A

New Species of *Liocichla* (Aves: Timaliidae) from Eaglenest Wildlife Sanctuary, Arunchal Pradesh, India," in *Indian Birds* (2 [4], 2006).

With regard to the human type specimen: Stearn, William Thomas: "The Background of Linnaeus's Contributions to the Nomenclature and Methods of Systematic Biology," in: *Systematic Zoology* (Vol. 8, 1959); Psihoyos, Louie / Knoebber, John, *Hunting Dinosaurs* (London 1994); Spamer, Earle E., "Know Thyself: Responsible Science and the Lectotype of *Homo sapiens* Linnaeus, 1758," in: *Proceedings of the Academy of Natural Sciences of Philadelphia* (Vol. 149, 1999).

With regard to Carl Linnaeus: Goerke, Heinz, *Carl von Linné. Beiträge über Zeitgeist, Werk und Wirkungsgeschichte* (Carl Linnaeus: Reports on Zeitgeist, Corpus, and Impact) (Göttingen 1980) and many other biographies.

With regard to anthropometry: Gould, Stephen Jay, *The Mismeasure of Man* (W.W. Norton & Company, 1981); Spitzka, Edward Anthony, "A Study of the Brains of Six Eminent Scientists and Scholars Belonging to the American Anthropometric Society, Together with a Description of the Skull of Professor E.D. Cope," in: *Transactions of the American Philosophical Society* (xxi, 4 1907).

Chapter 5: The Curio Collection of Animal Names

All of my information on Benedykt Dybowski is drawn from the works of Carsten Eckert, in particular from his article, "Die 'zweite Entdeckung' des Baikalsees durch die Brüder Dybowski" ("The 'Second Discovery' of Lake Baikal by the Dybowski Brothers"), in: *Natur und Museum* (No. 137, 2007), and from Dybowski's memoir (edited by Eckert, Daniel Schümann, and Christian Prunitsch), *Transbaikalien. Erinnerungen an meine sibirische Verbannung* (Transbaikalia: Memories of My Siberian Exile) (Bamberg 2013). The nomenclature commission's "Opinion 105" can be found online (http://biostor.org/reference/67131), as can Dybowski's original articles.

Many lists of unique animal names, both annotated and not, can be found online. The most extensive of these lists is probably "Curiosities of Biological Nomenclature" (http://www.curioustaxonomy.net), while that with the most interesting names is Doug Yanega's "Curious Scientific Names" (http://cache.ucr.edu/~heraty/yanega.html).

Worth reading is a highly amusing article on bizarre names by entomologist May Berenbaum, who is known (among other things) for her column

"Buzzwords" in *American Entomologist*, a quarterly magazine for bug enthusiasts. The article, titled "Apis, Apis, Bobapis," appears alongside a selection of other columns Berenbaum compiled in her book, *Buzzwords: A Scientist Muses on Sex, Bugs, and Rock 'n' Roll* (Washington 2000). "Apis, Apis, Bobapis" also provided the story that Hermann Haupt was attempting to rename *Roechlingia hitleri*.

Arthur Maitland Emmet's *The Scientific Names of the British Lepidoptera: Their History and Meaning* (Colchester 1991), from which I quoted the crossword analogy, is a must-read. Other books and articles include etymological explanations for certain animal groups, but it's a fairly modest number. Whenever I had an etymological analysis in hand, I would avoid researching the original publication containing the respective name, which is otherwise standard practice. A good example is the etymology of the snakefly names penned by Horst and Ulrike Aspöck, which was published recently and is a lot of fun to read: "Where Do the Names Come From? The Valid Extant Taxa of the Snakeflies of the World: Systematic List and Etymology," in: *Entomologica Austriaca* (No. 20, 2013).

Chapter 6: "I Shall Name This Beetle After My Beloved Wife ..."

The incredibly informative webpage "History of the Atlantic Cable & Undersea Communications" (http://atlantic-cable.com) closely documents the numerous attempts to lay the transatlantic cable.

Much has been published on *Bathybius haeckelii*. Stephen J. Gould takes on two of these chimeras at once (*Bathybius* and *Eozoon*) in his collection of essays, *The Panda's Thumb* (W.W. Norton & Co., 1980). The original description can be found here:

Huxley, Thomas H., "On Some Organisms Living at Great Depths in the North Atlantic Ocean," in: *Quarterly Journal of Microscopical Science* (New Series 8, 1868).

I also availed myself of two further works:

Rehbock, Philip F., "Huxley, Haeckel, and the Oceanographers: The Case of *Bathybius Haeckelii*," in: *Isis* (No. 66, 1975).

Rupke, Nicholas A., "*Bathybius Haeckelii* and the Psychology of Scientific Discovery," in: *Studies in the History and Philosophy of Science* (No. 7, 1976).

Peter Jäger's extensive study of the huntsman spider genus *Heteropoda* can be read in its entirety here: Jäger, Peter, "Revision of the Huntsman

Spider Genus *Heteropoda* Latreille 1804: Species with Exceptional Male Pal-
pal Conformations from Southeast Asia and Australia," in: *Senckenbergiana
biologica* (No. 88, 2008).

I selected and researched the individual examples of patronyms according to my own tastes entirely. A complete bibliography would exceed the
scope of these notes, and I'm sure readers can manage to find the species
descriptions that interest them.

Beyond the original description of *Anophthalmus hitleri,* I read a number
of articles and blog posts on "Nazi beetles," for instance, "Fans exterminate
'Hitler' beetle" (http://www.independent.co.uk/news/world/europe/fans
-exterminate-hitler-beetle-6232054.html).

The letters from the proud strawberry and rose breeders who wanted
to name their creations after Hitler but weren't allowed to were drawn
from *Die Rückseite des Hakenkreuzes. Absonderliches aus den Akten des Dritten
Reiches* (The Backside of the Swastika: Oddities from the Files of the Third
Reich, not yet translated) (Wiesbaden 2005), edited by Beatrice and Helmut
Heiber.

Chapter 7: "A New Species a Day"

While I was writing this book, the hundredth anniversary of Alfred Russell Wallace's death was celebrated. In his honor, a number of books were
published, including a work mentioned in this chapter and written by my
friend and colleague Matthias Glaubrecht, which should be highlighted
and recommended once more: *Am Ende des Archipels. Alfred Russell Wallace*
(At the Archipelago's End: Alfred Russell Wallace) (Berlin 2013). Furthermore, Wallace's own publications, numerous secondary sources, and lots
of additional information and links can be found on George Beccaloni's
webpage, "The Alfred Russell Wallace Project" (http://wallacefund.info).

The work of Daniel Bebber and others on the influence that "big hitters"
have on the discovery of botanical diversity was published under the title,
"Big Hitting Collectors Make Massive and Disproportionate Contribution
to the Discovery of Plant Species," in the *Proceedings of the Royal Society B:
Biological Sciences* (279/1736, 2012).

Pjotr Oosterbroek succinctly reported on the life and works of Charles P.
Alexander in his article, "On the 11,755 Insect Taxa Named by Charles P.
Alexander," in: *Zoosymposia* (No. 3, 2009).

Friendly (and less friendly) remembrances were published on Francis Walker's scientific legacy directly following his death, and thanks to his significance to so many insect groups, biographical pieces still pop up from time to time in connection with taxonomic works. The most balanced biography must be attributed to Oxford entomologist M. W. R. de V. Graham, whose article was published with the lovely title, "'Ambulator': Francis Walker, English Entomologist (1809–1848)" in the *Entomologist's Gazette* (No. 30, 1979). The article cross-references most of the obituaries written, including J. T. Carrington's famously scathing piece.

Robert Constantin provides a short biography of Maurice Pic in his article, "Mémorial des coléoptéristes français," in: *Supplément au Bulletin de Liaison de l'ACOREP* (No. 14, 1992).

Information on Thomas Lincoln Casey, Jr., was drawn from Lee H. Herman's "Catalog of the Staphylinidae (Insecta, Coleoptera): 1758 to the End of the Second Millennium. Vol. 1, Introduction, History," in: *Bulletin of the American Museum of Natural History* (No. 265, 2001).

Edmund Reitter's life story is told in his obituary by Franz Heikertinger: "Edmund Reitter. Ein Nachruf" ("Edmund Reitter: An Obituary"), in: *Wiener Entomologische Zeitung* (Viennese Entomological Newspaper) (No. 38, 1920).

I collected biographical information on Edward Meyrick from the introduction to the first volume of the *Catalog of the Type Specimens of Microlepidoptera in the British Museum (Natural History) Described by Edward Meyrick* (London 1969) by John Frederick Gates Clarke; from A. J. T. Janse's introduction to Edward Meyrick's work, *On the Types of South African Microlepidoptera* (Cape Town 1968); and from A. W. Hill's obituary, "Edward Meyrick: 1854-1938," in: *Obituary Notices of Fellows of the Royal Society* (2/7, 1939).

Chapter 8: Who Counts the Species, Names the Names?

A plethora of biographies and obituaries have been written on Walther Arndt, some emotionally overwrought—either given the writers' unfiltered alarm or the underlying influence of antifascist East German propaganda—whereas others focus more heavily on verifiable facts. I relied primarily on the following biographical texts:

Ferdinand Pax's "Walther Arndt: Ein Leben für die Wissenschaft" ("Walther Arndt: A Life Given to Science"), in: *Hydrobiologia: The International Journal of Aquatic Sciences* (4 [3], 1952).

"Walther Arndt, ein Opfer des faschistischen Gesinnungsterrors" ("Walther Arndt: A Sacrifice to Fascist Anti-Intellectual Terror") by Günther Peters, in: *Forschen und Wirken. Festschrift zur 150-Jahre-Feier der Humboldt-Universität zu Berlin, 1810–1960* (Research and Impact: Festschrift in Honor of the 150th Anniversary of Humboldt University, Berlin, 1810–1960) (Berlin, 1960), edited by Willi Göber and Friedrich Herneck.

Dietrich Kühlmann's "Professor Dr. Dr. Walther Arndt. Wissenschaftler und Antifaschist, Kustos am Museum für Naturkunde Berlin 1921-1944" ("Professor Dr. Dr. Walther Arndt: Scientist and Anti-Fascist, Curator at the Museum für Naturkunde, Berlin, 1921–1944") (Berlin 1985).

"Der Wissenschaftler und Antifaschist Professor Dr. Dr. Walther Arndt" ("Scientist and Anti-Fascist, Professor Dr. Dr. Walther Arndt"), a special publication by the Museum für Naturkunde at Humboldt University, Berlin, in 1983.

Martin Eisentraut's "Vom Leben und Sterben des Zoologen Walther Arndt. Ein Zeitdokument aus Deutschlands schwärzesten Tagen" ("On the Life and Death of Zoologist Walther Arndt: A Contemporary Document from Germany's Darkest Days"), printed in: *Sitzungsberichte der Gesellschaft naturforschender Freunde zu Berlin* (Proceedings of the Berlin Society of Friends of Natural Science) (New Series 26, 1986).

Finally, Günther Tembrock's remembrance, "Walther Arndt, eine Erinnerung an den 26. Juni 1944" ("Walther Arndt: Memories of June 26, 1944"), in: *Sitzungsberichte der Gesellschaft naturforschender Freunde zu Berlin* (New Series 33, 1994). Arndt's own publications are referenced clearly enough in the chapter to allow readers to find them. Reprints and originals can be found in the Museum für Naturkunde in Berlin.

The history of the German Zoological Society, with particular emphasis on its emergence, is detailed in Armin Geus and Hans Querner's book, *Deutsche Zoologische Gesellschaft 1890–1990. Dokumentation und Geschichte* (The German Zoological Society, 1890–1990: Documentation and History) (Stuttgart, New York 1990).

Colin Groves and Peter Grubb's *Ungulate Taxonomy* (Johns Hopkins University Press, 2011) was met with plenty of contrasting views, but I focused primarily on the article, "Are There Really Twice as Many Bovid Species as We Thought?" by Rasmus Heller et al. (in: *Systematic Biology* 62 [3], 2013). The discussion continues in this scientific journal and others to this day.

The sources I used for species number estimates and the rationale behind them should be cited well enough in the text to make them easy to find. Because not too many people have addressed this topic over the past 250 years, more recent authors can be relied on to reference the same sources, and that helps. The authors of the eighteenth century and their attempt to express nature in numbers are profiled in *The Quantifying Spirit in the Eighteenth Century* (University of California Press, Berkeley, Los Angeles, et al., 1990), edited by Tore Frängsmyr, Robin E. Rider, and J. L. Heilbron. The chapter written by Gunnar Broberg, titled "The Broken Circle," is an especially rich source of information on eighteenth-century encyclopedists.

Background information on Terry Erwin came from various sources, but most was drawn from Rob Dunn's wonderful book, *Every Living Thing: Man's Obsessive Quest to Catalog Life, from Nanobacteria to New Monkeys* (Harper-Collins, 2009).

Chapter 9: Naming Nothing

I highly recommend Frederik Sjöberg's books, which have been translated into English as *The Fly Trap* and *The Art of Flight*, which includes *The Raisin King*. Although *The Art of Flight* may be somewhat disappointing to readers interested in biology, Sjöberg's exploration of "strange passions" and the people subject to them—which parts of my book examine as well—is a true pleasure to read.

The anecdote about Hans Malicky's invented flea species comes from Horst Aspöck in Vienna, one of the best-known experts on the idiosyncrasies of Austrian entomology. He mentions the fleas explicitly in his article, "25 Jahre Österreichische Entomologische Gesellschaft" ("25 Years of the Austrian Entomological Society"), in: *Denisia* (No. 8, 2003). Otto Suteminn's publication, "Ergebnisse der zoologischen Forschungen von Dr. Z. Loew in Nepal" ("Results of Zoological Studies by Dr. Z. Loew in Nepal"), appeared in the *Zeitschrift der Arbeitsgemeinschaft Österreichischer Entomologen* (Journal of the Austrian Entomologists' Association) (No. 21, 1969), while F. G. A. M. Smit's bemused commentary, "Notes on Two Fictitious Fleas From Nepal," was printed in the *Entomologisches Nachrichtenblatt* (Entomological Bulletin) (19/3, 1972/1974).

Otherwise I used the following literature, usually including background information on individual works directly in the text:

Gordh, Gordon / Menke, Arnold S. / Dahms, E. C. / Hall, Jack C., "The Privately Printed Papers of A. A. Girault," in: *Memoirs of the American Entomological Institute* (No. 28, 1979).

Stümpke, Harald, *The Snouters: Form and Life of the Rhinogrades* (Natural History Press, 1967).

Geeste, Karl D. S., *Stümpke's Rhinogradentia. Versuch einer Analyse* (Stümpke's Rhinogradentia: An Attempt at Analysis) (Stuttgart 1988).

Fotheringham, Augustus C., *Eoörnis petrovelox gobiensis* (London 2007).

Ludovici, Anthony M., "Eugenics and Consanguineous Marriages," in: The *Eugenics Review* (No. 24, 1933/34).

Dixon, Dougal, *After Man: A Zoology of the Future* (St. Martin's Press, 1981).

Fross, Rank, "A New Species of Anuran, *Rana Magnaocularis*, the Pop-Eyed Frog," in: *The Journal of the Herpetological Association of Africa* (No. 17, 1978).

Scott, Peter / Rines, Robert, "Naming the Loch Ness Monster," in: *Nature* (No. 258, 1975).

Krantz, Grover S., *Big Footprints: A Scientific Inquiry into the Reality of Sasquatch* (Boulder, Colorado 1992).

Heuvelmans, Bernard, *Sur la piste des bêtes ignorées*, 2 volumes (Paris 1955), English translation: *On the Track of Unknown Animals* (London 1958).

Epilogue: On Labeling

The connection between linguistic and physical order in natural history collections is nicely presented in "Vorstoß ins Innere. Ein Cine-Interactive" ("Journey to the Interior: A Cine-Interactive") (Berlin 2011) by Juri Hwan and Andreas Kratky, a booklet accompanying the book *Journey to the Interior: A Tour Through Berlin's Museum für Naturkunde* (Berlin 2010) by Ulrich Moritz, Agnieszka Pufelska, and Hanns Zischler.

Index of Author Names

Relevant individuals are included in this index with the dates of their birth and death, as well as the first page on which they're mentioned. Secondary characters and those individuals who can be considered generally well known are not included in the list.

Ludovici, Anthony M. (1882–1971), 258
Ludwig, Hubert (1852–1913), 231

Marsh, Othniel Charles (1831–1899), 99
May, Robert M. (b. 1936), 238
Mayr, Ernst (1904–2005), 85
Meyrick, Edward (1854–1938), 201
Milne Edwards, Henri (1800–1885), 39
Milne-Edwards, Alphonse (1835–1900), 40
Möbius, Karl August (1825–1908), 229
Müller, Johannes (1801–1858), 211
Musschenbroek, Pieter (Petrus) van (1692–1761), 223

Neave, Sheffield Airey (1879–1961), 217, 247

Pic, Maurice (1866–1957), 200
Pohle, Hermann (1892–1982), 12

Ray, John (1627–1705), 222
Reichenow, Eduard (1883–1960), 231
Reitter, Edmund (1845–1920), 200
Rosenhof, August Johann Rösel von (1705–1759), 227

Schmidt, Christian (dates unknown), 51
Schulze, Franz Eilhard (1840–1921), 231
Sharp, Lester W. (1887–1961), 256
Simpson, Georg Gaylord (1902–1984), 255
Spengel, Johann Wilhelm (1852–1921), 231
Steiner, Gerolf (1908–2009), 254
Stümpke, Harald (nom de plume; see Steiner, Gerolf)

Taschenberg, Ernst Ludwig (1818–1898), 96
Thunberg, Carl Peter (1743–1828), 63

Valen, Leigh van (1935–2010), 173
Villers, Charles Joseph de (1724–1810), 63

Walker, Francis (1809–1874), 186, 195
Werner, Franz (1867–1939), 141
Werner, Fritz Clemens (1896–1975), 58
Wilson, Edward O. (b. 1929), 238

Zimmermann, Eberhard (1743–1815), 226